Patrick Miller

MRC Epidemiology Unit,
Royal Edinburgh Hospital.
EDINBURGH

Clinical Psychology and Medicine
a behavioral perspective

Clinical Psychology and Medicine

a behavioral perspective

Edited by

Chris J. Main
Gartnavel Royal Hospital
Glasgow, Scotland

Associate Editor

William R. Lindsay
Monklands District General Hospital
Airdrie, Scotland

PLENUM PRESS • NEW YORK AND LONDON

Library of Congress Cataloging in Publication Data

Main entry under title:

Clinical psychology and medicine.

Bibliography: p.
Includes index.
1. Clinical psychology. 2. Behavior modification. 3. Community psychology. 4. Medicine, Psychosomatic. 5. Psychology, Pathological. I. Main, Chris J. II. Lindsay, William R. [DNLM: 1. Behavior therapy—Congresses. 2. Psychology, Clinical—Congresses.
WM 105 C6414 1980]
RC467.C585   616'.001'9   81-19978
ISBN 0-306-40900-3   AACR2

© 1982 Plenum Press, New York
A Division of Plenum Publishing Corporation
233 Spring Street, New York, N.Y. 10013

Printed in the United States of America

For
DUNCAN J. H. MAIN

PREFACE

This book had its origins in a conference, organised by the Scottish Assocation for Behaviour Modification (SABM), which took place from September 29th to October 2nd, 1980 in Pitlochry, Scotland. The SABM was founded in the early 1970s to fulfil a teaching need and provide a forum at conferences in the Highlands and Islands of Scotland at which mainly clinical psychologists from Scotland and North-West England could discuss research. There have been four such major conferences over the years and the common feature has been the highlighting of research issues mainly in behavioural psychology.

At the 4th conference (Pitlochry, 1980), the general emphasis was on the assessment and treatment of chronic illness, although a number of other individual papers were presented. Chapters 4, 5, 8, 10 and 11 are based on papers from the full-day symposium on clinical psychology and physical illness (to which general medical practitioners were invited), although Chapter 8 in particular comprises a much wider review paper than the original conference paper; and Chapter 13 is also a much extended version of a paper accepted for, but not presented at, the conference. Chapters 15, 16, 18 and 19 are based on papers comprising the symposium on behavioural approaches to the care of the long-stay psychiatric patient. Chapters 2 and 3 are based on invited individual papers presented at the conference.

At the request of the publisher, additional material was commissioned. Chapters 9, 12 and 14 are review chapters while Chapters 1, 6, 7 and 17 contain in addition new empirical findings. Given the heterogeneity of the contributions both in terms of type and in terms of clinical context, the structuring of the book perhaps requires some explanation. Chapter 1 represents perhaps the widest perspective in that Main and Waddell attempt to integrate physical and psychological perspectives in a particular chronic disorder, but within a much more general framework. In Chapter 2, Wright and Ng write from a statistical perspective, but the implications of their analysis have wide-reaching implications for research in general medicine. In Chapter 3, Cullen presents a theoretical analysis of a specific debate current in behavioural psychology.

Chapters 4 to 9 deal mainly, although not exclusively, with clinical and methodological issues of particular relevance to community-based medicine. Chapters 10 to 13 concern patient problems normally necessitating the more specialised medical services, while Chapters 14 to 19 are of specific relevance to the treatment of the long-stay patient within the specialised psychiatric services. The intention of the book is to draw attention to recent advances in clinical psychology in multidisciplinary settings. No attempt has been made to incorporate the considerable clinical and research interest in anxiety and depression related disorders, or in many of the client problems, with which the psychologist may deal, on a one-to-one basis. Furthermore, research in a number of clinical fields, such as mental handicap, psychogeriatrics, adolescent or child problems, and neuropsychology is beyond the scope of this book. Within the general 'psychosomatic' area, however, an attempt has been made to present some of the theoretical issues facing the clinical psychologist, in the community and within specialised medical settings. Within the psychiatric realm, diverse approaches are presented to the fairly circumscribed yet extremely challenging set of problems posed by the institutionalised patient. Perhaps of most importance, however, is the discussion of methodological issues of relevance to the clinical psychologist in the design and analysis of applied clinical research.

I should like to thank Social Psychiatry and the British Journal of Psychiatry respectively for permission to reproduce Figures 1 and 2 in Chapter 6. As far as the SABM is concerned, its continuation over the years is in a large part due to the enthusiasm of a number of stalwarts, but mention must be made in particular of Dave Peck, Dave Whitlow and Chris Cullen. I should also like to thank Harry McAllister for help in the organisation of the 1980 conference.

Dr Robert Andrews of Plenum must be mentioned not only for his technical advice but for his patience and courtesy in dealing with what must have appeared at times to be simple-minded inquiries. Bill Lindsay's help in structuring the long-term section of the book is greatly appreciated as has been his general encouragement and willingness to help in reading drafts of papers and structuring part of the subject index.

My greatest debts undoubtedly, however, are to June McKill for an incredible level of dedication and professionalism in the preparation of the final manuscript and to my wife Carolyn not only for tolerating an incredible invasion of our private lives over the last few months, but for her active encouragement and help in proof-reading and preparing the subject index. Without the help of these ladies, the book certainly never would have been completed.

CONTENTS

CHRONIC PAIN, DISTRESS AND ILLNESS BEHAVIOR

Chris J Main

Psychology Department
Gartnavel Royal Hospital
Glasgow, Scotland

Gordon Waddell

University Department of Orthopaedic Surgery
Glasgow, Scotland

INTRODUCTION

At least one out of every two people in western society suffers
from back trouble at some time in their life. Along with respiratory
disease, heart trouble and arthritis or rheumatism, backache is one
of the commonest causes of morbidity, disability and perceived threat
to health, particularly in the most active middle years of life
(Rowe, 1969; Benn and Wood, 1975; Wood, 1976; DHSS, 1979). In the
United Kingdom, backache causes more time off work than strikes and
each year some 12 million working days are lost by a third of a
million people with backache. 1.1 million patients consult their
family doctor, 0.3 million are referred to hospital out-patient
departments, 30,000 are admitted to hospital and 5,000 have an
operation on their back. Between 20 and 35% of all new orthopaedic
referrals concern backache. Cumulatively there are 80,000 people
in the United Kingdom (about 0.015%) permanently disabled by backache and arguably the worst back cripples result from the 10-15%
of operations which fail and lead to repeated back surgery (Waddell
et al, 1979). In North America, the chances of an individual coming
to back surgery are six times greater than in Europe (Kane, 1980).
The total annual cost of backache in Britain is at least £320 million
and on a world scale, the annual toll of backache includes many
billions of dollars and some quarter of a million operations, yet
many millions of people remain disabled. Paradoxically, despite

1

the efforts of modern medicine, the problem appears greatest in the
quarter of the world's population living in western 'civilisation',
while the rest of mankind seems to cope with backache despite an
almost total lack of social security, technologically orientated
medicine or back surgery.

Treatment of Backache

There are a multitude of treatments for backache and most
careful trials show little or no difference in their effectiveness
(Doran and Newell, 1975; Nachemson, 1976). Most treatments can be
classified as radical or conservative methods of treatment. 5-10%
of chronic backache patients will be treated radically, usually by
a neurosurgeon or orthopaedic surgeon using a variety of sophisticated surgical procedures. Frequently, however, surgery is
considered only after failed conservative treatment, which may be
pharmacological (analgesic, anti-inflammatory, muscle relaxant or
hypnotic drugs); mechanical (plaster of paris jackets and lumbosacral supports); physiotherapeutic (exercises, manipulation, heat
treatment and hydrotherapy), or may include nerve-blocking or nerve-
stimulating techniques frequently prescribed in special pain clinics.
While most of the above treatments are available through the National
Health Service (NHS) in the UK, there are in addition a number of
further treatments formerly available only outside the NHS: such
as manipulation, acupuncture and hypnosis, now sometimes available
within the NHS. Other recent developments include Multidisciplinary
Back Education classes, operant techniques (Fordyce, 1976) and the
setting up of self-help groups. There have been in addition numerous
articles in popular magazines and recently a number of paperbacks
devoted to the subject of backache. The aforementioned is testimony
not only to the prevalence of backache and the suffering which it
occasions, but also to the inadequacy of our range of treatment
techniques to meet patients' clinical needs.

It is perhaps difficult to understand the comparative failure
of treatment for chronic backache given the considerable increase
in pain research over the last 20 years but part of the answer may
be in the assumptions we make about pain itself and the nature of
current research into the topic. The First World Congress of Pain
recently described itself as "the largest and most extensive multidisciplinary meeting of professional people who have a special
interest and expertise in pain research or pain therapy, or both,
that has ever been assembled anywhere" (Bonica and Albe-Fessard,
1976). During the $3\frac{1}{2}$ days of the conference, 18 special lectures,
250 individual papers, 6 motion pictures and 4 workshops were
presented. The scientific committee then selected the best 112
papers (based on two or three independent evaluations by the
editorial board). While the original submission of papers may not
be an accurate representation of research in the world, and while

the proportion of papers finally published may not exactly mirror the proportion of topics submitted to the conference, an examination of the contents of the book is illuminating. The vast proportion of studies are physiological, neuro-anatomical or neuro-chemical in nature, and are directed at increasing our understanding of the nervous system, the mechanisms whereby a painful stimulus leads to the experience of pain, and the effect of a variety of physical techniques (such as neurosurgery, acupuncture and pharmacology) on these relationships. Twelve of the papers (about 11%) were in any way psychological or psychiatric.

According to Sternbach (1978) "This incomplete translation of research findings to clinical applications may be due in part to the fact that most research has been on acute pain, and the clinical problems are usually chronic in nature. And it may be due in part to the lack of awareness on the part of clinicians of the implications of these research findings. However, some recognition must be given the fact that the human patient which chronic pain due to illness or injury is unlike the subject in the laboratory" (p.241). The differences between clinical and experimental pain, between human and animal pain, and between acute and chronic pain are real but difficult to articulate. The general purpose of this chapter is to attempt to increase our understanding of chronic backache by looking at physical and psychological factors with an attempt to estimate the relative importance of each, but before presenting clinical data, we should like to evaluate attempts to assess clinical pain and to review the assessment of psychological factors in backache.

The Assessment of Pain

Graphic and Verbal Self-Ratings. The use of simple rating scales to assess subjective feelings has a long history (Hayes and Patterson, 1921). More recently Aitken (1969) advocated the use of a 100 mm line in the assessment of mood. Their use in drug trials are recommended by Bond and Lader (1974), although the statistical results in the latter study are somewhat equivocal. The validity and reliability of the Visual Analogue Mood Scale is comprehensively analysed elsewhere (Luria, 1975) and will not be discussed further here.

One of the earliest attempts to obtain a measure of pain severity using such scales was by Hardy et al (1952) who developed a subjective Dol Scale, discussed by Woodforde and Merskey (1972) who incorporated Clarke and Spear's analogue scale. The advantages of such scales are obvious: they are simple to use, have high face validity, good test-retest reliability and a high compliance rate. Doubts, however, have been raised about the extent to which pain is indeed unidimensional or, in the case of chronic pain, can be

represented adequately by one mark at a fixed point in time
(Melzack, 1975). Pain seems to be influenced in addition to sensory
input, by many factors such as culture, emotion, psychological
processes and reinforcement contingencies (Beecher, 1959; Melzack,
1973; Sternbach, 1978). Alternatives to the simplest visual analogue
scale are graphic rating scales which have descriptive terms placed
at intervals along the line. In a sophisticated comparison of six
different types of scales, Scott and Huskisson (1976) found only the
simple visual analogue scale and one of the graphic rating scales
to be satisfactory in terms of the distribution of scores and
sensitivity.

The Pain Drawing (Ransford et al, 1976) was devised specifically
for patients with low back pain. The patient is asked to represent,
using a variety of symbols, on outlines of the body (both posterior
and anterior), the location and quality of his pain. The drawing
is then scored for poor anatomical localisation, "expansion" or
"magnification" of pain; specific emphases; and additional painful
areas in the body indicative of a tendency toward total body pain.
The authors claimed a high correlation with the Hypochondriasis (Hs)
and Hysteria (Hy) scores of the Minnesota Multiphasic Personality
Inventory (MMPI), but this has recently been questioned (Doxey et al,
1979) and since the MMPI is itself a weak predictor of outcome of
treatment, the utility of the Pain Drawing in the prediction of
outcome is still unproven.

According to Agnew and Merskey (1976, p. 80) attempts to classify pain words date from Tichener (1920) and Dana (1911) and Dall-
enbach's list of pain words serves as a model for the studies of
Melzack and Torgerson (1971)". They identified three major classes of pain words: sensory, affective, and evaluative. As Bailey
and Davidson (1976) point out, however, that Melzack and Torgerson's
(1971) assumption of an underlying dimension of intensity had not
been empirically verified. Bailey and Davidson (1976) in a factor-
analytic study of two separate samples, found only a relatively
small intensity factor on which loaded affective and evaluative
rather than sensory adjectives. Leavitt et al (1978) identified
seven distinguishable patterns in patients' descriptions of back
pain. The first factor, accounting for 38% of the variance, con-
stituted an entirely sensory class of factors. Crockett et al (1977)
on a further factor analysis of data from experimental pain subjects
and back pain patients identified a set of factors having a slightly
different blend of sensory, evaluative and affective components.
Prieto et al (1980), however, criticised the latter two studies on
methodological grounds, and in a study of 198 patients from a back
pain clinic, identified four major factors accounting for the
majority of the variance. Three of the factors were defined solely
by sensory, affective and evaluative sub-classes, while the fourth
factor was composed of both affective and sensory components. They
concluded that "the results appeared to provide strong support for

Melzack's 3-factor conceptualisation of the MPQ" (p.17). Graham
et al (1980) confirmed the replicability of the MPQ indices and
robustness over form of administration, but illustrated problems in
the use of the test as a way of summarising pain retrospectively and
when patients had experienced pain of fluctuating intensity. They
also drew attention to the need for additional psychometric refinement (the number of sub-classes devoted to each factor is disproportionate, as is the number of words in each sub-class).

A card sort method of pain assessment was also devised (Reading
and Newton, 1978) and consists of an adaptation of the Personal
Questionnaire technique (Shapiro, 1961) and while it shows promise
in the description of pain for gynaecological patients, it has not
so far been used with back pain patients. Given the complexity of
its administration, there may well be difficulties in obtaining
patient compliance and in its use in a much larger psychological
battery. Leavitt and Garron (1979b) have continued to advocate the
use of their Back Pain Classification Scale (BPCS). Recently
Duncan et al (1978) devised a computerised system for the assessment
of chronic pain, and while automated models may well be a development in the near future, the utility of the Pain Profile in routine
clinical settings is hard to imagine in the near future (especially
with the British National Health Service). Nonetheless, as a
research tool, the approach would appear to have considerable
promise.

It has been demonstrated that there is more than one component
in the verbal description of pain and that certain assessment methods
seem to be highly influenced by affective factors. The choice of
a measurement tool must depend on the purposes of the assessment.
Reading (1979) has criticised the use of a single unidimensional
measure to represent pain, and we certainly agree that quantitative
and qualitative aspects of pain must be distinguished. Since it
has been shown (Agnew and Merskey, 1976) that words are not adequate
as measures of severity and that factor analysis of verbal descriptions shows a tendency to use affective rather than sensory terms
(Crockett et al, 1977), we agree with Sternbach (1978) that graphic
or visual analogue representations of pain would appear to be
superior to simple verbal terms for the assessment of clinical pain
intensity per se.

Experimental Methods. Of cross-modality matching methods,
perhaps the best known are the pain threshold and pain tolerance
techniques. In such techniques the patient is required to estimate
the intensity of his clinical pain produced by experimental stimuli.
A number of numberal estimates such as pain threshold, pain tolerance
and pain ratio are then derived. These techniques are reviewed by
Sternbach (1974, 1978). As Weisenberg (1977) has indicated, perhaps
the most important feature of these techniques has been the
experimental derivation of the distinction between the original pain

sensation and the reaction component. "Three major classes of
reaction identified by Beecher are: (a) skeletal muscle reactions,
(b) autonomic nervous system reactions, and (c) processing of the
original stimulus by the central nervous system, which determines
the absence or presence of suffering. According to Beecher most
clinically effective pain drugs, such as narcotics, affect the
reaction component of the original pain sensation" (Weisenberg,
1977, p.1013).

     Varieties of pain stimuli include pressure techniques, elec-
trical current, extremes of temperature and chemically induced pain.
There have been considerable administrative, ethical and methodological problems, however, in the evaluation. Beecher (1966) and
Sternbach (1974) have both advocated the sub-maximum effort
tourniquet technique (Smith et al, 1968) which has the advantage
that the pain slowly builds up and so both the pain stimulus and the
subject's threshold and tolerance can be assessed fairly accurately.
While electrical stimulation techniques (Tursky, 1974, 1977) have
some advantages in the degree of control over the stimulus, there
are perhaps ethical problems in their routine clinical use and
problems also with patient compliance. Sophistication in the
measurement of pain reactions has arrived with the application of
signal detection or sensory decision theory (Clark, 1974; Chapman
et al, 1976). Rollman (1979) illustrated the major theoretical and
methodological difficulties of the approach.

     Of the experimental methods available at the moment, the
ischaemic pain produced by the sub-maximum effort tourniquet would
appear to be best analogue of clinical pain, but further studies
are needed not simply of its pharmacological sensitivity but of its
utility in the prediction of outcome of treatment, as a measure of
change over time, and its incremental validity in comparison with
simpler methods of estimating clinical pain intensity. To conclude,
"Using experimental pain models reliable results are not to be
expected as anxiety fluctuates intra- and inter-individually in an
unpredictable and uncontrollable manner" (von Graffenfried et al,
1978, p.253).

THE ASSESSMENT OF PSYCHOLOGICAL FACTORS

Introduction

     Patients with low back pain are difficult and challenging
diagnostic problems and, even with the newest and most sophisticated
clinical laboratory techniques, there are a substantial number of
patients suffering from the disorder for whom organic pathology
cannot be demonstrated (Wolfkind and Forrest, 1972) and there are
frequent reports (Sternbach, 1974; Engel, 1959) of patients in whom
the reaction to the pain or the presenting disability is considered
excessive in relation to the level of organic involvement. Given

the high failure rate of treatment for backache, and the limitations of our physical understanding, it is not surprising that clinicians began to look for possible psychological explanations for this failure. An unfortunate consequence of this search has been the frequent adoption of a dichotomy of 'functional' versus 'organic', although, the term 'functional' is frequently synonymous with the absence of physical findings, or lack of physical findings sufficient to account for the degree of expressed pain or reported disability. The diagnosis 'functional' is frequently a diagnosis 'by exclusion' rather than one based on the presence of significant psychological features and frequently has pejorative overtones. The simplistic dichotomy is paralleled by the equally inappropriate division into 'imaginary' and 'real' pain. Patients are frequently resentful when they suspect that their pain has been classified as imaginary, with the implication that they are either mad or malingering. Three somewhat different perspectives have come to bear on the role of psychological factors.

Experimental Studies

The reaction to pain has been shown to vary with demographic, social, ethnic and cognitive factors. Sex and age differences in pain threshold, pain tolerance and analgesic effects are reviewed by Weisenberg (1977, pp.1011-1019).

Perhaps of more clinical relevance are studies derived from cognitive dissonance and attribution theory. Typically these studies incorporate experimental manipulation of attitudes using socio-psychological techniques. As in the previous set of studies, the dependent variable is frequently pain threshold or pain tolerance. Blitz and Dinnerstein (1971) reviewed the role of attentional factors as mediators; Horan and Dellinger (1974) found emotive imagery effective in increasing pain tolerance; and Nisbet and Schachter (1966) in a celebrated experiment, demonstrated a clear relationship between pain tolerance, beliefs concerning the induced physiological arousal and fear. It would appear that in certain controlled experiments, pain tolerance is affected by subjects' belief about the situation, but the relevance of these findings for chronic pain patients is as yet unproven.

Several studies have incorporated the augmentation-reduction concept devised experimentally by Petrie (1967) to categorise styles of responding to painful stimulation. Augmenters characteristically overestimate stimulation while reducers underestimate (and show greater pain tolerance). The dimension has been linked with styles of managing stress.

"Sensitizers and copers tend to respond to external stimulation and cope with stress by trying to deal with it. Reducers or avoiders

play down external stimulation and tend to cope with stress by denial
and avoidance (cf Goldstein, 1973)" (Weisenberg, 1977, p.1021).

It seems that individuals who rely on denial (avoiders) to cope
with anxiety respond poorly to surgery when given detailed information about it (Andrew, 1970; De Long, 1970) and show better adjustment to that specific stress when not given information about it
(Cohen and Lazarus, 1973). Sensitisers on the other hand seem to
benefit from prior information. Patients intermediate on the
repression-sensitisation dimensions, or reporting intermediate levels
of pre-operative anxiety seem to recover well irrespective of
preparatory information. Davidson and Bobey (1970) and Neufeld and
Davidson (1971) confirmed the link between this dimension and
response to experimental pain stimulation. It seems clear that in
certain situations, cognitive styles are predictive of response to
stress and Weisenberg (1977) has expressed the opinion that knowledge of coping style may be a better predictor than knowledge of
immediate emotional arousal.

Other cognitive dimensions, such as field dependence-independ-
ence and lateral dominance are reviewed by Weisenberg (1977), but
the relationship of either to experimentally induced pain is unclear.

Perhaps best known of the cognitive dimensions, however, is
locus of control (Rotter, 1966). Rotter maintained that people can
be classified along a continuum according to the extent to which
they perceive what happens to them as being under their personal
control. The "internal" will be confident that he can bring about
changes in his environment and in his own behaviour, while the
"external" will feel comparatively powerless to produce change. The
subject has been extensively reviewed (Lefcourt, 1966, 1972; Joe,
1971) and the subject of numerous doctoral dissertations, concerned
with social learning theory, locus of control has been related to
depression (Prociuk et al, 1976); to neurotic symptomatology
(Feather, 1967); and anxiety (Watson, 1967; Ray and Katahn, 1968),
although the relationship of the locus of control to the latter is
unclear (Joe, 1971). It has recently been used in the study of
chronic pain (Block et al, 1980b).

The scale has been criticised, however, on the grounds that it
confuses personal and societal or political control (Gurin et al,
1969; Lao, 1970; Mirels, 1970; Thomas, 1970) and some studies
(Feather, 1967; Altrocchi et al, 1968) have shown it to be affected
by social desirability.

Recently Wallston et al (1976) devised a Health Locus of Control
(HLC) scale following a trend towards the development of less general, more specific measures of assessment, but the scale has not
yet been used with pain patients, nor has one specificially for
chronic pain been devised as yet.

Conclusion. In general it would appear that there is some relationship between cognitive variables and people's responses to a number of pain related situations. Most of these experiments have taken place in experimental rather than a clinical setting and so it remains to be determined the extent of their explanatory power in the much more highly emotionally charged clinical context.

Psychiatric Approaches

The derivation of the differential diagnosis into 'functional' and 'organic' pain and its limitations have already been discussed. While major psychiatric illnesses such as schizophrenic psychosis, and manic depressive psychosis are extremely rare in patients presenting with backache (Bond, 1979) organic psychoses, however, may be produced by acute systemic diseases such as infection or disseminated malignancy. Underlying physical pathology, therefore, must be excluded prior to urgent psychiatric assessment.

More commonly, chronic patients present with symptoms sugges-tive of neurotic disorder. The neuroses commonly associated with chronic pain are anxiety, depression, hypochondriasis and hysteria. The descriptions of hypochondriasis and hysteria overlap considerably and clinically, patients present frequently with a mixture of symptoms. Sternbach (1978) distinguishes acute and chronic pain on the basis of experimental and clinical findings.

"Acute pain, meaning pain of recent onset or of short duration, is typically associated with changes in autonomic activity roughly proportional to the intensity of the stimulus. The overall pattern is one of emergency response, the fight or flight reaction. It is also the pattern of responses seen in anxiety attacks. Patients with acute pain usually experience anxiety, either about the severity of the pain itself or about the meaning of pain.

"Chronic pain, meaning pain of at least several months' dura-tion, presents a rather different picture. Constant rather than intermittent, there appears to be a habituation of autonomic responses. A pattern of vegetative signs emerges; patients report sleep disturbance, appetite changes, decreased libido, irritability, withdrawal of interests, weakening of relationships and increased somatic preoccupation." (Sternbach, 1978, p.243). Sternbach (1978) refers to studies showing that treatment of depression alleviates pain (Bradley, 1963; Merskey and Hester, 1962; Taub and Collins, 1974) but also points to evidence that pain reduction reverses neurotic depression (Bond, 1973; Sternbach and Timmermans, 1975).

Individuals prone to the development of anxiety when stressed are known to have increased sensitivity to pain (Schalling and Levander, 1964) and the relationship between pain, anxiety (or

failed coping) and information given about surgery has already been
discussed above. The relationship between pain and depression in
cancer patients was studied by Woodforde and Fielding (1970) and
Bond (1980) concludes:

"The authors were uncertain whether depression was primary or
secondary event but commented that the combination of intractable
pain and depression indicates a state of helplessness, of inability
to cope with the disease, damage to the body and threat to life,
and that this is a response to having a progressive and potentially
fatal illness" (p.6). A general discussion of the relationship
between pain and depression is presented in Sternbach (1974, chapter
6).

Hypochondriacal and hysterical features are frequently used
diagnostic labels, but as Bond (1980) points out are sometimes used
in a pejorative rather than a diagnostic sense. Kenyon (1976)
demonstrates how the varied historical background has led to a
confusing variety of usages. Thus it can be used as a term of
abuse, as a psychiatric defence mechanism or as a type of body image
disorder in its own right. Stoeckle (1966) discusses four types:
bodily complaints, attitudes and beliefs about the body, concerns
about illness and the act of complaining (too often) to the doctor.
Hypochondriacal symptoms are common features of many presentations,
particularly depression. They have been attributed to loneliness
(Van der Bergh, 1963), dissatisfactions with body image (Schwab
and Harmeling, 1968), athletes' neurosis (Little, 1969), limited
intelligence (Martin and Swenson, 1966). They have been implicated
in 'unnecessary' or 'non-organic' operations (Wahl and Golden, 1966;
Zwerling et al, 1955; Merskey and Spear, 1967). Attempts have been
made (Pilowsky, 1971) to distinguish between primary and secondary
hypochondriasis, but doubts have been raised about the status of
hypochondriasis as a distinct clinical entity (Mayou, 1976).

It was at one time believed that hypochondriasis was simply the
male form of hysteria. The term 'hysteria' confuses several different usages: personality-type, conversion hysteria, anxiety-
hysteria, a psychopathological mechanism, a narrowly defined syndrome
or the simple everyday usage of the term (Reed, 1975; Lewis, 1974).
The reliability of any of these terms as a clinical diagnosis is
open to doubt. The terms will be discussed further in the section
on assessment of personality.

Unfortunately, methodological problems limit confidence in the
use of such clinical information in a research context. Many of
the early observations, particularly in the surgical literature,
were unconfirmed speculations frequently based on clinical impressions derived from a small number of cases. The diagnosis of unknown
reliability and the classification system derived from studies of
psychiatric populations seem ill-suited for chronic pain patients.

Perhaps of more value have been the studies incorporating psychometric measures of personality.

Assessment of Personality

    MMPI. Most research into the role of personality in back pain
has either consisted of attempts to describe differences in clinical
presentation of pain, frequently classified as 'organic' or 'functional', or attempted to predict outcome of treatment, usually
surgery, by psychometric traits.

    As mentioned above, the organic/functional distinction is
frequently made simply on the grounds of the presence or absence of
physical criteria considered sufficient to account for degree of
reported pain or disability. Attempts to describe psychological
factors have usually used the MMPI (Dahlstrom and Welsh, 1960).
Indeed one of these earliest studies (Hanvik, 1951) attempted to
distinguish on the basis of MMPI profiles between 'functional' and
'organic' low back patients. Statistically significant differences
were found on a number of scales and 'conversion - V' configuration
featuring elevations on the Hy and Hs scales, with a less elevated
but still elevated Depression (D) scale was identified as
characteristic of the functional group. Sternbach et al (1973) in
a mixed group of 117 patients confirmed the elevation of the Hs and
Hy scales and, as did Hanvik (1951), found a somewhat less elevated
D scale but not showing a clear 'psychosomatic - V' supposedly
characteristic of conversion hysteria. He concluded that "the
traditional attempt to distinguish between an 'organic' or
'functional' low back is useless" (p.227) (as there were no essential
differences between the patients with physical findings and those
without such findings). Pichot et al (1972) developed a 63-item
MMPI scale to differentiate between functional and organic patients,
but they in fact compared functional with non-pain patients rather
than with organic patients, and the scale they produced was relatively independent of Hanvik's low back scale. Both had a high
misclassification rate, although the two scales in conjunction were
better than either singly. Carr et al (1966) found the 'conversion
profile' in both 'functional' and 'organic' patients on the MMPI
and demonstrated that certain symptoms of emotional disturbance were
more characteristic of patients with relatively little evidence of
an organic basis, but "on each of these scales (Hs and Hy), approximately 25-30% of the functional patients scored below the mean of
the organic patients, and a similar percentage of organic patients
scored above the mean of the functional patients" (p.77). Freeman
et al (1976) and Wiltse and Rocchio (1975) have also confirmed that
some differentiation is possible among clinical groups with the
MMPI, but according to Leavitt and Garron (1979) "the actual existence of psychopathology is assumed from the absence of organic
pathology rather than demonstrated in its own right, that is, none
of the MMPI studies provide independent evidence of psychological
disturbance in patients whose low back pain is classified as
functional" (p.150).

   Studies using the MMPI to predict outcome have found a relationship between Hs and Hy scales and functional success after
chemonucleosis (Wiltse and Rocchio, 1975), post-surgery outcome at
6 months' follow-up (Blumetti and Modesti, 1976); spinal fusion
outcome (Wilfling et al, 1976) and there seem to be complicated
interactions between types of personality disturbances and different
measures of outcome (McCreary et al, 1979). Success in prediction
of response to rehabilitation programmes and return to work again
has been equivocal. Philips (1964) found higher Hs, D and Hy scales
among those who took longer to return to work, but Gentry et al
(1977) in an important study was not able to differentiate among
patients with successful and unsuccessful outcomes.

   It can be concluded that on theoretical grounds that, while as
a group test, elevations on the Hs, Hy and D scales have some relationship with outcome, there is a high level of misclassification in
the individual case, there are probably interactions between type of
profile and type of outcome measure used, and the test is at best
a weak predictor of outcome. Practical problems also limit its
usefulness. In its 555-item form, it takes a long time to administer
and therefore effectively precludes the use of less global, more
sensitive measures; there are no British norms for the test and it
has a relatively poor compliance rate. (In a pilot study of 30
British NHS patients with chronic backache, the present authors
found 30% were either unable or unwilling to complete the test.
Indeed some patients found it offensive to be asked so many clearly
psychological questions.) Although short forms have been devised,
their reliabilities vary widely and seem to depend on a particular
clinical population under consideration (Graham, 1977).

   Other General Personality Questionnaires. The most widely used
personality tests in Britain are Cattell's 16PF Questionnaire and
Eysenck's series of questionnaires. The 16PF, although American in
origin, has a set of British norms but has not been shown to be of
relevance to low back pain and will not be discussed further.

   Of the Eysenck scales, best known are neuroticism and extraversion. Level of neuroticism, defined by Eysenck as liability to
emotional breakdown under stress, was measured originally using the
Maudsley Personality Inventory (MPI) but this evolved into the
Eysenck Personality Inventory (EPI) using which most of the early
British personality research was conducted (Eysenck and Eysenck,
1964). Neuroticism has been related to pain severity (Lynn and
Eysenck, 1961; Pilling et al, 1967; Bond and Pearson, 1969; Bond,
1971; Bond, 1973; Bond, 1976; Bond et al, 1976). These findings
are summarised by Sternbach (1978): "they found that the degree of
pain experienced is positively correlated with the degree of
neuroticism, but the complaint of pain (and the receipt of analgesics) is associated with the degree of extraversion. Of those with
the greatest amount of pain (by rating), the amount of pain expres-

sion seemed to be a function of extraversion" (p.244). The implication that pre-existing personality traits may have a causal relationship with sensitivity to and reaction to pain, however, has been
questioned. Relief of pain is associated with a fall in levels of
neuroticism and anxiety (Kissen, 1964; Sternbach and Timmermanns,
1975) suggesting that the raised anxiety level may in fact result
from illness and pain. Similarly, the association between pain
complaint and extraversion may be explained simply by the wider range
of social activities chosen by extraverts and the correspondingly
wider spread of illness effects and disability for a given level of
physical impairment or experienced pain. It may be also that there
are interactions among pain complaint, type of pain problem (ie,
whether acute, chronic or terminal) and locus of pain (head, back
etc). The role of such general personality dimensions would seem to
need further investigation, although it may be, as is argued later,
that more specific measures are needed.

Hypochondriasis and Illness Behaviour. There have been two
main strands in the development of psychometric measures of
hypochondriasis and illness behaviour. Factor-analytic approaches
to the study of depression had frequently identified factors of
somatic concern, preoccupation with physical health, prolonged ill-
health and multiplicity of complaints (Kessell, 1968; Friedman et
al, 1963; Rosenthal and Gudeman, 1967; Hordern et al, 1965; Hunt
et al, 1967; Lorr et al, 1967; Kay et al, 1969). The scales of the
MMPI have already been reviewed. The Hs scale is essentially a
symptom inventory and does not include items tapping individual's
attitudes to disease, or assessing the reactions of other people in
the patient's environment.

Attempts have been made, however, to assess the individual's
perception of disease, and the effects on his life. Mechanic and
Volkart (1960) devised a scale to measure the degree to which a
person tends to classify himself as sick and adopt the sick-role
("sick-role tendency") and other studies (Thurlow, 1971; Spilken
and Jacobs, 1971) have attempted to examine the notion of illness
behaviour. More recently Pritchard (1974, 1979) has attempted to
assess illness behaviour among patients on haemodialysis and
awaiting cardiac surgery. He incorporated a 'Response to Illness'
questionnaire (RIQ) to assess both the meaning of the illness to the
patient and his affective, cognitive and behavioural response styles,
and produced eight dimensions of illness behaviour. His work has
not so far been replicated by independent authors, nor has his
system been used with back patients.

Perhaps best known, however, is the work of Pilowsky. Using
Raven's (1950) method of comparative matching, Pilowsky (1967)
produced a 20-item questionnaire which was then given to 200
psychiatric patients, of which 100 had been identified as having
hypochondriacal symptoms, and of which the other 100 had little or

none. Hypochondriasis was defined as: "a persistent preoccupation with disease despite reassurance given after thorough medical examination" (p.90).

Seventeen items originally discriminated between the groups, and of these, 14 items were factor analysed. The three emergent factors were described as bodily preoccupation, disease phobia and disease conviction. This index has been used in the investigation of pain in female patients with malignant disease (Bond, 1971) and in a comparison of the effectiveness of treatment by chiropractors and physicians (Kane et al, 1974). In another factor-analysis, Bianchi (1973) produced five configurations of hypochondriasis, but the statistics are questioned by Kenyon (1976).

By far the best known of the hypochondriacal measures, however, is the Illness Behaviour Questionnaire (IBQ), (Pilowsky and Spence, 1975), a derivation of the original Whitley Index. This 52-item questionnaire has been shown to comprise of seven factors, the most important of which are described as: general hypochondriasis characterised by phobic concern about one's state of health; disease conviction with accompanying somatic preoccupation; and a bipolar dimension contrasting somatic as opposed to psychological perception of illness. The scales have been shown to differentiate between intractable pain patients and a mixed group of physically ill outpatients (Pilowsky and Spence, 1976a); to be unrelated to chronicity (Pilowsky and Spence, 1976b); and to permit the classification of individuals into two general types of reaction to illness: relatively non-neurotic reality-orientated attitudes to illness, and types of abnormal illness behaviour (Pilowsky and Spence, 1976c). The earlier version of the scale was shown to correlate highly with independent assessment by spouses, and to have satisfactory test - re-test reliability (Pilowsky, 1967). Other studies using the IBQ are reviewed in Pilowsky and Spence (1981).

Finally, Sternbach (1974) devised a Health Index (HI) consisting of four sections designed to assess not merely hypochondriasis and depression, but also the "half-conscious embarking on a 'dropping out' style of life" (Sternbach et al, 1973). The invalidism scale was based on nine items from the Cornell Medical Index, Section J with the addition of a tenth item. The next 20 items were adopted from the Zung Self-Rating depression scale (Zung, 1965). The content of each was kept the same, but the format changed to be the same as the invalidism items. The final two sections comprised a 10-item pain-game scale designed to reflect the kinds of "hostile manipulation and 'doctor-patient' jousting that might go on if pain games were, in fact, being played" (Sternbach et al, 1973, p.55).

Somatic Awareness. The relationship between pain and affective states such as anxiety and depressed mood has already been discussed. Such states are frequently represented by collections of items in

measures of general emotional disturbance. Commonly, however, pain
patients do not acknowledge or complain of anxious mood despite
evidence of physiological hyperactivity or over-arousal during a
systemic inquiry. Clinically the diagnosis of somatic anxiety may
be made if a sufficient number of each symptoms are apparent. Reliance on questionnaires placing emphasis on underlined subjective anxiety, may
miss somatic components of anxiety. Similarly certain populations
such as military groups (Aitken et al, 1981) may appear within the
normal range as far as neuroticism is concerned, but show a significant number of somatic symptoms. Perhaps the best known measure of
anxiety is the Taylor Manifest Anxiety Scale (TMAS) (Taylor, 1953)
but according to Fenz and Epstein (1965), although the three original
sub-scales (striated muscle tension, autonomic arousal and feelings
of fear and insecurity) can be justifiably combined to produce an
overall measure of anxiety, there is in addition a specific muscle
tension factor. In an early study (Mandler et al, 1958), Mandler
investigated the perception of autonomic activity using the
Autonomic Perception Questionnaire (APQ) which consisted of several
open-ended questions about pleasure, happiness or state of wellbeing, and a second set concerning anxiety, apprehensiveness and
tension. There followed a series of visual analogue scales, anchored
at each end by adjectives, investigating the perception of a wide
range of body activities accompanying either anxious or happy mood.
Small, but significant, correlations between perceived and actual
autonomic reactivity during stress were discovered in a second study
(Mandler and Kremen, 1958). The APQ has also been found to be
related to performance in heart-rate-control tasks (Bergman and
Johnson, 1971; Blanchard et al, 1972). Borkovec (1976) has advocated
the differentiation of physiological, cognitive and overt behavioural
components of anxiety in response to external and internal fear cues.
In view of the aforementioned general lack of subjective anxiety
among chronic pain groups, except at times of clearly defined stress
(such as prior to surgical operations), it was decided to modify the
APQ to assess the role of somatic awareness in chronic pain.

DEMOGRAPHIC, SOCIAL AND CULTURAL INFLUENCES ON PAIN

Sex and Age

Notermans and Tophoff (1967) found that males showed significantly greater pain tolerance, though not pain threshold. Studies
of pain populations have generally shown a higher level of pain
reporting in females (Robins, 1973; Merskey and Spears, 1967;
Laskin, 1969; Schwartz, 1959; Bakal, 1975). Differences have also
been found in effect of analgesics (Loan and Morrison, 1967) and in
the quantity of analgesics prescribed (Pilowsky and Bond, 1969).
Studies of the effect of age on various pain measures are reviewed
by Weisenberg (1977). He mentions the important study by Clarke

and Mehl (1971) which showed that most of the apparent increase in
pain threshold with age could be accounted for by the reluctance to
label the noxious stimulus as pain rather than due to a change in
sensitivity.

Social Factors

   Experimental Approaches. Craig and Prkachin (1980) in a
transactional analysis of pain identified a number of social factors
affecting pain behaviour. "These social reactions would appear to
depend on a variety of factors including the situational context in
which they occur, attributes of all those present at the time
distress is signalled, and characteristics of the manner in which
pain is displayed, including its intensity, frequency and chronicity.
In turn, the social consequences are likely to exert reciprocal
influence, provoking immediate and long-term effects on the expressions themselves" (pp.58-59). The importance of social learning has
been illustrated in a series of investigations and shown the importance of modelling (Craig and Weiss, 1971, 1972), evaluated its
importance on a variety of dimensions of the experience of pain
(Craig and Prkachin, 1978), and examined other influences that may
modulate the effects of modelling (Craig, 1978). Craig and Prkachin
(1980) conclude: "The research program has been relatively consistent
in finding that exposure to tolerant and intolerant models respectively decreases or increases pain reports and produces alterations
in avoidance behaviour consistent with the altered reports" (p.61).

   Clinical Approaches. Most of the studies just mentioned were
designed from an experimental rather than clinical perspective.
Fordyce (1976) has attempted, however, to produce a treatment
approach to chronic pain from a learning theory perspective. In his
operant analysis of pain behaviour, social behaviour both of the
patient and of those in his environment is of paramount importance.
Unfortunately, he treats 'psychogenic' and 'operant' as diagnostic
rather than clinical dimensions (admittedly of a psychological
rather than a psychiatric type). The reliability with which specific
'respondent pain behaviours' and 'operant pain behaviour' can be
identified is not known; and while Fordyce stresses the importance
of adequate selection of patients for treatment (following a detailed
behavioural analysis), it is far from clear how to do this. In a
pilot study of about 20 NHS patients by the present authors, it
proved exceedingly difficult to obtain accurate information from
the patients about even the characteristics of their own pain
behaviour, quite apart from that of their relatives, and convincing
patients, and their families, to accept an in-patient programme of
the sort described by Fordyce seems a major problem. Private patients in the United States are, of course, quite a different population. Recently Leavitt et al (1979) using the Social Readmustment
Rating Scale (SRRS) investigated the relationship between recent

life stresses and the experience of low back pain, and found, somewhat surprisingly, changes in life events were associated with some
sensory attributes, but not others, not with purely affective
attributes and not with intensity. The authors admit the need to
refine psychological assessment techniques and suggest sub-division
of non-organic groups into at least two sub-groups; "one characterised by psychogenic syndromes and the other free of psychological
overlay" (p.55). While we agree about the necessity of clarifying
psychological assessment, and indeed go some way towards this in
the study reported below, it seems unlikely that the study of life
events per se will contribute more than a small amount to the
explanation of clinical pain.

Cultural Factors

The discussion of cultural factors is reviewed by Craig and
Prkachin (1978) and Wolff and Langley (1968), but while cultural
differences undoubtedly exist in beliefs about disease and communication about pain, the interpretation of cultural differences in the
individual back pain patient would seem to require the establishment
of adequate cultural norms for the variables of interest prior to
the examination of differences in patterns of inter-relationships
relating specifically to cultural rather than to sub-cultural
factors. Bond (1980b) presents a historical perspective on the
social development of attitudes to the suffering of pain and
concludes: "It is clear that there are several conceptual frameworks
within which pain problems and the suffering associated with them
may be analyzed and treated, namely, the neurobiological, psychodynamic, behavioural, and ethico-religious paradigms. This observation is central to the understanding of pain and suffering and one
which has only recently begun to filter into the minds of those who
care for individuals in pain" (p.60).

This brief review suggests that social and demographic factors
may be important to the expression of pain, but further studies of
clinical populations are needed, and further refinement in assessment techniques (particularly in the analysis of operant pain and
in the study of familial perspectives on pain) required to produce
instruments of use in a scientific framework. In the meantime, the
examination of simple social and demographic variables to identify
differences in the relationships among clinical variables may suggest
further avenues of inquiry and, in some circumstances, the production
of a general model partialling out differences in social and
demographic variables, may be appropriate.

PURPOSE OF STUDY

The general aim of the study was to examine the relationship between degree of physical impairment and severity of illness among chronic back patients. Several measures of severity were considered, but disability was finally chosen as being of special importance in clinical decision making and since it is of considerable importance in medico-legal practice where financial compensation often has to be considered.

It was hypothesised firstly that reported disability would be significantly predicted by degree of objective physical impairment and other illness characteristics; secondly, that occupational and demographic factors would increase the power of the prediction; and thirdly, that the inclusion of psychological measures would markedly increase the strength of the prediction even after these other factors had been taken into account.

The construction of the assessment measures will first be described; the general hypotheses will then be examined; the significance of two new types of psychological information will be discussed; disability will be compared with other measures of severity; and a tentative model will be offered to account for the relationships identified.

MATERIAL AND METHODS

Selection of Subjects

The patients for this study came from two sources. They were either referred directly by their general practitioner for assessment of treatment for backache to the Department of Orthopaedic Surgery (primary referrals); or were re-referred by other specialists (generally orthopaedic or neurological consultants, with a small number from rheumatological and general surgical consultants) to the Problem Back Clinic (secondary referrals). The primary referrals were allocated randomly to one of 8 orthopaedic consultants, and the patients in this study were those referred to one of the consultants (GW). There is no reason to suspect that this sample is in any way unrepresentative of the pool of primary referrals. The secondary referrals were re-referred usually because of problems, either surgical or psychological, in the assessment of their suitability for treatment.

Pilot studies of normal subjects had shown that the incidence of a number of features: physical impairment, reported disability, inappropriate symptoms and general somatic complaints; rose sharply after the age of 55 years. Older patients had difficulty with the psychological assessment and, most importantly, the incidence of serious spinal pathology rose markedly above the age of 55 years (Waddell et al, 1981). It was decided, therefore, in this study, to restrict our investigations to patients between the ages of 18 and 55 years.

Patients with an inability to read, brain damage, history of psychosis or formal psychiatric treatment were excluded. Furthermore all patients were of British extraction and had English as their native language.

Of the initial 332 patients, 34 (10.2%) were excluded because of age, 25 (7.5%) because of difficulties with language, comprehension or compliance, and 73 (22.0%) because of spinal pathology (tumour, infection, inflammatory disease, spondylolisthesis and osteoporotic or traumatic fracture). The final 200 subjects otherwise are representative of chronic backache (duration more than 3 months) related to mechanical derangement of the lumbosacral region due to trauma and/or degenerative changes.

An additional group (n = 141) who had a complete clinical assessment but not the psychometric battery (mainly as a result of either language related problems or administrative difficulties in obtaining complete proformas at the clinic) were used to cross-validate the internal consistency of the clinical assessment measures described below.

A number of other pilot studies were carried out to establish the discriminative validity of particular scales or methods of assessment. A detailed discussion of these is beyond the scope of the present chapter but will be reported elsewhere (Waddell et al, 1981). They will be referred to, where appropriate, in other parts of the text.

Clinical Assessment

The clinical examination consisted of obtaining demographic details, history of presenting problem, a general systemic inquiry, including personal and familial medical history, the elicitation of signs of physical impairment, inappropriate physical signs, and the determination of inappropriate symptomatology and chronic disability, based on the patient's report.

Special scales were constructed for the assessment of objective physical impairment, inappropriate physical signs, inappropriate symptomatology and chronic disability. Each of these now will be described in turn.

Demographic and Clinical Characteristics. Selected demographic and clinical characteristics of the main group are presented in Table 1. The mean age is slightly lower than would be expected. This is explained by the exclusion of more patients over 55 years than under 18 years. The relatively high proportion of Social Class 2 females is largely explained by female nurses, which will be commented upon later. Medico-legal involvement was not a feature

Table 1. Demographic and Clinical Characteristics

	Total (N = 200)	Males (n = 117)	Females (n = 83)
Age in Years	39.2 +/- 9.0	39.3 +/- 9.0	38.9 +/- 9.1
Social Class (Reg. Gen. Classif.) 1	7.6%	5.2%	11.69%
2	21.1%	12.9%	34.8%
3	9.7%	4.3%	18.8%
4	31.4%	41.4%	14.5%
5	14.6%	16.4%	11.6%
6	15.7%	19.8%	8.7%
Source of Referral			
Primary (GP)	39.5%	38.5%	41.1%
Secondary (other consultants)	60.5%	61.5%	59.0%
Medical Legal Status (past, present or planned)	9.0%	14.6%	1.2%
Major Presenting Problem			
Back pain	20.5%	24.3%	15.0%
Back pain + referred thigh pain	55.4%	48.7%	65.0%
Root pain + paraesthesia	23.6%	27.0%	18.7%
Neurological	0.5%	0%	1.2%
Type of Onset			
Spontaneous	34.9%	36.0%	33.3%
Lifting	18.7%	17.5%	20.5%
Bending	6.8%	4.4%	10.3%
Direct Blow	10.9%	14.9%	5.1%
Other	28.6%	27.2%	30.8%

Table 1. (continued)

	Total (N = 200)	Males (n = 117)	Females (n = 83)
Duration of Symptoms in Months	63.5 +/- 35.8	62.6 +/- 35.4	64.7 +/- 36.4
Number of Previous Back Operations			
0	85.0%	88.0%	80.7%
1	9.5%	6.8%	13.3%
2	4.0%	3.4%	4.8%
3	1.5%	1.7%	1.2%
Time Pattern			
Intermittent	28.0%	31.6%	22.9%
Continuous (more than 3 months)	72.0%	68.4%	77.1%
Type of Work			
Sedentary	19.4%	17.1%	22.8%
Housewife	12.8%	0%	31.6%
Driving	8.2%	12.8%	1.3%
Light Manual	28.6%	23.9%	35.8%
Heavy Manual	31.1%	46.2%	8.9%
Time Off Work (Continuously) in Months	10.3 +/- 17.1	9.3 +/- 13.2	12.3 +/- 23.2

of this group and its low incidence precluded its retention for
further investigation. Most patients presented with back pain,
usually accompanied by referred thigh pain. Only one patient had a
neurological diagnosis. Type of onset proved unrelated to any other
variable and was excluded. Duration of symptoms (mean of 63.5
months) is partly explained by the exclusion from the study of patients with acute pain (ie duration of less than 3 months' continuous
back pain). The number of previous back operations was small, but
the variable was retained as failed surgical treatment has been shown
to be of considerable psychological significance (Waddell et al,
1979). The majority of patients described their pain as continuous
rather than as intermittent. Proportions in various types of work
are as expected, as is the sex difference on this variable. The
high average time off work is partly a function of the exclusion of
patients with acute backache, but suggests also that many of the
group will have already lost their jobs or be in danger of doing so.

Physical Impairment. Clinical examination of the back provides
information about the back itself and the lumbar and sacral nerve
supply. Physical assessment of the spine, its mechanical disorders
and any neurological involvements, supplemented where necessary by
the appropriate radiological and other investigations, was standardised using two independent examiners and a scale contructed using
those variables having satisfactory discriminant validity (in comparison with normals), inter-rater reliability (using independent
examiners) incidence (to permit the variable in a factor-analysis)
and validity (having a satisfactory factor loading in the final
scale). After a series of sequential pilot studies, a final scale
was produced of 6 items referring to change in curvature of the
spine, listing, localised tenderness, limited lateral flexion and
limited straight leg raising (left and right). Principal Component
Analysis produced a first factor accounting for 32.3% of the variance
and having reasonable, if not high, internal consistency ($\Theta = 0.58$).
Details of this scale are described fully (Waddell et al, 1981).

Inappropriate Signs. The identification of physical signs
during examination of the back has already been described. Because
patient and observer interact in the course of medical examination,
however, most physical signs contain some non-organic element.
Wing et al (1977) found, for example, that lumbar flexion correlated
with neuroticism and straight leg raising with pain tolerance.
Selected physical signs which appeared to have a predominantly non-
physical interpretation were described earlier this century in a
medico-legal context. Clinical attention to these signs was drawn
by Walters (1961, 1973). Such signs are inappropriate in that they
are clearly distinguishable from the standard clinical signs of
physical pathology (described above) and correlate with other
psychological data (Waddell et al, 1979). They do not occur in
normal subjects, although multiple false positive signs do occur in
elderly patients with difficulty standing because of acute pain.

The present set of inappropriate, or non-organic signs (described in detail by Waddell et al, 1980) includes superficial or non-anatomical tenderness, pain on axial loading or rotation (simulation tests designed to appear as if they ought to produce pain), straight-leg raising under conditions of distraction (where a physical sign previously examined directly is now examined in the guise of another), widespread regional disturbance inconsistent with neuro-anatomical structure, and over-reaction (frequently non-verbal) to the examination procedure.

All items had a high inter-rater reliability (K = 0.60-0.67, p < .001 in all cases), high discriminatory validity (correlating insignificantly with objective physical impairment) and the final scale of 7 items had a high internal consistency (Θ = 0.83) which was replicated in a cross-validation group (Θ = 0.87). Further details are presented in Waddell et al (1980, 1981).

Inappropriate Symptoms. The entire clinical practice of medical diagnosis and management is based on the occurrence of common and hence recognisable patterns of disease. The anatomical and temporal patterns of back pain, its characteristics, and the way in which patients present and describe their symptoms usually approximate to such clinical patterns. Occasionally, however, patients offer descriptions which clearly do not fit general clinical experience. Certain specific symptoms appear to be particularly inappropriate and are related to psychological features (Brown et al, 1954; Walter, 1961; Merskey, 1965a, 1965b; Wing et al, 1977). They are generally vague, ill-localised and lack the normal relationships to time, physical activity and anatomy. Twenty-four inappropriate symptoms were initially identified from a review of the clinical literature (Brown et al, 1954; Walters, 1961; Guze and Perley, 1963; Merskey, 1965a, 1965b) and the medico-legal literature (McKendrick, 1912; Collie, 1913; Jones and Llewellyn, 1917; Collie, 1932; Huddleston, 1932; Miller, 1961). The list was submitted to 22 experienced orthopaedic and neurosurgical consultants who were asked to rank the inappropriateness of each symptom on the basis of their clinical experience. The incidence of the symptoms was then examined in a pilot study of 182 consecutive chronic back pain referrals. Fifteen of the symptoms were rejected because of rarity, high incidence in normal subjects, ambiguous clinical interpretations or lack of any relationship to any of the other psychological measures. The final group referred to symptoms affecting the whole leg, such as pain, numbness and collapsing; and other symptoms - tailbone pain, lack of pain-free spells, intolerance of any treatment and emergency admissions to hospital. There was high inter-rater agreement of the individual symptoms (K = 0.58-1.00, all significant at least at p < 0.01), and high discriminatory validity (very low incidence in normals). The final 7-item scale had a reasonable internal consistency (Θ = 0.66) which was cross-validated on a further sample of 141 subjects (Θ = 0.69) and did not correlate significantly with objective physical impairment (r = -0.02, NS).

The inappropriate symptoms although correlating with the inappropriate signs (r = 0.53, p < .001) were clearly separable from them. When the two sets of items were factor analysed together, two clear factors representing the signs and the symptoms emerged which accounted for 25.7% and 16.6% respectively of the total variance. The details are discussed elsewhere (Waddell et al, 1981).

Disability. Disability should be clearly distinguished from physical impairment which is an anatomical or pathological abnormality leading to loss of normal bodily ability (JAMA, 1958; Garrad and Bennett,1971) and has been defined as "diminished capacity for everyday activities and for gainful employment" (Martinat, 1966). Clinically it can be thought of as limitation of a patient's performance when compared with a fit person (Garrad and Bennett, 1971) but unlike physical impairment which is an objective structural impairment, disability is assessed on the basis of patient's verbal assessment of his difficulties. A previous check-list of functional disability (Wing et al, 1973, 1977) was used as a basis for the scale. The 20 items on Wing's scale, however, included items relating to work loss, financial consequences and social factors not necessarily directly proportional to functional disability and it was felt these would be better assessed separately. Items of physical impairment and pain severity were excluded for the same reason. A number of the items relating to general quality of life and ability to do household chores were felt to be imprecise and better excluded as secondary derivatives of the more basic functions.

The remaining 8 items particularly relevant to chronic disability were used as the basis for the 9-item scale which assessed problems lifting heavy weights, sitting, standing, walking or travelling difficulties; disturbed sleep, sexual problems, restricted social life, and specific difficulty dressing. The individual ratings were made by the surgeon on the basis of the patients' descriptions of their difficulties. The individual items were reliable (K = 0.41-0.78, p < .05 in all cases), as a scale had satisfactory internal consistency (θ = 0.79), which was cross-validated in a further sample of 141 patients (θ = 0.82) and correlated highly (r = 0.70) with a similar backache disability self-report questionnaire devised in Oswestry, England (Fairbank et al, 1980). In fact, it had a higher completion rate, was quicker to complete and produced a better spread of scores than the Oswestry questionnaire. The relationship of the other major variables to chronic disability will be the main purpose of the study.

Psychometric Variables

Pain Scale. Prior to the clinical examination, the patient was asked to complete a pain scale, a visual analogue measure with verbal end-points as used by Sternbach (1974) and described above.

Pain Drawing. At the same time, the patient filled in the pain drawing (Ransford et al, 1976) following the standard procedure and scored according to his instructions.

Locus of Control. Problems with the validity of the Rotter IE scale have already been discussed. Furthermore, a pilot study by the present authors of pain patients in the West of Scotland showed that a significant proportion of pain patients found it difficult to complete or were irritated by it. A new personal locus of control scale constructed to overcome the problems of confusing political and personal control, and social desirability bias, and for which general population norms are available (Cooke, in preparation) was used in this study. The 16-item scale in fact proved to be unrelated to any of the major variables in the study (apart from a modest correlation with extraversion) and so the details will not be presented here.

Eysenck Personality Questionnaire (EPQ). The utility of general personality traits was examined using the EPQ, the latest in Eysenck's series of personality tests. It gives measures of extraversion (EPQE) and neuroticism (EPQN) which are highly correlated with the traits as identified by the previous versions of the tests. It incorporates a new psychoticism scale (EPQP) which is something of a misnomer as the dimension seems to be more a measure of psychopathic tendencies than psychotic illness. Finally, the test includes a Lie Scale (EPQL) which seems to be a measure of social desirability rather than malingering (as might be implied by the title).

Depression. Since depressed mood is a well recognised concomitant of all sorts of pain (Sternbach, 1974) it was decided to include a measure of depression. The Zung Self-Rated depression scale (Zung, 1965; Zung et al, 1965) has been used in general population studies in nine different countries to date (Zung, 1967, 1969, 1971, 1972; Zung and Durham, 1973; Blumenthal and Dielman, 1975; Henderson et al, 1979). The particular advantage of the Zung is that it does not include any items specifically concerning pain and so it is useful in examining the relationship between depressed mood and pain. It has been used in other pain studies (Block et al, 1980a, 1980b; Sternbach, 1974). Following Blumenthal's (1975) suggestion, Cooke (1980) improved the Zung by the addition of three items. Since general population norms are available for the West of Scotland, it was decided to use Cooke's modification of the Zung scale in this study.

Somatic Awareness (MSPQ). Prior to the present studies, a 43-item modified MSPQ was developed by one of the authors (CJM). Items were drawn from several anxiety questionnaires and those items selected which were rated independently by seven judges as measuring perception of body activity. The 43-item questionnaire was given to 140 patients having a diagnosis of anxiety and to 100

consecutive hospital visitors. 33 items were retained as distinguishing satisfactorily between anxious patients and normals. The
33-item version was then given to a pilot series of 100 consecutively
referred back patients and those items having a satisfactory
incidence retained. Finally, the questionnaire was given to a further series of 40 back pain patients who filled in the questionnaire
at the clinic and again 24-48 hours later and unstable items
excluded. During these stages a further 20 items were rejected
leaving a 13-item scale which was factor-analysed and had a high
internal consistency ($\theta = 0.79$). The final set of items included
cardiovascular, cortical, gastro-intestinal and muscular variables,
but not items of subjective anxiety. The scale is being prepared
for publication (Main, 1982).

Illness Behaviour Questionnaire (IBQ). Pilowsky's IBQ has
already been described in the literature review. It was included
here as the best measure of general hypochondriasis. The original
52-item questionnaire had been criticised on the grounds that only
the first three scales had a reasonable number of items. Ten items
were added to the questionnaire to expand some of the smaller scales,
and responses to the 62-item IBQ were obtained from pain clinic
family general practice groups in two large cities (Adelaide,
S. Australia and Seattle, Washington) and while Pilowsky (1981)
claims that "the descriptions that the profiles provided are consistent with earlier work based on the 52-item IBQ" (p.4), he appears
to have added the items somewhat arbitrarily. At the time of
planning the present study, the only information concerning the
revised factor structure appeared to be based on myocardial infarction patients (Byrne and White, 1979). The studies on coronary
artery by-pass patients (Pilowsky et al, 1979) and on general
practice patients (Pilowsky, 1981) were not at that time available.
It was decided therefore to restrict our attention in the main to
the first three scales of the 52-item version, although the first
two scales are identical in both versions and the third scale has
the addition of only one item.

Sternbach's Health Index. In addition to the Zung, it was
decided to examine the other three scales from Sternbach's Health
Index: invalidism, pain communication and pain games scale although
the construct validity and statistical properties of these scales
have not so far been reported.

The internal consistency of the three scales was determined
from the first unrotated factor in separate principal component
analyses. The invalidism scale had highest construct validity
($\theta = 0.76$), followed by the pain communication scale ($\theta = 0.69$) and
the pain games scale ($\theta = 0.67$). It was decided therefore to
include the three scales in the study although it was felt likely
that there would be some overlap between the first two of these
scales and the first two of the IBQ.

Statistical Methodology

In view of the multivariate relationships, it was decided to use multiple regression as the main statistical method. It has procedures directly equivalent to analysis of variance techniques, and permits the inclusion of nominal or ordinal variables coded as dummy variables into the regression equation (Cohen and Cohen, 1975). It is possible to find either the best overall set of predictors of the dependent variable simultaneously or evaluate the increase in prediction obtained by adding each variable sequentially.

Since the basic purpose of the study was to evaluate the relative importance of certain types of variable to the prediction of disability, variables representing each of these differing conceptual domains were selected. An a priori order of entry into the equation was determined on the basis of clinical importance and ease of obtaining the information. Thus illness characteristics were evaluated prior to occupational and demographic characteristics and clinical psychological information (obtained by examination) prior to psychometric evaluation. Where necessary, for clarification purposes, and to elucidate certain redundancies (particularly among the psychometric variables) several orders of entry into the equation were compared.

Independent Variables: First Stage. Degree of physical impairment, type of major problem, number of previous back operations, duration of symptoms and time pattern (whether chronic or recurrent) were chosen to represent illness characteristics.

Sex, age, social class, work-loss and work-type were chosen to represent demographic and occupational factors.

Inappropriate signs and inappropriate symptoms were retained as two measures of magnified illness presentation.

The EPQ was retained as a measure of general personality structure; the locus of control scale as a cognitive dimension of personality; the modified Zung as a measure of depressed mood; the MSPQ for the perception of somatic activity; and the two sets of three scales (Pilowsky and Sternbach) as alternative measures of aspects of hypochondriasis and beliefs about disease.

Preliminary Results

The correlations of most of the variables (nominal variables excluded) with degree of disability are shown in Table 2 for the total group and for males and females separately.

It can be seen that age, EPQE, EPQP, locus of control and IBQ1

Table 2.   Correlations with Disability

	Total (N = 200)	Males (n = 117)	Females (n = 83)
Physical impairment	27*	25	30*
Previous back operations	33*	33*	34*
Duration of symptoms	15		
Time pattern	36*	31*	40*
Sex	-17	-	-
Age			
Social class	20*	27*	26
Work-loss	44*	44*	45*
Work-type			
Inappropriate signs	52*	48*	55*
Inappropriate symptoms	61*	59*	61*
EPQE			
EPQN	23*		28
EPQP			
EPQL	14		
Locus of control			
Depression	49*	43*	51*
MSPQ	47*	37*	52*
IBQ1 (Gen. hypochon.)			
IBQ2 (Dis. convict.)	39*	25	59*
IBQ3 (Somat. perc.)	-36*	-36*	-40*
Invalidism	47*	45*	49*
Pain communication	59*	54*	65*
Pain games			32*
Pain scale	39*	29*	29*
Pain drawing	30*	24	29*

All entries correlation significant p < .05
           * correlation significant p < .01
(values are Pearson corrs X 100)

(general hypochondriasis) bear no relationship with disability and were not considered further. Work-type just failed to reach significance but was retained in that there seemed to be a marked difference between the sexes.

In view of the high correlations with disability and to permit the construction of a more general model, it was decided to examine pain scale, pain drawing, Sternbach pain communication scale and work-loss as alternative measures of severity, as their inclusion at this stage in the analysis would account for so much variance in the dependent variable as to make it impossible to examine the four classes of variable selected for the study. The results for the other measures of severity, with implications for the assessment of severity will be discussed later.

Further Statistical Analysis

Number of previous back operations, social class, and work-type were coded as dummy variables and entered into regression equations with disability as the dependent variable and independent variables entered in the four classes already described (illness characteristics; occupational and demographic; magnified illness presentation and psychometric).

Clear differences were found between the scales on the psychological variables, and as would be expected, on work-related variables. In order to produce a general model of disability, therefore, sex was included as the first term in the regression equation and interaction terms (for various independent variables with sex) included as appropriate.

After a further series of regression equations, it was established that duration of symptomatology was entirely explained by degree of physical impairment and number of previous back operations; and EPQN was entirely explained by depressed mood and heightened somatic awareness. These variables were excluded from further analysis.

RESULTS

The Prediction of Disability

The results are shown in Table 3. It can be seen that disability is significantly predicted by degree of objective physical impairment. Type of major problem is irrelevant, but previous surgery and time pattern (whether intermittent or continuous) significantly improve the prediction. Of the demographic and

Table 3. The Prediction of Disability

Independent Variables	Class	$\%R^2$	$\%R^2$ch	F
Sex	D&O	3.1	3.1	12.40**
Physical impairment	IC	10.4	7.3	29.20**
Major problem	IC	12.0	1.6	2.13
Previous surgery	IC	17.1	5.1	10.20**
Time pattern	IC	25.0	7.9	31.60**
Work-type	D&O	27.6	2.6	2.60*
Work-type X Sex	D&O	31.9	4.3	4.30**
Social class	D&O	34.5	2.6	2.08
Social class X Sex	D&O	36.0	1.5	1.20
Inappropriate signs	MIP	46.5	10.6	42.40**
Inappropriate symptoms	MIP	57.6	11.1	44.40**
Depression	P	61.5	3.9	15.60**
Somatic awareness	P	61.7	0.2	0.80
Invalidism	P	63.0	1.3	5.20*

 * F Ratio to enter significant at $p < .05$
** F Ratio to enter significant at $p < .01$
IC - Illness characteristics
D&O - Demographic & occupational characteristics
MIP - Magnified illness presentation
P   - Psychometric variables

occupational variables, only sex, work-type and their interaction improve the prediction. Both types of magnified illness presentation greatly increase the prediction. Depressed mood and self-concept of invalidism add slightly more, even after the major amount of variance explained by magnified illness presentation.

It can be concluded that while many variables correlate signif-icantly with disability (Table 2), there is a large measure of redundancy among them. When differences in illness characteristics and demographic or occupational have been removed, psychological variables are still of major importance. In the specific model tested above, the effect of magnified illness presentation was considered prior to the routine psychometric measures, as it can be assessed quickly and reliably by the surgeon in the clinic without psychometric technology or expertise. If depressed mood, somatic awareness and invalidism are entered into the equation prior to the inappropriate signs and symptoms, the significance of these psycho-

Table 4. Correlations Among 4 Major Variables and Psychometric Measures

	Physical Impairment			Inappropriate Signs			Inappropriate Symptoms			Disability		
	Tot.	Male	Fem.	Tot.	Male	Fem.	Tot.	Male	Fem.	Tot.	Male	Fem.
EPQE												
EPQN							25*		23	23*		28*
EPQP												
EPQL							17					
Locus of control												
Depression				38*	46*	27	30*	29*	23	49*	43*	51*
MSPQ				35*	23	42*	45*	36*	45*	47*	37*	52*
IBQ1												
IBQ2				28*	25*	35*	31*	31*	35*	39*	25*	59*
IBQ3			-23	-27*	-22	-38*	-28*	-25*	-36*	-36*	-36*	-40*
Invalidism				29*	25*	31*	35*	34*	35*	47*	45*	49*
Pain communication		20		35*	32*	27	37*	34*	40*	59*	54*	65*
Pain games				21*		25	16	21		27*	24	32*
Pain scale	20*		26*	36*	26*	44*	36*	20	44*	39*	29*	47*
Pain drawing				22*		25	39*		51*	30*	24	29*

All entries correlation significant p < .05
* correlation significant p < .01
(Values are Pearson corrs X 100)

metric measures is heightened; but the inappropriate signs and symptoms remained of major importance even when entered last in the equation. Most of the psychometric variables added next to nothing when added at the fourth stage, although somatic awareness was a good predictor when entered prior to depressed mood into the equation.

Magnified Illness Presentation. The relationship between the psychometric variables and the four major variables are shown in Table 4.

It can be seen that most of the psychometric variables correlate significantly with inappropriate signs, inappropriate symptoms and disability; but hardly at all with the degree of physical impairment. The inappropriate signs are similar to the objective physical signs (physical impairment) in that they are elicited on clinical examination and in that the precise nature of the examination is unclear to the patients. Both the inappropriate symptoms and the disability index, however, are more closely based on the patient's self-report and the intention of the inquiry is much more evident to the patient.

It is clear from the correlation matrix that there may be a large measure of redundancy among the psychometric variables. In an attempt to distinguish further between the inappropriate signs and symptoms, it was decided to carry out separate regression analyses on each, and further regressions of males and females separately. The order of variables was once more specified a priori. To simplify presentation, only the % change in R^2 is presented (Table 5).

It can be seen that as far as general personality variables are concerned, neither extraversion, locus of control or "psychoticism" are of any relevance. Neuroticism is linked with both inappropriate signs and inappropriate symptoms, and there is also evidence of a differential sex effect (correlating significantly with signs and men, and symptoms among women). The symptoms would also appear to be affected by social desirability (lie scale) although the effect reaches significance only in the total group.

Depressed mood and somatic awareness are clearly of importance in both signs and symptoms (even with the prior removal of the effect of neuroticism). Depressed mood is more important in men (especially for the signs) while somatic awareness is more important for women for both variables (although somatic awareness is also of some importance in the prediction of the inappropriate symptoms among men).

General hypochondriasis (IBQ1), invalidism, disease conviction (IBQ2), pain communication, IBQ3 (somatic perception of problems) and pain games have no additional predictive value whatsoever.

Table 5. Regression Analyses of Inappropriate Signs and
Inappropriate Symptoms with Psychometric Variables

$\%\ R^2$ Change

	Inappropriate Signs			Inappropriate Symptoms		
	Total	Males	Females	Total	Males	Females
EPQE	0.1	0.1	0.8	0.3	0.0	0.6
Locus of control	0.0	0.6	0.1	0.2	1.1	0.0
EPQL	2.0	0.3	2.7	3.0*	0.9	1.5
EPQP	0.0	0.0	1.5	0.8	1.8	1.3
EPQN	3.1*	3.4*	1.5	5.2**	2.1	4.9*
Depression	10.6**	18.8**	4.9*	2.5*	5.0**	0.9
MSPQ	3.2*	0.5	11.1**	10.6**	6.3**	14.1**
IBQ1 (General hypochondriasis)	1.6	2.3	0.9	0.1	0.1	0.2
Invalidism	1.9	0.9	0.1	1.7	2.5	2.3
IBQ2 (Disease conviction)	0.4	0.7	0.8	0.9	2.6	0.2
Pain Communication	0.5	0.2	2.3	1.9	0.8	1.7
IBQ3 (Somatic perception)	1.3	0.1	3.2	1.1	0.9	6.5
Pain Games	0.0	0.0	2.2	0.0	0.0	0.0

*   F Ratio to enter significant at p < .05
** F Ratio to enter significant at p < .01

Both the inappropriate signs and the inappropriate symptoms would appear to be related primarily to depressed mood and heightened somatic awareness. The possible significance of these findings will be discussed below.

Measures of Severity

Although perhaps the most important, functional disability is but one measure of severity of illness. In Table 6, the relative predictive value of the four classes of variable (as before, in the order given) for different measures of severity are given. It should be stressed of course that we are attempting predictions with a small number of classes of variable and a small number of variables. For the purpose of this comparison, only those variables contributing significantly to variance in the dependent variable are included in the computation.

Work-loss is explained entirely by classes IC and D&O and the overall level of prediction (20.0%) is low. Pain scale and pain drawing, both measures of pain intensity rather than its consequences, give similar levels of prediction (25.7% and 23.4% respectively), but differ markedly in the importance of class IC. The greater importance of class D&O to the pain drawing is almost entirely explained by the marked sex difference.

Table 6. Types of Variable and Measures of Severity

| Class of variable | % of Variance Explained | | | | |
	Work-loss	Pain Scale	Pain Drawing	Pain Communication	Disability
IC	11.1	14.1	2.0	13.0	20.3
D&O	8.9	9.3	15.4	6.3	7.4
MIP	0	2.3	6.0	9.0	21.7
P	0	0	0	20.5	1.3
TOTAL	20.0	25.7	23.4	48.8	50.7

IC - Illness characteristics
D&O - Demographic & occupational characteristics
MIP - Magnified illness presentation
P   - Psychometric

Sternbach's pain communication scale is much more an estimate of pain effects than of pain intensity per se and is comparable to disability in terms of its overall predictability (48.8% and 50.7% respectively). Unlike the other measures the pain communication scale is highly predicted by class P (in fact entirely accounted for by depressed mood); but although depressed mood is also highly correlated with disability, it adds only little when added after magnified illness presentation.

Considered from another viewpoint, illness characteristics are fairly important to the prediction of all the measures of severity with the exception of the pain drawing (which raises a doubt about the validity of the pain drawing). Demographic and occupational factors are about equally important for all measures of severity (with an enhanced effect due to sex with the pain drawing). Magnified illness presentation, in the form of anatomically inappropriate signs and symptomatology, does not help in the prediction of work-loss and hardly at all in the simple rating of pain intensity, but becomes increasingly important with increasing generality in the measure of severity. Psychometric measures of subjective distress (mainly depressed mood) are of no help in increasing the prediction of the more objective measures (work-loss and pain ratings) but are highly important in predicting the reporting of pain effects and disability (correlating 0.59 and 0.40 respectively) although in the latter case, magnified illness presentation has accounted for most of their incremental predictive value.

DISCUSSION

Constraints

There were a number of constraints on the present study. The entire clinical assessment, psychometric investigation and exclusion of pathology took between $1\frac{3}{4}$ and $2\frac{1}{2}$ hours to complete. It was simply not feasible either in terms of further patient compliance or in terms of the administration of the out-patient clinic to gather any more information.

Secondly, information gathered depended mainly on clinical examination, self-reports and medical case sheets. It was beyond the resources of the present investigators to obtain routine information from patients' families or gather social background reports about patients from community agencies.

Thirdly, the main purpose of this study was to investigate patients referred for assessment of treatment for surgery. The aforementioned time constraints effectively precluded more widespread psychological investigations, such as one might wish in the assessment of suitability for psychological treatments (such as counselling or operant approaches).

Fourthly, this chapter reports on the identification of, and relationships among, various pain related variables and classes of variable. The identification of <u>individuals</u> of various types will be considered in conjunction with the outcome study, of these patients, at present still in progress.

Fifthly, in view of the expressed objectives of the study and the request for compliance with the extensive assessment procedure in the interests of research rather than simply clinical treatment, the incorporation of clinical pain estimation procedures (pain tolerance, pain threshold and electromyogram investigations of muscle tension in the back) was possible in only a sub-group of these patients and will be reported elsewhere.

Sixthly, as mentioned above, the investigation was restricted to British, English language speaking chronic backache patients between the ages of 18 and 55 able to comply with assessment procedures.

Seventhly, a longitudinal study of patients was not possible in the time available for this study. The hazards of inferring causal relationships from correlational analysis are well known, although determining redundancy among different types of information gathered at the same time would seem to be a worthwhile exercise.

Finally, all the patients were NHS (non-private) patients from the West of Scotland being seen at time of first referral to a specialist orthopaedic department for chronic backache. Generality of the findings to other patient populations and cross-cultural groups remains to be determined (although the data collection for a study of other chronic orthopaedic conditions has been just completed).

Choice of Dependent and Independent Variables

The choice of disability as the major dependent variable seemed important both on grounds of clinical decision making and with a view to future studies of compensation patients or groups in which the assessment has legal or financial implications. It has been shown, however, that the precise relationship between physical impairment and severity of illness is highly dependent on the particular measure of severity used, with the effect of psychological factors ranging from negligible to highly important.

The choice of independent variables was made on the basis of current clinical practice, previous research findings and pragmatic considerations resulting from the constraints on the study. Attempts were made to sample different 'conceptual domains' so that inter-relationships could be examined. In a clinical study of this nature, data collection is time consuming and expensive to gather. A balance has to be found between the breadth of the information sampled and the number of subjects assessed. Given a sample size of 200, it was clearly possible to include analysis of only a certain number of domains and of only a small number of variables representing each of these.

Conceptual Domains (classes of variable). Illness characteristics (IC) were represented by a relatively small number of variables, and of these, degree of physical impairment, previous back surgery and time pattern (whether intermittent or continuous) were of importance. In a separate study (Waddell et al, 1981) the assessment of illness history is discussed. Major problems were found in obtaining valid and reliable information concerning illness history and in fact three successive pilot studies were necessary to produce an instrument of satisfactory reliability. Items tapping previous illness experience (both personal and familial) were also problematic. Previous response to treatment (of various kinds) would again seem to be useful clinical information, but rigorous statistical cross-checks would seem to be advisable in this field.

Of the demographic and occupational characteristics (D&O) the only variables of importance seemed to be sex and type of work (rated according to its requirement of physical effort, on an ordinal scale). There is clearly a need to develop this 'module'. In a sub-group of patients work stress and risk of job loss would seem to be important, although clinical questioning may not be the best way of determining such information. In this study, attempts to investigate such domains were made, but valid and reliable indices would seem to require not merely a clinical screening of such problems, but a specially designed structured interview. In general it would appear that differences in quasi-sociological variables such as social class or socio-economic grouping are accounted for mostly by more specific work related variables.

Magnified illness presentation (MIP) (inappropriate signs and inappropriate symptoms) was highly predictive of the more generalised measures of severity. A lot of effort has been expended by the authors in developing this particular domain, and we are confident that the measures will stand up to replication. Still to be determined is the relative utility of each of these in identifying particular clusters of patients, its use at various stages in the development of chronicity, and power in the prediction of response to treatment.

Clearly, the design of the study enabled the examination of only the incremental value in the prediction of severity of illness of the psychometric variables (P). One might equally well consider the incremental value of the inappropriate signs and symptoms, for example, over and above the psychometric measures. While such

models in fact were investigated, and produced an enhancement in
the predictive value of the psychometric variables, as a class they
proved less important than the inappropriate signs and symptoms.
For this particular population, it would appear likely that only
clinically focussed psychometric measures such as depressed mood,
possibly somatic awareness and perhaps self-concept of invalidism
will be of value. Personality structure and cognitive measures
(such as locus of control) would seem to exert extremely weak effects,
if any at all, in these particular circumstances. Clearly, however,
of all the domains, this one is perhaps the widest and, of course,
only a small number of variables have been sampled. Nonetheless it
certainly would not seem worth excluding more immediate clinically
relevant information for variables constructed on non-clinical
populations unless there are extremely sound theoretical reasons
for pursuing that particular avenue of inquiry.

New or Additional Conceptual Domains. The investigation of the
social, economic and familial consequences of chronic pain was not
investigated in detail in this study (partly because of the aforementioned time constraints). A pilot study by the present authors
into the identification of illness effects has been undertaken
recently with a view to determining the clinical significance of
disparity among various types of pain effect. In order to validate
such information, however, it would appear necessary to cross-
validate information given by the patient with information obtained
from family members, social acquaintances and workmates. The
practical and ethical problems of obtaining such information would
appear to be considerable.

As already mentioned, conceptual domains relevant to psychological methods of treatment will need to be developed. Again,
problems in obtaining valid and reliable information in such areas
abound. A detailed operant analysis is extremely time consuming
and, in the present author's (CJM) experience, fraught with difficulty from a research or evaluative point of view. Apart from the
considerable quantity of missing data in a general behavioural
screening, the relative importance of specific variables to an
'operant dimension' has never been established, nor has a classification or typology for individuals been clearly worked out. It is
beyond the scope of this chapter to consider further psychological
treatments.

Of experimental approaches, pain threshold and pain tolerance
are perhaps of value in the estimation of severity of pain (although
limitations on the extent of inferences from experimental to chronic
clinic pain have been highlighted already). Their incremental value
over routine clinical assessment procedures has yet to be established, as has their comparative utility in the prediction of
outcome of treatment. The present authors have carried out a
pilot investigation of pain threshold, pain tolerance, pain ratio

and EMG determined muscle-tension levels, in certain of the back muscles, in 44 of the 200 subjects of the main study, but the results are as yet unanalysed.

Of the many other possible domains of investigation, the medico-legal domain is perhaps of most importance. Several of the earliest clinical studies (discussed above) on psychological factors in backache tried to identify malingering among back patients. There is no doubt that social factors exert a profound influence on the course of illness and a survey of 12 separate studies showed that the success rate of any form of treatment for backache is approximately one-third lower in compensation patients than in non-compensation patients (Waddell et al, 1979). Magnified illness presentation might seem to be a measure of malingering or consciously exaggerating the extent of the problem, but MIP seems to be equally common in medico-legal cases, compensation cases and in other problem patients for which neither factor operated. There is only a moderate correlation between MIP and medico-legal factors and regression analysis in an early study (Waddell et al, 1980) showed that medico-legal factors accounted for only a very small proportion of the total variance. Furthermore MIP neither correlates with the MMPI validity scores (F and K) which are generally accepted as detecting unreliable answers, attempts to give socially acceptable answers or deliberate exaggeration; nor with the lie score of the EPQ. Conscious magnification of symptoms may of course occur in situations, particularly medico-legal or compensation situations, when there may be considerable discrepancy between objective physical impairment and subjectively reported disability, but complex patterns of MIP cannot be explained simply as malingering. It would seem necessary to investigate their role in a specific study of medico-legal or compensation patients and develop appropriate assessment methods for the financial, occupational and legal implications of chronic pain.

Finally, it has been emphasised that this study has concerned itself with chronic pain patients referred for the first time to a department of orthopaedic surgery funded by the NHS. The generality of the findings to private or fee-paying patients is as yet unknown but would merit investigation. Such an inquiry might entail the alteration of old modules or the development of new ones in order to fit the clinical findings into a socio-economic context.

Research Design. Many alternative research designs are possible. The one selected for this study seemed to be most appropriate in this context. A strategy of continual development and redevelopment of variables and classes of variables has been recommended. Such an open-ended approach would seem to permit the integration of the latest research findings within an existing framework. Of paramount importance is the establishment of the construct validity, perhaps face validity and certainly incremental

validity of any new measures used. Different models using different
a priori order of classes of variable or indeed variables within
classes are possible with the same data base. As steps in the
development of modules for psychological treatments, small group or
single-case designs may help refine new domains of clinical interest.
At some point, however, some attempt will have to be made to
integrate them into a pre-existing framework, or where necessary
into a revised general framework.

The original diagnosis 'functional', representing very much
'diagnosis by exclusion', has certainly been improved by the attempts
to identify positive psychological features. We must beware,
however, of attempting to produce simplistic two-dimensional models
of pain and looking to psychometric measures exclusively to provide
an additional dimension to supplement a physical or organic one.
The specific psychometric approaches so far developed certainly may
be further refined, but personality traits, or even clinical mood
scales, are but one further set of investigations of a particular
type. A genuine multidimensional model with conceptually and
statistically distinct domains of inquiry would seem to be required.

Finally, the incorporation of interactions among relevant
clinical domains may turn out to be of interest in addition to their
main effects, although the statistical requirements as far as
quantity of data is concerned are fairly considerable.

CONCLUSION AND IMPLICATIONS

Firstly, it has been shown in this study that pathology, as
assessed by illness characteristics, is distinguishable from magnified illness presentation in the form of the reporting of inappropriate symptoms of backache and inappropriate responses to clinical
examination. Part of the explanation for the unsatisfactory success
rate for the treatment of chronic backache may lie in the failure
to distinguish pathology from illness behaviour. Indeed attempting
to treat illness behaviour, mistaking it for indications of trauma
or disease, will not only fail to alleviate the problem but may in
fact worsen it.

Secondly, there is only a relatively small relationship between
extent of physical impairment and subjectively reported disability.
The effect of failure to obtain relief from chronic pain may not
only result in depressed mood but also lead to a general sensitising
of the patient to all sorts of physiological events (heightened
somatic awareness), leading to inappropriate pain perceptions or
reports (inappropriate symptoms), inappropriate responses to physical
examination (inappropriate signs) and resulting in a marked exacerbation of the extent of disability for a given level of objective
physical impairment.

Thirdly, it cannot be assumed that even relatively simple items of clinical information are reliable until so demonstrated. Nonetheless, with the appropriate statistical safeguards, it is possible to identify clusters of variables representing discrete domains of clinical relevance in chronic backache.

The traditional role for the clinical psychologist in the field of backache needs re-examination. The interpretation of personality profiles such as the MMPI would appear to be of limited usefulness, although the development of more clinically relevant scales will undoubtedly happen. Indeed it has been suggested that the search for the definitive psychometric profile or set of profiles is perhaps an illusory quest. On the other hand, there would seem to be an important statistical and methodological contribution to be made not only in the processing of medical information and the construction of valid and reliable scales, but also in the design and interpretation of multidisciplinary research. Equally important, perhaps, is the development of psychological treatment techniques, incorporating concepts and clinical methods from other areas of clinical psychology. The same caveats about the identification of salient variables or domains of inquiry apply of course to psychological as well as medical treatment.

In other areas of medicine, there may be evidence of magnified illness presentation. The impetus to develop such concepts in backache has undoubtedly stemmed in part from the sheer extent of the problem and relative failure to treat it successfully. It seems likely that in chronic illness especially, inappropriateness of symptomatology particularly (assuming this can be adequately identified) would seem worth investigating both in terms of prediction of outcome of treatment and in identifying individuals for whom further psychological investigation might lead to educational or clinical counselling rather than traditional medical treatment.

The divisions among sociological, psychological and medical definitions of illness seem to be becoming increasingly blurred. It would seem important to identify the specific contribution of various specialties to human suffering but admit that the alleviation of the ills of mankind and the unhappiness occasioned by occupational, economic or political stress is likely always to be beyond the limits of technological medicine or clinical psychology.

REFERENCES

Agnew, D.C., and Merskey, H., 1976, Words of chronic pain, Pain, 2:73-81.
Aitken, R.C.B., 1969, Measurement of feelings using visual analogue scales, Proc. Roy. Soc. Med., 62:989-993.

Aitken, R.C.B., Lister, J.A., and Main, C.J., 1981, Identification
    of features associated with flying phobia in aircrew,
    Brit. J. Psychiat., in press.
Altrocchi, J., Palmer, J., Hellmann, R., and Davis, H., 1968,
    The Marlowe-Crowne, Repressor-Sensitizer and Internal-External
    scales and attribution of unconscious hostile intent, Psychol.
    Rep., 23:1229-1230.
Andrew, J.M., 1970, Recovery from surgery, with and without prepar-
    atory instruction, for three coping styles, J. Pers. & Soc.
    Psychol., 15:223-226.
Bailey, Carole A., and Davidson, P.O., 1976, The language of pain:
    Intensity, Pain, 2:319-324.
Bakal, D.A., 1975, Headache: a biopsychological perspective,
    Psychol. Bull., 82:369-382.
Beecher, H.K., 1959, "Measurement of Subjective Responses,"
    Oxford University Press, New York.
Beecher, H.K., 1966, One mystery solved, Science, 151:840-846.
Benn, R.T., and Wood, P.H.N., 1975, Pain in the back: an attempt to
    estimate the size of the problem, Rheumatol. & Rehab., 14:
    121-128.
Bergman, J.S., and Johnson, H.J., 1971, The effects of instructional
    set and autonomic perception on cardiac control, Psychophysiol.,
    8:180-190.
Bianchi, G.N., 1973, Patterns of hypochondriasis: a principal
    components analysis, Brit. J. Psychiat., 122:541-548.
Blanchard, E.B., Young, L.D., and McLeod, P., 1972, Awareness of
    heart activity and self-control of heart-rate, Psychophysiol.,
    9:63-68.
Blitz, B., and Dinnerstein, A.J., 1971, Role of attentional focus
    in pain perception: Manipulation of response to noxious stimula-
    tion by instructions, J. Abn. Psychol., 77:42-45.
Block, A.R., Kremer, E.F., and Gaylor, M., 1980a, Behavioural
    treatment of chronic pain: the spouse as a discrimination cue
    for pain behaviour, Pain, 9:243-252.
Block, A.R., Kremer, E.F., and Gaylor, M., 1980b, Behavioural
    treatment of chronic pain: variables affecting treatment
    efficacy, Pain, 8:367-375.
Blumenthal, M.D., 1975, Measuring depressive symptomatology in a
    general population, Arch. Gen. Psychiat., 32:971-978.
Blumenthal, M.D., and Dielman, T.E., 1975, Depressive symptomatology
    and role function in a general population, Arch. Gen. Psychiat.,
    32:825-991.
Blumetti, A.E., and Modesti, L.M., 1976, Psychological predictors
    of success or failure of surgical intervention for intractable
    back pain, in: Advances in Pain Research and Therapy, Vol. 1,"
    J.J. Bonica & D. Albe-Fessard, eds., Raven Press, New York.
Bond, Alyson and Lader, M., 1974, The use of analogue scales in
    rating subjective feelings, Brit. J. Med. Psychol., 47:211-218.
Bond, M.R., 1971, The relation of pain to the Eysenck Personality
    Inventory, Cornell Medical Index and Whitely Index of
    Hypochondriasis, Brit. J. Psychiat., 119:671.

Bond, M.R., 1973, Personality studies in patients with pain secondary
    to organic disease, J. Psychosom. Res., 17:257-263.
Bond, M.R., 1976, Pain and personality in cancer patients, in:
    "Advances in Pain Research and Therapy, Vol. 1," J.J. Bonica &
    D. Albe-Fessard, eds., Raven Press, New York.
Bond, M.R., 1979, "Pain: Its Nature, Analysis and Treatment,"
    Churchill Livingstone, Edinburgh.
Bond, M.R., 1980, Personality and pain: the influence of psycholog-
    ical and environmental factors upon the experience of pain in
    hospital patients, in: "Persistent Pain: Modern Methods of
    Treatment, Vol. 2," Sampson Lipton, ed., Academic Press,
    New York & London.
Bond, M.R., 1980b, The suffering of severe intractable pain, in:
    "Pain and Society," H.W. Kosterlitz & L.Y. Terenius, eds.,
    Dahlem Konferenzen, Verlag Chemie GmbH, Weinheim.
Bond, M.R., Glynn, J.B., and Thomas, D.J., 1976, The relation between
    pain and personality in patients requiring pentazocine after
    surgery, J. Psychosom. Res., 30:369.
Bond, M.R., and Pearson, I.B., 1969, Psychological aspects of pain
    in women with advanced carcinoma of the cervix, J. Psychosom.
    Res., 13:13.
Bonica, J.J., and Albe-Fessard, D., 1976, eds., "Advances in Pain
    Research and Therapy, Vol. 1," Raven Press, New York.
Borkovec, T.D., 1976, Physiological and cognitive processes in the
    regulation of anxiety, in "Consciousness and Self-Regulation:
    Advances in Research, Vol. 1," G.E. Schwartz & D. Shapiro,
    eds., Plenum, New York.
Bradley, J.J., 1963, Severe localised pain associated with the
    depressive syndrome, Brit. J. Psychiat., 109:741-745.
Brown, T., Barr, J.S., Nemiah, J.C., and Barry, H., 1954,
    Psychological factors in low-back pain, New Engl. Med. J.,
    251:31.
Byrne, D.G., and White, H., 1979, Severity of illness and illness
    behaviour: a comparative study of coronary care patients,
    J. Psychosom. Res., 23:57-62.
Carr, J.E., Brownsberger, C.N., and Rutherford, R.S., 1966,
    Characteristics of symptom-matched psychogenic and real pain
    patients on the MMPI, Proc. of 74th Ann. Conv. of Amer.
    Psychol. Assoc., pp.215-216.
Chapman, C.R., Wilson, M.E., and Gehrig, J.D., 1976, Comparative
    effects of acupuncture and transcutaneous stimulation on the
    perception of painful dental stimul, Pain, 2:265:283.
Clark, W.C., 1974, Pain sensitivity and the report of pain: an
    introduction to sensory decision theory, Anaesthesiology,
    40:272-287.
Clark, W.C., and Mehl, L., 1971, Thermal pain: a sensory decision
    theory analysis of the effect of age and sex on d', various
    criteria, and 50% pain threshold, J. Abn. Psychol., 78:202-212.
Clarke, P.R.F., and Spear, F.G., 1954, Reliability and sensitivity
    in the self-assessment of well-being, Bull. Brit. Psychol. Soc.,
    17:55.

Cohen, J., and Cohen, P., 1975, "Applied Multiple Regression/Correlation Analysis for the Behavioural Sciences," Lawrence Erlbaum Assoc., Hillsdale, New Jersey.

Cohen, F., and Lazarus, R.S., 1973, Acting coping processes, coping disposition and recovery from surgery, Psychosom. Med., 35:375-389.

Collie, J., 1913, "Malingering and Feigned Sickness," P.B. Boeber, New York.

Collie, J., 1932, "Fraud in Medico-Legal Practice," Edward Arnold Co., London.

Cooke, D.J., 1980, The structure of depression found in the general population, Psychol. Med., 10:455-463.

Cooke, D.J., (in preparation), A personal locus of control scale, Psychology Department, Gartnavel Royal Hospital, Glasgow, U.K.

Craig, K.D., 1978, Social disclosure, coactive peer companions and social modelling determinants of pain communications, Canad. J. Beh. Sci., 19:91-104.

Craig, K.D., and Prkachin, K.M., 1978, Social modelling influences on sensory decision theory and psychophysiological indices of pain, J. Pers. & Soc. Psychol., 36:805:815.

Craig, K.D., and Prkachin, K.M., 1980, Social influences in public and private components of pain, in: "Stress and Anxiety, Vol. 7," I. Sarason & C.D. Spielberger, eds., Hemisphere Publishing Co., Washington.

Craig, K.D., and Weiss, S.M., 1971, Vicarious influences on pain-threshold determinations, J. Pers. & Soc. Psychol., 19:53-59.

Craig, K.D., and Weiss, S.M., 1972, Verbal reports of pain without noxious stimulation, Perc. & Mot. Skills, 34:943-948.

Crockett, D.J., Prkachin, K.M., and Craig, K.D., 1977, Factors of the language of pain in patient and volunteer groups, Pain, 4:175:182.

Dahlstrom, G.W., and Welsh, G.S., 1960, "An MMPI Handbook," University of Minnesota Press, Mineapolis.

Dana, C.L., 1911, The interpretation of pain and the dyaesthesias, J. Amer. Med. Assoc., 56:787-791.

Davidson, P.O., and Bobey, M.J., 1970, Repressor-sensitizer differences on repeated esposures to pain, Perc. & Mot. Skills, 31:711-714.

De Long, R.D., 1970, "Individual Differences in Patterns of Anxiety-Arousal, Stress-Relevant information and Recovery from Surgery," Unpublished doctoral dissertation, University of California, Los Angeles.

DHSS (Cochrane Report), 1979, "Working Group on Back Pain," HMSO, London.

Doran, D.M.L., and Newell, D.J., 1975, Manipulation in treatment of low back pain: a multicentre study, B.M.J., 2:161-164.

Doxey, N.C.S., Mitson, G.L., and Robson, M.J., 1979, The pain drawing as a predictor of psychogenic involvement in low back pain patients, Unpublished paper presented to the Ontario Psychological Association, Toronto, Canada.

Duncan, G.H., Gregg, J.M., and Ghia, J.N., 1978, The pain profile:
    a computerized system for assessment of chronic pain, Pain,
    5:275-284.
Engel, G.L., 1959, Psychogenic pain and the pain prone patient,
    Amer. J. Med., 26:899-918.
Eysenck, H.J., and Eysenck, S.G.B., 1964, "Manual of the Eysenck
    Personality Inventory," University of London Press, London.
Fairbank, J.C.T., Davies, J.B., Couper, J., and O'Brien, J.P., 1980,
    The Oswestry low back pain disability questionnaire,
    Physiother., 66:271-273.
Feather, N.T., 1967, Some personality correlates of external control,
    Aust. J. Psychol., 19:253-260.
Fenz, W.D., and Epstein, S., 1965, Manifest anxiety: unifactorial
    or multifactorial composition,, Perc. & Mot. Skills, 20:773-780.
Fordyce, W.E., 1966, "Behavioural Methods for Chronic Pain and
    Illness," C.V. Mosby Co., St Louis.
Freeman, C., Calsyn, D., and Louks, J., 1976, The use of the MMPI
    with low back pain patients, J. Clin. Psychol., 32:294-298.
Friedman, A.S., Cowitz, B., Cohen, H.W., and Granick, S., 1963,
    Syndromes and themes of psychotic depression - a factor
    analysis, Arch. Gen. Psychiat., 9:504-509.
Garrad, J., and Bennett, A.E., 1971, A validated interview schedule
    for use in population surveys of chronic disease and disability,
    Brit. J. Prev. & Soc. Med., 25:97-104.
Gentry, W.D., Newman, M.C., Goldner, J.L., and Von Baeyer, C., 1977,
    Relation between graduated spinal block technique and MMPI for
    diagnosis and prognosis of chronic low-back pain, Spine,
    2:210-213.
Goldstein, M.J., 1973, Individual differences in response to stress,
    Amer. J. Commun. Psychiat., 1:113-137.
Graham, C., Bond, S.S., Gerkovich, M.M., and Cook, M.R., 1980,
    Use of the McGill pain questionnaire in the assessment of
    cancer pain: replicability and consistency, Pain, 8:377-387.
Graham, J.R., 1977, "The MMPI: A Practical Guide," Oxford University
    Press, New York.
Gurin, P., Gurin, G., Lao, R., and Beattie, M., 1969, Internal-
    external control in the motivational dynamics of negro youth,
    J. Soc. Issues, 25:29-53.
Guze, S.B., and Perley, M.J., 1963, Observations on the natural
    history of hysteria, Amer. J. Psychiat., 119:960-965.
Hanvik, L.J., 1951, MMPI profiles on patients with low-back pain,
    J. Consult. Psychol., 15:350-353.
Hardy, J.D., Wolfee, H.G., and Goodell, H., 1952, "Pain Sensations
    and Reactions," Hafner, New York.
Hayes, M.H.S., and Patterson, D.G., 1921, Experimental development
    of the graphic rating method, Psychol. Bull, 18:98-99.
Henderson, S., Duncan-Jones, P., Byrne, D.G., Scott, R., and
    Adlock, S., 1979, Psychiatric disorder in Canberra: a
    standardized study of prevalence, Acta Psychiat. Scand.,
    60:355-374.

Horan, J.J., and Dellinger, J.K., 1974, 'In vivo' emotive imagery:
     a preliminary test, Perc. & Mot. Skills, 39:359-362.
Hordern, A., Burt, C.G., and Holt, N.F., 1965, "Depressive States,
     a Pharmacotherapeutic Study,"
Huddleston, J.H., 1932, "Accidents, Neuroses and Compensation,"
     Williams & Wilkin Co., Baltimore.
Hunt, S.M. Jnr., Singer, K., and Cobb, S., 1967, Components of
     depression, identified from a self-rating depression inventory
     for survey use, Arch. Gen. Psychiat., 16:441-447.
JAMA, 1958, A guide to the evaluation of permanent impairment of
     the extremities of the back. A Report by the Committee on
     Medical Rating of Physical Impairment, J. Amer. Med. Assoc.,
     Special Edition, 166:1-122.
Joe, V.C., 1971, Review of the internal-external control construct
     as a personality variable, Psychol. Rep., 28:619-640.
Jones, A.B., and Llewellyn, L.J., 1917, "Malingering or the
     Simulation of Disease," William Heinemann, London.
Kane, R.L., Leymaster, C., Olsen, D., Wooley, F.R., and Fisher, F.D.,
     1974, Manipulating the patient, Lancet, 1:1333-1336.
Kane, W.J., 1980, The incidence rate of laminectomies in the USA,
     Paper presented to the International Society for the Study of
     the Lumbar Spine, New Orleans, USA.
Kay, D.W.K., Roy, J.R., and Beamish, P., 1969, Endogenous and
     neurotic syndromes of depression: a 5-to-7 year follow-up of
     104 cases, Brit. J. Psychiat., 115:389-399.
Kenyon, F.E., 1976, Review article: hypochondriacal states,
     Brit. J. Psychiat., 129:1-14.
Kessell, A., 1968, Parameters of research into the depressive states,
     Aust. & N.Z. J. Psychiat., 2:272-288.
Kissen, D.M., 1964, The influence of some environmental factors on
     personality inventory scores in psychosomatic research,
     J. Psychosom. Res., 8:145.
Lao, R.C., 1970, Internal-external control and competent innovative
     behaviour among negro college students, J. Pers. & Soc. Psychol.,
     14:263-270.
Laskin, D.M., 1969, Etiology of the pain-dysfunction syndrome,
     J. Amer. Dent. Assoc., 79:147-153.
Leavitt, F., and Garron, D.C., 1979a, The detection of psychological
     disturbance in patients with low back pain. J. Psychosom. Res.,
     23:149-154.
Leavitt, F., and Garron, D.C., 1979b, Validity of a back pain and
     classification scale among patients with low back pain not
     associated with demonstrable organic disease, J. Psychosom.
     Res., 23:301-306.
Leavitt, F., Garron, D.C., and Bieliauskas, L.A., 1979, Stressing
     life events and the experience of low back pain, J. Psychosom.
     Res., 23:49-55.
Leavitt, F., Garron, D.C., Whisler, W.W., and Sheinkop, M.B., 1978,
     Affective and sensory dimensions of back pain, Pain, 4:273-281.
Lefcourt, H.M., 1966, Internal versus external control of reinforce-
     ment: a review, Psychol. Bull., 65:206-220.

Lefcourt, H.M., 1972, Recent developments in the study of locus of
    control, in: "Progress in Experimental Personality Research,
    Vol. 6," B. Maher, ed., Academic Press, New York.
Lewis, W.C., 1974, Hysteria: the consultant's dilemma, Arch. Gen.
    Psychiat., 30:145-151.
Little, J.C., 1969, The athlete's neurosis - a deprivation crisis,
    Acta Psychiat. Scand., 45:187-197.
Loan, W.B., and Morrison, J.D., 1967, The incidence and severity
    of postoperative pain, Brit. J. Anaesth., 39:695-698.
Lorr, M., Sonn, T.M., and Katz., 1967, Towards a definition of
    depression, Arch. Gen. Psychiat., 17:183-186.
Luria, R.E., 1975, The validity and reliability of the visual
    analogue mood scale, J. Psychiat. Res., 12:51-57.
Lynn, R., and Eysenck, H.J., 1961, Tolerance for pain, extraversion
    and neuroticism, Perc. & Mot. Skills, 12:161.
McCreary, C., Turner, J., and Dawson, E., 1979, The MMPI as a
    predictor of response to conservative treatment for low back
    pain, J. Clin. Psychol., 35:278-284.
McKendrick, A., 1912, "Malingering and its Detection,"
    E. & S. Livingstone, Edinburgh.
Main, C.J., 1982, The modified somatic awareness scale (MSPQ),
    in preparation.
Mandler, G., and Kremen, I., 1958, Autonomic feedback: a correlation
    study, J. Pers., 26:388-399.
Mandler, G., Mandler, J.M., and Uviller, E.T., 1958, Autonomic feed-
    back: the perception of autonomic activity, J. Pers. & Soc.
    Psychol., 56:367-373.
Martin, H.R., and Swenson, W.M., 1966, Limited intelligence as a
    psychodynamic stress in patients with physical symptoms,
    Postgrad. Med., 39:240-245.
Martinat, E.H., 1966, Evaluation of permanent impairment of the
    spine, J. Bone & Joint Surg., 48A:1204-1210.
Mayou, R., 1976, The nature of bodily symptoms, Brit. J. Psychiat.,
    129:55-60.
Mechanic, D., and Volkart, E.H., 1960, Illness behaviour and medical
    diagnoses, J. Health & Hum. Beh., 1:86.
Melzack, R., 1973, "The Puzzle of Pain, " Penguin Books,
    Harmondsworth, London.
Melzack, R., 1975, The McGill pain questionnaire: major properties
    and scoring methods, Pain,'1:277-279.
Melzack, R., and Torgerson, W.S., 1971, On the language of pain,
    Anaesthesiology., 34:50-59.
Merskey, H., 1965a, Psychiatric patients with persistent pain,
    J. Psychosom. Res., 9:299-309.
Merskey, H., 1965b, The characteristics of persistent pain in
    psychological illness, J. Psychosom. Res., 9:291-298.
Merskey, H., and Hester, R.N., 1972, The treatment of chronic pain
    with psychotropic drugs, Postgrad. Med. J., 48:594-598.
Merskey, H., and Spear, F.G., 1967, "Pain: Psychological and
    Psychiatric Aspects," Bailliere, Tindall & Cassell, London.

Miller, H., 1961, Accident neuroses, B.M.J., 1:919-925; 992-998.
Mirels, H.L., 1970, Dimensions of internal versus external control,
    J. Cons. & Clin. Psychol., 34:226-228.
Nachemson, A., 1976, A critical look at conservative treatment for
    low back pain, in: "The Lumbar Spine and Back Pain," M. Jayson,
    ed., Sector Publishing Ltd., London.
Neufeld, R.W., and Davidson, P.O., 1971, The effects of vicarious
    rehearsal on pain tolerance, J. Psychosom. Res., 15:329-335.
Nisbett, R.E., and Schachter, S., 1966, Cognitive manipulation
    of pain, J. Exp. Soc. Psychol., 2:227-236.
Notermans, S.L.H., and Tophoff, M.M.W.A., 1967, Sex differences in
    pain tolerance and pain appreciation, Psychiat. Neurol.
    Neurochir., 70:23-29.
Petrie, A., 1967, "Individuality in Pain and Suffering," University
    of Chicago Press, Chicago.
Phillips, E.L., 1964, Some psychological characteristics associated
    with orthopaedic complaints, Curr. Pract. Orthop. Surg.,
    2:165-176.
Pichot, P., Perse, J., Kekeous, M.O., Dureau., J.L., Perez, C.I.,
    and Rychewaert, A., 1972, La personalite des sujets presentant
    des douleurs dorsales fonchonnelles valeurde l'inventair
    Multiphasique De Personnalite Du Minnesota, Rev. de Psychol.
    Appliq., 22:145-172.
Pilling, G.L.F., Brannick, T.L., and Swenson, W.M., 1967, Psycholog-
    ical characteristics of psychiatric patients having pain as a
    presenting symptom, Canad. Med. Assoc. J., 97:387.
Pilowsky, I., 1967, Dimensions of hypochondriasis, Brit. J. Psychiat.,
    113:89-93.
Pilowski, I., 1970, Primary and secondary hypochondriasis, Acta
    Psychiat. Scand., 46:273-285.
Pilowski, I., and Bond, M.R., 1969, Pain and its management in
    malignant disease: elucidation of staff-patients transactions,
    Psychosom. Med., 31:400-404.
Pilowski, I., and Spence, N.D., 1975, Patterns of illness behaviour
    in patients with intractable pain, J. Psychosom. Res., 19:279-
    287.
Pilowski, I., and Spence, N.D., 1976a, Pain and illness behaviour:
    a comparative study, J. Psychosom. Res., 20:131-134.
Pilowski, I., and Spence, N.D., 1976b, Is illness behaviour related
    to chronicity in patients with intractable pain, Pain, 2:167-
    173.
Pilowski, I., and Spence, N.D., 1976c, Illness behaviour syndromes
    associated with intractable pain, Pain, 2:61-71.
Pilowski, I., and Spence, N.D., 1981, "Manual for the Illness
    Behaviour Questionnaire (IBQ)," Unpublished manuscript,
    Department of Psychiatry, University of Adelaide, S. Australia,
    5000.
Pilowski, I., Spence, N.D., and Waddy, J.L., 1979, Illness behaviour
    and coronary artery bypass surgery, J. Psychosom. Res., 23:
    39-44.

Prieto, E.J., Hopson, L., Bradley, L.A., Byrne, M., Geisinger, K.F., Midax, D., and Marchisello, P.J., 1980, The language of low back pain: factor structure of the McGill Pain Questionnaire, Pain, 8:11-19.

Pritchard, M.J., 1974, Reaction to illness in long-term haemo-dialysis, 1974, J. Psychosom. Res., 18:55-67.

Pritchard, M.J., 1979, Measurement of illness behaviour in patients on haemodialysis and awaiting cardiac surgery, J. Psychosom. Res., 23:117.

Prociuk, T.J., Breen, L.J., and Lussier, R.J., 1976, Hopelessness, internal-external locus of control and depression, J. Clin. Psychol., 32:299-300.

Ransford, A.O., Cairns, D., and Mooney, V., 1976, The pain drawing as an aid to the psychological evaluation of patients with low-back pain, Spine, 1:127-134.

Raven, J.C., 1950, The comparative assessment of personality, Brit. J. Psychol., 11:115-123.

Ray, W.J., and Katahn, M., 1968, Relation of anxiety to locus of control, Psychol. Rep., 23:1196.

Reading, A.E., 1979, A comparison of pain rating scales, J. Psychosom. Res., 24:119-124.

Reading, A.E., and Newton, J.R., 1978, A card sort method of pain assessment, J. Psychosom. Res., 22:503-512.

Reed, J.L., 1975, Hysteria, in: "Comprehensive Psychiatry," T. Silverstone & B. Barraclough, eds., Brit. J. Psychiat., Spec. Publ., No. 9, Headley Bros. Ltd., Ashford, Kent.

Robins, A.H., 1973, Functional abdominal pain, S. African Med. J., 47:832-834.

Rollman, G.B., 1979, Adaptation level effects in the rating of acute pain, in: "Advances in Pain Research and Therapy, Vol. 3," J.J. Bonica, J.C. Liebeskind, & D.G. Albe-Fessard, eds., Raven Press, New York.

Rotter, J.B., 1966, Generalised expectancies for internal versus external control of reinforcement, Psychol. Monogs: Gen. & Appl., 80 (whole no. 609).

Rosenthal, S.H., and Gudeman, J.E., 1967, The endogenous depressive pattern - an empirical investigation, Arch. Gen. Psychiat., 16:241-249.

Rowe, M.L., 1969, Low back pain in industry, J. Occup. Med., 11:161-169.

Schalling, D., and Levander, S., 1964, Ratings of anxiety proneness and responses to electrical pain stimulation, Scand. J. Psychol., 5:1.

Schwab, J.J., and Harmeling, J.D., 1968, Body image and medical illness, Psychosom. Med., 30:51-61.

Schwartz, L., 1959, "Disorders of the Temperomandibular joint," W.B. Saunders Co., Philadelphia.

Scott, J., and Huskisson, E.G., 1976, Graphic representation of pain, Pain, 2:175-184.

Shapiro, M.B., 1961, "Personal Questionnaire," Unpublished manual,
    Institute of Psychiatry, London.
Smith, G.M., Lowenstein, E., Hubbard, J.H., and Beecher, H.K., 1968,
    Experimental pain produced by the submaximum effort tourniquet
    technique: further evidence of validity, J. Pharmacol. & Exp.
    Therapeut., 163:468-474.
Spilken, A.Z., and Jacobs, M.A., 1971, Prediction of illness behaviour
    from measures of life crisis, manifest distress and maladaptive
    coping, Psychosom. Med., 33:251-264.
Sternbach, R.A., 1974, "Pain Patients, Traits and Treatment,"
    Academic Press, New York.
Sternbach, R.A., 1978, Clinical aspects of pain, in: "The Psychology
    of Pain," R.A. Sternbach, ed., Raven Press, New York.
Sternbach, R.A., and Timmermans, G., 1975, Personality changes
    associated with reduction of pain, Pain, 1:177-181.
Sternbach, R.A., Wolf, S.R., Murphy, R.W., and Akeson, W.H., 1973,
    Traits of pain patients: the low-back 'loser', Psychosom.,
    14:226-229.
Stoeckle, J.D., 1966, Hypochondriasis, Int. J. Psychiat., 22:330-331.
Taub, A., and Collins, W.F. Jnr., 1974, Observation on the treatment
    of denervation dyesthesia with psychotropic drugs: postherpetic
    neuralgia, anesthesia dolorosa, peripheral neuropathy, in:
    "Advances in Neurology, Vol. 4, International Symposium on
    Pain," J.J. Bonica, ed., pp.309-316, Raven Press, New York.
Taylor, J.A., 1953, A personality scale of manifest anxiety,
    J. Abn. & Soc. Psychol., 48:285-290.
Thomas, L.E., 1970, The I-E scale, ideological bias and political
    participation, J. Pers., 38:273-286.
Thurlow, H.J., 1971, Illness in relation to life situation and sick
    role tendency, J. Psychosom. Res., 15:73-88.
Tichener, E.B., 1920, Notes from the psychological laboratory of
    Cornell University, Amer. J. Psychol., 31:212.
Tursky, B., 1974, Physical, physiological and psychological factors
    that affect pain reaction to electric shock, Psychophysiol.,
    11:95-112.
Tursky, B., 1977, The measurement of pain reactions: laboratory
    studies, in: "Pain: New Perspectives in Therapy and Research,"
    M. Weisenburg & B. Tursky, eds., Plenum Press, New York.
Van den Bergh, R.L., 1963, Loneliness - its symptoms, dynamics and
    therapy, Psychiat. Quart., 37:466-475.
Von Graffenfried, B., Adler, R., Abt, K., Nuesch, E., and
    Spiegel, R., 1978, The influence of anxiety and pain sensitiv-
    ity on experimental pain in man, Pain, 4:253-263.
Waddell, G., Kummell, E.G., Lotto, N.N., Graham, J.D., Hall, H.,
    and McCulloch, J.A., 1979, Failed lumbar disc surgery and
    repeat surgery following industrial injuries, J. Bone & Joint
    Surg., 61A:201-207.
Waddell, G., McCulloch, J.A., Kummell, E., and Venner, R.M., 1980,
    Nonorganic physical signs in low-back pain, Spine, 5:117-125.

Waddell, G., Main, C.J., Venner, R.M., Morris, A.W., and Gray, I.G., 1981, Clinical assessment of psychological factors in backache, in preparation.

Wahl, C.W., and Golden, J.S., 1966, The psychodynamics of the polysurgical patient: report of 16 patients, Psychosom., 7:65-72.

Wallston, B.S., Wallston, K.A., Kaplan, G.D., and Maides, S.A., 1976, Development and validation of the Health Locus of Control (HLC) Scale, J. Cons. & Clin. Psychol., 44:580-585.

Walters, A., 1961, Psychogenic regional pain alias hysterical pain, Brain, 84:1-18.

Walters, A., 1973, Psychiatric consideration of pain, in: "Neurological Surgery," J.R. Youmans, ed., W.B. Saunders Co., Philadelphia.

Watson, D., 1967, Relationships between locus of control and anxiety, J. Pers. & Soc. Psychol., 6:91-92.

Weisenberg, M., 1977, Pain and pain control, Psychol. Bull., 84: 1008-1044.

Wilfling, F.J., Klonoff, H., and Kokan, P., 1973, Psychological, demographic and orthopedic factors associated with prediction of outcome of spinal fusion, Clin. Orthop., 90:153-160.

Wiltse, L.L., and Rocchio, P.D., 1975, Preoperative psychological tests as predictors of success of chemonucleosis in the treatment of the low back syndrome, J. Bone & Joint Surg., 57A:478-483.

Wing, P.C., Wilfling, F.J., and Kokan, P.J., 1973, Psychological, demographic and orthopaedic factors associated with prediction of outcome of spinal fusion, Unpublished manuscript.

Wing, P.C., Wilfling, F.J., and Kokan, P.J., 1977, "Comprehensive Analysis of Disability Following Lumbar Inter-vertebral Fusion," Unpublished manuscript, Vancouver.

Wolff, B.B., and Langley, S., 1968, Cultural factors and the response to pain: a review, Amer. Anthrop., 70:494-501.

Wolfkind, S.N., and Forrest, A.J., 1972, Low back pain: a psychiatric investigation, Psychosom. Med., 48:76-79.

Wood, P.H.N., 1976, Epidemiology of back pain, in: "The Lumbar Spine and Back Pain, Chap. 1," M.I.V. Jayson, ed., Sector Publishing Ltd., London.

Woodforde, J., and Fielding, J., 1970, Pain and cancer, J. Psychosom Res., 14:365.

Woodforde, J.M., and Merskey, H., 1972, Some relationships between subjective measures of pain, J. Psychosom. Res., 16:173-178.

Zung, W.W.K., 1965, A self-rated depression scale, Arch. Gen. Psychiat., 32:63-70.

Zung, W.W.K., Richards, C.B., and Short, M.J., 1965, Self-rating depression scale in an out-patient clinic, Arch. Gen. Psychiat., 13:508-515.

Zung, W.W.K., 1967, Depression in the normal aged, Psychosom., 8:287-292.

Zung, W.W.K., 1969, A cross-cultural survey of symptoms in
    depression, Amer. J. Psychiat., 126:116-121.
Zung, W.W.K., 1971, Depression in the normal adult population,
    Psychosom., 12:164-167.
Zung, W.W.K., 1972, A cross-cultural survey of depression symptomat-
    ology in normal adults, J. Cross-Cult. Psychol., 3:177-183.
Zung, W.W.K., and Durham, N.C., 1973, From art to science: the
    diagnosis and treatment of depression, Arch. Gen. Psychiat.,
    29:328-337.
Zwerling, I., Titchener, J., Gottschalk, L., Levine, M.,
    Culbertson, W., Cohen, S.F., and Silver, H., 1955, Personality
    disorder and the relationship of emotion to surgical illness
    in 200 surgical patients, Amer. J. Psychiat., 112:270-276.

THREE METHODS FOR AIDING CLINICAL DECISION MAKING

George Wright

Department of Behavioural Sciences
Huddersfield Polytechnic, England

Kee-On Ng

Sub-department of Clinical Psychology
Liverpool University, England

INTRODUCTION

The mathematical techniques to be presented are intended as aids to the clinician's decision making.[1] The methods to be introduced do not imply that a mathematical model or theory implemented by computer can replace the clinician. The work we are about to discuss shows that decision aids, utilising the clinician's knowledge and expertise, can improve on unaided judgement and choice. Diagnosis, prognosis and treatment decisions made under conditions of uncertainty and including the clinician's differential valuation of the consequences of the decisions, can be improved. This extra precision is due to the optimal combination of the information the clinician already possesses rather than the clinician's access to extra information.

This paper does not assume any familiarity with the literature and at the same time takes a non-mathematical approach illustrated by practical examples. In this way we hope to give a fairly complete

---

[1] See Brown et al (1974) for a review of the practical application of decision analysis in business settings and Raiffa (1968) for a more detailed discussion of the techniques involved.

overview of "the state of the art" in Decision Analysis, Bayesian
Revision of Opinion and Linear Additive Modelling.

DECISION ANALYSIS

Training gives the clinician instruction in the various indices
of a disease or condition and also teaches the possible positive and
negative outcomes of various forms of treatment. These considerations are, of course, essential but the clinician must also be able
to weigh and combine information to reach appropriate decisions concerning patient management.

As Sir William Osler once said "Medicine is a science of uncertainty and an art of probability". Decision Analysis performs
the optimal integration of the uncertainty, risks and benefits present in a decision using the principle of Subjective Expected Utility
(SEU) maximisation. Although decision analysis has been fruitfully
applied in industrial management, economics and government until
recently only a few studies have attempted to apply it to medicine
and clinical psychology.

Figure 1 presents a clinical decision problem adapted from
Christensen-Szalanski and Bushyhead (1979). This is a decision
analytic representation of the physician's decision of whether to
assign a pneumonia diagnosis, or assign a non-pneumonia diagnosis.
For each course of action there are two possible outcomes: the patient does have pneumonia, or the patient does not have pneumonia.

The physician is first required to estimate the subjective
probability that the patient has pneumonia (P). Given this subjective probability estimate and the physician's utility for the possible
consequences of the decision (A-D) it is then possible to calculate
the expected utility for each diagnostic assignment. The act, or
in this case the diagnosis, with the highest expected utility is
then chosen.

Both probabilities and utilities are crucial in determining the
decision. As Christensen-Szalanski and Bushyhead note, the physician
could appropriately assign a pneumonia diagnosis even when he or she
believes it less likely to be correct than the non-pneumonia diagnosis. Similarly two physicians may estimate the same probability
of a patient having pneumonia but still assign different diagnoses
because they value the consequences differently. If a physician
is making many diagnoses of the absence or presence of a specific
disease or illness, where the set of utilities for the possible
consequences of the diagnoses remain unchanged, it is a straight-
forward extension of the decision analytic approach to calculate a
critical probability for diagnosis. At the critical probability
neither diagnosis would be favoured. After a critical probability

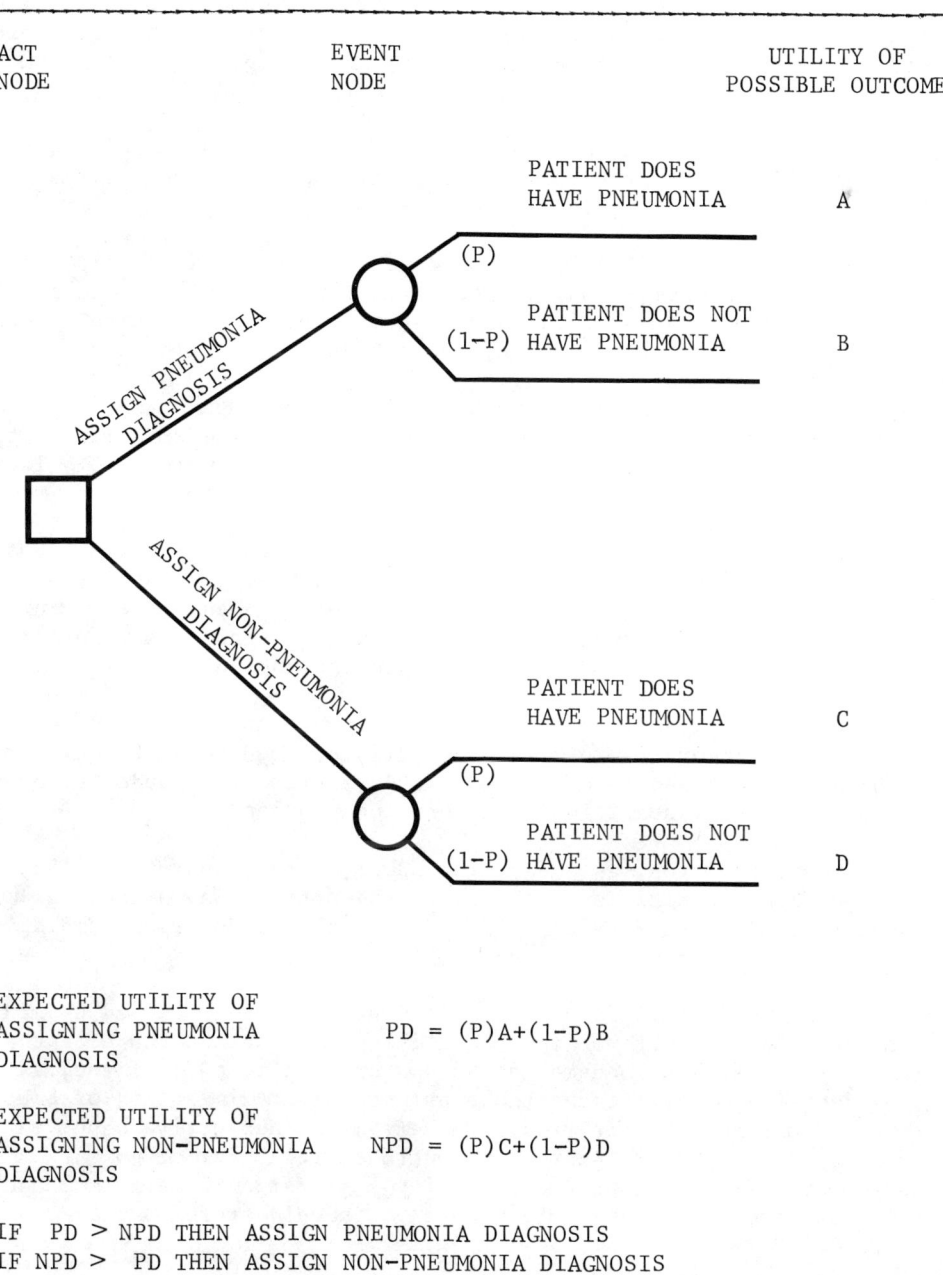

ACT   EVENT   UTILITY OF
NODE   NODE   POSSIBLE OUTCOME

PATIENT DOES
HAVE PNEUMONIA   A

(P)

PATIENT DOES NOT
(1-P) HAVE PNEUMONIA   B

ASSIGN PNEUMONIA
DIAGNOSIS

ASSIGN NON-PNEUMONIA
DIAGNOSIS

PATIENT DOES
HAVE PNEUMONIA   C

(P)

PATIENT DOES NOT
(1-P) HAVE PNEUMONIA   D

EXPECTED UTILITY OF
ASSIGNING PNEUMONIA   PD = (P)A+(1-P)B
DIAGNOSIS

EXPECTED UTILITY OF
ASSIGNING NON-PNEUMONIA   NPD = (P)C+(1-P)D
DIAGNOSIS

IF PD > NPD THEN ASSIGN PNEUMONIA DIAGNOSIS
IF NPD > PD THEN ASSIGN NON-PNEUMONIA DIAGNOSIS

Fig. 1.   Decision Analysis applied to pneumonia diagnosis problem.

has been established precise specification of probability of illness
for future patients is unnecessary, all the physician has to do is
to assess whether the probability that a given patient has pneumonia
falls above or below the critical probability.

The pneumonia example is a very simple application of decision
analysis using the principle of subjective expected utility maximisation as a choice criterion.

Emerson et al (1974) have used decision analysis to aid the
decision of whether to apply prophylactic heparin therapy to prevent
possible pulmonary embolism following myocardial infarction. Heparin
therapy itself may cause death from a bleeding complication. In
their study Emerson et al calculated the probability of death for
patients of different ages on the basis of previous actuarial data
which was available, rather than on more subjective criteria. Utilities for the possible consequences in this study were simply 1 or
0 - the patient lives or the patient dies.

Pliskin and Beck (1976) applied decision analysis in a situation
where all the probabilities utilised were subjective estimates. This
was because the specific characteristics of a given patient did not
enable the use of actuarial tables. Explicit tradeoffs were made
between two utility dimensions of longevity and quality of life.

Schwartz et al (1973) presented an overview of the application
of decision theoretic techniques to clinical judgement. They noted
that several sequences of acts and events are often needed to provide
an adequate representation of a decision problem.

Why should you, as a decision maker, accept that the prescription of SEU and decision analysis is the optimal way of making
decisions under uncertainty? What if intuitive decisions and SEU
prescribed decisions conflict?

The argument in favour of following the act specified by maximisation of subjective expected utility is based on the acceptability of certain fundamental axioms or principles. If you, as
the decision maker, accept these axioms then maximisation of SEU is
the optimal choice criterion. The axioms of subjective expected
utility theory are relatively uncontroversial. For example, one
axiom, transitivity, states that if you prefer outcome A to B and
you also prefer outcome B to C then you should prefer outcome
A to C.[2]

---

[2] For a more detailed consideration of the axiom system underlying
SEU, see Edwards, Lindman and Phillips (1966).

Studies that have attempted to investigate whether maximisation of SEU is descriptive of human decision behaviour have found that, in detail, it is not. Peterson and Beach (1967) concluded "Experiments that have compared human inferences with those of statistical men show that the normative model provides a good first approximation for a psychological theory of inference. Inferences made by subjects are influenced by the appropriate variables in appropriate directions".

Slovic (1972) and Hogarth (1975) have marshalled the research evidence in support of the notion that limited capacity in terms of memory, attention and reasoning capabilities lead the decision maker to be sub-optimal. SEU aids the decision maker by "dividing and conquering" - the decision maker's estimates of probabilities and utilities are recomposed by subjective expected utility theory to specify the optimal decision.

In terms of decision analysis an ability to assess realistic probabilities is obviously very desirable. Lichtenstein et al (1977) have developed a measure of the realism of assessed probabilities which they have labelled calibration. A person is perfectly calibrated if for all those events assessed as having .XX probability of occurrence, XX% actually occur. For example, if 10 separate events were each assessed as having a .7 chance of occurrence 7 out of the 10 should actually occur.

In the medical setting illustrated in the decision analysis example above, Christensen-Szalanski and Bushyhead (in press) examined the probability estimates given by 9 physicians to 1531 patients. Each patient was examined by only one physician. The physicians were required to estimate the probability that the patient had pneumonia. Because most physicians consider the chest x-ray to be the definitive test for pneumonia, chest x-rays were taken of all the patients in the study. Radiologists then examined each patient's x-ray and decided whether the patient had pneumonia. The radiologist made the criterion diagnosis without any knowledge of the patients or of the physicians' probability estimates.

The calibration of the physicians' assessed probabilities were, generally, "overconfident". For example, for those probability assessments of a .7 chance of pneumonia only about 12% were confirmed by the radiologists. Were the physicians acting cautiously because of the risk of a false negative, ie, assigning a non-pneumonia diagnosis when the patient did in fact have pneumonia? Christensen-Szalanski and Bushyhead tested for a motivation bias by asking the physicians to list their utilities for the possible outcomes of the decision and found that the overall utilities for the two possible diagnoses balanced. They concluded that the overconfidence bias must be cognitive rather than motivational.

Overconfidence is not limited to physicians! Lichtenstein et al (1977) have documented the generality of this effect with psychologists, the general public, civil servants, insurance underwriters and, of course, the average university student. There are individual differences in overconfidence and it is true that the type of task also has an effect. As yet it is impossible to predict, on the basis of personality/cognitive tests, who will be best calibrated (Wright and Phillips, 1979).

Why aren't we better calibrated? - why don't we learn from experience? Fischhoff and Beyth (1975) have found that when decision makers are told which event actually occurred - for instance the results of the chest x-rays - and are then asked to recall their original subjective probabilities, most decision makers exhibit the "I knew it all along effect". For example, given that an x-ray was positive the physician's recalled probability would be near 1.0 (or certainty) than the physician's original probability estimate.

Clearly we don't learn from experience. Fischhoff, has argued that if you want to get an accurate picture of your own calibration you should keep a tally of your probability assessments and construct a personal calibration chart when the true outcomes are known. Once a calibration chart is constructed it's then possible to externally recalibrate your own probability assessments and hence improve your decision making. For instance, if you are only correct 80% of the time you say you are 100% sure, you should say 80% sure every time you think you are 100% sure. These personally adjusted probabilities can then be utilised in an improved decision analysis.

BAYES' THEOREM

Bayes' theorem is another 'normative' approach to decision making, this time to the combination of the prior probability (for example, the base-rate incidence of a disease within a given population) with case-specific information (for example, individual patient symptom data) to obtain an individual patient diagnosis.

Graham and Kendall's (1960) Memory-for-Designs Test has been used to diagnose brain damage. Graham and Kendall found that 50% of brain damaged people scored above a criterion level while 4% of people who were functionally ill scored above this level.

Imagine that a psychiatrist makes a preliminary diagnosis of a patient as either functionally ill or brain damaged. After a preliminary investigation he is about equally sure of either diagnosis. He then gives the Memory-for-Designs Test to the patient and the patient scores above the criterion level. How sure should the psychiatrist now be about each of the two possible diagnoses?

Table 1.   Calculation of Posterior Opinion with 50-50 Prior Opinion

Hypotheses	Priors	Likelihoods	Priors X Likelihoods	Posteriors
Functional Illness	0.5	0.04	0.02	$\frac{0.02}{0.27} = 0.07$
Brain Damage	0.5	0.50	0.25	$\frac{0.25}{0.27} = 0.93$
			Sum = 0.27	Sum = 1.00

Bayes' theorem states that our prior opinion multiplied by our likelihood gives us our posterior opinion.[3]   Table 1 sets out the calculations with 50-50 prior opinion.   In this example posterior odds have been converted to posterior probabilities.

Therefore, after seeing the test result the psychiatrist is 7% sure the patient is functionally ill and 93% sure of brain damage. Prior uncertainty of 0.5-0.5 has changed to posterior uncertainty of 0.07-0.93.

So, posterior probabilities or degrees of belief depend not only on the likelihoods but also on prior opinion.

Suppose the psychiatrist consulted the records of the hospital to provide a basis for assessing these prior probabilities and that he discovered that only 20% of the patients at the hospital in the past have been functionally ill, and that 80% were brain damaged. Next, suppose he used these figures as his prior probabilities. Let's see what effect this change in prior opinion has on his posterior opinion.   Table 2 sets out the calculations.

After seeing exactly the same test result the psychiatrist is 2% sure the patient is functionally ill and 98% sure of brain damage. The test, patient and psychiatrist are identical in the calculations of Tables 1 and 2, only the prior opinion has changed.

Next consider the case where the patient does not score above the criterion level.   The appropriate calculations are given in Table 3.

---

[3] For a formal derivation of Bayes' theorem see Phillips (1973). Phillips also gives similar numerical examples.

Table 2. Calculation of Posterior Opinion with 80-20 Prior Opinion

Hypotheses	Priors	Likelihoods	Priors X Likelihoods	Posteriors
Functional Illness	0.2	0.04	0.01	$\frac{0.01}{0.41} = 0.02$
Brain Damage	0.8	0.50	0.40	$\frac{0.40}{0.41} = 0.98$
			Sum = 0.41	Sum = 1.00

This time prior probabilities of 0.2-0.8 have changed to posteriors of 0.32-0.68. It is important to notice that the psychiatrist's posterior probabilities still favour the diagnosis "brain damage" even though the patient did not show a score indicating brain damage. The Bayesian psychiatrist would conclude that the test would not change his prior probabilities enough to warrant its use.

Other important points to note are that prior opinions and likelihoods need not be based on "actuarial" or relative frequency data as they are in this example. Bayes' theorem applies equally well to the revision of subjective probabilities in the light of new information. This fact is especially useful where base-rate data is non-existent or believed to be unreliable.

One important question remains to be answered. Is opinion revision performed by Bayes' theorem more valid than the intuitive revision of opinion? Two types of evidence answer this question in the affirmative.

Table 3. Calculation of Posterior Opinion Where the Patient Does
           Not Score Above the Criterion Level

Hypotheses	Priors	Likelihoods	Priors X Likelihoods	Posteriors
Functional Illness	0.2	0.96	0.19	$\frac{0.19}{0.59} = 0.32$
Brain Damage	0.8	0.50	0.40	$\frac{0.40}{0.59} = 0.68$
			Sum = 0.59	Sum = 1.00

First, Bayes' theorem is derived from certain axioms or basic principles in a similar way to SEU theory. For instance, one axiom is "The probability of any one event occurring from among n mutually exclusive events is equal to the sum of the probabilities of the individual events". For example, the probability of a specified side of the six sides of a die landing facing up is 1/6 .'. the probability of any one side of a die landing facing up is 1, or certainty. If you, as a decision maker accept the various axioms of Bayes' theorem (and they are all relatively innocuous) then it follows that Bayes' theorem is the "normative" or optimal method for your opinion revision.[4]

The second type of evidence supporting the use of Bayes' theorem in opinion revision involves empirical studies. Decision theorists have compared intuitive revision of subjective probability with that performed by Bayes' theorem where Bayes' theorem combines subjective prior opinions with subjective likelihoods to give posterior opinions which are then the prior opinions ready for combination with further likelihoods. The general finding is that both intuitive opinion revision and Bayes' theorem eventually favour the same hypothesis but Bayes' theorem gets there first. In other words unaided decision makers fail to extract the maximum amount of information from data, intuitive decision makers are "conservative" in their opinion revision. Currently there are several explanations of the locus of conservatism. Some theories point to the limited capacity of the human mind to aggregate information. Whatever the reason the fact remains that human decision makers are suboptimal in revising their opinion in the light of new information.

In a medical setting, Diamond and Forrester (1979) note that the diagnosis of coronary heart disease has become increasingly complex. Many different results obtained from diagnostic tests with substantial imperfections, must be integrated into a diagnostic conclusion about the probability of coronary-artery disease in a given patient. These authors collected data on the pretest likelihood of the disease (defined by age, sex, and symptoms) and the sensitivity and specificity of four diagnostic tests: stress electro-cardiography, cardiokymography, thallium scintigraphy, and cardiac fluoroscopy. With this information, test results of an individual patient can be analysed by use of Bayes' theorem. The authors point out the advantages of this approach and state that it may assist in decisions on cost effectiveness of diagnostic tests.

Computers have been used to perform the tedious calculations of posterior probabilities in medical diagnosis with the clinician

---

[4] Phillips (1973) outlines the axioms of Bayes' theorem in more detail.

and/or actuarial tables inputing prior opinion and likelihoods. Uses include diagnosis of thyroid disease, causes of acute renal failure and paternity evaluation.[5]

ADDITIVE LINEAR MODELS

One of the major data bases used for experimentation with linear models has been that collected by Meehl (1959). The judgemental problem used was that of differentiating psychotic from neurotic patients on the basis of their MMPI profiles. Fig 2. sets out the basic paradigm.

Each patient upon being admitted to hospital had taken the MMPI. Expert clinical psychologists believe (or at least used to believe) that they can differentiate between psychotics and neurotics on the basis of profile of the 11 scores. Meehl (1959) noted "because the differences between psychotic and neurotic profile are considered in MMPI lore to be highly configural in character, an atomistic treatment by combining scales linearly should be theoretically a very poor substitute for the configural approach".

Initially researchers tried to "capture" or "model" expert judges by a simple linear regression equation. These judgemental representations are constructed in the following fashion. The clinician is asked to make his diagnostic or prognostic judgement from a previously quantified set of cues for each of a large number of patients. These judgements are then used as the dependent variable in a standard linear regression analysis. The independent variables in this analysis are the values of the cues. The results of such an analysis are a set of regression weights, one for each cue, and these sets of regression weights are referred to as the judge's "model" or his "policy".

How do these models make out as predictors themselves? That is, if the regression weights (generated from an analysis of one clinical judge) were used to obtain a "predicted score" for each patient would these scores be more valid, or less valid, than the original clinical judgements from which the regression weights were derived? To the extent that the model fails to capture valid non-linear variance in the judges' decision processes, it should perform worse than the judge to the extent that it eliminates the random error component in human judgements, it should perform better than the judge.

---

[5]See Beach (1975) for a review of these studies.

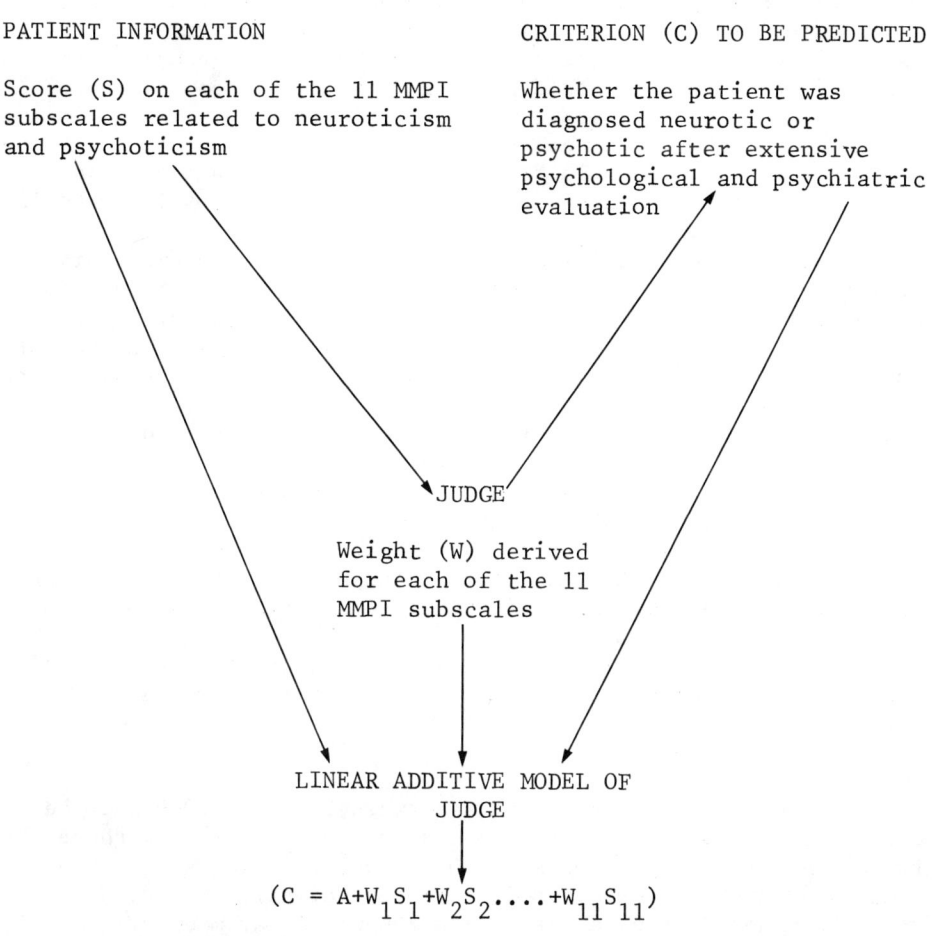

PATIENT INFORMATION

Score (S) on each of the 11 MMPI subscales related to neuroticism and psychoticism

CRITERION (C) TO BE PREDICTED

Whether the patient was diagnosed neurotic or psychotic after extensive psychological and psychiatric evaluation

JUDGE

Weight (W) derived for each of the 11 MMPI subscales

LINEAR ADDITIVE MODEL OF JUDGE

$$(C = A + W_1S_1 + W_2S_2 \ldots + W_{11}S_{11})$$

Fig. 2. Basic Paradigm for the Construction of a Linear Additive Model of a Judge

What were the results of this research? The overwhelming conclusion was that the linear model of the judge's behaviour outperformed the judge. Dawes (1975) noted that "I know of no studies in which human judges have been able to improve upon optimal statistical prediction". Dawes concluded "A mathematical model by its very nature is an abstraction of the process it models; hence if the decision maker's behaviour involves following valid principles but following them poorly these valid principles will be abstracted by the model".

Goldberg (1965) reported on intensive study of clinical judge-

ment, pitting experienced and inexperienced clinicians against linear
models and a variety of non-linear or configural models in the
psychotic/neurotic prediction task. He was led to conclude that
Meehl chose the wrong task for testing the clinicians' purported
ability to utilise complex configural relationships. The clinicians
achieved a 62% but rate whilst the simple linear composite achieved
70%. A 50% hit rate could have been achieved by chance as the
criterion base-rate was approximately 50% neurotic, 50% psychotic.

Dawes and Corrigan (1974) have called the replacement of the
decision maker by his model "bootstrapping". Belief in the efficacy
of bootstrapping is based on a comparison of the validity of the
linear model of the judge with the validity of his or her wholistic
judgements. However, as Dawes and Corrigan (1974) point out, that
is only one of two logically possible comparisons. The other is
between the validity of the linear model or the judge and the validity of linear models in general. That is, to demonstrate that bootstrapping works because the linear model catches the essence of a
judge's expertise and at the same time eliminates unreliability, it
is necessary to demonstrate that the weights obtained from an
analysis of the judge's behaviour are superior to those that might
be obtained in another way - for example, obtained randomly.

Dawes and Corrigan (1974) constructed random linear models to
predict the criterion. The sign of each predictor variable was
determined on an a priori basis so that it would have a positive
relationship to the criterion.

On the average, correlations between the criterion and the
output predicted from the random models were higher than those obtained from the judge's models. Dawes and Corrigan also investigated
equal weighting and discovered that such weighting was even better
than the model of the judges or the random linear models. In all
cases equal weighting was superior to the models based on judges'
behaviour.

Dawes and Corrigan concluded that the human decision maker need
specify with very little precision the weightings to be used in the
decision - at least in the context studied - what must be specified
are the variables to be utilised in the linear additive model. It
is precisely this knowledge of "what to look for" in reaching a
decision that is the province of the expert clinician. Again, as
shown in the previous sections of this paper, it is not in the
ability to integrate information that the decision maker excels.

The distinction between knowing what to look for and the ability
to integrate information is illustrated in a study by Einhorn (1972).
Expert doctors coded biopsies of patients with Hodgkin's disease and
then made an overall rating of severity. These overall ratings were
very poor predictors of survival time but the variables the doctors

coded made excellent predictions, when utilised in a linear additive model.

In conclusion we can say that in a multivariate prediction task only the knowledge of which variables to include in the prediction equation is important. Clinical expertise is, of course, the source of this knowledge - without it the linear models could not work. However, the clinician's importance weightings are not at all crucial. This result remains true in all the contexts so far investigated.

CONCLUSIONS

Decision Analysis, based on SEU, is the optimal way for the clinician to make decisions which involve uncertainty and the differential valuation of possible outcomes. Although initially derived in an economic context, decision analysis is suitable for clinical decision making where utilities of outcomes can be expressed, for example, in terms of longevity, and quality of life as well as, or perhaps instead of, cost of treatment. Although probability assessments are, generally, overconfident[6] and as such may bias the results of any decision analysis, intuitive or wholistic decision making can be seen to be prone to these and other more significant limitations.

Bayes' theorem is the normative method of revising probabilistic opinion in the light of new information. Input probabilities can be purely actuarial, subjective, or a mixture of the two. Human opinion revision is "conservative" compared to Bayes' theorem in that Bayes' theorem extracts much more information from the data. One use of Bayes' theorem is to decide when test administration is unnecessary because the weight of prior opinion will remain unchanged whatever the test result. Another use is to stop the administration of diagnostic tests when a threshold probability level, eg 95% sure of a diagnosis, is reached.

Repetitive predictions based on multivariate indices are better made by a regression equation based on the indices the clinician thinks relevant rather than by the clinician's unaided wholistic judgement. The relative weighting of the indices is essentially unimportant, prediction is best when the weights are equal. The combination of scores on the indices should be performed by a computer programmed with the linear additive model.

One question remains to be answered, if these decision aids are so good why aren't more clinicians using them? In a business context Brown et al (1974) have reported that the absence of top-level

----

[6] Other common heuristics and biases in probability assessments, not discussed here, are given by Tversky and Kahneman (1973).

decision makers familiar with the techniques and the bad experiences of decision makers who have tried the aids by themselves without proper training have restricted their acceptance. Slovic et al (1977) commented that decision makers may reject the logical implications of decision aids if the decisions specified by the aids were unintuitive or too difficult to explain and justify to others. According to Schwartz (1979) physicians complain that decision analysis takes the art out of clinical judgement, dehumanises patient care and takes too much time to apply. We hope that this presentation of decision aiding techniques has resolved some of these problems and at the same time has shown the usefulness of the aids in a variety of clinical contexts.

REFERENCES

Beach, B.H., 1975, Expert judgement about uncertainty: Bayesian decision making in realistic settings, Org. Beh. & Hum. Perf., 14:10.

Brown, R.V., Kahr., A.S., and Peterson, C., 1974, "Decision Analysis for the Manager," Holt, Rinehart & Winston, New York.

Christensen-Szalanski, J.J.J., and Bushyhead, J.B., 1979, Decision analysis as a descriptive model of physician decision making, Technical Rep., 79-45, Department of Health Services Research, University of Washington.

Christensen-Szalanski, J.J.J., and Bushyhead, J.B., in press, Physicians' use of probabilistic information in a real clinical setting, J. Exp. Psychol.

Dawes, R.M., 1975, Graduate admission variables and future success, Science, 187:721.

Dawes, R.M., and Corrigan, B., 1974, Linear models in decision making, Psychol. Bull., 81:95.

Diamond, G.A., and Forrester, J.S., 1979, Diagnosis of coronary heart disease, New Eng. J. Med., 300:1350.

Edwards, W., Lindman, H., and Phillips, L.D., 1966, Emerging technologies for making decision, in: "New Directions in Psychology 11," T.M. Newcomb, ed., Holt, Rinehart & Winston, New York.

Emerson, P.A., Teather, D., and Handley, A.J., 1974, The application of decision theory to prevention of deep vein thrombosis following myocardial infarction, Quart. J. Med., New Series, XLIII, 171:389.

Fischhoff, B., and Beyth, R., 1975, I knew it would happen: Remembered probabilities of once-future things, Org. Beh. & Hum. Perf., 13:1.

Goldberg, L.R., 1965, Diagnosticians versus diagnostic signs: the diagnosis of psychosis versus neurosis from the MMPI, Psychol. Monogs., 79:602.

Graham, R.K., and Kendall, B.S., 1960, Memory-for-designs test: revised general manual, Perc. & Mot. Skills, 11:147.

Hogarth, R.M., 1975, Cognitive processes and the assessment of subjective probability distributions, J. Amer. Stat. Assoc., 70:721.

Lichenstein, S., Fischhoff, B., and Phillips, L.D., 1977, Calibration of probabilities: the state of the art, in: "Decision Making and Change in Human Affairs," H. Jungerman & G. de Zeeuw, eds., D. Reidel, Amsterdam.

Meehl, P.E., 1959, A comparison of clinicians with five statistical methods of identifying psychotic MMPI profiles, J. Coun. Psychol., 6:102.

Peterson, C.R., and Beach, L.R., 1967, Man as an intuitive statistician, Psychol. Bull., 68:29.

Phillips, L.D., 1973, "Bayesian Statistics for Social Scientists," Nelson, London.

Pliskin, J.S., and Beck, C.H., 1976, Decision analysis in individual clinical decision making: a real world application in treatment of renal disease, Methods Info. Med., 15:43.

Raiffa, H., 1968, "Decision Analysis: Introductory Lectures on Choices Under Uncertainty," Addison-Wesley, Reading, Mass.

Schwartz., W.B., 1979, Decision analysis: a look at the chief complaints, New Eng. J. Med., 300:556.

Schwartz, W.B., Gorry, G.A., Kassirer, J.P., and Essig, A., 1973, Decision analysis and clinical judgement, The Amer. J. Med., 55:459.

Slovic, P., 1972, From Shakespeare to Simon: speculations – and some evidence – about man's ability to process information, Oregon Research Institute, Res. Bull., 12.

Slovic, P., Fischhoff, B., and Lichtenstein, S., 1977, Behavioural decision theory, Ann. Rev. Psychol., 28:1

Tversky, A., and Kahneman, D., 1974, Judgement under uncertainty: Heuristics and biases, Science, 185:1124.

Wright, G.N., and Phillips, L.D., 1979, Personality and probabilistic thinking: an exploratory study, Brit. J. Psychol., 70:295.

QUESTIONING THE FOUNDATIONS OF COGNITIVE BEHAVIOR MODIFICATION

Chris Cullen

Hester Adrian Research Centre
University of Manchester

In recent years, an apparently new field has opened for clinical psychologists and other therapists. An endeavour which purports to reach the parts which behaviour therapies cannot reach, while retaining the rigour which many have claimed distinguishes behaviour therapies from other forms of psychotherapy. This new field is cognitive behaviour modification, and since the publication in 1974 by Mahoney of his oft-quoted book "Cognition and Behaviour Modification", there have appeared many books and articles debating the practical and conceptual issues involved.

It would be possible and usual to next give a sample list of references here, but I choose not to do so. The main reason is that this paper is not an examination of the practical utility of cognitive behaviour modification versus any other kind of behaviour modification. Indeed, I start from the premise that precious few forms of intervention have had any real and lasting impact on many clinical populations. As I write this, I have to hand a paper by Bernal et al (1980) on a comparison of 'behavioural parent training and client-centred parent counseling for children with conduct problems'. They found that parents trained in a behavioural group reported fewer child problems after treatment than did the client-centred group, but home observation data
  "... indicated that there was no advantage of behavioural treatment as demonstrated by either child or parent behaviours over the comparison treatment group." (p.687. My emphasis)
Furthermore, these authors were unable to assert the supremacy of either of the two forms of intervention at 6 and 12 months' follow-up! A similar set of conclusions could be found in almost any study addressing the issues of comparative and long-term evaluation. As therapists, we work in very complicated clinical situations, and

69

examining the efficacy of different forms of intervention has led
us only to self-doubt and despair. The position taken in this paper
is that almost all therapy involves people talking to each other,
and that the protagonists in the battle between cognitive behaviour
modification and behaviour therapy have made one or both of two
fundamental errors:
   behaviour therapists have ignored the fact that they usually
   talk to their clients, and cognitive behaviour modifiers have
   tended to concentrate only on this.

The importance of the verbal relationship between client and
therapist has been consistently acknowledged by no less a behaviourist than C.B. Ferster (Tryon et al, 1980), and this paper echoes the
message spelt out by him.

THE FOUNDATIONS OF COGNITIVE BEHAVIOUR MODIFICATION

A field which has become as widespread as the cognitive-behavioural therapies have is unlikely to have a single determining
source, but the place of Lloyd Homme is undisputed. His 1965 paper,
Control of Coverants, the Operants of the Mind, is usually referred
to as a germinal influence. It is interesting, therefore, to look
again at the content of such an important paper.

The first thing to strike the reader is the lack of any data
on which the arguments in the paper might be founded. The second
thing is the almost "tongue-in-cheek" manner which certain portions
of the paper seem to be written in. He refers to his "sparkling new
ideas" in an introductory footnote. Much of his discussion of weight
control is about "... those people (many consider them fortunate)
who find it nearly impossible to gain weight" - not a problem referred to many therapists! The final section of the paper seems to
be aimed at establishing a manic-depressive repertoire. Now, it may
be that I am guessing wrongly at the determinants of Homme's behaviour, but some aspects of the paper seem decidedly unusual.

Taking the (unobjectionable) line that private events have no
special properties other than their inaccessibility (Creel, 1980,
for a full discussion of the radical behaviourist position), Homme
proceeds to argue that there are two reasons for the failure of
behaviourists to deal with what are, for most people, very important
aspects of being human, ie thinking, feeling, etc. Firstly, it is
difficult to detect the occurrence and describe the topography of
private events, and second, even if that one were solved, there is
a problem in the availability and control of contingent reinforcers.

Homme goes on to suggest solutions to these two problems. In
the first place we can ask the client when he is thinking, feeling,
etc, and what he is feeling or thinking about. Response identifica-

tion and definition is essentially a pseudo-problem. His solution
to the difficulty with reinforcers is to utilise the Premack principle
- for any pair of responses, the more probable one will reinforce
the less probable one, and moreover, this rule holds true regardless
of response topography. However, to complicate the issue, Homme
adds, in a footnote:

"The probability referred to here, of course, is not based on
   formal frequency or duration data; it is a kind of phenomen-
   ological probability estimate." (Homme, 1965, p.504).

For therapy, therefore, the therapist has to identify coverants
which are incompatible with the problem behaviour and then strengthen
them using a reinforcer identified by asking the client what he would
rather be doing. This therapy is based on the interesting (though
mistaken) assumption that:

"... contingency management in general has no technology for
   'getting rid' of a response. [It] has only a technology for
   strengthening a behaviour which is incompatible with the response to be eliminated." (Homme, 1965, p.505).

Homme goes on to outline therapies for smoking and for weight
control. In the former case, the incompatible coverant might be
thinking about cancer, early death, etc. The reinforcer might be
anything the client would sooner do, such as having coffee, visiting
the cinema and so on. Smoking a cigarette is, of course, not allow-
able! To prevent adaptation to the aversive properties of the coverant, Homme (1965) suggests: (1) using as many, anti-smoking coverants
as possible, and (2) following the anti-smoking coverant with a pro-
non-smoking coverant and then allowing the reinforcer to occur. For
weight control, similar procedures are used, such as thinking of the
consequences of being overweight followed by thinking of the advantages of being slim. Eating would not be acceptable as a reinforcer, although presumably smoking a cigarette would?

        Homme concludes:
"... the requirements for coverant control can reasonably be
   met and ... although only a bare beginning has thus far been
   made, a technology for the control of frequency of coverants
   is indeed feasible." (Homme, 1965, p.511).
Although no real evidence was presented by Homme, clearly the chall-
enge was open for clinicians to assess the validity of the claims
and assumptions made. So, what happened next?

The Covert Conditioning Therapies

     In the years following the publication of Homme's (1965) paper,
there was an increasing number of attempts to treat private events
as if they were essentially similar to public events. In essence
a relatively simple "lever-press" model was assumed. First identify
the important coverant, then increase or decrease its frequency by
the use of suitable reinforcing or punishing events. The reinforcers

or punishers might initially be public, but the aim was ultimately
to make them private. Some examples will suffice to indicate the
flavour of the approach.

Thought-Stopping. This is a procedure used with clients who
have obsessional ruminations. Stripped of procedural complexities,
the therapy is remarkably simple. The rumination is treated as a
(private) problem behaviour, and is punished. Initially, the therapist administers the punishing stimulus by shouting STOP! when the
client signals that a rumination is occurring. Gradually, control
is taken by the client, who, by eventually sub-vocalising the phrase
STOP! is able to punish his own ruminations. It is an elegantly
simple application of the "lever-press" model. However, it appears
not to work. Even in 1974, Mahoney commented:

"Unfortunately, the empirical evidence on the effectiveness of
thought stopping is very meagre. ... Poor operational definitions, the absence of within-subject control procedures, and
the lack of follow-up measurements are only a few of the
methodological problems which have characterised many of the
case-study applications of thought stopping." (Mahoney, 1974,
pp. 83-84).

Covert Sensitisation. This is a procedure developed by
J.R. Cautela, and it enjoyed some notoriety in the late 1960s and
early 1970s. It shares the same assumptions, as do most of the
covert conditioning therapies, as set out in Homme (1965). Essentially, the imagined rehearsal of a problem behaviour is paired with
an unpleasant imagined event. For those of an iron constitution,
typical instructions given to an obese client are illustrative:

"I want you to imagine you've just had your main meal and you
are about to eat your dessert, which is apple pie. As you
are about to reach for the fork, you get a funny feeling in
the pit of your stomach. You start to feel queasy, nauseous
and sick all over. As you touch the fork, you can feel some
food particles inching up your throat. You're just about to
vomit. As you put the fork into the pie, the food comes up
into your mouth. You try to keep your mouth closed because
you are afraid that you'll spit the food out all over the
place. You bring the piece of pie to your mouth. As you're
about to open your mouth, you puke; you vomit all over your
hands, the fork, over the pie. It goes all over the table,
over the other people's food. Your eyes are watering. Snot
mucus is all over your mouth and nose. Your hands feel sticky.
There is an awful smell. As you look at this mess you just
can't help but vomit again and again until just watery stuff
is coming out. Everybody is looking at you with a shocked
expression. You turn away from the food and immediately
start to feel better. You run out of the room, and as you
run out, you feel better and better. You wash and clean
yourself up and it feels wonderful." (Cautela, 1967, p.462).

Mahoney (1974) reviews more of the covert conditioning therapies, and there is also available a more recent review by Kazdin and Smith (1979). Mahoney (1974) summarises his discussion by stating that:
"... the empirical evidence on the effectiveness of procedures derived from the covert conditioning model tentatively suggests that its clinical utility may be problem-specific and summarily modest." (p.122).

At this stage, then, in the mid-1970s, much effort had been expended on clinical procedures which were less useful than many had hoped and were certainly no more effective than the therapies they purported to replace. If just the clinical utility of a handful of intervention procedures was at stake, then there would have been no problem. After all, much of science is 'suck it and see', and many ineffective tools are discarded. However, the cognitive behaviour modification movement was founded on the premise that these procedures were derived from a conceptual base which was superior to "ordinary behaviourism". The theoretical baby was in danger of being thrown out with the clinical bathwater. Even if the therapies didn't really work, the conceptual basis had to be saved at all costs. And that is what seemed to happen. But to do this, cognitive behaviour modification had to make a subtle change in direction, and had to incorporate therapies which, ten years before, might not have been allowed into the fold.

Writing this in 1981, it is obvious that what goes by the name of cognitive therapy or cognitive behaviour modification is indeed multi-faceted. So much so that what one therapist calls by one name, another will refer to as something else. The remainder of this paper will address over-simplified caricatures of two of the therapeutic paradigms which came to be called by the name of cognitive behaviour modification. These are rational-emotive therapy and self-instructional training. If space allowed, a third might well have been Beck's cognitive therapy for depression (Beck, 1976), but I hope that it will become clear that arguments similar to those I will present might apply to this and indeed to any other therapy. To pre-empt my main point
"The important questions do not concern whether ... therapies are effective but the limits of their effectiveness and how they achieve their effects." (C.B. Ferster. In Tryon et al, 1980, p.13).

Rational-Emotive Therapy

This is a therapeutic school which existed pre-cognitive behaviour modification, but which has been eagerly welcomed under the umbrella. Obviously, it is not possible in the space of a few paragraphs to even begin to do justice to such a complex system, but at the risk of oversimplifying too much, the main therapeutic principle seems to be that men are troubled not by things, but by their perception of these things. Most of us have irrational and erroneous ideas about the world and how it works, and these ideas underlie our distress and unhappiness. The therapeutic task is to identify the irrational ideas and to replace them with rational ones (Ellis, 1970). Some examples of irrational ideas might be:

- It is dire necessity for an adult to be loved by everyone for everything he does.
- If something is or may be dangerous or fearsome one should be terribly upset about it.
- One should be thoroughly competent, intelligent, and achieving in all possible respects.
- Human happiness can be achieved by inertia and inaction.

A more comprehensive list and outline of rational-emotive therapy is to be found in Ellis (1970).

Armed with, among other things, a list of irrational ideas and the "I think, therefore I feel" philosophy, the therapist goes into battle. What form does the battle take? Again, to do no justice at all to the model, a simple caricature will serve:

- Listen to what the client is saying, or watch what he does.
- Make an inference about which irrational ideas are causing trouble.
- Inform the client of this irrational idea, and present him with a more rational alternative.
- Give homework assignments for the client to do.
- Analyse the client's new repertoires for evidence of the new, rational ideas.

Rachlin (1977) has identified two important aspects of this therapy: first, the irrational ideas are usually expressed by the therapist, and rarely by the client. They are inferences drawn from the client's behaviour and then used to explain it. Second, therapy doesn't stop at the stage of rational and irrational ideas - therapy largely consists of homework assignments, ie getting the client to behave. Probably, much of what goes on is pretty similar to what a behaviour therapist might suggest. (In all recent reviews of the efficacy of different therapies, it is acknowledged that performance-based therapies are more successful.)

Rational-emotive therapy may or may not be effective, but it is very difficult to see what is particularly non-behavioural about it, especially when we concentrate on what the therapist and client actually do, rather than on what they say about what they do. When clinicians learn how to use rational-emotive therapy, part of their training is listening to and watching audio and videotapes of therapy sessions. Mahoney (1974) describes a form of rational-emotive therapy which he calls "cognitive re-structuring". He uses the mnemonic label ADAPT to help his clients remember the coping skills:

A   Acknowledge the sensation
D   Discriminate the private events occurring
A   Assess the logical basis of the images
P   Present alternatives
T   Think praise

Presented below is an illustrative therapist-client interchange:

CLIENT: I got really depressed on Wednesday night - almost called you but I felt too bad to even do that.

THERAPIST: Did you remember to use any of the "cognitive" skills we have been talking about in the last few sessions?

CLIENT: You mean the ADAPT stuff? Yeah. I tried it but couldn't seem to figure out what was bothering me. You know, it just seemed like everything was shitty.

THERAPIST: Had anything happened earlier in the day that made you feel bad?

CLIENT: Nope ... it was one of my routine crappy days. Two classes in the morning, bussing trays at the cafeteria all afternoon, and a boring evening of television and books. I called the Self-Report Service at about 11.30 and turned in before midnight.

THERAPIST: Yes. I listened to your self-monitoring messages just before coming in here. It seems to me that you had said something about Sally being over Wednesday night ...?

CLIENT: Oh, yeah, she came over. We watched All in the Family and listened to a couple of albums.

THERAPIST: Is that it? No arguments? discussions? sex?

CLIENT: Yeah, we balled a little.

THERAPIST: What does "a little" refer to?

CLIENT: Well, it was pretty short. I mean I had studying to do and she had to get going.

THERAPIST: When did you first notice that you were depressed?

CLIENT: Um... let's see ... I'd been kind of mellow all day; not high or low ... until evening.

THERAPIST: Before or after Sally?

CLIENT: I see what you're getting at. Yeah, it was after she
             left. We had made love and then she had to go right
             away to catch her bus. But why would that make me
             depressed? Balling is a high.

THERAPIST: You had no problems or disappointments in making love?
             Both of you enjoyed it and felt good afterward?

CLIENT: Well, like I said, it was brief. I had to come pretty
             quick, even though I could have waited.

THERAPIST: Did Sally enjoy it?

CLIENT: I don't know ... I guess so. She didn't say much before
             she left.

THERAPIST: And did that bother you ... the fact that she didn't say
             much?

CLIENT: Well, kind of. I was a little worried about whether I
             had done okay ... you know. It wasn't as if I didn't
             want her to feel good or couldn't have held off my climax
             until she came.

THERAPIST: You say you "worried" about it ... Give me some specif-
             ics. What do you mean?

CLIENT: Well. I thought about it a lot. Couldn't get back to
             the books. I kept ... Hey! I see what you're getting
             at! I was saying a lot of negative things to myself!
             Like "Jesus, she is going to think I'm a premature
             ejaculator or a 'slam-bam' baller - somebody who just
             wants to get their rocks off and doesn't care about how
             she feels."

THERAPIST: Good ... you're getting pretty "insightful". Now let's
             see how well you've done your cognitive homework. Give
             me a brief summary of what happened and why you may have
             felt depressed.

CLIENT: Well. Sally is usually pretty expressive. You know,
             telling me that I made her happy and that she enjoyed it.
             I initiated sex and she reminded me that we only had a
             little time before her bus arrived. We "had at it" ...
             very little foreplay ... I came, we washed up, and she
             left. Then I started feeling kind of bad; worried about
             whether Sally had enjoyed it and what she was thinking of
             me. I gave myself hell for being a horny klutz who
             couldn't wait until we had more time for love-making.

THERAPIST: Excellent! Now that we have some of the facts on what
              probably made you depressed, let's look at whether or
              not you should have felt bad. Is occasionally being a
              "horny klutz" grounds for feeling totally wiped out?
              Should your sexual performance be an absolute standard
              for self-acceptance? (Mahoney, 1974, pp.175-177).

This presumably does not allow us to sample all the complexities
of this young man's problems, but even from this example a perfectly
reasonable interpretation could be offered which does not appeal to
the re-structuring of faulty cognitions. Here we have a man who
usually has a satisfactory sexual relationship, and particular setting
conditions lead to an encounter which shared few of the characteristics of his normal sexual encounters with Sally. Her reaction on
that occasion is likely to act as a punisher, (since she was usually
very expressive) and some (large) part of his repertoire will then
decrease in probability. Typical private events associated with a
repertoire loss are often labelled as "depression" in our culture
(Skinner, 1945, 1974, pp.58-59). Now, this may not be the whole
story, but then we don't have all the important details. What is
clear is that there is probably no need to appeal to irrational ideas
in order to understand the behaviour presented. It is important to
reiterate here that I am not claiming that the rational-emotive therapist is not successful, or that a behaviourist would be more
successful, but that the failure or success of either may be understood without recourse to fictional entities.

Self-Instructional Training

A currently popular form of cognitive behaviour modification is
self-instructional training, discovered almost by accident by
Donald Meichenbaum in 1969, and previously discovered by Soviet
psychologists A. Luria (1961) and L. Vygotsky (1934). The interested reader might also turn to Carnegie (1948) and Skinner (1957).

Meichenbaum (1969) was teaching schizophrenics to "give healthy
talk", and he noted that many of his subjects would help themselves
by repeating the experimental instructions "give healthy talk, be
coherent and relevant". This seemed to him to be a reasonable way
of helping people to achieve a self-control target - teach them to
instruct themselves to achieve their goal.

The best known procedures for self-instruction were devised by
Meichenbaum and Goodman (1971) for use with children. Essentially
the steps in the programme are:

- Child observes therapist doing a task while talking out loud.
- Child performs the task with instruction from the therapist.
- Child performs the task instructing himself out loud.
- Child performs the task, whispering the instructions.
- Child performs the task silently.

Typical instructions for a line copying task would be:
"Okay, what is it I have to do? You want me to copy the picture with the different lines. I have to go slow and be careful. Okay, draw the line down, down, good; then to the right,
that's it; now down some more and to the left. Good, I'm
doing fine so far. Remember go slow. Now back up again. No,
I was supposed to go down. That's okay. Just erase the line
carefully ... Good. Even if I make an error I can go on
slowly and carefully. Okay, I have to go down now. Finished.
I did it!" (Meichenbaum and Goodman, 1971, p.8).

There is a burgeoning literature in this area now, and a news-
letter giving details of published, unpublished and in press research
is edited by Meichenbaum. The current status of self-instructional
training may be summarised as follows:

- Such training can improve the performance of clinical populations
  (eg hyperactive children, schizophrenics and mentally handicapped
  adults).
- The majority of tasks used have had little practical use, so the
  clinical utility of the procedures has yet to be established.
- Generalisation and maintenance of change is still an unsolved problem (as is the case for most therapeutic interventions).

So, here we have a paradigm which promises to be useful, yet to
return to Ferster's (1980) concern: how does it work? Is there anything here which delivers a death blow to behaviourism? Sadly (for
some) the answer is 'no'. Here we have a series of demonstrations
that what we say to ourselves is likely to act as a determinant of
more of our behaviour. Nothing more, nothing less. No need to
appeal to cognitions or other fictional entities.
"Any actual formulation of the relationship between a response
and its consequences (perhaps simply the observation 'Whenever I respond in this way such and such an event follows')
may of course function as a prior controlling stimulus."
(Skinner, 1969, p.147).

In an analysis of self-instructional training which is in perfect accord with the one presented here, but which is considerably
more comprehensive and scholarly, Lowe and Higson (in press) write
that the position of behaviourists such as Skinner, as well as the
Soviet psychologists Luria and Vygotsky, on self-talk, may be summarised as:
"In the lifetime of the 'normal' individual (i) the world
exists prior to his being able to talk, (ii) the world,
that is his particular social environment, establishes the
skill of his being able to talk about the world and himself, and (iii) being able to speak about his interactions
 with the environment has a profound effect on the way he
behaves; his actions and the consequences of these actions
 determine what he says to himself." (Lowe and Higson, in press).

SYNTHESIS

So far, I have considered two forms of cognitive behaviour modification: rational-emotive therapy and self-instructional training.
There are others I have omitted (in particular Beck's cognitive therapy for depression), but similar points apply. I have deliberately
not attempted to comment on the success or failure of these therapies, since that is irrelevant to the points I am making here.

These therapies are being set up by many to be in opposition
to radical behaviourism (as described by Skinner, 1974), and indeed
are said to demonstrate that the philosophical and conceptual foundations of radical behaviourism are somewhat inadequate. In this paper
I have suggested that whatever goes on in rational-emotive therapy
or in self-instruction training can be understood in the terms and
concepts of radical behaviourism, with reference to private events,
but without recourse to fictional entities. So why has there been
such antagonism from the cognitive behaviour modifiers? I believe
that the commonly held view that radical behaviourism cannot deal
with feelings, emotions, images, etc, is based largely on ignorance
and misunderstanding.

Consider the following quotation from Mahoney:
"Watson and Skinner have been among the more outspoken pro-
 ponents of a non-mediational approach to human behaviour.
 In brief, their arguments have included assertions that
 (a) science can only deal with publicly observable events
 and (b) inferential accounts of behaviour are to be avoid-
 ed because they are unparsimonious." (Mahoney, 1977, p.9).
I do not wish to comment on the position of Watson, but is Mahoney
referring to the same Skinner who wrote:
"Behaviourists have, from time to time, examined the problem
 of privacy, and some of them have excluded so-called sensations, images, thought processes, and so on, from their de-
 liberations. When they have done so not because such things
 do not exist but because they are out of reach of their
 methods, the charge is justified that they have neglected
 the facts of consciousness. The strategy is, however, quite
 unwise. It is particularly important that a science of behaviour face the problem of privacy. It may do so without
 abandoning the basic position of behaviourism. Science
 often talks about things it cannot see or measure. When a
 man tosses a penny into the air, it must be assumed that he
 tosses the earth beneath him downward. It is quite out of
 the question to see or measure the effect on the earth, but
 the effect must be assumed for the sake of a consistent
 account. An adequate science or behaviour must consider
 events taking place within the skin of the organism not as
 physiological mediators of behaviour, but as part of behaviour itself. It can deal with these events without assuming

that they have any special nature or must be known in any
special way. The skin is not that important as a boundary.
Private and public events have the same kinds of physical
dimensions." (Skinner, 1969, pp.227-228).
This is one of many possible quotations I could have chosen, but it
serves the purpose well enough. Quite clearly there is some misunderstanding and a good deal of ignorance regarding the radical
behaviourist position on the nature and role of private events.

Postscript

At this stage, I would hope that most readers would accept the
following summary of my position: the different forms of cognitive
behaviour modification may or may not be clinically effective - that,
in most cases, still has to be demonstrated. When 'effective' is
taken to refer to establishing coping repertoires which are enduring,
the same comment would apply to most forms of therapy currently in
use. Whatever the form of therapist-client relationship, it has
not been demonstrated that radical behaviourist concepts cannot describe what is going on, and attempts to assert this proposition are
generally based on ignorance and misunderstanding. In the words
of C.B. Ferster:
"We need to know how therapy increases the overall frequency
of the patient's verbal behaviour, how the verbal interaction
helps the patient to observe the events there, and how a
repertoire developed in the consulting room influences the
pressing events in the patient's life that brought him or her
to therapy." (Tryon et al, 1980, p.13).
It is my contention that a return to the philosophy of radical behaviourism is likely to help us in this task. But could the cognitive behaviour modifiers be persuaded of this?

In a recent paper, Mahoney (1979) has expressed dissatisfaction
with current cognitive therapies. His concerns are centred on particular theoretical and procedural issues, and I would like to
suggest that, in many cases, whereas the cognitive therapies may well
be guilty of the sins outlined by Mahoney, radical behaviourism
comes off much better, and might be a possible avenue for explora-
tion!

Consider the following theoretical problems raised by Mahoney
(1979):

1.   'Cognitive-behavioural therapies tend to overlook, disregard
and sometimes openly attack the potential importance of unconscious
processes'. Radical behaviourism has always acknowledged the importance of 'unconscious processes' (while eschewing the elaborate
fictional structures postulated by Freud). A single quote will
illustrate:

"It is often said ... that behaviourism cannot deal with the
unconscious. The fact is that, to begin with, it deals with
nothing else. The controlling relations between behaviour
and genetic and environmental variables are all unconscious
and it was Freud who emphasised that they need not be observed (that is, conscious) to be effective." (Skinner,
1974, p.153).

2.   'Cognitive-behavioural therapies tend to narrowly view feelings
as phenomenal artifacts that are to be controlled rather than experiences'. Mahoney is here complaining of an over-emphasis in cognitive therapies on thoughts, but for the radical behaviourist, all
private events are treated as useful in therapy (Cullen, 1980;
Goldiamond, 1974). What private events can help us with is in
identifying environmental contingencies before those contingencies
start to have a major impact on one's repertoire. In this respect,
'feelings' (broadly speaking, autonomic responses) are likely to be
more useful than thoughts (often private verbal behaviour).

3.   'Cognitive-behavioural therapies are poorly integrated with
current theories of cognition'. This may well be true, but it is
certainly possible to have a therapy which is well integrated with
the philosophy of radical behaviourism (Cullen et al, in press;
Goldiamond, 1974; Schwartz and Goldiamond, 1975).

4.   'Cognitive-behavioural therapies place an excessive emphasis
on the isomorphism between words and beliefs'. In other words, there
is considerable naivety in assuming that one has full and accurate
knowledge about one's private events. Radical behaviourism has
always acknowledged the impossibility of a person 'knowing accurately' his inner world (Skinner, 1945) and has always emphasised the
multiple determination involved in verbal behaviour (Skinner, 1957).
When I say "I feel happy" or "I believe in God', some of the determinants may be private events, but many will be public environmental events, most of which I am not aware of (cf point 1 above).

5.   'Cognitive-behavioural therapies place an excessive emphasis
on the role of rationality in adaptation'. Presumably Mahoney is
here describing the 'absolutist' position held by some therapists
that there is a right and a wrong way to go about living. Although
Skinner is often hard to understand on this point, radical behaviourism is clearly not an 'absolutist' philosophy, but asserts that
nature has no absolute values. We call things 'good' or 'right' or
'rational' for many reasons, most of which are cultural (Hocutt,
1977).

6.   'Cognitive-behavioural therapies implicitly endorse a judgemental distinction between therapist and client'. Apparently,
many of the therapists Mahoney is familiar with pretend that they
have no problems of their own. I would imagine that behaviourist

therapists are no exception to this complaint. However, what behaviourism does allow the therapist to do, since he has to acknowledge
that he, like his client, is a behaving organism, is to examine the
determinants of his own therapeutic practices. In that sense, then,
there is no distinction between therapist and client.

7.   'Cognitive-behavioural therapies are developing a potentially
dangerous orthodoxy and defensiveness'. That may well be so. Few,
though would describe radical behaviourism as orthodox and defensive.
As an approach to understanding human behaviour, it often seems to
fly in the face of traditional wisdom and common sense. Neither are
its adherents noticeably defensive. Skinner in particular has taken
the view that criticisms are usually based on misunderstanding, and
consequently are best ignored! The philosopher Willard Day has also
commented on the ways in which radical behaviourism can be distinguished from orthodox approaches in psychology, in particular cognitive psychology and methodological behaviourism (Day, 1977).

CONCLUSION

     Human behaviour is complex and multiply determined. There is
no doubt at all that we have progressed only a little way along the
road to understanding, although time and again extravagant claims
are made for this or for that therapy. It is my view that the
'cognitive view' gives us an illusory understanding of behaviour by
encouraging us to deal in metaphor and invented structures. There
is no evidence that 'cognitive' approaches have had a greater practical impact than 'behavioural' approaches in any sphere of the
science of behaviour. Indeed, the practical impact of any approach
is still very small.

     However, certain things are known. It is clear, for example,
that performance-based therapies have more effect than talk-based
therapies. I have also argued that, whenever clinical change is
observed, it can be understood by reference to the conceptual framework of radical behaviourism without recourse to fictional entities.
This does not mean, of course, that radical behaviourism is in any
sense "right" or "the answer". Indeed, it would be surprising if the
conceptual system were to not change as empirical and philosophical
advances are made. There does not seem to be enough reason though
to declare radical behaviourism dead and gone. For the last thirty-
five years, it has provided a clear framework within which to interpret human behaviour.

     This paper has not provided a comprehensive literature review,
nor has it addressed the question of which forms of therapy are
most effective. Instead, I have argued that the important question
is: when interventions succeed in changing behaviour, what are the
functional relationships involved? Central to any attempt to answer
this question is the need to have a conceptual system to do the job.
My own preference is for radical behaviourism.

ACKNOWLEDGEMENTS

The author gratefully acknowledges the agreement of
Prentice-Hall Inc. for permission to quote material from B.F. Skinner,
CONTINGENCIES OF REINFORCEMENT: A Theoretical Analysis, copyright
1969, pp.227-228; of Ballinger Publishing Company for permission
to quote material from M.J. Mahoney, COGNITION AND BEHAVIOUR
MODIFICATION, copyright 1974, pp.175-177; is grateful to Alison Heard
for helpful comments and to Sheila Watt for preparing the manuscript.

REFERENCES

Beck, A.T., 1976,"Cognitive Therapy and Emotional Disorders,"
    International Universities Press, New York.
Bernal, M.E., Kinnert, M.D., and Schultz, L.A., 1980, Outcome
    evaluation of behavioural parent training and client-centred
    parent counseling for children with conduct problems,
    J. App. Beh. Anal., 13:677-691
Carnegie, D., 1948, "How To Stop Worrying and Start Living,"
    Simon & Schuster, New York.
Cautela, J.R., 1967, Covert sensitisation, Psychol. Rep., 20:459-468.
Creel, R., 1980, Radical epiphenomenalism: B.F. Skinner's account of
    private events, Behaviourism, 8:31-53.
Cullen, C., 1980, Therapeutic paradigms: radical behaviourism,
    New Forum: J. Psychol. & Psychother. Assoc. 1980, 7:35-38.
Cullen, C., Hattersley, J., and Tennant, L., in press, Establishing
    behaviour: the constructional approach, in: "Applications of
    Conditioning Theory," G. Davey, ed., Methuen, London.
Day, W., 1977, On the difference between radical and methodological
    behaviourism. Invited address at the meeting of the Midwestern
    Assoc. of Beh. Anal., Chicago, May, 1977.
Ellis, A., 1970, "The Essence of Rational Psychotherapy: A Comprehen-
    sive Approach to Treatment," Institute for Rational Living,
    New York.
Goldiamond, I., 1974, Toward a constructional approach to social
    problems. Ethical and constitutional issues raised by applied
    behaviour analysis, Behaviourism, 2:1-84.
Hocutt, M., 1977, Skinner on the word 'good': a naturalistic
    semantics for ethics, Ethics, 87:319-338.
Homme, L.E., 1965, Perspectives in psychology: XXIV Control of
    coverants, the operants of the mind, Psychol. Rec., 15:501-511.
Kazdin, A.E., and Smith, G.A., 1979, Covert conditioning: a review
    and evaluation, Adv. Beh. Res. & Ther., 2:57-98.
Lowe, C.F., and Higson, P.J., in press, Self-instructional training
    and cognitive behaviour modification: a behavioural analysis,
    in: "Applications of Conditioning Theory," G. Davey, ed.,
    Methuen, London.
Luria, A., 1961, "The Role of Speech in the Regulation of Normal and
    Abnormal Behaviour," Liveright, New York.

Mahoney, M.J., 1974, "Cognition and Behaviour Modification,"
    Ballinger Publishing Company, Cambridge, Mass.
Mahoney, M.J., 1977, Reflections on the cognitive-learning trend in
    psychotherapy, Amer. Psychol., 32:5-13.
Mahoney, M.J., 1979, Psychotherapy and the structure of personal
    revolutions, in: "Cognition and Clinical Science," M.J. Mahoney,
    ed., Plenum, New York.
Meichenbaum, D.L., 1969, The effects of instructions and reinforce-
    ment on thinking and language behaviour of schizophrenics,
    Beh. Res. & Ther., 7:101-114.
Meichenbaum, D., and Goodman, J., 1971, Training impulsive children
    to talk to themselves: a means of developing self-control,
    J. Abn. Psychol., 77:115-126.
Rachlin, H., 1977, A review of M.J. Mahoney's "Cognition and Behav-
    iour Modification", J. App. Beh. Anal., 10:369-374.
Schwartz, A., and Goldiamond, I., 1975, "Social Casework: A
    Behavioural Approach," Columbia University Press, New York.
Skinner, B.F., 1945, The operational analysis of psychological terms,
    Psychol. Rev., 52:270-277.
Skinner, B.F., 1957, "Verbal Behaviour," Appleton-Century-Crofts,
    New York.
Skinner, B.F., 1969, "Contingencies of Reinforcement: A Theoretical
    Analysis," Appleton-Century-Crofts, New York.
Skinner, B.F., 1974, "About Behaviourism," Jonathan Cape Ltd.,
    London.
Tryon, W.W., Ferster, C.B., Franks, C.M., Kazdin, A.E., Levis, D.J.,
    and Tryon, G.S., 1980, On the role of behaviourism in clinical
    psychology, Pav. J. Biol. Sci., 15:12-20.
Vygotsky, L., 1934, "Thought and Language," Sovgiz, Moscow,
    (Wiley, 1962, New York).

THE ROLE OF THE CLINICAL PSYCHOLOGIST IN PRIMARY CARE - AN ANALYSIS OF CURRENT PRACTICE

Laurence E Burns

Psychology Department
Birchhill Hospital
Rochdale, England

Until the early 1970s, when there were just under 600 psychologists employed in the National Health Service, the profession of clinical psychology was closely allied with that of psychiatry. Most clinical psychologists worked in the fields of mental illness or mental handicap; indeed, according to a survey carried out by the British Psychological Society, some 95% of the patients seen by clinical psychologists were assigned to them by psychiatrists. Their role at that time consisted largely of undertaking routine and specialised diagnoses and assessments.

In the 1960s, however, there had been a substantial expansion in the body of psychological knowledge which had major implications for the treatment of patients with behavioural problems. Psychologists, by virtue of their training and skills in the problems of the scientific investigation of human behaviour, had made significant contributions to the development of a new form of treatment, behaviour therapy. Indeed, as Burns et al (1970) pointed out, the phenomenal growth in behaviour therapy had probably no parallel in the fields of clinical psychology or psychiatry, as the 1960s had seen more change in our approach to the psychological causation and modification of behavioural disturbances than in the whole of history. An important factor accounting for this rapid advancement was undoubtedly the disquiet felt by many clinicians with the methodological inadequacies of the psychodynamic approach arising from the work of Freud. By the end of the decade, behaviour therapy was rapidly gaining recognition as an applied science and, when used judiciously, could often effect a rapid improvement in the patient's condition which might have taken years to achieve, if at all, using older psychotherapeutic methods.

Thus, in view of these and other developments, the roles of clinical psychologists began to change. In order to consider these developing roles a sub-committee of the National Health Service Standing Mental Health Advisory Committee was established. The sub-committee was chaired by Professor Trethowan, Professor of Psychiatry at Birmingham University, and first met in December, 1972. The work of the sub-committee generated very considerable interest both within and outside the profession of clinical psychology, with evidence submitted by a large number of organisations and individuals and in 1977 the report was finally published (Trethowan, 1977).

There was a consensus of opinion that the contributions of psychologists in the National Health Service fell short of what the profession potentially had to offer; clinical psychologists had a contribution to make in many fields of health care and their services tended to be very restricted. The sub-committee recognised that this state of affairs was partly attributable to the small size of the profession which, in turn, was partly the result of an inadequate career structure, a matter which the Department of Health and Social Security has not rectified.

The report recognised that trained clinical psychologists were a scarce resource; most psychologists were still involved in the fields of mental illness and mental handicap but that there had been a considerable evolution in their roles. The report indicated that full professional status should be accorded to clinical psychologists and that this should be reflected in the organisation of their services. Psychology should not be regarded as an adjunct to any other profession but psychologists should be recognised as constituting a responsible group having specific skills and expertise to contribute to patient care within a multidisciplinary framework.

The report stated that there was scope for a greatly increased contribution by psychologists in a number of fields of health care in addition to mental illness and mental handicap, such as, physical handicap, child and adolescent health problems, neurology, general medicine, geriatrics, community medicine and general medical practice. Ideally the head of each of these sections would be a psychologist of at least Principal Grade. The sub-committee saw the future role of psychologists in community-based work as an important one in making a significant contribution to both illness prevention and to primary care. The sub-committee looked forward to developments in this area in the reasonably near future.

Even before the Trethowan Committee published the report many hospital-based clinical psychologists were receiving direct referrals from general practitioners and some had provided services within group practices and health centres. Indeed, in October 1973, a clinical psychologist was appointed to the first post in the UK

which had been specifically established in a primary health care
setting, at Craigshill Health Centre, Livingston, (McAllister et al,
1975). Her remit was to develop new areas of psychological service.
Kat (1979) gives a review of the development of psychology services
in primary care. It is interesting to note that, in 1973, a WHO
working party on psychiatry and general medical care recommended
that closer links should develop between psychiatry and primary
medical care and that this should be brought about by psychiatrists
working in primary care.

ADVANTAGES OF PSYCHOLOGICAL SERVICES AT PRIMARY CARE LEVEL

What are the advantages to patients, to members of the primary
health care team and to psychologists themselves of having psychological services at the primary care level as compared to centrally
organised services? Johnston (1978), Kincey (1974), Broome (1979)
and others have listed a number of potential advantages:-

1)   There may be greater accessibility to psychological services.
Such services are more likely to be available to patients as the
group practices or health centres will probably be nearer the
patients' homes; attendance at a centrally based clinic may be
difficult owing to travelling time, time off work, physical
disability or travelling difficulties of a phobic nature.

2)   Psychological services within the primary health care setting
may permit greater continuity of care of the patients. Thus, in
dealing with a problem such as agoraphobia, which is notorious for
fluctuating in severity on a day-to-day basis, there is an increased
likelihood of regular treatment.

3)   There are greater possibilities of liaising with general
practitioners, health visitors, and other members of the health care
professions, and thus facilitating the more appropriate medical
management of a patient, such as gradually reducing the use of
tranquillisers.

4)   Another consideration relates to the problem of stigma for the
patient. The patient may well have fewer doubts about seeing a
clinical psychologist within a group practice or health centre than
at a hospital-based department, even though, in our experience,
patients have fewer reservations in attending a psychology department than a psychiatry department. Thus, the psychologist is
identified more with the general practitioner and the provision of
primary health care services.

5)   If the clinical psychologist is based on the premises there is
the possibility of the patient being seen at an earlier date as
fewer administrative arrangements may need to be made. The earlier

the therapeutic involvement, the less likely the patient's problems
will become firmly entrenched. This has important preventative
implications for, if there is not early intervention, the problem
may increase in severity and become an established part of the
patient's life style and, accordingly, may be more difficult to
treat.

6)   Working in a health centre may lead to the development of new
therapeutic and assessment approaches more relevant to the problems
presenting in primary care, and facilitate, for example, more
effective doctor-patient communication, better patient compliance
with the doctor's instructions, or the detection and management of
emotional disturbance.

7)   Many of the behaviour therapy techniques used by clinical
psychologists involve therapeutic agents; for example, spouses may
be used in the treatment of sexual dysfunction, marital problems and
phobic anxiety states, and parents in the management of childhood
behaviour problems such as temper tantrums, enuresis and anxiety.
Working in the primary health care setting affords the possibility
of establishing and maintaining greater rapport with, and,
therapeutic involvement of, the patient's family.

8)   Because of the likelihood of closer contact with the patient
and his family, there is a greater possibility that the monitoring
of difficulties arising from the implementation of the therapeutic
programme and the evaluation of therapeutic progress will be
facilitated. These aspects have significant ethical implications
as there is a need to evaluate carefully the effectiveness of the
approaches being used and that the patient is making progress towards
clearly defined treatment objectives.

9)   A further advantage concerns reduced administrative and
ambulance service costs. It would appear that psychological treatment within the health centre setting is cost effective although
this is an empirical question and further data needs to be obtained.

10) Provided there is earlier intervention, greater continuity of
care and improved liaison, there may be less need for referral to
other agencies.

11) General practitioners and other members of the primary health
care team can learn at first hand of the distinctive nature of
clinical psychology and the special features which characterise it
as a discipline; in particular, its systematic methods of scientific
enquiry into different aspects of human behaviour. There is likely
to be an increased acceptance of other-than-illness models for
behaviour disorders.

12) Finally, of all the settings in which clinical psychologists

work, it is difficult to envisage an environment, other than a group
practice or health centre, where the range of problems with both
adults and children will be so diverse; those who work in these
settings are well aware that the challenges, but also the levels of
job satisfaction, are high.

DISADVANTAGES OF PSYCHOLOGICAL SERVICES AT PRIMARY CARE LEVEL

What are the disadvantages of clinical psychologists working in
primary care? As trained clinical psychologists are a scarce
resource and as most would regard the provision of services in the
primary care as an attractive proposition, fewer services may be
provided to less attractive areas; such as, the rehabilitation of
chronic patients, or psychogeriatric services. There seems little
evidence at present to support this possibility. Not all patients
are suitable for treatment within a primary care setting. Thus, as
few health centres have been designed with the needs of clinical
psychologists in mind, it may be necessary to treat some patients,
for example patients with severe anxiety, in the central department
where more appropriate facilities exist. Even in these cases,
however, there are considerable advantages to establishing initial
contact with the patient in an environment with which he is
familiar.

PREVALENCE OF PSYCHOLOGICAL PROBLEMS

The great majority of psychological problems, of course, are
dealt with by general practitioners in the primary care setting
without the specialist facilities provided by clinical psychologists
or psychiatrists. Estimates of the prevalence of such problems are
as low as 9.4% (Kessel, 1960). Shepherd et al (1966), in a survey
of 50 London practices, found a prevalence rate of 14%; only 5% of
these cases were referred elsewhere for specialist assistance.
However, other studies report a much higher prevalence rate;
Hewetson et al (1963), for example, report 23.2% and Hopkins (1955,
1956) reports 42.8%; 11.1% for formal psychiatric illness and a
further 31.7% for other stress disorders. General practitioners
regard psychological problems as more difficult to treat and manage
than other types of cases, and in a study by Cooper (1964) many felt
insufficiently trained for the treatment of psychological problems.
Treatment was often inadequate, (Shepherd et al, 1966). Since these
surveys were carried out considerable efforts have been made to
increase the training of undergraduate medical students in the
behavioural sciences. There is, however, still a need for improved
training and a need for further investigation into the prevalence
of emotional disturbance in primary health care, (Lamberts, 1979).

THE NATURE OF PSYCHOLOGICAL SERVICES

What type of services can the clinical psychologist provide in group practices or health centres? In considering this question reference will be made to services which are provided at area or district departments. In response to a question posed by the Trethowan Committee on the desirable division of the psychologist's time spent in the provision of services, the British Psychological Society suggested the following breakdown:-

Assessment and diagnosis	10%
Treatment and rehabilitation	45%
Research	20%
Teaching	15%
Administration, etc	10%

Quite clearly these categories are not mutually exclusive and it would be inappropriate to give a precise significance to the percentages but they may broadly reflect the relative importance assigned to the different areas of expertise.

In order to provide a guide to the range of primary referral problems, a survey was conducted in the Out-Patient Department of Clinical Psychology, Rochdale Area Health Authority, at Birch Hill Hospital, Rochdale, covering a 6 months' period. The results are shown in Table 1. The figures in Table 1 neither take into account referrals to specialised clinics such as enuresis and anti-smoking, nor in-patient referrals. Approximately 100 out-patient referrals were received per month; over 82% of the referrals were for treatment. 17.5% of patients were referred for more than one problem. Children under the age of 16 years accounted for 45% of the referrals. 56% of the referrals were made by general practitioners, the rest being made by paediatricians, psychiatrists, physicians, surgeons, neurologists, and other medical specialists.

McPherson and Feldman (1977) considered that, if clinical psychologists were to make a useful contribution to primary care, some basic information was needed concerning the nature of the psychological problems presented to the general practitioner and the methods of treatment which could be applied. Research into these issues involved a psychologist sitting in, as a non-participant observer, with four general practitioners in two group practices differing considerably in size and social characteristics. The psychologist and general practitioners independently rated the relevance of psychological factors in the problems presented by the patients on a 4 point scale from 1 = not relevant to 4 = highly relevant. Patients were asked if they would be prepared to be interviewed at home for the purpose of obtaining additional information if they were rated 3 or 4 on the scale.

Table 1. Primary Referral Problems - 6 months' period
from 1st January, 1980

Problems	%
Anxiety states	20.2
Psychological assessment (including educational attainment, assessment for organic brain damage, developmental assessment of children under 2 years of age, assessment for mental handicap, etc)	17.5
Obesity; compulsive eating	8.4
Phobias and fears (including school phobia)	7.4
Multiple behaviour problems in children, (including hyperactivity, stealing, tantrums, etc)	6.4
Sexual dysfunction (impotence, frigidity, etc)	4.7
Depression	4.0
Anti-smoking referrals	4.0
Aggressive behaviour (including violence)	3.4
Agoraphobia	3.0
Problems of social inadequacy	2.7
Learning disabilities (including dyslexia, etc)	2.4
Marital problems	2.4
Headaches (tension, migraine)	2.4
Overdose; suicide attempt; self-inflicted wounds	2.0
Encopresis	1.7
Personality disturbance (including psychopath)	1.7
Problems of epileptics	1.4
Speech disfluencies	1.0
Obsessive/compulsive disorders	1.0
Alcoholism; heavy drinking	0.7
Sleep disturbance	0.7
Sexual deviancy	0.7

On this basis 40 patients were selected (20 from each practice) out of a total population of 366 patients seen at 22 surgeries. The male/female ratio was 1 : 4; the mean age was 40.5 years. There was a satisfactory level of agreement between the psychologist and general practitioners regarding the relevance of psychological factors. The majority of the problems were categorised under headings of anxiety and depression and involved phobias, insomnia, obesity, alcohol abuse, marital and sexual problems and problems related to children and elderly people. 70% of the problems had a duration of greater than one year, indicating that psychological problems in primary care do not tend to be of a transient nature.

McPherson and Feldman (1977) estimated that the clinical psychologist could make a useful contribution in the management of the presenting problem in 77% of the cases in the sample. In a further 16% of the cases the problem did not appear to be sufficiently troublesome to warrant psychological intervention. In only 7% of the cases was it felt that the psychologist could make no useful contribution. Thus, in considering the total number of patients (366) seen at the two practices during the survey, it was estimated that a useful contribution could be made by clinical psychologists in 8.4% of cases.

An implication of this study is that there is a very significant number of potential referrals to clinical psychologists in primary health care settings. An estimate of one full-time psychologist per two practices seems conservative; this level of staffing would give a national total approaching three-and-a-half-thousand clinical psychologists in primary care settings.

Broadhurst (1977) carried out a survey in order to assess the volume and range of the work of clinical psychologists in relation to the community, the general practitioner being viewed as the major deliverer of health services in the community. The findings indicated that the majority of psychologists (51.9%) worked to some extent with general practitioners. The initiative for such relationships was made by the psychologists although, in 14% of cases, the initial contacts were made by medical practitioners. 56.9% reported referrals for individual treatment of patients with behavioural problems; 14.4% for referrals for group treatment; 38.4% for referrals for individual assessment and 27.3% indicated involvement for research. The types of cases most frequently referred included phobias (42.1%), general anxiety (31.5%), sexual dysfunction (32.4%) and marital discord (29.6%). Vocational guidance (24.1%) and educational assessments (18.1%) were significant reasons for referral. Collaborative research projects involved treatment outcome studies and patient change during drug treatment trials. Teaching was another major commitment both at undergraduate and postgraduate levels.

The survey indicated that the reactions of colleagues to psychologists' work with general practitioners was generally favourable. No problems concerning general practice contracts were encountered by 88.4% of those working with general practitioners and virtually all respondents would like to see psychologists having some permanent attachment to health centres.

Davidson (1977) reported a survey among general practitioners working within the boundaries of the Croydon Area Health Authority on the kinds of working relationships they would like to have with psychologists. Seventy-six practitioners participated in the survey. The largest demand was for treatment facilities, especially for sexual/marital problems, phobic states, addictive problems, obesity, obsessional states and behavioural training in mental handicap. Interest in teaching facilities, particularly as part of regular courses, was expressed by a significant number of general practitioners.

A number of general practitioners have written about their experiences in working with psychologists in primary care. For example, Taylor (1979) sees benefits in mixing with a health professional whose views of psychiatric illness and its treatment are very different from those received during medical training. Taylor believes that there is an important role for clinical psychologists in educating doctors about the behavioural and other psychological methods. An article on the clinical psychologist as part of the primary health care team appeared in Update (September, 1980). The paper reports on psychological services over a 12 months' period, services which were regarded as being particularly success- ful. Details of the functions of the clinical psychologist are given also in the paper together with a breakdown of referral problems.

Further evidence on the value of psychological services in general practice is provided by two studies. Ives (1979) reports having seen 238 patients over a 26 months' period. Treatment methods included counselling, anxiety management methods, relaxation training, biofeedback, social skills training, etc. Of the patients completing therapy 72% had made satisfactory progress. In the 3 months following the completion of treatment patients made significantly fewer (36%) visits to the surgery; they received significantly fewer (50%) prescriptions for psychotropic drugs than in the 3 months before referral. Twelve-to-fifteen months' follow-up studies indicated that progress had been maintained. The author concludes that, besides filling an important gap in services, the evidence suggests that psychological services in general practice appear to be greatly worthwhile.

Similar results were reported by Koch (1979) and are discussed in the next chapter. Koch believes that there is a need for clinical psychologists to have close liaison with general practitioners within a multidisciplinary team framework and that this will be of great benefit to continuing health care.

After 10 years of experience in working closely with general practitioners I can endorse these views. The particular expertise which clinical psychologists possess in the fields of behavioural assessment, treatment and research should contribute greatly to patient care. However, although the initial clinical and research evidence for the value of clinical psychology services in primary health care is encouraging, there is an urgent need for well controlled studies for, as Hood (1979) cautions, the onus is largely on clinical psychologists to demonstrate the usefulness of their services.

REFERENCES

Broadhurst, A., 1977, What part does general practice play in community clinical psychology?, Bull. Brit. Psychol. Soc., 30:305-309.
Broome, A., 1979, A psychologist's view of GPs. work in psychology and primary care, Leicester: Division of Clinical Psychology, Brit. Psychol. Soc., pp.11-20.
Burns, L.E., and Worsley, J.L., 1970, "Behaviour Therapy in the 1970s," J. Wright, Bristol.
Cooper, B., 1964, General practitioners attitudes to psychiatry, De Medicine Tuenda, 1:43-48.
Davidson, A.F., 1977, Clinical psychology in general practice: a preliminary enquiry, Bull. Brit. Psychol. Soc., 30:337-338.
Hewetson, J.C., McEwan, J.A., and Ollendorf, R.H.V., 1963, The incidence of psychiatric disorders in general practice, Practitioner, 190:127.
Hood, J.E., 1979, Clinical psychology and primary care: a plea for restraint, Bull. Brit. Psychol. Soc., 32:422-423.
Hopkins, P., 1955, "The General Practitioner and the Psychosomatic Approach in Modern Trends in Psychosomatic Medicine," Butterworth, London.
Hopkins, P., 1956, Referrals in general practice, B.M.J., 2:873.
Ives, G., 1979, Psychological treatment in general practice, J. Roy. Coll. Gen. Pract., 29:343-351.
Johnston, M., 1978, The work of a clinical psychologist in primary care, J. Roy. Coll. Gen. Pract., 28:661-667
Kat, B., 1979, Psychology and primary care: a review in psychology and primary care, Leicester: Division of Clinical Psychology, Brit. Psychol. Soc., pp.3-10.
Kessel, W.I.N., 1960, Psychiatric morbidity in a London general practice, Brit. J. Prev. & Soc. Med., 14:16.
Kincey, J.A., 1974, General practice and clinical psychology - some arguments for a closer liaison, J. Roy. Coll. Gen. Pract., 24:882-888.
Koch, H.C.H., 1979, Evaluation of behaviour therapy intervention in general practice, J. Roy. Coll. Gen. Pract., 29:337-340.
Lamberts, H., 1979, Problem behaviour in primary health care, J. Roy. Coll. Gen. Pract., 29:331-335.
McAllister, T.M., and Philip, A.E., 1975, The clinical psychologist in a health centre: one week's work, B.M.J., 4:513-514.
McPherson, I.G., and Feldman, M.P., 1977, A preliminary investigation of the role of the clinical psychologist in the primary care setting, Bull. Brit. Psychol. Soc., 30:342-346.
Shepherd, M., Cooper, B., Brown, A.C., and Kalbon, G.W., 1966, "Psychiatric Illness in General Practice," Oxford University Press, London.

Taylor, G., 1979, A GP's view of the psychologist's work, in: "Psychology and Primary Care," Brit. Psychol. Soc. Publications, Leicester, pp.21-28.

Trethowan, W.H., 1977, "The Role of Psychologists in the Health Services: Report of the Sub-Committee," H.M.S.O., London.

Update (September, 1980), City practice revealed. Our team - the clinical psychologist, Update - The J. Post-Grad. Gen. Pract., pp.483-487.

CLINICAL PSYCHOLOGY IN PRIMARY CARE - ISSUES IN THE

EVALUATION OF SERVICES

DWA Jerrom, D Gerver, RJ Simpson, and DA Pemberton

Forth Valley Health Board and the University of Stirling

CLINICAL PSYCHOLOGY IN PRIMARY CARE - AN EVALUATION

As Burns already suggested in the previous chapter, it has become fashionable for clinical psychologists to work in primary care settings, and although there are only a handful of clinical psychologists working exclusively in primary care, most area psychology departments have members who work in health centres on a sessional basis. Though Hood (1979) and McPherson (1980) have both recently suggested that the traditional individual treatment model is inappropriate for the psychologists working in primary care, it is not yet clear what the best role for the psychologist should be in these settings. However in this discussion we will not enter into the debate regarding roles, but will rather review the comparatively recent literature on the work of clinical psychologists in primary care. We will also present some preliminary data on the Forth Valley Health Board Stirling Health District Community Clinical Psychology Project.

Several of the papers we will review are descriptive rather than evaluative in nature, and in our view further evaluation of psychological treatments is necessary before any planning of psychological resources for primary care is undertaken. Various authors have suggested that the incidence of psychological problems in primary care is so great that it is impossible for the National Health Service to supply the number of psychologists required to

The Community Clinical Psychology Service discussed in this paper is supported by the Forth Valley Health Board.

meet the potential demand. We consider this assumption to be premature until the therapeutic role of the psychologist in primary care has been properly evaluated.

Clinical Psychologists in Primary Care - Descriptive Studies

A number of authors have published descriptions of their clinical work in primary care. McAllister and Philip (1975) reported on one year's work at Craigshill Health Centre, Livingston. The six general practitioners in the health centre referred 94 cases during 1974 to the clinical psychologists attached to the centre. The main types of problems for which referral were made involved problems of behaviour and cognitive development in children, and phobias and anxiety states in adults. 52% of the cases referred were under 16 years of age. When asked by McAllister and Philip how they would have dealt with the cases had they not been able to refer them to the psychologist, the general practitioners replied that they would have retained 46% of the cases in their own care, with the remainder being referred to a variety of specialist services.

Kat (1978) discussed the problem of the psychologist finding his "place in the team" in primary care, and classified the cases he had been dealing with into three approximate groups: sexual and marital problems, psychotropic complaints, and anxiety problems. Taylor (1979), one of the general practitioners in the practice to which Kat had been offering a clinical psychology service, reviewed the service after a period of 3 years. During the 3 years Taylor and his colleagues referred 64 patients to the psychologist, he classified these patients' problems as follows: 19 cases of chronic anxiety, 11 phobics, 16 cases of marital and sexual problems, 2 bereavement reactions, 4 patients with dependency problems and lastly a heterogenous group of 9 patients. Taylor reported on outcome for each of these groups. At the time Taylor made his enquiry 2 of the chronic anxiety cases had left the practice, but the remaining 17 patients were still taking Benzodiazepines or Tricyclics. Taylor considered that 2 of the latter group had shown enduring improvement since psychological treatment. 6 of the 11 phobic cases had improved during treatment, but 4 of these had relapsed since discharge. There was no evidence of improvement in any of the cases of marital problems, though 3 of the 8 couples with sexual problems had shown improvement. In fairness to the psychologist, Taylor repeatedly makes the point that these cases were "the tip of the iceberg", and therefore probably the most severe and chronic. It should be pointed out, however, that Taylor presents a clinical review of treatment rather than an objective assessment, and that the only objective data discussed concerned drug intake. Furthermore, data relating to drug intake is only reported for a third of the sample, and even then only related to whether the patient was still taking medication or not.

Johnston (1978) reported on 116 cases treated at Wellingford Community Hospital, and gives detailed information on the age/sex distribution of these patients (88% females), their main referring problem, the types of treatment used, and the general practitioner's assessment of the severity of those aspects of the patients' problems for a sub-group of 24 patients. Johnston reports on treatment outcome for 20 agoraphobic patients in concrete terms (viz for one case: best achievement pre-treatment = cycled to local shops alone and best achievement post-treatment = took train to London to collect son), but gives no other information on outcome. Bhagat et al (1979) report on their clinical work in primary care in Yorkshire and give seven detailed case histories to illustrate different aspects of the psychologist's role. Clark (1979) surveyed 42 consecutive referrals by general practitioners to his department in the North of Scotland, 24 for treatment and 18 for assessment only. He evaluated outcome by taking the opinion of both the psychologist and the patient as to how much improvement had been brought about by treatment, and also by judging the patient's continued reliance on drugs or other means of support. Using this assessment method Clark considered that 12 of the treatment cases had "greatly improved" following treatment and a further 9 were "slightly improved".

Two psychologists have produced evaluations of their work in primary care using the patients' consultation rates at the surgery and the level of drug intake as outcome measures. Koch (1979) reports on 30 patients treated at a University teaching practice in Leicester, and found that GP consultation rate dropped from an average of 9.27 visits during the year prior to treatment to an average of 5.46 visits for the year post-treatment. The number of repeat prescriptions for these two periods also dropped from 3.03 to 1.93. Treatment thus produced a 50% drop in GP attendance rate and a 30% drop in the number of prescriptions issued. Koch classified consultations into four classes: advice only, psychotropic prescription, physical drug prescription and mixed prescription, and demonstrated that the reduction in attendance rate resulted from significant reductions in the first two types of consultation. Overall Koch estimates that 73% of the patients improved as a result of treatment. Ives (1979) reports on 2 years' work in two group practices in Sheffield. During this time he saw 246 patients, and he reports outcome data on three sub-groups of these patients. He had discharged 149 cases at the time of writing his paper and classifies the outcome of treatment as follows: patient free, or almost free, of presenting symptoms = 32%; good progress = 28%; little or no progress = 23%; drop out = 17%. Ives presents data on both consultation rate and number of prescriptions for psychotropics during the 3 months before and after treatment for a group of 109 patients. Attendance rate dropped by 36% from an average of 3.53 to 2.26 post-treatment. The number of prescriptions issued dropped by 50% from an average of 1.88 to 0.94 for the same 3 month periods. Ives also gives data on 12-15 months' follow-up of 49

patients showing that these improvements were maintained. A further
interesting finding was that the referral rate from one of the
practices to the local psychiatric services did not change after
Ives began to work in the practice, suggesting that in this case the
general practitioners would either have retained the care of these
patients themselves or been unable to offer treatment.

Both Ives and Koch are aware of the limitations of their studies
and both suggest that future work should use no-treatment groups to
control for spontaneous remission and individual measures of severity
made by the therapist, the patient, the patient's relatives, and most
desirably, by an independent assessor blind to whether the patient
was in a treatment or a control group.

Lay Counsellors in General Practice

The papers reported above are all of the published accounts,
except one controlled study to be mentioned below, concerning the
work of the clinical psychologist in Britain. At the same time as
psychologists have been invited by general practitioners to provide
a specialist service in primary care other groups of mental health
workers, social workers, psychiatrists and lay counsellors, have
also begun to work in health centre settings, the latter two groups
tending to see the same types of patients that a psychologist would
treat. Two papers have now been published in Britain concerning
the evaluation of the work of lay counsellors in general practice.
Anderson and Hasler (1979) report on the work of one counsellor in
a group practice in South Oxfordshire. The counsellor involved was
a trained marriage guidance counsellor and held a nursing
qualification. It is obvious from their report both that the
counsellor was seeing similar types of patients to those a
psychologist would see and that she was also occasionally using the
same techniques a psychologist would use. The treatment offered
was described thus: "The counsellor's main aim is to offer the
patients support and insight. The patient is also given the chance
to learn new skills such as relaxation techniques .... a
behavioural approach has been found useful in the management of
phobias." (Anderson and Hasler, 1979, p.352). Anderson and Hasler
present outcome data on 80 patients. All patients were sent a
detailed questionnaire about "personal development", 55 returned
them. In response to the crucial question "Has there been any
improvement in the way you feel about yourself?", 64% of the patients
replied "Yes", 78% of respondents indicated that they would use the
counselling service again, whilst 84% said they would recommend
counselling to relatives or friends. The general practitioners
also reported improvement in their patients and were satisfied with
the service provided. Anderson and Hasler report consultation rates
for the 3 months before and after treatment. The patients who
returned the questionnaire reduced their average number of consulta-

tions by 67%, non-responders reduced their consultations by 54%.
The average rates for the two groups were 3.3 down to 1.1, and
3.5 down to 1.6 respectively. Anderson and Hasler do not give full
information on drug intake but they report that over half of the
total sample were not taking psychotropics at any point, and that
20 patients had either reduced or stopped their medication by the
time of the 3 month follow-up.

Waydenfeld and Waydenfeld (1980) report on a larger study of
counselling in 9 North London practices involving 9 counsellors and
99 patients. The counsellors were all trained marriage guidance
counsellors but in this study were treating patients with similar
types of problems to those that a psychologist would normally treat,
the most frequent presenting symptoms being anxiety and depression.
Waydenfeld and Waydenfeld used a 6 point improvement scale ranging
from "deteriorated" to "very much improved" which was completed by
the counsellor, the general practitioner and the patient in each
case. The ratings were made independently by the general
practitioner and counsellor and show remarkable agreement, general
practitioners rating 32% of the patients as very much improved and
counsellors rating 34% as very much improved. 53% of the patients
returned their questionnaires about treatment; 80% of these
respondents reported that they were "very much" or "somewhat"
improved. Waydenfeld and Waydenfeld report that the patients'
consultation rate was an average of 4.5 visits for the 6 months
before treatment, and this had dropped by 31% to an average of 3.1
consultations during the 6 months post-treatment. They also found
a dramatic reduction in the attendance rates of the patients'
spouses and children, with spouses' consultation rate dropping from
3.8 to 0.4 during the same period, while the average attendance rate
of the patients' children dropped from 4.4 to 0.8. The numbers of
prescriptions given to patients during the 6 months pre- and post-
treatment were compared. There was a 30% reduction in the number of
prescriptions issued for psychotropics, and a 48% reduction in
prescriptions for other drugs. These studies suggest that lay
counsellors are as effective as clinical psychologists in treating
psychological problems in primary care. This concurs with the
conclusions of Durlak's (1979) review of the relative efficacies of
professional and para-professional workers in the mental health
field. Reviewing 42 studies which have compared the effectiveness
of para-professionals or lay counsellors to that of professionals
he concludes that: "Para-professionals achieve clinical outcomes
equal to or significantly better than professionals." (Durlak, 1979).
However we do not consider that lay counsellors are interchangeable
with clinical psychologists in primary care as there are certain
types of problem for which psychologists possess particular skills
of analysis and treatment, whereas counsellors have no experience
or training in the treatment of these problems. Examples of such
problems would be the treatment of sexual dysfunction, obsessional
ruminations and obsessional compulsions, and of patients with social

skills deficits. In addition the assumption that because lay counselling is at present free it is therefore more cost effective for the National Health Service than treatments conducted by either psychologists or social workers will not always be the case: "Should surgery counselling become a widely accepted practice, something will have to be done about the position of counsellors, because the increased demand for counselling will not be met by voluntary workers and a new method will have to be devised for paying them." (Waydenfeld and Waydenfeld, 1980, p.676).

Psychological Treatments – Controlled Studies

Two controlled studies of the effectiveness of psychological treatments in general practice have now been conducted in this country, one involving a social worker using a case work approach and the other a psychologist using behavioural treatments. The first of these two studies, Cooper et al (1975), examined the work of a social worker attached to one general practice in Croydon. 92 patients with a diagnosis of "chronic neurotic illness", the criteria for this being the presence of continuous symptoms and/or dependence on psychotropic drugs for at least 12 months, formed the treatment group, while the control group consisted of 97 neurotic patients from 8 surrounding practices. A psychiatrist conducted a psychiatric assessment of all 189 patients at entry to the study, and then again one year later. The authors emphasise that their study is not a simple comparison of social case work with no treatment, but is rather a comparison between social case work together with existing services and existing services alone. At one year follow-up .the treatment group showed significant improvements in symptoms and social adjustment scores when compared to the control group, these changes being significant at the .01 level and .001 level respectively. 38% of the treatment group had been taken off psychotropic drugs, as against 25% of the controls; this difference was significant at the .05 level. Cooper et al do not report consultation data for the two groups. A problem with the study is that the bulk of the outcome data comes from psychiatric interviews, and the psychiatrist knew whether the patient belonged to the treatment or control groups. Earll and Kincey (1980) have recently reported a study of behaviour therapy in general practice. This work has not yet been published so we will not review it in detail here. Suffice it to say that Earll and Kincey found no significant differences in outcome between their treatment (N = 23) and control (N = 19) groups, except that the treatment group received significantly fewer prescriptions for psychotropics between the point of referral and discharge than the no-treatment control group did during the same period. The method of assessment used was again principally a structured interview carried out by the second author who was blind to the experimental condition of the patient.

Discussion

To conclude: the effectiveness of psychological treatment in primary care has not yet been properly measured, the papers discussed above can only be regarded as preliminary reports. Four studies, two involving psychologists and two counsellors, have produced highly significant reductions in both consultation rate and drug intake. The two controlled studies reviewed above produced contradictory results. Cooper et al (1975), in the best designed study so far carried out in this area, found small but statistically significant differences between a social case work treatment group and a no-treatment control group. However in a more recent but smaller study Earll and Kincey (1980) failed to find any enduring difficulties between a behaviour therapy treatment group and a no-treatment control group.

There are some general criticisms which can be levelled at all of the research to date. Firstly the two most commonly used outcome measures, drug intake and consultation rate, have not yet been shown to be valid indices of symptomatic improvement. It is well known that patients with psychological problems consult their general practitioners more often than "normals" (Hassall and Stilwell, 1977), but it has not yet been demonstrated that a reduction in the former group's attendance rate correlates with symptomatic improvement. The same point can be made about psycho-tropic drug usage. The reasons for the selection of these two measures by researchers are obvious: they are objective measures of behaviour, they are relevant to general practitioners' needs and interests, they are easy to obtain and they seem likely to prove valid as measures of improvement. It needs to be demonstrated that drug intake and consultation rate are truly valid measures of symptomatic improvement. The second general criticism of these studies is that none have attempted to relate patient variables to the outcome of treatment. If psychological treatment in primary care is to become more widespread it is obviously crucial to dis-cover which type of patient will benefit the most.

Recommendations

We therefore make the following suggestions concerning future research studies on psychological treatments and counselling in primary care:

1)   They should employ a no-treatment control group obtained by either randomised allocation or a matching procedure.

2)   They should use the following outcome measures: the patients' assessment of the severity of their problems before and after the experimental period, a structured interview conducted by a blind

assessor with the patient before and after the experimental period,
the patients' consultation rates and data on psychotropic and other
drug usage.

3)   They should investigate the relationship between patient
variables, such as type, severity and chronicity of problem, and the
outcome of treatment.

4)   They should attempt to assess how durable the effects of treatment are over follow-up periods of greater than one year.

5)   They should compare the efficacies of differing psychological
treatments, the most obvious candidates for the first comparison
being behaviour therapy and counselling.

The goal of the types of research suggested above would be to
discover whether the introduction of psychologists and counsellors
into primary care benefits either the group of moderately and
severely neurotic patients involved, or their general practitioners.
Whilst we would agree with the various authors who have suggested
that mental health care in the community should primarily be the
responsibility of the general practitioner (viz Shepherd, 1980),
we suggest that a sub-group of the general practitioner's patients
with psychological problems may benefit in the long term from
psychological treatment.

FORTH VALLEY COMMUNITY CLINICAL PSYCHOLOGY PROJECT

Background

The research to be discussed below was carried out within the
context of a project set up in January 1979 by Forth Valley Health
Board, in collaboration with the University of Stirling, involving
the development and assessment of a community based clinical
psychology service for the Stirling District of the Forth Valley.
A team was set up consisting of a senior psychologist appointed to
develop the service and a consultant psychiatrist, a general
practitioner and a senior lecturer in psychology to work as a
support group. The psychologist is based in one health centre, but
has clinics in six other health centres on a regular basis and visits
two further health centres occasionally.

The Stirling Health District has a population of 127,600, and
25 practices which refer to the sector psychiatrists. The psychology
service is open to referrals from the 77 general practitioners from
these practices, the sector psychiatrists and medical staff at the
local general hospital.

Initial Referral Pattern

During the first 22 months of the service 17 practices referred to the psychology service, 5 out of the 7 non-referring practices were rural ones. 51, or 66% of the 77 general practitioners working in the health district have now referred patients. By the end of November 1980, 409 patients had been referred, equivalent to an average referral rate of 4.3 cases per week. The average waiting list time has varied between 3 weeks and 7 weeks for different months during the project so far, depending on such factors as the fluctuation in the number of referrals, the number of discharges and the number of cases accumulated at particular health centres used for consultation. As the project has progressed urgent referrals have become more common, for instance, during August 1980 4 patients were seen within one week of referral as the general practitioner had asked for the case to have urgent attention.

Preliminary Results

Table 1 gives a breakdown of the number of patients discharged from the service by the end of October 1980, and these are shown under the 11 categories we have been using for classifying dis- charges. The chief aim of using these categories is to sort patients into those groups which have received treatment and are therefore to be followed up as part of the evaluation of the service. All patients from the first 6 categories are followed up 6 months after discharge.

Table 1. Patients Discharged by November, 1980

	Status	No.	%
1.	Discharged improved	67	28
2.	Discharged unimproved	18	8
3.	Drop out	67	28
4.	Discharged counselled	10	4
5.	Student	2	0.5
6.	Crisis over	4	2
7.	Referred on	16	7
8.	Moved/Died	13	5.5
9.	Psychological assessment	11	5
10.	Refused treatment	3	1
11.	No show	25	11
		236	

The criteria for including patients in these categories are as
follows: "Discharged improved" refers to cases where the patient
and the psychologist agree that the presenting problem had entirely
gone, or where the patient felt that any remaining difficulties could
be overcome unaided. "Discharged unimproved" refers to cases where
the patient and the psychologist agreed that treatment had so far
produced no benefit, and that further sessions would be a mutual
waste of time. Patients are classified as "Drop outs" if they enter
treatment but at some stage fail to keep two consecutive appointments
at the clinic without making contact before or afterwards. Patients
who do this are automatically discharged unless they are agoraphobic,
in which case they are offered a home visit. "Discharged counselled"
refers to the small group of patients who were not offered any formal
treatment, but who simply discussed their problem with the psychologist; usually these patients only attended for one appointment.
The special category "Student" refers to students from Stirling
University who have broken off treatment at the end of one semester
and have not restarted treatment in the next semester. Three
patients in the "Crisis over" group came into treatment because of
an obvious stress in their environment and then lost their symptoms
as soon as this problem was removed. Patients from the 4 remaining
groups, "Referred on", "Moved/Died", "Psychological assessment" and
"Refused treatment" are not followed up after discharge. Patients
in the "No show" group did not keep their first appointment. Table 1
shows that 236 patients were discharged by November 1980, leaving
173 active cases.

Assessment of Outcome

Three types of follow-up data are being gathered:

1)   Consultation rate for the 6 months' period prior to referral,
during treatment and for the 6 months following discharge.

2)   The patients' own ratings of the severity of their problem and
the extent to which treatment has been of benefit.

Table 2. Patients' Average Consultation Rates,
Pre, During and After Treatment

	6 months pre-treatment	During treatment	6 months post-treatment
Monthly	0.9	0.49	0.5
Yearly	10.8	5.9	6.2

3)   Patient levels of psychotropic drug usage which can then be compared to drug usage at admission.

54 patients have now been followed up and we have attained GP attendance data and drug intake data on 47 of these cases, and patients' own ratings of their condition for 33 cases.

Consultation Rate. Table 2 shows a 43% reduction in attendance rate between the 6 months prior to treatment and the 6 months following discharge (Wilcoxon P < .001). It is interesting to note that pre-treatment these patients were consulting their doctors at nearly four times the average annual rate for the general population, and even though their consultation rate following treatment was nearly halved it is still twice the national average. 33 patients have now returned their follow-up questionnaires which asked them to rate the extent to which treatment has "helped" them on a 4 point scale, and to rate the severity of their problem on a 5 point scale. These responses are presented in Table 3.

Patients' Self-Ratings. Inspection of Table 3 shows that 31 of the 33 respondents (94%) considered psychological treatment to have helped them to some extent, whilst 29 respondents (87%) rated their problem as having improved to various degrees. During 1980 we have begun asking all patients to complete 6 point self-rating scales for up to three separate problems at admission, discharge and follow-up. The first 22 patients to complete their scale at both admission and discharge gave an average problem rating of 3.55 at admission and an average rating of 1.48 at discharge. This 58% reduction in self-rated problem severity is statistically significant (Wilcoxon P < .001). These results must be regarded with some reserve as they may either reflect spontaneous remission, or a therapist "halo" effect.

Table 3. Patient Self-Ratings at Follow-up (N = 33)

"Helping" rating:
Seeing the psychologist helped me a lot	=	45%
Seeing the psychologist helped me a bit	=	49%
Seeing the psychologist did not help me	=	6%
Seeing the psychologist made me worse	=	0%

"Problem" rating:
The problem is completely gone	=	3%
The problem is a lot better	=	56%
The problem is a bit better	=	28%
The problem is the same	=	13%
The problem is worse	=	0%

Psychotropic and Analgesic Usage. Drug intake data has been obtained for psychotropics and analgesics on 52 patients at admission, discharge and follow-up: 21 patients were taking drugs neither on admission nor on follow-up; of the remaining 31 patients, 15 who were taking drugs at admission stopped taking all medication by follow-up, 7 patients were on the same medication and 2 patients had changed their medication. A further 2 patients who were not taking drugs at admission had started medication by the time of follow-up. Lastly, 5 patients who were taking drugs at admission were still taking the same drugs at follow-up but had decreased their dose. No patients who were taking medication at admission had increased their dosages by follow-up. Thus 39% of patients had either with-drawn from drugs completely, (Wilcoxon P < .05) or decreased their dosage between admission and discharge, 21% of patients were taking the same dosage, had changed to another drug or had begun to take medication, and 40% of patients were not taking medication at any point.

Consultation Rate of Spouses and Children

The reader will recall our reviewing Waydenfeld and Waydenfeld's data on the consultation rate of the patients' spouses and children. 13 married patients from one of the health centres used in the study have now completed the 6 month follow-up period, and 8 of these patients have children below the age of 16. The consultation rates for these patients, their spouses and children are shown in Table 4.

These figures show that while the patients reduced their attendance rate by 47% there was no significant reduction in the consultation rate of the patients' spouses and children. It is of interest to note, however, that during the 6 months pre-treatment the patients were attending twice as often as their spouses, but after treatment they were attending at the same rate.

Table 4. Patient, Spouse and Children Consultation Rates

	6 months pre-treatment	6 months post-treatment	Wilcoxon P.
Patient (N = 13)	4.23	2.23	<.01
Spouses	2.23	1.92	N.S.
Children (N = 11)	2.09	1.64	N.S.

Table 5. Patients' Major Problem as Defined
by Psychologist

Problem	%
Anxiety	26
Agoraphobia	13
Social phobia	11
Sex	8
Focal phobia	7
Somatic symptoms	7
Depression	7
Pain/Headache	5
Obsessions	4
Drink/Drugs	3
Other	9

Kincey Categories:

A	Anxiety and stress	69%
B	Habit disorders	7%
C	Interpersonal, social and marital	22%

The final data we wish to present about the results of the project so far concern the types of problem dealt with.

Types of Psychological Problems Referred

A 24 category classification system for "priority problems" has been employed, and Table 5 shows the frequency of the 10 most commonly referred problems so far. The Table also groups these patients' problems into the categories: A - Anxiety and stress, B - Habit disorders, and C - Interpersonal, social and marital, suggested by Kincey (1974). These percentages are remarkably similar to those reported by Koch (1979) for his much smaller sample.

Research in Progress

By the end of 1981 it is hoped to include the following areas of assessment in evaluation of the work of the clinic:

1) Consultation rates for 6 months before and after treatment for all patients discharged by June 1981 (N = approximately 250). Drug intake data between admission, discharge and follow-up will also be obtained for these patients.

2)   Problem severity ratings and General Health Questionnaire responses on admission, discharge and follow-up will be obtained from a sample of patients.

3)   The relationship between demographic factors and other patient variables and measures of outcome will be examined, with a view to defining prognostic indicators for treatment.

4)   A comparison of outcome between a treatment group and a no-treatment control group over a 3 month period.

5)   Consultation rates for 6 months before and after treatment for the families of a series of 50 patients, and prescribing for the patients' families during the same periods will also be investigated.

6)   The durability of treatment effects will be examined by a 2 year follow-up of the patients discharged during the first year of the project. The patients' attendance rate over this 2 years and their drug usage at admission, discharge, 6 month follow-up and 2 year follow-up will be reported.

7)   A survey of the satisfaction of the general practitioners with the service provided, using an anonymous questionnaire.

CONCLUSION

In this chapter we have reviewed publications concerning the work of the clinical psychologist in primary care, have made some suggestions concerning future research, and have presented some early data from our own project. It could be suggested, although no author has done so, that because psychological treatments have been well evaluated in their traditional psychiatric out-patient setting there is no need for further evaluation in primary care. We disagree with this on two grounds. Firstly, the patients the psychologist sees in primary care do not necessarily have the same types of problem as the patients a hospital based psychologist sees; some patients have been referred to our project who would un-doubtedly, for a variety of reasons, not have seen either a psychiatrist or a psychologist if our service did not exist. Secondly, general practitioners have different criteria for evaluating treatment from those used in the published literature to date. In particular they are interested in whether psychological treatment can reduce the dependence of the patient with emotional problems upon the services of the primary care team. Fortunately this is an area of clinical psychology where there is much research in progress, and we are confident that in a further 5 years' time many of the issues referred to in this paper will have been clarified.

REFERENCES

Anderson, S., and Hasler, J.C., 1979, Counselling in general practice, J. Roy. Coll. Gen. Pract., 29:352-356.
Bhagat, M., Lewis, A.P., and Shillitoe, R.W., 1979, Clinical psychologists and the primary health care team, Update, pp.479-488.
Cooper, B., Harwin, B.G., Depla C., and Shepherd, M., 1975, Mental health care in the community: an evaluation study, Psych. Med., 5:372-380.
Clark, D.F., 1979, The clinical psychologist in primary care, Soc. Psy. & Med., 13A:707-713.
Durlak, J.A., 1979, Comparative effectiveness of paraprofessional and professional helpers, Psychol. Bull., 86:80-92.
Earll, L., and Kincey, J., 1980, A controlled trial evaluation of psychological intervention at primary care level. Paper read at the Brit. Psychol. Soc. Conf., Aberdeen, March 1980.
Hassall, C., and Stilwell, J.A., 1977, Family-doctor support for patients on a psychiatric case register, J. Roy. Coll. Gen. Pract., 27:605-608.
Hood, J.E., 1979, Clinical psychologists in primary care: a plea for restraint, Bull. Brit. Psychol. Soc., 32:422-423.
Ives, G., 1979, Psychological treatment in general practice, J. Roy. Coll. Gen. Pract., 29:343-351.
Johnston, M., 1978, The work of a clinical psychologist in primary care, J. Roy. Coll. Gen. Pract., 28:661-667.
Kat, B., 1978, Primary health care: on finding one's place in the team, Bull. Brit. Psychol. Soc., 31:154-156.
Kincey, J., 1974, General practice and clinical psychology - some arguments for a closer liaison, J. Roy. Coll. Gen. Pract., 24:882-888.
Koch, H.C.H., 1979, Evaluation of behaviour therapy intervention in general practice, J. Roy. Coll. Gen. Pract., 29:337-340.
McAllister, T.A., and Philip, A., 1975, The clinical psychologist in a health centre: one year's work, B.M.J., 4:513-514.
McPherson, I., 1980, Clinical psychology in primary care - another case of innovation without change? Paper read at Brit. Psychol. Soc. Conf., Aberdeen, March 1980.
Shepherd, M., 1980, Mental health as an integrant of primary medical care, J. Roy. Coll. Gen. Pract., 30:657-663.
Taylor, G., 1979, A GP's view of the psychologist's work, in: "Psychology and Primary Care," Brit. Psychol. Soc. Publications, Leicester.
Waydenfeld, D., and Waydenfeld, S.W., 1980, Counselling in general practice, J. Roy. Coll. Gen. Pract., 30:671-677.

LIFE EVENTS AND PSYCHOLOGICAL DISTRESS: SOME PROBLEMS IN DESIGN AND ANALYSIS

David J Cooke

Psychology Department
Gartnavel Royal Hospital
Glasgow, Scotland

The hypothesis that stressful life events may engender psychological disturbance currently receives considerable attention and considerable uncritical support. Cooper and Shepherd (1972), in their historical review, suggested that this has not always been the case; the extent to which psychological distress has been attributed to the experience of stressful life events has varied throughout history. They indicated that during the great plagues of the middle ages contemporary social historians perceived a link between the concomitant stress and strife and the occurrence of "great madness". Given this early perception, it is curious that during the first world war, the link between the stress of combat and the acute neurotic breakdowns of aircraft pilots, was not generally perceived. Indeed these neurotic reactions were attributed to noise, cold, oxygen lack and lack of moral fibre.

Currently, the view that there is an aetiological link between stressful life events and psychological distress holds favour. Despite the popularity of this view, Dohrenwend and Dohrenwend (1978), in a detailed review suggested that this view is founded more on faith than scientific evidence. While this contention has a certain validity, over the last one and a half decades, the systematic study of everyday stressful life events has developed substantially and certain general principles regarding the appropriate methods of design and analysis have emerged.

In this chapter I hope to outline some of the pitfalls and difficulties in carrying out research in this field. I hope, in addition, to provide a theoretical account of the principles that will aid the shift from faith towards evidence. The practical application of these principles is described in the next chapter on

113

the influence of life events during the climacterium. The bourgeoning literature is now so large to be beyond review in the space available and thus the general principles will be illustrated from the literature on psychological distress in general and depressive disorders in particular.

I will examine the difficulties inherent in operationalising the dependent and independent variables and the impact that their characteristics may have in the detection of an aetiological link between events and symptoms.

DEVELOPING SUITABLE DEPENDENT VARIABLES

One Dependent Variable or Many?

When an investigator starts to operationalise his hypotheses perhaps his first decision relates to the number of dependent variables that are required. Rabkin and Struening (1976) indicated that a large body of literature demonstrates that psychological distress is heterogenous in quality; it is heterogenous both in terms of symptomatology and in terms of aetiology. Depressive disorders, for example, are characterised by symptoms as diverse as weight loss, poor concentration and feeling of hopelessness, while aetiological factors as diverse as genetic, hormonal and social environmental have been implicated. Rabkin and Struening (1976) argued that failure to constrain this heterogeneity can frequently lead to erroneous and misleading conclusions. Thus steps must be taken to reduce this heterogeneity.

Reducing Symptom Heterogeneity

In developing suitable dependent variables the researcher's first problem is deciding which characteristics, behaviours or experiences characterise the essence of the condition of interest and which are merely correlates. No a priori rules exist for distinguishing between core features and correlates, however, some guidelines are available. Derogatis et al (1972) and Ni Bhrolchain (1979) have cogently argued that advantages accrue from restricting consideration to clinical signs and symptoms. Within the context of depressive disorders, restriction to clinical signs and symptoms would entail consideration of symptoms such as depressed mood, fatigue irritability, hopelessness and weight loss. These symptoms, although heterogenous in nature exemplify those symptoms generally considered to characterise the core defining features of depression. Restriction to clinical signs and symptoms would, however, exclude the consideration of demographic, personality, social adjustment and life event variables. These factors may be considered, on

a priori grounds, to be antecedents or consequences of depressive
disorders rather than core defining features. The principal advantage that accrues from this approach, therefore, is that it allows
clear demarcation between the putative aetiological agent and its
putative effect viz psychological distress. Lack of clear demarcation has been a problem in life event research. Schless et al
(1977) indicated that there are certain phenomena that, on a priori
grounds, can be equally well regarded as either symptoms or antecedents of psychological distress. Even if detailed contextual information is available it is frequently impossible to determine whether,
for example, "marital difficulties" should be regarded as a cause
or a concomitant of depressive disorder. Restricting the dependent
variable to clinical signs and symptoms reduces the potential for
such contaminative effects.

When the characteristic behaviours and experiences of psychological distress are distilled to the essential features an unacceptable
level of heterogeneity will generally still remain. It is necessary,
therefore, to further condense and clarify the information.

In describing the classification of symptoms, Eysenck (1970),
Garside et al (1971) and Garside and Roth (1978) indicated that it
entails two necessary and discrete steps. The first step involves
the identification of syndromes, syndromes being composed of symptoms
that are highly correlated amongst themselves but relatively un-
correlated with other symptoms. The second step requires the
generation of a subject classification in relation to the derived
syndromes. This second step demonstrates whether a dimensional or
a categorical model of describing psychological disturbance is
most parsimonious and the form of model that is identified has
implications for our understanding of the impact of life events.

Cattell et al (1966) and Garside and Roth (1978) have indicated
that Principal Component Analysis (PCA) can be used to delineate
syndromes as defined above. This first step in deriving a descriptive system provides information about the number of syndromes present
and the nature of their defining characteristics.

Syndromes derived by PCA not only summarise the observations
obtained but also they can be regarded as unidimensional hypothetical
constructs. Eysenck (1953) stated that each syndrome represents
"a hypothetical causal influence underlying and determining the
observed relationship between a set of variables" (p.110). It was
noted above that a variety of aetiological factors are thought to
underpin the distribution of depressive symptoms. Following
Eysenck, it may be argued that particular syndromes, defined by
PCA, may be linked to specific aetiological factors. In the most
simple hypothetical form, psychosocial factors may influence one
syndrome or symptom complex, while hormonal factors may influence
another syndrome.

The application of PCA, therefore, will reduce the level of symptom heterogeneity and facilitate the identification of links between potential aetiological factors and particular symptom clusters.

The second step in deriving a classification system based on symptoms involves determining whether subjects fall into discrete subject categories or whether they fail to cluster and appear to simultaneously experience differing degrees of all extant syndromes.

This issue can be tackled by considering the multivariate distributions of subjects' component scores. Weckowicz (1973) argued that three general forms of component score distribution may emerge: (a) n – variate rectangular, (b) n – variate unimodal, (c) n – variate multimodal. The first distribution implies that the subjects are distributed evenly within the component spaces; the second that there is highest density in the centre thinning towards the periphery; and the third that there are several high density clusters of subjects in different areas of the component space. Cattell et al (1966) and Eysenck (1970) indicated that the occurrence of either of the first two forms implies that a dimensional view of illness is most parsimonious whereas the occurrence of a multimodal distribution implies that a categorical view of illness is most parsimonious.

The two necessary and discrete steps inherent in the reduction of symptom heterogeneity are important in the identification of the links between life events and psychological distress.

Failure to carry out the first step may have important implications. If the investigator uses generalised measures of psychiatric or psychological distress such as the General Health Questionnaire (eg Andrews et al, 1976), Zung Self Rating Depression Scale (eg Henderson et al, 1980) or Hamilton Depression Scale (Surtees and Ingham, 1980) without differentiating symptoms into specific syndromes, then he may fail to detect links between life events and the critical syndrome. If symptoms, that are outwith the relevant aetiological chain are included in the dependent variable then they are embued with the qualities of error variance. The inclusion of such epiphenomena will tend to cloud or attenuate the link between the putative aetiological agent and the relevant syndrome.

In a general population study the present author identified four syndromes of depression (Cooke, 1980a, 1981a). Only one of these syndromes was related to life stress (Cooke, 1981b). Failure to distinguish amongst these four syndromes would have both obscured the specificity of the link between life events and only one syndrome and mislead the investigator to assume a lower level of covariation between events and depressive symptoms. This attenuative effect of the irrelevant symptoms is particularly critical in the life event field because the level of covariation between dependent and

independent variables is generally low. Two sets of reviewers have
recently highlighted this point. Cochrane and Sobol (1980) suggested
that on average 10% of the variance is explained by the covariation,
whereas Lin et al (1979) provided a lower estimate of between 4
and 8% of the variance being shared.

Errors may also arise in the interpretation of covariation of
the dependent and independent variables, if the second step in the
development of a classification system is ignored. A priori
assumptions regarding the presence of discrete subject categories
can obscure the differential impact of life stresses. This problem
is well illustrated in the work of Brown and Harris (1978) and
Brown et al (1979).

Brown et al (1979) examined the relationship between life stress
and the traditional psychotic-neurotic dichotomy in depressive
disorders. The psychiatric tradition is that neurotic depression
is a consequence of life stress whereas psychotic depression results
from a variety of processes intrinsic to the organism. Brown et al
(1979) concluded that this tradition is misleading and that both
forms of depression are 'reactive' in quality.

Brown and Harris (1978) made the a priori assumption that the
111 patients in their cohort fell into one of two diagnostic categories and condensed the two necessary but discrete steps of
classification into one. They carefully examined the relationships
between life stress and several discriminant functions which mar-
ginally discriminated between these two diagnostic categories.
Their ability to discriminate appeared to be poor as the maximum
amount of variance explained by the diagnostic dichotomy, adjusted
for chance effects, was only 24% (corrected R^2). This lack of clear
discrimination into discrete diagnostic categories was further
confirmed by their descriptions. Brown and Harris (1978) noted
that "clinical differences between the 'endogenous' and 'reactive'
groups were few indeed" (p.217) and further that " 'typical'
symptoms of either group can occur in the other ....." (p.40).

Given this, it is likely that their data fit a unimodal bi-
variate distribution as stylised in Fig 1. On Fig 1 subjects A and
D will experience significant degrees of either psychotic or neurotic
depression.   Subject B, however, will experience equally severe
degrees of both psychotic and neurotic depression, whereas subject
C will experience equally low degrees of both. If a patient (Pp)
in the psychotic group is contrasted with a patient (Pn) in the
neurotic group, then it is clear that both patients (Pp and Pn)
experience high levels of each syndrome, and, they differ merely in
terms of which syndrome predominates. In contrasting such patients,
the differential effects of life stress must be obscured as their
level of neurotic (reactive) depression are not substantially
different. This is true for all patients who lie near the cutting

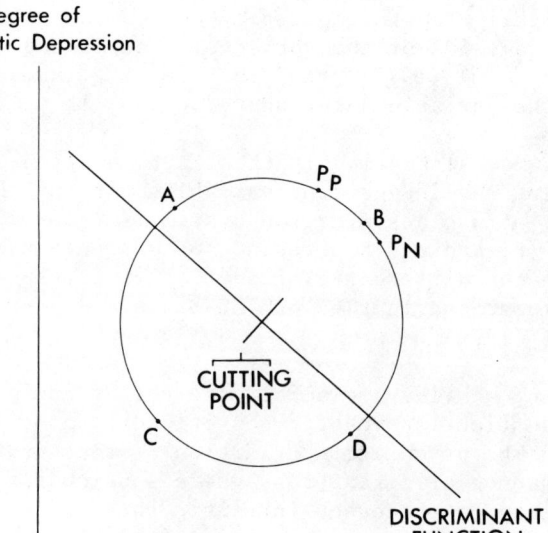

Fig. 1. Patterns of patients' symptomatology in relation
to their location on a discriminant function.

score of the discriminant function, whether they are experiencing
equally high, moderate or low degrees of each syndrome. The confusion of the two processes of classification must perforce lead to
confusion in the linking of potential aetiological mechanisms
(see Cooke (1981b) for fuller discussion of these issues).

The Dependent Variable: Caseness Versus Continuous Measurement

The above approach to the reduction of symptom heterogeneity
results in a set of continuous dependent variables. There has been
a tendency, however, in the life event literature to use the
dichotomous 'case-versus-non-case' distinction as the dependent
variable (eg Brown et al, 1975; Andrews et al, 1976, 1978). The
debate on the use of categorical as against dimensional description
of psychological disorders has a long history, and the theoretical
and practical advantages of each approach are well reviewed by
Williams et al (1980). Given the existence of this review and the
current strictures of space, I will merely examine the advantages
of the dimensional approach as it directly affects our understanding
of the link between life events and psychological distress.

In developing their 'case versus non-case' distinctions many
investigators deliberately dichotomise essentially continuous
variables. The first practical disadvantage that emerges from this
dichotomisation of continuous variables is that there is a substantial loss of statistical power. Loss of statistical power may lead
the investigator to either underestimate the level of covariation
between his dependent variable and his life event measure, or, more
importantly, result in him failing to detect any significant covariation.

Cohen and Cohen (1975) argued that reducing a graduated, many
valued scale to a 2-point scale results in a wilful loss of information. The magnitude of this loss of information can be substantial.
To illustrate the strength of this effect Cohen and Cohen (1975)
indicated that "median cuts of two normally distributed variables
will result in an r^2 between them ($r^2\phi$) which is only 40% as large
as r^2 would be in the original variables" (p.300, footnote). The
loss of power may be even greater with the non-normal distributions
that are characteristic of measures of psychological distress.
Therefore, while nominalisation of quantitative variables may have
merits in simplifying descriptive accounts of data, it may have
the unfortunate consequence of the investigator underestimating the
level of covariation present.

Problems in Causal Inference and Dichotomous Variables

Researchers in the life event field are concerned, either
implicitly or explicitly, with the divining of causal links between
life events and psychological disturbance. It is in this endeavour,
perhaps, where the use of dichotomous dependent variables poses the
most significant difficulties for workers in this field.

Thus, in this section a more fundamental question is posed,
whether causal modelling is possible with data that are tabulated
in dichotomous contingency tables.

In attempting to make causal statements about life events
Bebbington (1980), amongst others, has attempted to apply the principles of formal logic to data. He argued that the 2 X 2 contingency
tables, commonly used in psychiatric epidemiology, represent the
relationship between two variables in a manner analogous to the
truth tables of formal logic. He has argued that the analysis of
contingency tables can lead to the corroboration of one causal model
rather than another.

Novack (1960, 1976), Blalock (1964), Cook and Campbell (1979)
and Cooke (1980b), however, have indicated that causal analysis of
empirical data, based on the principles of truth tables, is fraught
with difficulties. Both truth tables and the contingency tables

with which we are concerned depend on dichotomous classifications.
Pearson (1957) argued that dichotomisation is often merely a crude
procedure for handling continuous variables. Blalock (1964)
indicated that, while it is technically possible to think always in
terms of dichotomies, difficulties may arise because they are frequently the result of an essentially artificial cutpoint on some
quantitative variable.

Blalock (1964) illustrated these difficulties. Given two
continuous variables, one a hypothetical causal agent and the other
its postulated effect then the best fitting curve, be it linear or
non-linear, represents a continuous causal function linking the
postulated cause and effect.

For the purpose of illustration the regression line is plotted
in Fig 2, sample fluctuation being ignored. Examination of Fig 2
illustrates that our decision regarding the arbitrary point at which
to dichotomise the variables dramatically influences the entries in
the truth table and the resulting causal inference made.

If fortuitously the intersection of our dichotomising lines
falls precisely on the regression line then Fig 2a results. When the
cause is absent the effect is also absent, when the cause is present
the effect is present. The resulting truth table implies that the
cause is both necessary and sufficient.

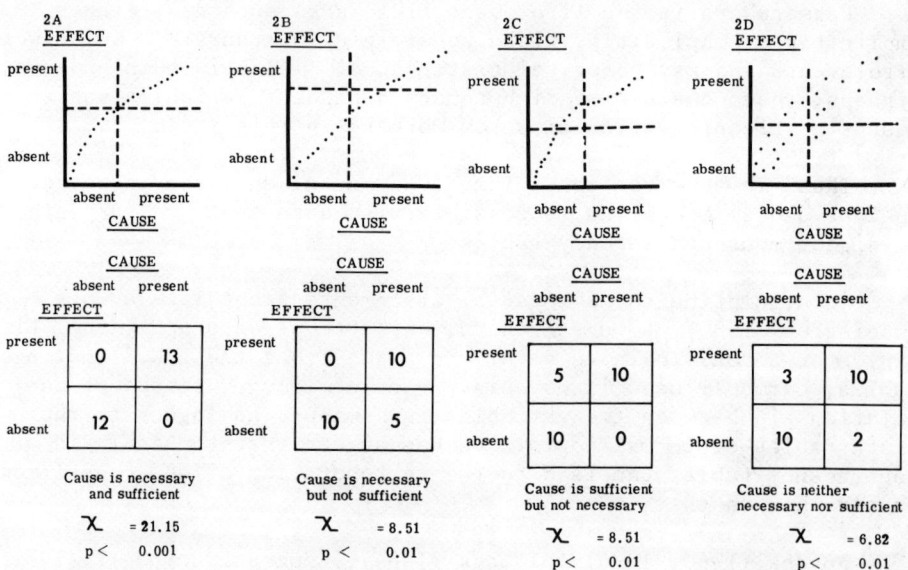

Fig. 2. Demonstration of the effect that arbitrary dichotomisation
of continuous variables has on causal inference.

If, however, the intersection of the dichotomising lines crosses above the regression line then different entries appear in the truth table (Fig 2b). In this case when the cause is absent, the effect is absent, when the cause is present, however, the effect only appears spasmodically. The resulting truth table suggests that the cause is necessary but not sufficient. When the intersection of the dichotomising lines falls below the regression line a new set of entries is placed in the truth table (Fig 2c). When the cause is absent the effect appears spasmodically, however, when the cause is present the effect is always present. This truth table implies that the cause is sufficient but not necessary.

Sampling fluctuations and other factors entailed in any empirical distribution will tend to result in truth tables of the form 2d. This table, the most common form in studies of psychological distress (Susser, 1973), suggests that causes are neither necessary nor sufficient.

It must be contended, therefore, that the entries in tables and the inferences made from them are critically influenced by essentially arbitrary decisions regarding the point of dichotomisation of continuous cause and effect variables. Even given that empirical data will inevitably result in truth tables without empty cells, the relative proportion of the entries in the cells critically affects inferences made about causal processes.

Relevance to the Interpretation of Life Events

The above argument clearly entails the assumption that cause and effect are best conceptualised as continuous variates and not attributes. The relevance of this problem for the life event literature will be considered by examining the example used by Bebbington (1980).

Bebbington applied his principles of analysis to the data published by Brown et al (1975). Brown et al (1975) initially considered the link between the experience of life events (postulated cause) and caseness (postulated effect).

Brown and his colleagues dichotomised their example into those subjects who had experienced no provoking agents and those subjects who had experienced one or more provoking agents. The critical question is whether the relationship between provoking agents and caseness is continuous or all or none; that is, for example, is the risk of becoming a case greater for a subject experiencing three provoking agents than for a subject experiencing one provoking agent. Brown and Harris (1978), referring to this property of the relationship as additivity, suggests that their data supports the absence of an all or none effect even although "our method of measuring

threat probably rules out finding an 'additive effect' should one
exist" (p.109). Miller and Ingham (1979) and Surtees and Ingham
(1980), using similar threat measures, on different populations,
identified similar 'additive' effects. This would tend to imply
that the hypothetical causal variable ie number of life events does
not act in an all or none fashion, and it may therefore tend towards
a continuum. Dichotomising the number of provoking agents experience
by subjects into zero and non-zero probably involves an essentially
arbitrary division of a continuous variable. Brown and his colleagues regarded psychiatric caseness, as defined by the Present State
Examination, (Wing et al, 1977), as their 'effect' variable. The
use of the concept of 'caseness' might superficially tend to suggest
a qualitative rather than a quantitative distinction between cases
and non-cases. Closer examination of Brown's and his colleagues'
position, however, indicates that they view caseness as a continuum
not as a qualitative distinction. Brown and Harris (1978) described
caseness as "something we have hypothesised as not a categorical
distinction but as a continuum representing a dimension of some sort
of severity of symptomatology" (p.583). The approach is consistent
with that described and advocated by William et al (1980), in their
review of case definition problems in psychiatric epidemiology.
They contended that caseness should be viewed as a continuum with
psychiatric patients acting as a caseness criterion, with the case-
finding instrument measuring the subjects closeness to this
criterion.

The effect variable, used by Brown and his colleagues, would
appear to be continuous in quality. The relevant question in this
context then is whether the 'case' 'non-case' distinction is
arbitrary. Brown et al (1975) confirm that it is arbitrary, "There
is evidently an arbitrary element in choosing a cut off point between
a case and a borderline (case)" (p.229).

There thus appears to be clear support for the view that the
'cause' and 'effect' variables used by Bebbington in his examples
are essentially arbitrarily dichotomised continuous variables. His
approach to causal analysis is therefore subject to the deficiencies
demonstrated above.

The use of dichotomous variables can thus critically mislead
us in our attempts to understand the impact of events on psychological disorder.

I have used what is perhaps a disproportionate amount of space
to discuss the problems in developing suitable dependent variables
in this field. There has, however, been a tendency to take scales
'off the shelf' rather than tailor them to the particular needs of
this particular field. This emphasis has perhaps come about because
of the substantial problems inherent in measuring life events
adequately and researchers have tended to focus on this side of the

equation. Some problems in the measurement of life events will now
be considered.

DEVELOPING SUITABLE MEASURES OF LIFE EVENTS

Holmes and Rahe (1967) made what was perhaps the first substantial step towards the development of a useful quantitative measure
of life stress and despite the significant difficulties of this
method it had a formative impact on the field. Brown and his colleagues (Brown, 1972, 1974; Brown et al, 1973b) have played central
roles in the attempts to overcome the substantial inadequacies of
the early assessment methods and to improve the quality of life event
information. The principal pitfalls inherent in developing measures
of life events will now be outlined.

Reducing Unreliability

The researcher's ability to detect significant level of covariation between the dependent and the independent variables is
substantially reduced if his measures are unreliable. Brown (1974)
considered the problems involved in developing reliable life event
ratings. Using the Schedule of Recent Experiences (SRE) developed
by Holmes and Rahe (1967) as an exemplar, he argued that vagueness
in defining life events contributed to substantial random error
variance. Brown (1974) indicates that random error occurs due to
variability in response to an item such as "Change in health in
Family member". Variability in a subject's interpretation of what
constitutes a "change in health" and who should be regarded as a
"family member", can lead to an increased error variance and a
concomitant lowering of reliability. Brown indicated that the
reliability of life event measures can be enhanced by the use of
specific definitions. Paykel et al (1976) developing a life event
inventory incorporated a similar item but defined a 'major physical
illness' as requiring hospitalisation, surgery or one month's
absence from work and 'close family member' as a parent, sibling or
other close person, eg fiance. Clearer specification tends to
enhance reliability although rigid application of this principle
could tend to make life event schedules unwieldy and reliability
may be reduced due to subject fatigue.

Assessing the Plausibility of a Causal Link

The detection of a significant degree of covariation between
life events and a dependent variable does not necessarily indicate
the existence of a plausible causal link. Cook and Campbell (1979)
argued that in assessing the plausibility of any aetiological link
it is necessary to rule out competing explanations for the observed
covariation. Thus the variables may covary because symptomatology
leads to events, rather than vice-versa, or because they both
correlate with some third variable. The problem of the direction
of effect will be examined first.

It is necessary, as Susser (1973) indicated, to demonstrate asymmetry in the relationship between putative cause and putative effect. That is, a change in the cause variable should 'produce' a change in the effect and not vice-versa. Most life event studies fail to counter this threat to the interpretation of an aetiological link and it may be that insidious onset of psychosocial disturbance leads to an increase in event frequency.

Brown and Birley (1968) argued that only events that occurred before the onset of the disorder should be considered and that this would impose the necessary asymmetry on the relationship. There are significant practical and logical difficulties with this approach (see Miller and Ingham, 1979) particularly when the onset of disturbance is insidious rather than acute.

Brown and Birley (1968), acknowledging that difficulties in identifying insidious onsets might threaten the validity of interpretations, introduced the notion of 'illness-independent' events. 'Illness-independent' events are regarded as events, that on logical grounds, are unlikely to have been caused by the insidious onset of psychological disturbance. The death of the subject's parent is unlikely to be a consequence of the subject's psychological disturbance and, thus, this would be regarded as an independent event. 'Loss of job' or 'marital separation' however, may come about because of the subject's disturbance and these are thus regarded as 'illness-dependent' events. The inclusion of 'illness-independent' events in any analysis results in a breakdown of the necessary asymmetry in the relationship between cause and effect and may mislead the investigator into the assumption of an aetiological link.

Brown and Harris (1978) noted that this approach, despite its advantages, has the disadvantage that events that are probably causal are disregarded, with a concomitant lowering of the estimate of any aetiological effect.

The introduction of the notion of 'illness-independent' events is a useful way of imposing the necessary asymmetry as the event-syndrome link. As an approach, however, it is not without difficulties. Surtees (1978), in a prospective study of hospitalised depressives, demonstrated that he could predict the frequency of 'illness-independent' events recorded at follow-up, by using the level of prior depressive symptoms. The results might imply, as Miller and Ingham (1979) have indicated, that personality and social or life circumstances may influence the occurrence of both events and symptoms, and that the apparent aetiological link between events and symptomatology merely represent a spurious correlation.

Cook and Campbell (1979) indicated that the evaluation of the plausibility of aetiological statements entails determination of the extent to which explanations of observed covariation, in terms of 'third variable explanations', can be ruled out. That is, it involves deciding whether the putative cause and putative effect variables appear to covary merely because they are both related to some third variable. Brown (1974) published a seminal paper on this problem and this discussion leans heavily on his principles. Brown identified three general problems: 'Direct Contamination', 'Indirect Contamination' and 'Spuriousness'.

Direct Contamination. This occurs when the subjects' symptomatology leads them to report an excess of events, or stimulates the interviewer to probe more thoroughly for undisclosed events. Brown (1974) argued that the 'check-list' approaches to the measurement of life events as exemplified by the 'Schedule for Recent Life Experiences' (SRE) are particularly prone to this form of contamination although approaches using interviews are not free of this problem. How can this threat be countered? Brown (1974) argues that interviews are necessary and that careful pre-interview description of the events should be carried out. The subject should not decide which events occurring to which elements of their social circle should be reported, but rather, this should be prescribed in detail before the interview is initiated. In addition, during the interview, the interviewer, should be required to concentrate on the fact of the occurrence of all the events before pursuing issues concerning the meaning of the events for the individual. Brown (1974) also argued that the 'severity' of the events should be assessed in the absence of information about the respondent's psychological state. Brown achieved this by having independent ratings of the events. However, this can be achieved by applying consensually derived weights from independent studies (eg Paykel et al, 1976).

Indirect Contamination. This may occur in prospective studies with the measurement of life events, at the initial interview, being influenced by the investigator's awareness of the subject's anxiety. The interviewer may elicit more events from an anxious subject, or the anxious subject may endorse more events on a check-list. At a later date, the anxious subject may show more intense psychological disturbance and the presumption of cause between events and symptoms may be made. This would merely reflect indirect contamination. Brown (1974) argued that such threats could be countered using the procedures outlined above.

Spuriousness. The problem of spuriousness, or the possibility that the correlation between two measures is a result of their mutual correlation with a third variable, is a more serious threat to internal validity and it is not a result of faulty measurement processes. Brown (1974) indicated the spuriousness can occur even with perfect measurement of the putative cause and effect variables. Thus a third factor, such as high general anxiety or neuroticism, may increase the frequency of events a subject experiences and the probability of psychological disturbance. Thus, as Miller and

Ingham (1979) suggested, the correlation between events and
psychological disturbance might not be causal but rather it merely
reflects mutual correlations with the subject's personality
characteristics and life stress variables.

Brown (1974) and Brown and Harris (1978) were unable to provide
a totally satisfactory solution to the problem of spuriousness.
Brown (1974), rather optimistically argued that "since actual experience of the event is ignored, we can hope to rule out the possibility that some unknown factor is influencing both onset and reporting
or experience of events (ie to rule out indirect contamination and
spuriousness)" (p.229).

While these precautions might counter threat of spuriousness
to some extent, a more powerful, yet not foolproof, procedure would
be to measure intervening variables that potentially have a spurious
impact. These measures could be used as control variables. Blalock
(1964) suggested that spurious relationships can be detected by
controlling for intervening variables in statistical analysis and
determining whether this results in the original correlation between
the putative cause and effect disappearing. This again is only a
partial solution as there are large numbers of variables that could
be considered, at any particular level of reduction, to intervene
between cause and effect variables. The experimenter must be guided
by theory to allow the determination of which control variables
should be measured.

Hopefully the brief account given above indicates that while
the measurement of life events is not devoid of difficulty, there
are some tactics that can be applied to improve its quality. Within
the fairly short period of time since Holmes and Rahe's (1967)
seminal contribution, investigators have refined their methods to
counter some of the major threats to our interpretation of the oft
observed covariation between stressful life events and psychological
distress. This refinement of technique has entailed a shift from
the early simplistic check-list method towards the use of semi-
structured interviewing techniques. This development in procedure
is best exemplified in the work of Brown and Harris (1978), although
a simpler and perhaps more economical semi-structured interview
approach is applied in the next chapter (see Cooke (1980c) for a
detailed account of the interview).

CONCLUSIONS

Over the last two decades life events have acquired the status
of universal causes. They have been implicated in the processes of
a wide variety of pathological conditions: from schizophrenia to
depression, from diabetes mellitus through myocardial infarction to
the common cold. Many life event studies, however, failed to rule

out the many plausible non-causal hypotheses that might explain the
observed covariations between the dependent and independent measures
used. It is likely, therefore, that the detection of covariation
between putative cause and putative effect may be due to contamination effects. It is only through the careful development of both
the dependent and independent variables that these threats to
interpretation can be reduced. It is perhaps only then that the
researcher can profitably consider the effects that additional
variables have on the simple event-syndrome link. Only then should
he attempt to discover the conditions under which covariation occurs
and those conditions under which it does not occur.

REFERENCES

Andrews, J.G., Tennant, C.C., Hewson, D.M., and Vaillant, G.E., 1976,
    Life event stress, social support, coping style and risk of
    psychological impairment, J. Nerv. & Ment. Dis., 166:307-316.
Andrews, J.G., Tennant, C.C., Hewson, D.M., and Schonell, M., 1978,
    The relation of social factors to physical and psychiatric
    illness, Amer. J. Epidem., 49:72-83.
Bebbington, P., 1980, Causal models and logical inference in
    epidemiological psychiatry, Brit. J. Psychiat., 136:317-325.
Blalock, H.M., 1964, "Causal Inferences in Non-Experimental
    Research," The University of North Carolina Press.
Brown, G.W., 1972, Life events and psychiatric illness: some thoughts
    on methodology and causality, J. Psychosom. Res., 16:311.
Brown, G.W., 1974, Meaning, measurement and stress of life events,
    in: "Stressful Life Events Their Nature and Effects,"
    B.S. Dohrenwend & B.P. Dohrenwend, eds., John Wiley, New York.
Brown, G.W., and Birley, J.L.T., 1968, Crises and life changes and
    the onset of schizophrenia, J. Health & Soc. Beh., 9:203-214.
Brown, G.W., Harris, T.O., and Peto, J., 1973, Life events and
    psychiatric disorder: 2; Nature of causal link, Psychol. Med.,
    3:157-176.
Brown, G.W., and Harris, T.O., 1978, "Social Origins of Depression:
    A Study of Psychiatric Disorder in Women," Tavistock, London.
Brown, G.W., Ni Bhrolchain, M., and Harris, T.O., 1975, Social class
    and psychiatric disturbance among women in an urban population,
    Sociology, 9:225.
Brown, G.W., Ni Bhrolchain, M., and Harris, T.O., 1979, Psychiatric
    and neurotic depression: aetiological and background factors,
    J. Affect. Dis., 1:195.
Brown, G.W., Sklair, F., Harris, T.O., and Birley, J.L.T., 1973,
    Life events and psychiatric disorders, Part I: Some
    methodological issues, Psychol. Med., 33:74-87.
Cattell, R.B., Coulter, M.A., and Tsujioka, B., 1966, The taxono-
    metric recognition of types and functional emergents, in:
    "Handbook of Multivariate Psychology," R.B. Cattell, ed.,
    Rand McNally & Co., Chicago.

Cochrane, R., and Sobol, M., 1980, Personal distress and mental disorder, in: "The Social Psychology of Psychological Problems," M.P. Feldman & J.F. Orford, eds., Wiley, London.

Cohen, J., and Cohen, P., 1975, "Applied Multiple Regression/Correlation Analysis for the Behavioural Sciences," John Wiley & Sons, New York.

Cook, T.D., and Campbell, D.T., 1979, "Quasi-Experimentation, Design and Analysis Issues for Field Settings," Rand McNally College Publishing Co., Chicago.

Cooke, D.J., 1980a, The structure of depression found in the general population, Psychol. Med., 10:455-463.

Cooke, D.J., 1980b, Causal modelling with contingency tables, Brit. J. Psychiat., 137:582-584.

Cooke, D.J., 1980c, Some conceptional and methodological considerations of the problems inherent in the specification of the simple event syndrome link, in: "Stress and Anxiety," Vol. 7: 139-157, I.G. Sarason & C.D. Spielberger, eds., Wiley, New York.

Cooke, D.J., 1981a, Depression: demographic factors in the distribution of different syndromes in the general population, Soc. Psychiat., in press.

Cooke, D.J., 1981b, Life events and syndromes of depression in the general population, Soc. Psychiat., in press.

Cooper, B., and Shepherd, M., 1972, Life change, stress and mental disorder: the ecological approach, in: "Modern Trends in Psychiatry," F.H. Price, ed., Cambridge University Press, London.

Derogatis, L.R., Klerman, G.R., and Lipman, R.S., 1972, Anxiety states and depressive neurosis: issues on nosological discrimination, J. Nerv. & Ment. Dis., 155:392-403.

Dohrenwend, B.S., and Dohrenwend, B.P., 1978, Some issues in research of stressful life events, J. Nerv. & Ment. Dis., 166:7-15.

Eysenck, H.J., 1953, The logical basis of factor analysis, Amer. Psychol., 8:105-114.

Eysenck, H.J., 1970, The classification of depressive illness, Brit. J. Psychiat., 117:241-250.

Garside, R.F., Kay, D.W.K., Wilson, I.C., Deaton, I.D., and Roth, M., 1971, Depressive symptoms and the classification of patients, Psychol. Med., 1:333-338.

Garside, R.F., and Roth, M., 1978, Multivariate statistical methods and problems of classification in psychiatry, Brit. J. Psychiat., 133:53-67.

Henderson, S., Byrne, O.G., Duncan-Jones, P., Scott, R., and Adcock, S., 1980, Social relationships, adversity and neurosis: a study of associations in a general population sample, Brit. J. Psychiat., 136:574-583.

Holmes, T.H., and Rahe, R.H., 1967, The social readjustment scale, Psychosom. Med., 11:213-218.

Lin, N., Simeone, R.S., Ensel, W.M., and Wen, K., 1979, Social support, stressful life events and illness: a model and empirical test., J. Health & Soc. Beh., 20:108-119.

Miller, P.McC., and Ingham, J.G., 1979, Reflections on the life-event-to-illness link with some preliminary findings, in: "Stress and Anxiety," Vol. 6, I.G. Sarason & C.D. Spielberger, eds., John Wiley, New York.

Ni Bhrolchain, M., 1979, Psychotic and neurotic depression: I Some points of method, Brit. J. Psychiat., 134:87-93.

Novak, S., 1960, Some problems of causal interpretation of statistical relationships, Philos. Sci., 17:23-38.

Novak, S., 1976, "Understanding and Prediction: Essays in the Methodology of Social and Behavioural Theories," D. Reidel Publishing Co., Boston.

Paykel, E.S., McGuiness, B., and Gomez, J., 1976, An Anglo-American comparison of the scaling of life events, Brit. J. Med. Psychol., 49:237.

Pearson, K., 1957, "The Grammar of Science," Meridian, New York.

Rabkin, J.G., and Struening, E.L., 1976, Life events, stress and illness, Science, 194:1013-1020.

Schless, A.P., Teichman, A., Mendals, J., Weinstein, N., and Weller, K., 1977, Life events and illness: a three year prospective study, Brit. J. Psychiat., 131:26-34.

Surtees, P.G., 1978, "Psychosocial factors in Depression: A Follow-Up Study of Patients After Recovery," Ph.D. Thesis (unpublished), University of Edinburgh.

Surtees, P., 1980, Social support, residual adversity and depressive outcome, Soc. Psychiat., 15:71-80.

Surtees, P.G., and Ingham, J.G., 1980, Life stress and depressive outcome: applications of a dissipation model to life events, Soc. Psychiat., 15:21-31.

Susser, M., 1973, "Causal Thinking in the Health Sciences," Oxford University Press, New York.

Weckowicz, T., 1973, A multidimensional theory of depression, in: "Multivariate Analysis and Psychological Theory," A. Boyce, ed., Academic Press, London.

Williams, P., Tarnopolsku, A., and Hand, D., 1980, Case definition and case identification in psychiatric epidemiology: review and assessment, Psychol. Med., 10:101-114.

Wing, J.K., Nixon, J.M., Mann, S.A., and Leff, J.P., 1977, Reliability of the P.S.E. (ninth edition) used in the population study, Psychol. Med., 7:505-516.

PSYCHOSOCIAL FACTORS IN WOMEN DURING THE CLIMACTERIUM:

A COMMUNITY STUDY

John G Greene and David J Cooke

Psychology Department
Gartnavel Royal Hospital
Glasgow, Scotland

THE MENOPAUSAL SYNDROME

Physical and psychological symptoms, when experienced by women
in middle life are frequently attributed to the menopause, particularly if no clear medical nor psychiatric diagnosis can be made.
As a consequence, the term "menopausal syndrome" has come into
common usage and is often used as a "ragbag diagnosis", referring
as it does to a plethora of ill-defined physical, psychosomatic and
psychological symptoms. In a recent search of the clinical literature, one of the present authors arrived at a list of no less
than 45 symptoms all of which had been attributed to the menopause
by some writer at some time (Greene, 1976). These included headaches, palpitation, dizzy spells, poor concentration, lack of energy,
excitability, insomnia, irritability, anxiety, crying spells and so
on. Indeed the menopause has become an explanation for almost any
discomfort experienced by women in middle life. Yet the only
symptoms which are truly characteristic of the menopause are the
vasomotor ones, that is, disturbances in body temperature experienced
by women in the form of hot flushes and excessive sweating.

At the outset it is necessary to distinguish between the term
menopause and climacterium, which, as Neugarten and Kraines (1965)
have pointed out, are often used interchangeably in the literature.
The term menopause refers to cessation of menses, which occurs on
the average around the age of 50 years and is a fairly well-defined
point that may occur abruptly or may follow menstrual cycles of
increasing intervals with decreasing menstrual flow. The term
climacterium is a more general term and refers to the involution of
the ovaries and the various pathological and hormonal changes
associated with this. This is a prolonged affair, beginning perhaps

131

as long as 10 years before menses cease and continuing perhaps for
some 10 years thereafter. The main hormonal change is the fall in
the rate of production of oestrogen. This fall in oestrogen results
in atrophy of the urogenital tract and a rise in gonadotrophin, which
causes vasomotor instability, thereby inducing the unpleasant, and
at times distressing, experiences of hot flushes and cold sweats.
When the fall in oestrogen reaches a critical point, menses ceases.
The menopause is therefore a fairly circumscribed event, albeit a
biologically important one, occurring within the longer period of the
climacterium.

The term "menopausal syndrome" does not appear therefore to be
a valid one, if it is meant to refer to a unique constellation of
signs and symptoms by means of which the syndrome can be distinguished from others, and in which the menopause has some aetiological
significance. Apart from the vasomotor symptoms and atrophic
vaginitis (Beard, 1975; Rybo and Westerberg, 1971) there does not
appear to be any other specific physical or psychological symptom
not found in other conditions.

Symptoms at the Climacterium

Whether or not there is an increase in the incidence and
severity of these non-specific symptoms during the climacterium,
and if so, what temporal relation such an increase has to the
menopause, are more debatable questions. One reason for the uncertainty regarding these questions is that up to the mid-60s most
research on this subject had been carried out on clinical populations, that is, women attending gynaecological clinics or in some
cases general practitioners.

The literature covering this early period has been comprehensively reviewed by McKinlay and McKinlay (1973) in the form of an
annotated bibliography. Many of these studies of clinical groups
unfortunately amount to no more than reports based on clinical
experience and observation in which conclusions are largely
unsubstantiated by systematically gathered empirical data. Moreover
in those studies in which some attempt has been made to provide
empirical data, conclusions are limited because of the inadequate
design and analysis. The only clear and consistent findings emerging from studies of clinical populations that may have a bearing
on the questions posed above are those coming from clinical trials
of Hormone Replacement Therapy (HRT): that those oestrogen-based
preparations commonly in use act primarily on the vasomotor symptoms
and that any effect on symptoms other than these is less dramatic
and often little more than that produced by a placebo (Beard, 1975).
Indeed studies of clinical populations are incapable of answering
the key question regarding the incidence of symptoms, other than
the vasomotor one, at the menopause because these populations are
highly selected groups. To answer this question we must turn to
general population surveys.

A few surveys have been concerned solely with determining the age at which the menopause occurs. Suffice it to say that it is now substantiated that the median age at which the menopause occurs is around 50 years and that there is no foundation for the view that the age of the menopause has been increasing over the past century (McKinlay et al, 1972).

Others have been concerned mainly with establishing the incidence of various symptoms around the time of the menopause. Neugarten and Kraines (1965) examined the incidence of symptoms in a group of women in the United States across five age groups. Using a comprehensive check-list of symptoms it was found that the highest frequency of symptoms occurred at two points in life, adolescence and the climacterium. At adolescence symptoms were primarily emotional; at the climacterium they tended to be somatic. The Blatt Menopausal Index (Blatt et al, 1953), a measure weighted for endocrine-related changes, significantly differentiated the menopausal group from all other groups. A similar tendency for climacteric women to report somatic symptoms was found by Prill (1966) in a random sample of 2232 German women aged 45-55 years. Prill found, however, that the only symptoms elevated in menopausal women were those of rheumatic and degenerative skeletal conditions. There was no evidence that the incidence of psychosomatic and psychological symptoms increased in the menopausal group. Jaszmann et al (1969), reporting on the findings of a large population survey of 4584 Dutch women aged 42-62 years, found that only somatic symptoms of the vasomotor type showed a close temporal relationship to the menopause and that although some other symptoms such as depression, sleeplessness and palpitations showed some association, this relationship was less clear. Similarly Thompson et al (1973) found that among a group of 200 climacteric Scottish women aged 40-60 years, only vasomotor symptoms were definitely correlated with the menopause, and McKinlay and Jefferys (1974) in a postal survey of 638 women aged 45-54 in the London area found again that only vasomotor symptoms were clearly associated with the onset of the menopause and that these occurred, in varying degrees of severity, in the majority of women. Other symptoms showed no direct relationship to the menopause. Finally, in another postal survey, Ballinger (1975), using the General Hospital Questionnaire, a measure developed by Goldberg (1972) to detect psychiatric cases in the community, found an increased prevalence of minor psychiatric illness in women at the menopause in a sample of 534 Scottish women aged between 40-55. The rise in psychiatric morbidity, however, occurred prior to the actual menopause.

The general finding from these surveys is therefore that although there is a tendency for symptoms other than vasomotor ones to increase during the climacterium, their association with the event of the menopause is by no means clear.

Psychosocial Factors at the Climacterium

The climacterium can be defined in terms of well documented
biological changes, but these occur at a time when a variety of
psychosocial changes are also taking place, which may dramatically
effect a women's role in society. Dominian (1977) has aptly termed
this time of life a major period of "psychosocial transition", a
term originally coined by Parkes (1971) to refer to "changes in life
space which are lasting in their effects, which take place over a
relatively short period of time and which affect large areas of the
assumptive world" (p.103). The climacterium could be considered as
a major period of psychosocial transition, coinciding as it does
with a variety of such changes.

For the married woman, the major event of this psychosocial
transition is seen to be the departure of children from home and a
return to a one-to-one relationship with her spouse. How well a
woman adapts to this change will depend on a variety of factors,
some internal, others external. On the internal side much will
depend on the woman's willingness and ability to shift from a family
orientated lifestyle to one with satisfactory outlets outside the
home. Much will depend on prior preparation and the extent to which
this shift is likely to be an abrupt one. Her attitude to the
menopause itself and the extent to which she views the loss of child-
bearing ability as a threat to her sexual identity will also play
an important part in how well she adapts. Also critical will be
both the quality of the marriage and the degree to which children
have provided the sole emotional outlet for the couple.

Apart from these personal factors there may be a variety of
pressures coming from other sources. These could include problems
and a concern arising from teenage children. Her husband may well
be passing through a critical phase in his career or may suffer,
not uncommonly, from health problems. Elderly parents may be
nearing death or entering a stage of geriatric dependence.

Unfortunately empirical evidence relating psychosocial factors
to symptoms at the climacterium is conspicuously lacking. Of the
surveys reviewed in only two have the authors attempted to investigate possible aetiological factors underlying the increase in the
incidence of symptoms. In the McKinlay and Jefferys (1974) study
none of six sociodemographic variables, employment status, school
leaving age, social class, domestic work load, marital status and
pregnancy parity had any association with the reported frequency of
symptoms, while in the study by Ballinger (1975) it was found that
specific problems within the family, particularly with children,
were associated with increased psychiatric morbidity. More recent
surveys by the International Health Foundation (van Keep and
Kellerhals, 1974; Severne, 1977) in Switzerland and Belgium have
reported findings contrary to the former. Thus it was found that

symptoms among women at the climacterium were more numerous in women of lower social class, for women who did not have a job outwith the home and for those with reduced opportunities for social contacts.

Finally, evidence from cross-cultural studies have indicated that there is wide variation in attitudes and responses to the menopause across different cultures. In Israel, Maoz et al (1970) looking at symptoms and attitudes to the menopause among immigrant groups, found that women from Arab countries suffered little or no symptoms at that time. Nor was the menopause seen as a time of crisis. Similar findings have been reported by Flint (1980) in a study of Rajput women in India. The same researcher also found that Cuban women in the United States had a more negative attitude to the menopause than did Jewish women (Flint, 1980). All these researchers have concluded that women in each culture tend to respond to the menopause as their respective cultures expect them to respond.

Methodological Issues

In a recent survey of depression in the general population (Cooke, 1980) the opportunity arose to look at the sub-group of climacteric women in some detail and in particular at the relationship between symptoms and psychosocial change among such women. The model chosen within which to investigate this relationship was a life event one. There is now a considerable life event literature, and in recent years techniques for measuring life events have become considerably refined. Before describing the method and results of the survey, however, it is first of all necessary to consider some methodological issues both in relation to the study of the climacterium itself and of life events.

Operational Definitions of Key Terms. Surveys of the menopause have been subject to two fundamental difficulties. One of these is inconsistencies between studies in the determination of menopausal status. In many of the clinical studies, especially where the study has been carried out on patients attending an HRT clinic, menopausal status has been defined in terms of the presence of vasomotor symptoms, thereby ignoring age and including both younger women who may have had an artificial menopause and older women who may be postmenopausal. In other studies such as that of Neugarten and Kraines (1965), the menopausal group was self-defined, a subjective and unacceptable method. Others have categorised women as menopausal who have not had periods for some time, up to 5 years in some cases, thus confounding women whose periods have just stopped with women who are clearly postmenopausal. The most satisfactory method of defining menopausal status is that used by McKinlay and Jefferys (1974) and Ballinger (1975). This method, by limiting the age range from 40-55 years, includes only women "at risk" and distinguishes clearly between women who are currently menopausal

and those in varying stages of the pre- or postmenopause. The
criteria are:

Premenopausal. Menstruated within the last 3 months, with no
change in regularity or volume in the previous year.

Transitional. Menstruated within the last 3 months but with some
change in regularity or volume in the previous year.

Menopausal. Last menstruated between 3 and 12 months ago.

Postmenopausal. Last menstruated more than 12 months ago. This
category can be further subdivided according to the last menses.

Related to the problem of arriving at agreed criteria for
determining menopausal status is the need to clearly distinguish,
conceptually and operationally, between menopause and climacterium.
As pointed out at the beginning of this chapter, the terms are often
used interchangeably, but in practice most research has in fact been
carried out on the menopause, which is a specific event taking place
within the climacterium. For this reason there are really two
questions relating to severity and incidence of symptoms. One
concerns the increase in symptoms during the climacterium generally,
the other what particular association, if any, this increase may
have with the menopause. This means that in practice any survey of
symptoms in the general population must include a group of younger
women regarded as preclimacteric and a group of older women regarded
as postclimacteric.

To date in only one survey, that of Neugarten and Kraines
(1965), have such groups been included. This requires an operational
definition of the climacterium, the only feasible one at present
being in terms of age. Following Studd et al (1977) the climacterium
may therefore be considered to cover the period from the late 30s
to the early 50s. For the purposes of this study the climacterium
was taken to be the age range 35-54 years, although such age limits
are purely arbitrary and serve only as working definitions.

The Assessment of Climacteric Symptoms. The other major
methodological problem in climacteric research is the lack of a
satisfactory, agreed-on instrument for assessing symptomatology at
the climacterium. In most clinical studies and general population
surveys, symptomatology is generally assessed by a short check-list
of symptoms made up by the authors and consisting of what they
consider to be "typical menopausal symptoms". Symptoms are usually
responded to on a "yes" or "no" basis and treated separately in the
analysis. There is often no attempt to classify symptoms in any way
nor to assess their severity. The survey by McKinlay and Jefferys
(1974) is a typical example of this sort of study. The only
instrument used commonly in some research, mostly in clinical, has

been the Blatt Menopausal Index (Blatt et al, 1953). This consists
of a mixture of vasomotor, somatic, and psychological symptoms
weighted in an arbitrary fashion and summated to give an overall
"menopausal index". In the most comprehensive check-list used to
date, that of Neugarten and Kraines (1965), symptoms are classified,
again arbitrarily, into somatic, psychosomatic, and psychological,
with a separate score being given to each class. It would seem,
then, that a first step in the proper appraisal and assessment of
climacteric symptoms is the clarification of the relationships among
symptoms and the identification of those symptoms uniquely associated
with the vasomotor ones. One technique for doing this is factor
analysis. This method has proved to be of value in analysing
symptoms in other multisymptom conditions, notably in clinical
depression. Furthermore as a first step in the construction of a
proper assessment procedure, a study of the factorial structure of
a symptom complex is essential.

Such a study was carried out (Greene, 1976) with the objects of
investigating the interrelationships between symptoms presented by
women at the climacterium and of devising a more rational method of
assessing climacteric symptoms. Symptoms of 50 women attending an
HRT clinic were submitted to a principal factor analysis, using a
check-list of 45 symptoms, each rated in degree of severity on a
scale from 0 to 3. Two main independent factors emerged. One of
these had high loadings on such items as "feeling unhappy or
depressed", "attacks of panic", "crying spells", and "worrying need-
lessly" and was identified as a psychological factor. The other
had high loadings on such items as "feeling dizzy or faint", "headaches" and "parts of body feel numb or tingling". This was
identified as a somatic factor. A third and much smaller factor
emerged independent of the two main ones; this seemed to be a
specific vasomotor factor, having high loadings almost exclusively
on vasomotor symptoms. Thus vasomotor symptoms emerged as being
completely independent from other symptoms in this group of menopausal women.

On the basis of this factor analysis a final scale, easily
administered and scored, was constructed. This consisted of two
subscales, one measuring psychological the other somatic symptoms.
Within each subscale each symptom is rated in severity from 0 to 3
and weighted according to its factor loading. Test-retest reliability for a group of 30 women over a period of one week was 0.89 for
the psychological and 0.85 for the somatic subscale.

Assessment of Life Events. A detailed account of the general
rationale and philosophy underlying the approach used in the measurement of life events was provided in the previous chapter of this
book. Thus, this section will merely provide a brief outline of the
specific techniques used in this particular study (see Cooke (1980)
for a full account of the procedures).

An approach similar in principle, although less laborious than
that developed by Brown and his colleagues (Brown and Harris, 1978),
was adopted. Non-directive semi-structured interviewing strategies
were used, with careful probing to elicit accurate responses regarding the events experienced by the individual in the previous 12
months.

In the analyses to be described, only those events that were
rated by the interviewer as being "independent" of the symptoms were
included. In other words, events that might have been triggered by a
subject's symptoms were left out of account; for example, a person
may develop psychological symptoms and break off their engagement
as a consequence, rather than their symptoms being a consequence of
their broken relationship.

The level of overall life stress experienced was measured by a
Total Life Stress (TLS) score, calculated by summating the
consensually derived weights of the degree of upset produced by
particular events. The weights applied were published by Paykel
et al (1976). In this system of weighting events 'death of a child'
is given the maximum score of 20 and 'retirement' is given a score
of 10. In addition to this overall stress score, it is possible,
using this method, to obtain scores that estimate the amount of
stress arising from different types of events.

General Approach to Data Analysis.   Lin et al (1979) indicated
that the majority of life event studies rely on comparatively crude
data analysis techniques, such as tests of percentage differences
or tests of differences between means. They pointed out that,
despite their many advantages, the use of correlational methods is
rare. Multiple Regression Analysis (MRA) was used in the present
study as it has two major advantages for the analysis of data of
this type; namely statistical power and flexibility.

Firstly, MRA, based on continuous variables, has more statistical power than Analysis of Variance or most non-parametric
techniques (Cohen and Cohen, 1975). The advantage of using a more
powerful technique is that it increases the probability of detecting
small effects. This is particularly important in life event research
where the amount of variance explained in the dependent variable
by life event measures tends to be rather small. Cochrane and
Sobol (1980) and Linn et al (1979) indicated that the average amount
of variance explained is very small lying somewhere between 4 and
10%.

The second principal advantage of MRA is its flexibility. Its
flexibility allows the investigator to simultaneously consider the
impact of different types of life events. Thus the investigator
can evaluate the relative importance of different aspects of life
events and determine which particular characteristics make life

events stressful. In addition, MRA, is flexible in that it allows
the detection of interactive effects. It is therefore possible to
go beyond simple additive notions of more stress causing more
distress towards the detection of more complex multiplicative or
synergistic relationships amongst different categories of life
events. When synergistic effects are present the intensity of
psychological distress produced is greater than the sum of the
individual life event characteristics. Synergistic effects of this
type are not uncommon in the epidemiological literature (eg Rothman,
1976) and, as will be illustrated below, their detection increases
our understanding of the links between events and symptomatology.

A COMMUNITY STUDY OF WOMEN AT THE CLIMACTERIUM

Method

     In the previous section on Methodological Issues, operational
definitions of key terms have been presented, the methods of
assessing symptoms and life events described, and the method of
statistical analysis discussed. All that remains to be done is the
description of the survey method.

     The data were collected in the course of a survey carried out
within the catchment area of Gartnavel Royal Hospital, a Scottish
psychiatric hospital serving the Western District of the Greater
Glasgow Health Board, over a six month period from September 1977
to February 1978. Socially this is a mixed community and is fairly
representative of the city of Glasgow as a whole. The aim of the
survey was to investigate the relationship between various life
event characteristics, possible mediating factors and depressive
symptomatology. 408 subjects, selected by systematic sampling from
the electoral roll, were interviewed. The total sample was made up
of 3 replicated samples, replication being for the purpose of
estimating interviewer bias. The response rate was 77.3%, with a
refusal rate of 14.9%. The remaining 7.8% was made up of subjects
who could not be contacted or whose protocols were incomplete. The
interviews, which were fairly intensive and covered a variety of
material, were carried out by a team of psychologists, specifically
trained for the purpose. The majority of interviews, each of which
lasted about $1\frac{1}{2}$ hours, were carried out by two interviewers in
order that interrater reliability estimates could be obtained for
the relevant sections of the interview schedule. Semistructured
interview techniques were used to assess such matters as life stress,
social support and adjustment, while self-administered questionnaires
of known reliability and validity were used to assess symptoms and
personality factors. For a more detailed account see Cooke (1980).

Symptoms at the Climacterium

Inspection of age trends in the adult female sample (25-64
years) indicated that scores on both "menopausal" symptom subscales
tended to begin to rise around the late 30s, reach a peak in the
early 40s, decline slightly in the late 40s and early 50s and then
fall off more sharply in the late 50s and early 60s. These trends
are summarised in Fig 1 which graphs the means of women between
the age of 25 and 64 years, grouped into 10 year age bands for
each subscale. Differences between the means of the pre- and early
climacteric group were significant (Student's t-test) for both
psychological and somatic symptoms ($p < 0.05$ in both cases). A
significant difference occurred between the early and postclimacteric
groups for somatic symptoms only ($p < 0.02$). Thus for this group of
women there is an increase in the severity of somatic and psychological symptoms during the climacterium, especially in the early part
and therefore some time before the majority of women experience the
actual menopause itself.

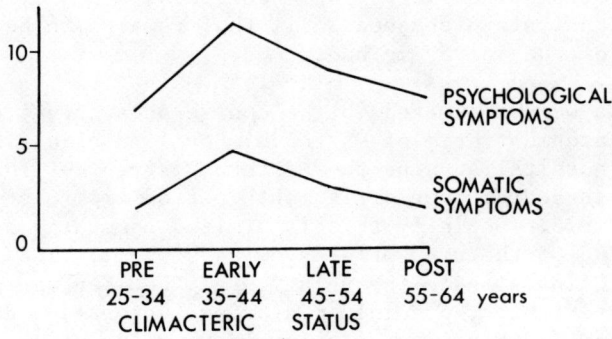

Fig. 1. Climacteric status and symptoms.

The Relationship Between Symptoms and Life Stress

Total Life Stress (TLS) scores at each age are shown in Fig 2.
As can be seen there is a tendency for TLS to increase during the
early climacteric period and fall off in the post climacterium.
None of these differences, however, reached the conventional significance levels. The relative relationship between TLS, menopausal
status and age and severity of symptoms within the climacteric
period (age range 35-54) was then examined by means of a hierarchical stepwise multiple regression analysis.

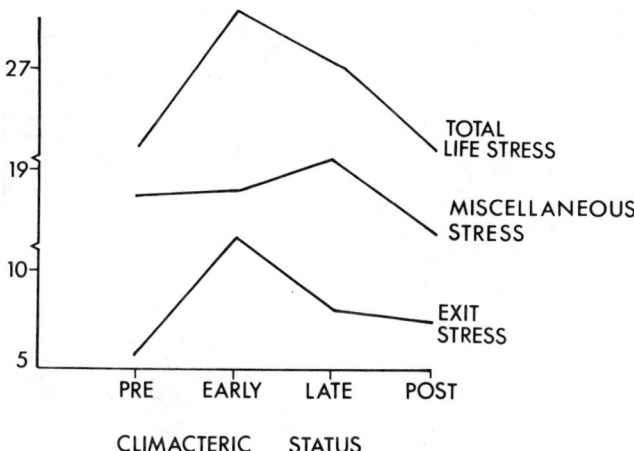

Fig. 2. Climacteric status and life events.

The analysis was carried out using the SPSS regression sub-
programme (Nie et al, 1975). First order effects were entered into
the regression equation initially, being followed by first order
and then second order interaction effects. The results of the two
hierarchical stepwise multiple regression are shown in Table 1.
In column 2 are the multiple correlations associated with each step
in the equation. In column 3 are the Beta coefficients (ie standardised partial regression coefficients) associated with each
variable after all the variables have been entered into the regression equations. The examination of these standardised regression
coefficients allows determination of the relative importance of each
variable in the equation (Dartington, 1968). In column 4 are the
F values for the significance test of the Beta coefficients.

The pattern of results for both classes of symptoms are
similar. The three independent variables, individually and in
combination account for 26% of the variance in psychological symptoms
and 30% of the variance in somatic symptoms. In both cases the TLS
scores account for a significant proportion of the variance. Neither
age nor menopausal status makes a significant contribution. However,
in both cases there was a significant interaction effect between
TLS and age with the younger of this group showing a significantly
higher relationship between symptoms and TLS than the older group.
None of the correlations between TLS scores and symptoms was significant within the early and the late climacteric groups all such
correlations were significant.

Table 1. Hierarchical Stepwise Multiple Regression Analysis of the Three Independent Variables Against Psychological and Somatic Symptoms for the 35 - 54 Age Range Groups

Order of Variables	Psychological Symptoms			Somatic Symptoms		
	Multiple R	Beta	F	Multiple R	Beta	F
Total Life Stress	0.38	2.04	5.39++	0.43	2.33	7.37+++
Age	0.44	0.19	0.56	0.46	0.28	0.41
Menopausal Status	0.46	1.01	0.96	0.47	0.65	1.24
Age/TLS	0.48	-2.00	4.03+	0.54	-2.11	4.68+
MS/TLS	0.50	-1.20	0.79	0.54	-0.76	0.33
MS/Age	0.50	-1.02	0.88	0.54	-0.60	0.32
Age/TLS/MS	0.51	1.66	1.23	0.55	0.97	0.46

(+ $p < 0.05$,   ++ $p < 0.02$,   +++ $p < 0.01$)

The absence of a significant relationship between menopausal status and symptoms was further investigated within both the early and late climacteric groups separately. This was done by testing the significance of the differences between the premenopausal, the menopausal and the postmenopausal group within each age range. None of these differences proved to be significant. Details of these findings can be found elsewhere (Greene and Cooke, 1980).

So far the results of this survey show that women in the general population experience an elevation in psychological and somatic symptoms during the climacterium and that the severity of these symptoms is associated more with a high degree of life stress than with the actual menopause. This occurs over a fairly wide age range, roughly between the ages of 35 and 54 years, with the early part, age range 35-44, being the most critical. In this early part, life stress is associated with symptom severity over and above that expected by a simple additive effect. No such relationship exists between symptoms and stress within the pre- nor postclimacteric periods. Paradoxically, however, there is no evidence that such life stress significantly increases at the climacterium. There are two possible, but not mutually exclusive hypotheses which could account for these findings. First, some women at that time of life may be particularly predisposed to react adversely to a high degree of life stress, with which at an earlier or later age they are able to cope. Alternatively, although there may be no significant increase in life stress during the early part of the climacterium, there may well be qualitative aspects to events at that time which hold a special significance for women at that age. Findings relating to this latter hypothesis are reported in the next section.

Types of Life Stress and Symptoms at the Climacterium

In writing about the life changes to which women at the climacterium are exposed, most writers regard such events as the departure of children from home and the illness and death of parents as the most critical of these changes. Such events are seen as effecting a profound change in the social role of the women. In the life event literature Paykel et al (1969) have identified an important group of life events known as exits. These are operationally defined as any event involving the departure of others from the social field of the subject. Such events have also been empirically shown to be associated with psychiatric depression (Paykel, 1974; Paykel, 1978). The concept of exits, as defined and measured by Paykel, would therefore seem appropriate to the study of the climacterium.

Fig 2 graphs mean scores of women between the ages of 25 and 64, grouped according to climacteric status, for TLS scores, for stress arising from exits and stress arising from other sources,

Table 2. Hierarchical Stepwise Multiple Regression Analysis of General Stress and Stress Arising from Exits Against Psychological and Somatic Symptoms for the Climacteric Group

Order of Variables	Psychological Symptoms			Somatic Symptoms		
	Multiple R	Beta	F	Multiple R	Beta	F
Miscellaneous Stress	0.39	0.32	5.29**	0.25	0.08	0.17
Exit Stress	0.39	-0.18	0.57	0.32	-0.24	0.99
Miscellaneous x Exit	0.40	0.19	0.57	0.40	0.54	4.47*

(* $p < 0.05$, ** $p < 0.025$)

referred to from hereon as miscellaneous stress. As can be seen the increase in TLS scores in both climacteric groups is almost entirely accounted for by stress arising from exits. A significant difference occurred between the pre- and early climacteric groups for exit stress ($p < 0.05$), none of the other differences being significant.

To determine the relative relationships between symptoms and stress arising from exits within the climacteric period another hierarchical stepwise multiple regression analysis was carried out, the results of which are shown in Table 2. The pattern of results vary depending on the class of symptom. In the case of psychological symptoms there is one significant main effect, that between miscellaneous stress and symptom severity. In the case of somatic symptoms there are no significant main effects but there is a significant interaction effect.

It was clear from inspection that the interaction effect was due to the mean of the group high on both miscellaneous and exit stress being considerably higher than those of the other three groups. This means that neither a high degree of stress arising from exits nor miscellaneous stress alone is associated with the severity of somatic symptoms. Both must be concomitantly high to produce an exacerbation of symptoms.

The reasons for this differential effect of events on symptoms was investigated by examining the event contributing to both types of stress. Inspection showed that events contributing to miscellaneous stress were of a heterogenous nature, there being no major differences between the climacteric group and the pre- or post-climacteric groups in the types of events being experienced. However, with regard to exit stress, it was found that the increase at the climacterium was largely due to stress arising from deaths. Fig 3 graphs the means over the entire age range for stress arising from exits, subdivided according to whether it arose from deaths or non-deaths. The mean of the preclimacteric group for stress arising from deaths is significantly different from the early climacteric group ($p < 0.01$). None of the other differences are significant.

In numerical terms, deaths accounted for some 60% of all exits in the climacteric group compared with only 5% of exits in the pre-climacteric group. These deaths were mostly those of members of the preceding generation, and included those of parents, uncles and aunts, many of whom, as might be expected, were reaching an age when the probability of death increases. There was only one death of a spouse and none of children. In addition more than two-thirds of these deaths were described as being those of a close friend or significant relative. This information had been obtained at the time of the interview and had been elicited by means of a number of probe questions designed to determine the closeness of the relationship with the deceased person. A second hierarchical stepwise

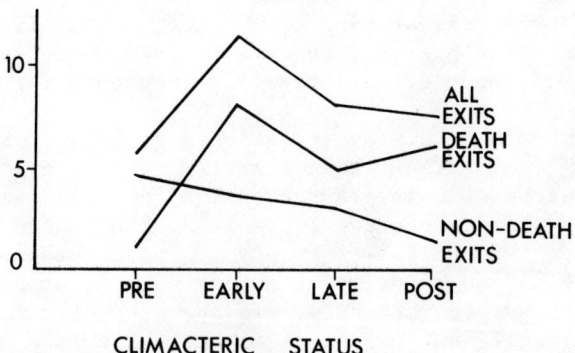

Fig. 3. Climacteric status and life events (exits).

multiple regression was carried out to determine the relationship
between symptoms and stress arising from deaths and miscellaneous
stress. The results, shown in Table 3, are similar to the results
of the other regression analysis with the corresponding F-ratios
being slightly increased. Details of these findings can be found
elsewhere (Cooke and Greene, 1981).

CONCLUSIONS AND IMPLICATIONS

     In this final section, the results of the research just
described will be discussed both with regard to its implications for
life event research in general, and its implications for our
understanding of adverse reaction during the climacterium in particular.

Life Event Research

     The results highlight two problems inherent in linking life
events to symptom patterns. These problems are the cumulative or
additive effect of events and the specificity of their effects.
These problems will be discussed in the context of the present
results and other life event research.

     Cumulative Effect of Events. Paykel (1978) has indicated that
in epidemiological work it is common to argue that aetiological
relationships should show dose-response characteristics, that is,
the risk or intensity of the disorder should increase as does the

Table 3. Hierarchical Stepwise Multiple Regression Analysis of General Stress and Stress Arising from Deaths Against Psychological and Somatic Symptoms for the Climacteric Group

Order of Variables	Psychological Symptoms			Somatic Symptoms		
	Multiple R	Beta	F	Multiple R	Beta	F
Miscellaneous Stress	0.39	0.34	6.56**	0.25	0.09	0.40
Death Stress	0.39	0.16	0.40	0.32	-0.27	1.36
Miscellaneous x Death	0.40	-0.13	0.28	0.40	0.56	5.10*

(* p < 0.05, ** p < 0.025)

intensity of exposure to the causal agent. Brown and Harris (1978)
however, in their influential book argue that the stressful effects
of events generally do not accumulate to increase the risk of
depression. Miller and Ingham (1980) and Surtees and Ingham (1980)
have however argued to the contrary. In the present study the
miscellaneous stress measure was linearly related to psychological
symptoms. The addition of quadratic or cubic miscellaneous stress
measures did not improve the goodness of fit of the regression
equation, implying the presence of a linear dose-response relationship. This result would tend to suggest that in some instances at
least, an additive relationship between events and symptoms may hold.

In the case of somatic symptoms, however, neither miscellaneous
stress nor exit stress alone were associated with symptom level, but
a concomitant increase of both types of stress were required. This
therefore could be interpreted as a multiplicative rather than a
linear effect. Here multiplicative is being employed in the sense
used by Blalock (1968), which implies that independent effects are
absent and that an increase in both independent variables must occur
in order to produce an effect on the dependent variable. In the
present context, the multiplicative effect is between different
types of events. These results suggest, therefore, that both
additive and multiplicative relationships may exist between events
and symptoms. The use of models with multiplicative terms thus
allows the detection of effects that otherwise would remain obscured,
thereby facilitating our understanding of the link between events and
symptoms.

Specificity of Event Effects. These results also indicate that
events may differentially influence different classes of symptoms.
Previously Paykel (1978) presented evidence of slight specificity
between exits and undesirable events and depression. Andrews and
Tennant (1978) and Brown et al (1979) on the other hand suggest that
life events do not have a specific effect. They argue that personality, demographic factors and early loss act as "symptom formation
factors". It is these factors that determine the nature of the
symptomatology, while life event stress acts merely to demoralise
the individual. More recently, however, Cooke (1981) has
demonstrated that within syndromes of depression found in the general
population, events have a specific effect in triggering off only one
of these syndromes.

The results described in this paper support the view that event
characteristics per se may educe certain types of symptoms.
Miscellaneous stress alone appears to directly influence only
psychological symptoms. Somatic symptoms, however, are elevated
only when, in addition, to a high level of miscellaneous stress,
exits are experienced.

The Climacterium

The results of this survey support the view that there is an elevation in psychological and somatic symptoms experienced by some women around the time of the climacterium. This occurs over a fairly wide age range roughly between the ages of 35 and 54 years. Furthermore, a considerable amount of this increase appears to be associated with the presence of a large number of stressful life events. Within this period the early part, age range 35-44, appears to be the most critical. At that time a high number of stressful life events is associated with an eleviation of symptoms over and above that expected by a simple additive effect.

There was no tendency for women at the menopause to experience any significant increase in symptoms. This, together with the finding that symptoms tend to peak prior to the menopause, clearly reduces the importance of this biological event in contributing, in any significant manner, to psychological difficulties at this time of life, and lends further support to the view that adverse reactions are more related to significant psychosocial changes in life space.

The results of the present study, however, indicate that the relationship between life events and symptoms at the climacterium is a complex one and depends both on the nature of the events and on the type of symptoms. Psychological symptoms at the climacterium are directly related only to the degree of miscellaneous stress being experienced, that is, stress coming from a variety of different sources but excluding exits, which are events having in common the departure of persons from the subjects' social field. Miscellaneous stress does not in fact increase during the climacterium, thereby suggesting that women at this time of life may become, for some reason, more vulnerable to this non-specific type of stress, stress with which, at an earlier age they are able to cope. This association occurs regardless of whether the woman is experiencing exits or not. Somatic symptoms on the other hand are directly associated neither with miscellaneous stress nor stress arising from exits alone. They increase in severity only when both categories of stress are concomitantly high, that is, before experiencing somatic symptoms a woman must be exposed not only to exits but also to a high level of miscellaneous stress. As the increase in stress arising from exits was largely due to deaths it seems reasonable to conclude that this effect on somatic symptoms is in some way linked to the illness or death of the deceased. This effect may further be enhanced by the fact that women at this age may be experiencing age related physical changes, in which case the effect of illness and death of others may act to exacerbate already existing somatic discomfort.

Furthermore, the finding that many of these deaths were described as being that of a significant person suggests a possible explanation for the interaction effect. Several researchers (Brown et al, 1975; Cobb, 1976; Miller and Ingham, 1976) have provided evidence demonstrating the importance of social support, in the form of friends and confidants, in ameliorating the event-syndrome link. Deaths of significant persons may therefore educe not merely an immediate bereavement reaction, but may also serve to deprive women at this time in their lives of the support necessary for them to cope with current and future adversity.

These hypotheses obviously require further empirical examination. Nevertheless the evidence provided here does suggest that the traditional medical view of the climacterium and more specifically the menopause requires to be re-evaluated. This view has long regarded difficulties among women at this time of life as being predominately due to biological processes and physical change. That these factors play an important role is not to be denied, but they must not be over-emphasised to the exclusion of the social and psychological context within which the changes take place. A much broader conceptualisation of the climacterium is required. This also of course has implications for how those professional groups should respond to women experiencing difficulties at this time of life. Such groups include marriage guidance counsellors, social workers, health visitors, general practitioners, gynaecologists, psychiatrists and clinical psychologists. It would no longer seem justified to dismiss such women as being "just menopausal" and prescribe hormone replacement therapy and/or tranquillisers. Some attempt should be made to elucidate the specific psychological problems that these women may be facing at that time of life in order to better counsel them.

REFERENCES

Andrews, G., and Tennant, C., 1978, Life stress and psychiatric illness, Psychol. Med., 8:545.
Ballinger, C.B., 1975, Psychiatric morbidity and the menopause: screening of a general population sample, B.M.J., 2:344-346.
Beard, R.J., 1975, The menopause, Brit. J. Hosp. Med., 13:631-637.
Blalock, H.M., Jnr., 1968, Theory building and causal inferences, in: "Methodology in Social Research," H.M. Blalock, Jnr. & A.B. Blalock, eds., McGraw-Hill, New York.
Blatt, H.G., Wiesbader, H., and Kuppermann, H., 1953, Vitamin E and the climacteric syndrome, A.M.A. Arch. Int. Med., 91:792-799.
Brown, G.W., 1972, Life events and psychiatric illness: some thoughts on methodology and causality, J. Psychosom. Res., 16:311.
Brown, G.W., and Harris, T., 1978, "Social Origins of Depression: A Study of Psychiatric Disorder in Women," Tavistock, London.
Brown, G.W., Ni Bhrolchain, M., and Harris, T.O., 1975, Social class and psychiatric disturbance among women in an urban population, Sociology, 9:225.

Brown, G.W., Ni Bhrolchain, M., and Harris, T.O., 1979, Psychiatric and neurotic depression: aetiological and background factors, J. Affect. Dis., 1:195.

Cobb, S., 1976, Social support as a moderator of life stress, Psychosom. Med., 38:300.

Cochrane, R., and Sobol, M., 1980, Personal distress and mental disorder, in: "Social Psychology of Psychological Problems," M.P. Feldman & J.F. Orford, eds., Wiley, London.

Cohen, J., 1968, Multiple regression as a general data-analytic system, Psychol. Bull., 70:426-433.

Cohen, J., and Cohen, P., 1975, "Applied Multiple Regression/Correlation Analysis for the Behavioural Sciences," Wiley, New York.

Cooke, D.J., 1980, Some conceptual and methodological considerations of the problems inherent in the specification of the simple event syndrome link, in: "Stress and Anxiety," Vol. 7, I.G. Sarason & C.D. Spielberger, eds., Wiley, New York.

Cooke, D.J., 1981, Life events and syndromes of depression, Soc. Psychiat., in press.

Cooke, D.J., and Greene, J.G., 1981, Types of life events and relation to symptoms of the climacterium, J. Psychosom. Res., 25:5-11.

Dartington, R.B., 1968, Multiple regression in psychological research and practice, Psychol. Bull., 69:161-182.

Dominian, J., 1977, The role of psychiatry in the menopause, Clin. Obstet. & Gynaec., 4:3-29.

Flint, M.P., 1980, Transcultural influences in peri-menopause, in: "Psychosomatics in Peri-Menopause," A.A. Haspels & H.M. Musaph, eds., MTP Press, Lancaster.

Goldberg, D.P., 1972, "The Detection of Psychiatric Illness by Questionnaire," Oxford University Press, London.

Greene, J.G., 1976, A factor analytic study of climacteric symptoms, J. Psychosom. Res., 20:425-430.

Greene, J.G., 1980, Stress at the climacterium: the assessment of symptomatology, in: "Stress and Anxiety," Vol. 7, I.G. Sarason & C.D. Spielberger, eds., Wiley, New York.

Greene, J.G., and Cooke, D.J., 1980, Life stress and symptoms at the climacterium, Brit. J. Psychiat., 136:486.

Jaszmann, L., Van Lith, N.D., and Zatt, J.C.A., 1969, The peri-menopausal symptoms, Med. Gynaec. & Sociol., 4:268-275.

Lin, N., Simeone, R.S., Ensel, W.M., & Wen, K., 1979, Social support, stressful life events and illness: a model and empirical test, J. Health & Soc. Beh., 20:108-119.

McKinlay, S.M., and Jefferys, M., 1974, The menopausal syndrome, Brit. J. Prev. & Soc. Med., 28:108-115.

McKinlay, S.M., Jefferys, M., and Thompson, B., 1972, An investigation of the age at menopause, J. Biosoc. Sci., 4:161;-73.

McKinlay, S.M., and McKinlay, J.B., 1973, Selected studies of the menopause, J. Biosoc. Sci., 5:533-555.

Maoz, B., Dowty, N., Antonovsky, A., and Wijsenbeek, H., 1970, Female attitudes to the menopause, Soc. Psychiat., 5:35.

Miller, P.McC., and Ingham, J.G., 1976, Friends, confidants and symptoms, Soc. Psychiat., 11:51-58.

Miller, P.McC., and Ingham, J.H., 1980, Reflections on the life-event-to-illness link with some preliminary findings, in: "Stress and Anxiety," Vol. 6, I.G. Sarason & C.D. Spielberger, eds., Wiley, New York.

Neugarten, B.L., and Kraines, R.J., 1965, Menopausal symptoms in women of various ages, Psychosom. Med., 27:266-273.

Nie, N.H., Hull, C.H., Jenkins, J.C., Steinbrenner, K., and Bent, D.H., 1975, "Statistical Package for the Social Sciences, McGraw-Hill, New York.

Parkes, C.M., 1971, Psychosocial transitions: a field study, Soc. Sci. & Med., 5:101-115.

Paykel, E.S., 1974, Recent life events and clinical depression, in: "Life Stress and Illness", E.K. Gunderson & R.N. Rahe, eds., Charles C Thomas, Springfield, Illinois.

Paykel, E.S., 1978, Recent life events in the development of depressive disorders, in: "The Psychobiology of Depressive Disorders: Implications for the Effects of Stress," R.A. Depue, ed., Academic Press, London & New York.

Paykel, E.S., McGuiness, B., and Gomez, J., 1976, An Anglo-American comparison of the scaling of life events, Brit. J. Med. Psychol., 49:237-247.

Paykel, E.S., Myers, J.K., Dienelt, M.N., Klerman, G.C., Lindentmal, J.J., and Pepper, M.P., 1969, Life events and depression: a controlled study, Arch. Gen. Psychiat., 21:753-760.

Prill, H.J., 1966, Die Beziehung von Erkrankungen und social psychologischen Faktoren zun Klimakterium, Medizinische Klinik, 61:1325-1330.

Rothman, K.J., 1976, Causes, Amer. J. Epidem., 104:587-592.

Rybo, G., and Westerberg, H., 1971, Symptoms in the post menopause: a population study., Acta. Obstet. Gynaec. Scand., 9:25-32.

Severne, L., 1977, "La Menopause: Etude effectuee en Belgigue aupres de 922 femmes entre 45 et 55 ans," International Health Foundation, Geneve.

Studd, J., Chakravarti, S., and Okram, D., 1977, The climacteric, Clin. in Obstet. & Gynaec., 4:3-29.

Surtees, P.C., and Ingham, J.G., 1980, Life stress and depressive outcome: applications of a dissipation model to life events, Soc. Psychiat., 15:21.

Thompson, B., Hart, S.A., and Durno, D., 1973, Menopausal age and symptomatology in a general practice, J. Biosoc. Sci., 5:71-82.

Van Keep, P.A., and Kellerhals, J.M., 1974, The impact of socio-cultural factors on symptom formation, Psychother. & Psychosom., 25:251-263.

CONSULTING WITH MILD SYMPTOMS IN GENERAL PRACTICE

Jack Ingham and Patrick Miller

Medical Research Council Unit for Epidemiological
    Studies in Psychiatry
University Department of Psychiatry
Edinburgh, Scotland

The act of going to the doctor is an important item of illness behaviour both for the individual and for society. It is important for the individual because upon it depends the likelihood of obtaining satisfactory treatment. Initiated appropriately, it can help to cure illness and save a great deal of time and effort. Initiated inappropriately, it can involve economic loss and, indeed, through the soliciting of unnecessary treatments, can increase the likelihood of iatrogenic illness. From society's point of view, health services are expensive and there is a clear need to concentrate resources where they are most needed. At the primary care stage, when patients first come under medical surveillance, there is complete dependence upon the individual's ability to recognise the symptoms of ill health and to be motivated by them to seek treatment.

SYMPTOM PREVALENCE AND SEVERITY

Many more people seem to believe they are suffering from ill health than actually present themselves in the general practitioner's surgery. In the General Household Survey of 1977, reported by the Office of Population Censuses and Surveys, it was reported that 85% of women and 77% of men thought they had a health problem. Studies using health diaries have reported high average symptom rates. In one instance, symptoms occurred on an average of 10 days out of the 28 studied (Banks et al, 1975; Beresford et al, 1977), and in another an average of 25 medical problems per individual were recorded during one month (Freer, 1980). Of course, a great deal depends upon how you ask the question and these may well be inflated values, but

153

there are clearly a lot of people who feel unwell from time to time
and who consult their doctors on only a small proportion of such
occasions. If symptoms are so common amongst people who do not consult their doctors, can we conclude that they are not effective as
motivators for consultation and that decisions to go to the doctor
depend more on other factors? This would be an over-simplification
because as was demonstrated by Ingham and Miller (1979) using data
from a random sample of a Scottish community, when non-consulters
do have symptoms, they tend to have them less severely. They
suggested that symptom severity increased the likelihood of surgery
attendance, often as a background factor rather than as a precip-
itant.

Hannay (1979) also took symptom severity into account in his
study of 1344 home interviews of patients registered in a Glasgow
health centre. He identified people whose self-referral behaviour
he considered incongruous in relation to the severity gradings that
the patients themselves had allocated to their symptoms. Of his
1183 patients who had one or more symptoms present, 26% came into
the 'iceberg' category of people with serious symptoms who had not
sought medical advice. There were 11% who had sought medical advice
with 'trivia', that is, symptoms rated by the subjects as not serious
and involving no pain or disability.

Ingham and Miller in their study took the matter a stage further
by examining the extent to which self-referral behaviour could be
explained by symptom severity alone. They divided their group of
consulting patients according to symptomatology and chronicity though
focussing on a small group of seven selected symptoms (Ingham, 1981).
The influence of symptom severity upon self-referral was greatest
when the presenting symptoms were acute anxiety or depression. In
two completely independent samples each divided into consulters and
controls, there were multiple correlation coefficients of more than
.6 predicting consulter-control status from information about symptom
severity. Groups of consulters presenting with other symptom patterns were not quite so effectively discriminated from controls, but
it is clear that symptom severity is a major determinant of consulting behaviour. Even for the consulting group as a whole, with
no account being taken of different presenting symptoms, it was
possible to explain approximately 10% of the discriminating variance
using severity measurements for only seven selected symptoms.
Another study in which the perceived seriousness of illness was found
to be an important determinant of help-seeking for physical conditions was that of Hulka (1972).

This brief review indicates that symptom severity is a major
determinant of consulting behaviour. On the whole, people visit
their doctors because they feel ill and the iller they feel the
likelier they are to go. Nevertheless, symptom severity is not the
only factor involved and it is necessary to consider what other
things determine people's decisions to consult their doctors.

CHARACTERISTICS OF THE ILLNESS

Severity is not the only illness variable that is likely to be involved in motivating the patient to seek help. An illness that has a seriously disrupting effect on a person's life, for example, may lead to a consultation more readily than another which might be more severe, but less incapacitating. Similarly, the amount of distress associated with an illness is not perfectly correlated with the severity of the symptoms. Mechanic and Greenley (1974) in their random sample of students found that 45% had abnormally high psychological stress scores compared with 75% amongst those who had sought treatment. The treatment seeking sample were much more likely to report that their problems had prevented activities; 50% did so compared with only 10% of the random sample. Tessler et al (1976) predicted the number of consultations made by patients to their doctors over a 12 month period using a number of social and clinical variables, apart from sex which is discussed below. The only variables that made significant contributions to the prediction were a measure of chronic illness and another of distress. They suggested that distress and consultation probably occurred in close temporal proximity and they regarded the use of medical services as a coping device helping people to deal with personal stress and present discomfort.

Rate of onset may also be an important factor. During insidious onset of a condition the patient may experience bouts of minor complaints, such as dizziness or mild low back pain, that last for short periods and seem amenable to self-treatment. The sufferer may then take little notice of them and tend to accept a gradual but increasing deviation from health as normal. This may lead some patients to put off their first consultation (Wadsworth, 1974).

STRESS

An idea similar to that of Tessler et al (loc. cit.), that a consultation may sometimes represent a coping device helping to deal with stress, played a significant role in the thinking that led up to two studies by the authors (Miller et al, 1976; Ingham, 1981). In the first investigation, which was a pilot study for the second, patients who had recently consulted at a general practice were compared with other individuals of the same age and sex who had not. Life events information was collected by an adaptation of the methods devised by Brown and colleagues (1973 and 1978). The index of stress discriminated significantly between consulters and non-consulters and was strongly associated with the severity of psychological symptoms like anxiety and depression. This was based on rather a small sample so it was not possible to make allowance for symptom severity. In the later study, information was available for a random sample of 706 individuals equally divided between new episode consulters and people who had not attended at the health centre within the previous three months. There was a significant, but small, association between life stress and consultation. However, a multiple regression analysis in which the stress and symptom variables were the independent variables showed that the stress items did not contribute significantly to the dependent variance once the symptom variables had been partialled out.

A possibility not often considered is that people consulting the primary care services do not form a homogeneous group with respect to non-illness determinants of consultation. Separate comparisons of groups consulting with each of a group of symptoms confirmed that different relationships do indeed hold for different symptoms. Patients attending with acute backache, for example, when compared with non-consulting controls, showed no evidence of psychological stress contributing to the dependent variance. For patients consulting with psychological symptoms, however, stress did make a significant contribution. In a multiple regression analysis of 397 individuals in which the dependent variable was consulting with acute anxiety or depression (compared with non-consulting controls), the stress variables accounted for about 7% of the dependent variance. The analysis was done by a hierarchical series of multiple regression equations and when the symptom variables were entered at an earlier step than the stress variables, the latter hardly contributed anything new. This was confirmed in an independent sample of 292 subjects, again equally divided into consulters with acute anxiety or depression and non-consulting controls. It seems likely that for people consulting primary care services with psychological symptoms, stress is indeed a factor that influences the decision to consult, but that its effect is mediated by the symptoms and distresses it produces. It is, of course, dangerous to infer causal relationships from regression analysis of cross-sectional data.

DEMOGRAPHIC VARIABLES - AGE AND SEX

There are social and demographic variables that have been shown by several authors to be associated with consultation. Usually it is the contact rate of patients registered on general practitioners' lists that has been the dependent variable, but symptom severity has not often been taken into account. Probably the two most firmly established variables in this area are age and sex. A consistent finding is that women have more contacts with their GPs than men, particularly in the 20-30 year age group (Banks et al, 1975; Ashford, 1972; Weissman and Klerman, 1977). In addition, there is a steady increase in consultation rates in adults of both sexes from early teens to old age. It is also well established that women have more symptoms, or at least admit to having more symptoms and to having them more severely on average than men. A question that clearly arises is whether this accounts for the higher consultation rate of women. Of course, most symptoms are subjective experiences of

distress and the differences may lie in the reporting of the experiences rather than the experiences themselves. In the absence of
objective information, however, there is little that can be done
about this and we must accept self-reported symptoms at their face
value for the time being.

A Study of Health Centre Patients

The authors' comparative study already referred to (Ingham and
Miller, 1979; Ingham, 1981) was a sampling investigation in which
random samples of male and female consulters with new episodes of
illness were selected over a period of one year. It was possible
to examine the data for the influence of age and sex upon consultation, taking symptom severity into account. These and other results
reported in the rest of this chapter have not been published previously so the investigation will be described in rather more detail.

The Samples. The target population comprised patients aged
between 16 and 75 and registered in one Scottish health centre during
a period of one year from March 1976 to February 1977 inclusive.
Two samples of consulters and two of controls were selected. Medical
Research Council (MRC) interviewers at the health centre identified
all new episode consulters, and a random sample of one in four men
and one in six women was drawn daily. For each patient a control
of the same sex and age group was selected at random from the list
of registered patients excluding those who had attended within the
previous three months. The sampling procedure was described in
detail by Ingham and Miller (1979).

Evidence from pilot studies suggested that there would be too
few patients consulting with anxiety or depression to serve our
purpose. For this reason, a further sample was selected comprising
all those consulters who, in response to the standard questioning
procedure, reported anxiety or depression as a symptom and, furthermore, that they intended to tell the doctor about it. All such
patients were included unless they had already been selected in the
random sample, and there was a further group of corresponding controls from non-attenders. In the event, rather more anxiety or
depression consulters appeared in the random sample than had been
feared, and the additional sample was used for cross-validation.

Results. The age and sex distributions of the population are
shown in Table 1. Details of refusal rates and lapses for other
reasons have been reported previously (Ingham and Miller, 1979).
Less than 1% of consulters visited at home refused to co-operate.
The true refusal rate, taking into account patients who would not
co-operate at the health centre, may have been as high as 18% but
this is probably an overestimate. The refusal rate for controls
was 9.9%. For a detailed analysis of all health centre attenders

a sample of six one-week units, selected at random from the year of
the study was used. This analysis provided an estimate of the
numbers of men and women per week attending with new episodes of
illness, with a correction for the small number of individuals who
refused to co-operate at the health centre or were missed for other
reasons (approximately 7%). The results are shown in the first row
of Table 1 as episodes per 12-week period and, as a first approximation, they provide base rates for consulters and controls in the
registered population. They probably represent an overestimate of
the number of patients per 12-week period because they fail to take
account of possible multiple episodes.

For sex differences these figures confirm earlier findings.
A higher proportion of women consulted with at least one new episode
of illness, especially in the younger age group. For age, however,
it was a different matter. The figures for the over 56 age group
are based on small numbers because this is a new town population in
which older people are under-represented compared with the population at large. The results are clearly at variance with what seemed
to be established findings and, at first sight, with common sense,
but a reason is not hard to find. It is not that the older people
have fewer consultations per annum. Indeed they probably have more,
as in other populations, but in this study it was new episodes of
consultation that were counted and clearly definable new illnesses
would arise less often in a group frequently consulting with chronic
conditions.

Table 1. Population Aged 16-75 Registered at Health Centre

| Sex | | Male | | | Female | |
Age	≤36	37-56	>56	≤36	37-56	>56
Estimated number of patients consulting with at least one new episode in 3 months*	339 (18.7%)	158 (16.5%)	28 (11.6%)	632 (31.4%)	195 (21.6%)	45 (14.0%)
Others	1469 (81.3%)	799 (83.5%)	214 (88.4%)	1379 (68.6%)	706 (78.4%)	276 (86.0%)
N	1808	957	242	2011	901	321

* Estimated from six-week sample corrected for refusals and patients
  missed at the health centre. Assumes same age distribution as in
  whole sample.

Consultation and Symptoms. The question at issue is whether
women consult more often because of their readiness to consult or
because they more often have symptoms. For the main random sample,
selected over the whole year, the percentage of people troubled by
each of the seven symptoms was known. It was possible, therefore,
to calculate from our base rates the number of people in the population within each group who had the symptom. For consulters, the
percentage who regarded the symptom as something they were consulting the doctor about was also known and could be applied to the base
rate. These figures are shown for every symptom in Tables 2a and
2b.

Taking backache as an example, if women are more likely to
consult their doctors with it than men are, then the proportion of
consulters amongst backache sufferers should be higher amongst women
than amongst men. Table 2 shows the percentage of consulters in
each group and it will be seen that it is uniformly higher for women
in both age groups. The presence of a symptom in a consulting patient does not necessarily mean that the patient sees that symptom
as a reason for consultation. A second figure for consulters, shown
below the first, refers to those patients who not only had the
symptom but said they were consulting about it and for these figures
the differences between males and females are less striking and less
consistent. In fact, for backache, the proportion of consulters is
actually greater for males than for females in both age groups.
Perhaps part of the excess of females over males that appears when
we analyse each symptom separately, exists because more women are
consulting with symptoms other than the one under consideration.
The difference is less marked when we restrict the symptom to one
that is seen by the patient as a reason for consultation though it
is still true to say that on balance a higher proportion of women
are consulting. The excess of women tends to be clearer for psychological symptoms than for physical symptoms.

Illness. The results presented so far have been concerned with
analysis at the level of single symptoms. Do we arrive at the same
conclusion when we consider prevalence and self-referral rates for
illnesses rather than symptoms? The authors had a special interest
in psychological illness and for a sub-sample of subjects a procedure
was used that has been claimed to provide a valid criterion of
minimal psychiatric illness. This was the DSSI/sAD inventory of
Foulds and Bedford (1978). Thirty-seven per cent of women who
reached the 'personally ill' criterion score on the sAD had consulted
their doctors, whereas for the men the figure was 22%, again con-
firming that the proportion of consulters amongst female 'cases'
was higher than that amongst men.

Our interest in differential selection into the psychiatric
services started with some work with which one of the authors was
associated in South Wales (Ingham et al, 1972). In one area of

Table 2a. Estimated Number of Symptom Sufferers Amongst Consulters and Controls* - Age ≤ 36

	MALE				FEMALE			
	N	Controls	Consulters	Consulters as % of N.	N	Controls	Consulters	Consulters as % of N.
All	1808	1469	339	19	2011	1379	632	31
Backache present	297	206	91	31	548	325	223	41
Doctor told			62	21			112	20
Tiredness present	346	259	87	25	660	389	271	41
Doctor told			63	18			178	27
Anxiety present	230	179	51	22	470	270	200	43
Doctor told			25	11			106	23
Headache present	264	173	91	34	596	342	254	43
Doctor told			62	23			145	24
Depression present	137	100	37	27	324	185	139	43
Doctor told			19	14			72	22
Irritability present	240	182	58	24	386	210	176	46
Doctor told			29	12			83	22
Dizziness present	81	41	40	49	208	80	128	62
Doctor told			29	36			85	41

* Estimated from Table 1 and from known percentages of symptom sufferers amongst main random sample of consulters and controls.

Table 2b. Estimated Number of Symptom Sufferers Amongst Consulters and Controls* - Age > 36

	MALE				FEMALE			
	N	Cont-rols	Consult-ers	Consulters as % of N.	N	Cont-rols	Consult-ers	Consulters as % of N.
All	1199	1013	186	15	1222	982	240	20
Backache present	244	192	52	21	419	317	102	24
Doctor told			34	14			43	10
Tiredness present	222	159	63	28	437	278	159	36
Doctor told			43	19			105	24
Anxiety present	185	142	43	23	357	238	119	33
Doctor told			18	10			66	18
Headache present	183	134	49	27	355	228	107	32
Doctor told			29	16			81	24
Depression present	115	92	23	20	257	169	88	34
Doctor told			12	10			48	19
Irritability present	143	108	35	24	256	159	97	38
Doctor told			11	8			48	19
Dizziness present	72	50	22	31	132	70	62	47
Doctor told			14	19			45	34

* Estimated from Table 1 and from known percentages of symptom sufferers amongst main random sample of consulters and controls.

South Wales, prevalence defined by specialist treated psychiatric
cases was substantially higher for women than for men. However,
taking into account severity for any given score on the Cornell Medical Index, men were more likely to become patients than women. In
other words, the preponderance of women amongst declared cases could
easily be accounted for by the greater prevalence and severity of
illness in the community amongst women. The writers were not able
to say, however, whether the differential selection, in this case
in favour of men, was occurring at entry into primary care services
or at transfer from primary care to specialist services.

   The selection process can be conceived as operating through a
series of filters intervening between the different levels of care
that patients may reach (Ingham and Miller, 1976). Goldberg (1980)
has argued that "in order to show that the first filter is more
permeable to women it would be necessary to show that the female to
male ratio at level 2 is higher than at level 1 and the available
evidence suggests that this is not so". The first filter is the
selection process that separates the community (level 1) from the
consulting population in primary care (level 2). There is now fairly
consistent evidence that the female to male ratio for rates of
psychiatric disorder in the whole community is roughly 2 : 1 for the
general population, whereas according to Goldberg (1978) it is
between 1.2 : 1 and 1.3 : 1 at level 2. This being so, he argues
"a symptomatic woman is less not more likely to attend than a
symptomatic man". There are two ways in which the apparent discrepancy between Goldberg's results and ours might be accounted for.
His case definition instrument was the General Health Questionnaire,
a symptom inventory with many items contrasting with the single
symptom assessments reported in Table 2. His technique was closer
to that of Ingham et al (1972). However, the sAD as used in the
present study is similar to the GHQ albeit with fewer items. An
explanation that seems more likely is that Goldberg used what we
believe to be a misleading denominator in calculating his rates for
level 2. It seems that his figures were based upon a sample of
consecutive attenders at general practices and rates were expressed
as a proportion of total number of attenders. The reduced preponderance of females compared with level 1 could, therefore, be due
not to fewer women consulting with psychiatric illness but to more
consulting with other things. Women are known to have higher prevalence rates in a very wide range of symptoms both physical and
psychological and it may be these rates that are higher compared
with men rather than the psychiatric illness rates that are lower
when level 2 is compared with level 1. It was possible to re-
calculate our own data using Goldberg's denominators for sAD personal
illness. This resulted in a female to male ratio of 2 : 1 in the
whole population and 2.1 : 1 in consulters, showing no difference
in first filter permeability, a conclusion that would be misleading.
We conclude, therefore, that although the preponderance of women
amongst people seeking help from the primary care services is to a

large extent attributable to the fact that women tend to suffer from more symptoms of ill health and to have them more severely (or at least to be more willing to acknowledge their existence), there is a further factor involved, namely a greater readiness on the part of women to go to the doctor when they feel ill.

OTHER SOCIAL AND PSYCHOLOGICAL VARIABLES

Anyone who attempts to review the literature dealing with social and individual factors determining primary care consultation finds himself faced with a bewildering array of such variables. The problem is not made any easier by the fact that most of the research deals with factors associated with frequency of consultation, rather than those that modify a tendency to consult on a specific occasion. Contacts with the doctor are not randomly distributed in time, but are grouped around episodes of illness. Ashford and colleagues (Ashford, 1972) presented a convincing argument that distributions of contact rates require two independent parameters to be represented adequately, one describing various degrees of predisposition to illness, and the other variations in the number of contacts arising from each episode. Most of the work in this field has been concerned with overall contact rates, but the two parameters required by the Ashford model may each have different associations. Bearing this in mind, there are a few variables that stand out as being associated with consultation rates. Marital status, education, occupation and social class have all been claimed by different investigators to be differentially associated with a demand for medical care, as have a number of personality factors. Kessel (1960) for example showed excessive attendance to be associated with neuroses, social problems, emotional disturbance and conflicts within the family. Other authors have shown the same variable to be associated in individuals (Watts, 1962; Brown and Fry, 1962; Ryle and Hamilton, 1962; Grad and Sainsbury, 1963; Balint, 1968). Polliak (1971) using the Cornell Medical Index, found consultation rates to be significantly associated with scores on the inventory, perhaps not surprising, as it is after all a symptom inventory, but it was particularly interesting that the consultation rates of children were associated with the inventory scores of each of their parents. Children may consult doctors largely on the incentive of adults around them. It would probably be worthwhile looking for an influence upon adult consultation rates from other adults in the immediate social environment. Unemployment and loneliness have been observed more often in patients with a high frequency of GP contacts (McArdle et al, 1974). Beresford et al (1977) found that women with poor housing amenities consulted their doctors more frequently than others and those who had lived longest in the area consulted less often.

A link between personality and consultation has been studied by Foulds and his colleagues. Mayo (1969), for example, compared

neurotic patients with people who had neurotic symptoms but had not
sought medical assistance for them. The instrument used was Foulds'
Hostility and Direction of Hostility Questionnaire (HDHQ). Both
neurotics and normals with symptoms had significantly higher total
hostility scores than normals without symptoms. However, those with
symptoms who had sought treatment were more likely to be intro-
punitive, that is to blame themselves for their problems. People
with the same symptoms who did not seek treatment, tended to blame
the outside world. There was some indication that the extrapunitive-
ness of normals with symptoms was reflected in their inter-personal
relationships. They showed poorer home adjustment on Bell's Adjustment Inventory. These findings were confirmed by Foulds and Bedford
(1977).

Hannay (1979) looked at a range of social variables to see if
they were associated with self-referral behaviour. Subjects were
asked to grade the severity of their symptoms and to state whether
they had referred them either to a friend or relative (lay referral)
or to a professional adviser (formal referral). From these, three
referral scores were derived: (1) mean referral score which was the
sum of medical referral gradings expressed as a ratio of the total
number of medical symptoms; (2) incongruous medical lay referral
score (symptom iceberg) which was the number of medical symptoms for
which there was no formal referral when the symptom was graded as
severe; (3) incongruous medical professional referral score (symptom
trivia) which was the number of medical symptoms formally referred
when the self-rating of a symptom was not serious. Apart from age
and sex already mentioned, several independent variables were associated with one or other of these three dependent variables. They
included unemployment due to illness, marital status, education,
religious allegiance, social class, housing, mobility, neuroticism,
availability of a telephone and distance from the health centre for
those who did not have a car. Because of the way the dependent
variables were defined it was difficult to know whether the associations were with self-referral behaviour or with symptom frequency
and severity. A multiple regression analysis did little to clarify
the picture.

Statistical Methodology

The present authors also analysed their results by multiple
regression using a hierarchical method in which the variables were
entered in a predetermined order based upon logical and theoretical
considerations rather than statistical criteria. The results are
shown in Table 3 to 7.

Each row of the table represents a set of one or more variables,
usually in the form of two-valued dummy variables representing the
nominal scale concerned. Social class, for example, comprises six

Hierarchical Multiple Regressions Dependent Variable:
Consulter/Control Status

Table 3. Complete Random Sample

Independent variables	R^2	Increment
Sex, age,) symptom variables)	.089	
Social class	.099	.010*
Marital status	.102	.003
Employment status	.106	.004*
Size of household	.107	.001
Distance from Health Centre	.110	.003*
Close social support	.113	.002
Diffuse social support	.116	.003
Concept of cause	.174	.058*
$N_{controls}$, $N_{consulters}$	707, 709	

* Statistically significant (P < .05)

such dummy variables, one for each social class up to 6. Sets of
variables were entered into the equation in the order listed. The
body of the table contains the multiple R^2 for each equation for
variables up to and including that row. These figures represent the
total dependent variance accounted for and the second column shows
the increment, the extra dependent variance accounted for by the set
of variables in that row. The order of entry into the equation
requires some explanation. In all the tables sex, age and symptom
variables have been entered together, first because our objective was
to see whether the social factors contribute independently to
consulter/control status. For example, if the unemployed are more
likely to consult their doctors than those in work and if, in addition, a high proportion of the unemployed are women, then a direct
causal link between unemployment and consultation can only be
established if sex is partialled out first. Similarly if the unemployed tend to have more symptoms then we can only establish the
direct link between unemployment and consultation by partialling out
symptoms. There is no implication in this argument that if the
partialling out of symptoms were to eliminate the association between
employment and consultation, we would therefore lose interest in
unemployment as a factor in the causal process. It would simply
mean that interest was now shifted towards the process whereby unemployment and symptoms were associated, which would be quite an

important clarification of the problem. Our purpose at this point
is to seek out the variables that are directly linked with the act
of consultation.

The principle determining the order in which the various social
variables were entered is less clear. As far as possible, the concept of weak causal ordering as used in path analysis was applied,
implying that variables higher in the list may well have some causal
influence upon lower variables, but not the other way round. Often,
however, the correct causal order is arguable and sometimes it is
completely indeterminate, so also taken into consideration was an
a priori assessment of the likelihood that each variable would turn
out to be significant as a predictor of consultation. In the interpretation of these results, the essential point to bear in mind if
a set of variables produces a significant contribution to the dependent variance as indicated in the right hand column, is that the
link cannot be caused or mediated by any of the prior variables in
the list.

Results

Table 3 shows the results of the analysis applied to the complete random sample of consulters and controls. The factor that
contributed most to the discrimination was the patient's own assessment of the likely cause of the trouble. Those who plumped for a
physical cause were more likely to consult than those who thought
a psychological cause more likely. Although less than 6% of the
dependent variance could be attributed to this self-concept of
cause, it was not only statistically significant but also much in
excess of any other social factor. Even more striking is the fact
that this variable was entered last into the equation, so it is unlikely to be caused by or mediated through any of the other variables. Social class, employment status and distance from health
centre also contributed significantly, though to a very minor degree.

Tables 4 to 7 refer to separate sub-samples of consulters defined according to the symptoms that, according to patients' own
statements, were reasons for the consultation though not necessarily
the only reasons. For ease of interpretation it was desirable to
make the consultation groups mutually exclusive so they were selected
from the whole sample by the presence of the symptoms concerned in
the order represented by the tables. The acute anxiety or depression
consulters, for example, were included even if the other symptom
of the pair was chronic and irrespective of what further symptoms
were present. An acute symptom was defined as one with an onset
within the previous twelve months. Consulters of Table 4 included
any who had consulted with anxiety or depression. Those of Table 6
excluded any who had consulted with anxiety or depression, whilst
Table 7 excluded also those who had irritability, tiredness, head-

Hierarchical Multiple Regressions Dependent Variable:
Consulter/Control Status

Table 4.   Random Sample: Controls/Consulters With
Anxiety or Depression

Independent variables	Acute		Chronic	
	R^2	Increment	R^2	Increment
Sex, age and appropriate) symptom variables)	.361		.081	
Social class	.371	.010*	.082	.001
Marital status	.373	.002	.083	.001
Employment status	.374	.001	.088	.005
Size of household	.374	.000	.100	.012*
Distance from Health Centre	.374	.000	.100	.000
Close social support	.380	.006	.111	.011*
Diffuse social support	.382	.002	.116	.006
Concept of cause	.394	.012*	.138	.022*
$N_{controls}$, $N_{consulters}$	707, 80		707, 43	

* Statistically significant (P < .05)

Table 5. Special Sample of Consulters With Anxiety
or Depression and Their Controls

Independent variables	Acute		Chronic	
	R^2	Increment	R^2	Increment
Sex, age and appropriate) symptom variables)	.442		.221	
Social class	.444	.001	.235	.013
Marital status	.444	.000	.238	.003
Employment status	.447	.003	.239	.001
Size of household	.451	.004	.250	.011*
Distance from Health Centre	.452	.001	.252	.001
Close social support	.455	.003	.253	.001
Diffuse social support	.459	.005	.255	.002
Concept of cause	.507	.048*	.290	.036*
$N_{controls}$, $N_{consulters}$	363, 213		363, 145	

* Statistically significant (P < .05)

Hierarchical Multiple Regressions Dependent Variable: Consulter/Control Status

Table 6.   Random Sample: Controls/Consulters With Irritability, Tiredness, Headaches or Dizziness

Independent variables	Acute		Chronic	
	R^2	Increment	R^2	Increment
Sex, age and appropriate) symptom variables)	.163		.051	
Social class	.169	.006	.065	.014
Marital status	.178	.009*	.066	.001
Employment status	.180	.002	.067	.001
Size of household	.181	.001	.069	.002
Distance from Health Centre	.182	.001	.069	.000
Close social support	.183	.001	.074	.005
Diffuse social support	.186	.003	.078	.004
Concept of cause	.244	.058*	.182	.104*
$N_{controls}$, $N_{consulters}$	707, 104		707, 102	

* Statistically significant (P < .05)

Table 7.   Random Sample: Controls/Consulters With No Target Symptom Other Than Backache

Independent variable	R^2	Increment
Sex, age and appropriate) symptom variables)	.065	
Social class	.073	.007
Marital status	.076	.003
Employment status	.079	.003
Size of household	.079	.000
Distance from Health Centre	.085	.006*
Close social support	.086	.001
Diffuse social support	.091	.005
Concept of cause	.135	.044*
$N_{controls}$, $N_{consulters}$	707, 380	

* Statistically significant (P < .05)

aches or dizziness.   Table 5 refers to a completely independent
sample of consulters and controls, the consulters being all those
consulting with anxiety or depression during the year of the study
who had not already been included in the random sample.   It is noteworthy that in Tables 4 to 7, self-assessed cause remains in every
instance not only statistically significant but also the largest
contributor to the dependent variance.   Other variables show no such
consistency.   Size of household was a significant variable for consulters with chronic anxiety or depression and as this was confirmed
in the additional independent samples (Table 5) it is probably a
reliable finding.   However, for consulters with acute anxiety or
depression and indeed with any other group of symptoms, household
size made a negligible contribution to consulter/control discrimination.   Distance from health centre was a significant variable for
patients consulting with backache or a wide range of undetermined
symptoms other than those selected for assessment in the study.
But for those attending with anxiety, depression, irritability,
tiredness, headaches or dizziness, its influence was negligible.
Marital status was a minor but significant influence for consulters
with any of the miscellaneous group of acute symptoms in Table 6.
It was the married, widowed, separated or divorced who were most
likely to be found amongst the consulters.

DISCUSSION

     Most of the work reviewed in this chapter has relied upon
estimates of association from cross-sectional enquiries.   The fallacy
of assuming that such associations indicate causal links is well
known and the link between life stress and consultation, probably
mediated through symptoms, is not necessarily causal.   Stress may
tend to produce symptoms and consultation but it is perhaps just as
plausible to suggest that those with a proneness to symptoms and
help-seeking, attributable to factors like personality and life style,
also tend, for the same reasons, to experience stressful life events
and difficulties.   If this is so, there is no reason to suppose that
an increase in stress for any one individual will necessarily lead
to an increased likelihood of consultation.   Covariation over time
is more difficult to investigate and naturally enough, fewer researchers have attempted it.   There are indications that the picture
revealed by intensive longitudinal studies may be very different
from the cross-sectional one.   For example, Roghman and Haggerty
(1972) asked a random sample of 512 mothers to keep a health calendar
over a period of 28 days and also to record any upsetting events at
work or in the family.   Each mother also recorded illness and use
of health services for all members of the family.   The association
between stress and illness was quite opposite in direction to that
shown by the other methodology.   Illness episodes accompanied by
stress had a lower chance of medical contact than illness episodes
without stress.   "The mother seems to realise stress as the cause

of these short illnesses and does not expect any help from the
physician." For longer illnesses stress seemed less important.
Numbers were small in this enquiry and the time period short, but
the message is clear. It is essential to pursue longitudinal investigations to reduce the number of explanatory hypotheses that cross-
sectional correlational studies leave behind as equally acceptable.
If this discussion drifts into wording that seems to assume causal
links, it is always with this strong proviso in mind.

Our studies have shown that people with symptoms are more likely
than other people to visit their doctors and the more severely they
rate their symptoms, the more likely they are to go. Figures for
the contribution of symptom variables in Tables 3 to 7 are minimum
estimates for two reasons. Firstly, only a few of the many different
symptoms that patients report to their doctors were included. Each
new symptom added to the equation contributed more to the discrimination between consulters and controls. Larger multiple correlations
could have been achieved if instead of assessing seven symptoms
using three different measures for each we had assessed 21 symptoms
using only one scale for each. Furthermore, only a limited aspect
of severity was tapped. No attempt was made, for example, to assess
the personal, social and occupational disruption produced by each
symptom and this also might have added substantially to the symptom
component of explained dependent variance. Despite these limitations,
symptom severity was the main determinant of consultation and the
other variables played only a minor role once the effect of symptoms
had been partialled out.

Assuming that the associative link between symptoms and self-
referral is causal, then we have shown that symptoms are strong
motivators of consultation. However, the symptom severity scales
extended over a wide range of values from complete absence of the
symptom to levels that everybody would consider to be highly distressing and outside the normal range of experience. No attempt was
made to define a point on the continuum beyond which normal variation became pathological. For convenience, the scales are labelled
symptom variables but it would be more accurate to refer to them as
distresses. The distinction becomes particularly difficult to make
for psychological symptoms like anxiety or depression. There is
little doubt that many of the patients who complained to their
general practitioners about anxiety or depression were experiencing
distressing but normal and adaptive psychophysiological responses
to stress. Any feeling of distress may be attributed by the sufferer
to illness and in the absence of other ways of coping with the source
of the distress, the sick role (Parsons, 1951) may be adopted in an
attempt to seek relief. This form of illness behaviour (Mechanic,
1962) is an attempt at coping with stress. Wadsworth and Ingham
(1981), discussing this aspect of consulting behaviour, wrote
"adopting the sick role is a modern institutionalised solution to
many present day problems. For example, the patient consulting the

doctor with typical early symptoms of depression, such as tiredness, insomnia, anxiety, headaches, inability to concentrate, lack of interest, feelings of being unable to cope with work, may well have experienced a number of life events of quite a threatening nature in the recent past. Is this an example of threat induced illness, of illness as a maladaptive coping response, or of institutionalised illness behaviour that solves, or partially solves, the environmental problem?" Answers to questions like this, asked of an individual patient consulting his doctor with his own unique set of problems, clearly have important implications for practical steps that can be taken to help him with these problems.

In the absence of any generally accepted formulation for dealing with such situations, a great deal must depend on the attitudes and judgements of individual practitioners and these tend to be crystallised around two points of view that have been widely reflected in both popular and medical press. Many patients who consult their doctors following stressful experiences, particularly when the anxiety and depression symptoms themselves are not major, are inclined not to mention them but to complain of physical symptoms that would not otherwise be seen by them as reasons for self-referral. Such complaints are sometimes seen by the general practitioners as trivial and estimates of the proportion of consultations falling into this category have varied widely from 10% to 90%. It is often suggested that consulters with trivial symptoms should be discouraged. Cartwright (1979), however, asserted that minor illness "can only be eliminated from the consulting room by adding to the iceberg of more serious untreated illness and at the expense of good patient-doctor relationships." If there are patients consulting their doctors unnecessarily, then there are certainly others in the community with illnesses that do require treatment and who are not seeking help. Hannay (1979) has suggested that this symptom "iceberg", which he defines as the percentage of patients with serious symptoms who do not seek medical advice, comprises a larger group than that consulting with symptom "trivia". These comparative figures must be arbitrary, because the point at which a symptom becomes serious enough to require medical intervention is only defined in an arbitrary way. It would certainly be unwise to argue from the size of the symptom iceberg that more individuals with symptoms should be urged to see their doctors. Our own results could be said to favour the status quo in the sense that, on balance, it seems that those who are most in need of treatment (symptoms most severe) are more likely to seek help than those who are least in need (symptoms least severe). With present knowledge, it is probably best to allow patients to decide for themselves the point at which they are in need of help. To encourage or discourage consultation would probably make matters worse, except when there are easily detectable symptoms of serious illness which are not in themselves very distressing, such as previously unnoticed lumps. According to Cartwright, it is lack of definition of the general practitioner's job and what can

be treated or counselled which "leads not only to minor illness in
the consulting room, but also to a failure to consult about some
major illness at an appropriate stage". If, as we suspect, a substantial proportion of the minor complaints result from personal
adversity and the distress arising from it, then one is forced to
question whether the primary care health service is the appropriate
agency for offering help. In practice it is often the only source
of help and even where non-medical intervention, such as counselling,
is appropriate, there are many advantages in providing it within the
framework of the Health Service. The symptoms that finally motivate
the help-seeking behaviour may be symptoms either of physical illness or personal stress and patients often attribute them incorrect-
ly. Furthermore, even when the real problem is non-medical, medicine
may still be helpful, for example in the cautious prescribing of
tranquillisers to help somebody over a particularly difficult period
of life.

Implications for Primary Care

We already have the beginnings of a service, within a few
centres of primary care, for helping people for whom the main problem
is one of adverse life events or difficulties. In some health
centres, counselling is offered by clinical psychologists, community
psychiatric nurses or social workers. What is required is a more
detailed assessment of need and intensive research on high risk
groups of primary care consulters. This seems to be the point at
which preventive intervention could have its greatest and most
economical impact and its greatest chance of reducing serious
psychiatric disorder.

All of this points to a need for a new preventive service to
be set up within the framework of primary care, but here it is
essential to strike a strong note of caution. Before such a service
can be established on anything other than a strictly limited and
experimental basis we must be able to define and de-limit the
problems with which it should deal and above all lay down clear
guide lines to specify unambiguously the people to whom the service
should be offered. We certainly do not have in mind the vague and
diffuse set of social problems which many writers seem to envisage
when they refer to the non-medical problems encountered by general
practitioners. Primary care patients are individual people seeking
treatment for their own illnesses and distresses and need help to
enable them to live their own lives without ill-health. Clearly
when the doctor recognises in the patient's environment a factor
that he believes to be causing ill-health, it is part of his job
to take whatever steps he can to help the patient to change things,
but it is not his job to smooth out the ups and downs that are in-
evitable and essential components of living. It is this sort of
stress that is responsible for much of the "trivial" consultation
that occurs. Many people cope with such stresses adequately without

any professional help, even when the adversity involved seems extreme. Others seek professional help, usually from their doctors,
and manage to get by. Some eventually break down and become psychiatrically ill in a way that is clear and obvious, at least to those
who know them well. Before the point of breakdown, they could be
helped to adjust their attitudes and coping strategies so that the
breakdown would be less likely. There is as yet no professional
group with the body of knowledge and techniques that fully qualifies
them to offer such a service but the professional best placed to
develop the necessary knowledge and skills is the clinical psychologist working in primary care. Enough is known of the psychology
of coping to enable some well-founded guidance and help to be given
(Coelho et al, 1974). Existing behavioural and cognitive techniques
will probably be appropriate in many instances, but it must be borne
in mind that at this level the needs may be very different from
those generally met in psychiatric patients. The immediate need is
for research aimed first at detecting those who are in greatest need
of such a service, secondly at developing and evaluating intervention
techniques on the basis of what knowledge already exists.

REFERENCES

Ashford, J.R., 1972, Patient contacts in general practice in the
      National Health Service, The Stat., 21:265-289.
Balint, M., 1968, "The Doctor, His Patient and the Illness,"
      2nd Edition, Pitman Medical, London.
Banks, M.H., Beresford, S.A.A., Morrell, D.C., Waller, J.J., and
      Watkins, C.J., 1975, Factors influencing demand for primary
      medical care in women aged 20-44 years: a preliminary report,
      Int. J. Epidem., 4:189-195.
Beresford, S.A.A., Waller, J.J., Banks, M.H., and Wale, C.J., 1977,
      Why do women consult doctors? Social factors and the use of the
      general practitioner, Brit. J. Prev. & Soc. Med., 31:220-226.
Brown, A.C., and Fry, J., 1962, The Cornell Medical Index Health
      Questionnaire in the identification of neurotic patients in
      general practice, J. Psychosom. Res., 6:185-190.
Brown, G.W., Sklair, F., Harris, T.O., and Birley, J.L.T., 1973,
      Life-events and psychiatric disorders Part I: some method-
      ological issues, Psychol. Med., 3:74-87.
Brown, G.W., and Harris, T., 1978, "Social Origins of Depression,"
      Tavistock Publications, London.
Cartwright, A., 1979, Minor illness in the surgery, in: "Management
      of Minor Illness," Ch.9, King's Fund Publishing Office,
      Pitman, London.
Coelho, G.V., Hamburg, D.A., and Adams, J.E., 1974, "Coping and
      Adaptation," Basic Books, New York.
Foulds, G.A., and Bedford, A., 1977, Personality and coping with
      psychiatric symptoms, Brit. J. Psychiat., 130:29-31.
Foulds, G.A., and Bedford, A., 1978, "DSSI (State of Anxiety and
      Depression Manual)," NFER Publishing Co., London.

Freer, C.B., 1980, Self-care: a health diary study, Med. Care, 18:853-860.

Goldberg, D., 1978, "Manual of the General Health Questionnaire," National Foundation for Educational Research, Slough.

Goldberg, D., and Huxley, P., 1980, "Mental Illness in the Community: The Pathway to Psychiatric Care," Tavistock, London.

Grad, J., and Sainsbury, P., 1963, Mental illness and the family, Lancet, 1:544-547.

Hannay, D.R., 1979, "The Symptom Iceberg," Routledge Kegan Paul, London.

Hulka, B.S., 1972, Determinants of physician utilization, Med. Care, 10:300.

Ingham, J., 1981, Neurosis: disease or distress?, in: "What is a Case? Problems of Definition in Psychiatric Community Surveys," P. Bebbington, ed., Grant McIntyre,

Ingham, J.G., and Miller, P.McC., 1976, The concept of prevalence applied to psychiatric disorders and symptoms, Psychol. Med., 6:217-225.

Ingham, J.G., and Miller, P.McC., 1979, Symptom prevalence and severity in a general practice population, J. Epidem. & Comm. Health, September, Vol. 33, 3:191-198.

Ingham, J.G., Rawnsley, K., and Hughes, D., 1972, Psychiatric disorder and its declaration in contrasting areas of South Wales, Psychol. Med., 2, 3:281-292.

Kessel, W.I.N., 1960, Psychiatric morbidity in a London general practice, Brit. J. Prev. & Soc. Med., 14:16-22.

McArdle, C., Alexander, W.D., and Murray Boyle, C., 1974, Frequent attenders at a health centre, The Pract., November, pp.696-702.

Mayo, P.R., 1969, Women with neurotic symptoms who do not seek treatment, Brit. J. Med. Psychol., 42:165-169.

Mechanic, D., 1962, The concept of illness behaviour, J. Chron. Dis., 15:189-194.

Mechanic, D., and Greenley, J.R., 1974, The prevalence of psychological distress and help-seeking in a college student population, Soc. Psychiat., 11:1-14.

Miller, P.McC., Ingham, J.G., and Davidson, S., 1976, Life events, symptoms and social support, J. Psychosom. Res., 20:515-522.

Office of Population Censuses and Surveys, 1977, "General Household Survey".

Parsons, Tacott, 1951, "The Social System," Ch. X, The Free Press, Glencoe.

Polliak, M.R., 1971, The relationship between Cornell Medical Index scores and attendance rates, J. Roy. Coll. Gen. Pract., 21:453-459.

Roghman, K.J., and Haggerty, J., 1972, Family stress and the use of health services, Int. J. Epidem., 1:279-286.

Ryle, A., and Hamilton, M., 1962, Neurosis in fifty married couples, J. Ment. Sci., 108:265-273.

Tessler, R., Mechanic, D., and Dimond, M., 1976, The effect of
    psychological distress on physician utilization: a prospective
    study, J. Health & Soc. Beh., 17:353-364.
Wadsworth, M.E.J., Butterfield, W.J.H., and Blaney, R., 1971,
    "Health and Sickness," Tavistock Publications, London, pp.1-4.
Wadsworth, M.E.J., 1974, Health and sickness, J. Psychosom. Res.,
    18:271-276.
Wadsworth, M.E.J., and Ingham, J.G., 1981, How society defines
    sickness, in: "Foundations of Psychosomatics," M.J. Christie &
    P.G. Mallet, eds., Wiley, London and New York.
Watts, C.A.H., 1962, Psychiatric disorders, in: "Morbidity Statistics
    from General Practice, Vol. III (Disease in General Practice),
    the Res. Comm. of the Council of the Coll. of Gen. Prac.,
    Studies in Medical and Population Subjects, No. 14," H.M.S.O.,
    London.
Weissman, M.M., and Klerman, G.L., 1977, Sex differences and the
    epidemiology of depression, Arch. Gen. Psychiat., 34:98-111.

BEHAVIORAL BIBLIOTHERAPY: THEORETICAL AND METHODOLOGICAL ISSUES

IN OUTCOME RESEARCH INTO SELF-HELP PROGRAMS

Michael GT Dow

Psychology Department
Gartnavel Royal Hospital
Glasgow, Scotland

INTRODUCTION

Although the term "bibliotherapy" probably smacks of contemporary "psychobabble", like the technique to which it refers, it has
a lengthy history. It first appeared in Dorland's Illustrated Medical Dictionary in 1941 and was defined as 'the employment of books
and the reading of them in the treatment of nervous diseases' - a
definition which was expanded twenty years later to include physical
disorders. The therapeutic use and value of books have been recognised since ancient times. Tews (1970) reports that the libraries
of three millennia bore the inscription in Greek, 'Medicine (or
remedy) for the soul', and she notes that records of early Roman
encyclopaedists 'leave little doubt that books were made to serve
curative objectives, particularly in the treatment of the emotionally
disturbed patient' (p.173) and in the sixteenth century Rabelais
(1494-1553) prescribed literature for his patients as part of their
treatment (Schneck, 1944). Of course, the theoretical rationale for
their use in treatment has changed throughout history. Originally,
the therapeutic emphasis was mainly on the act of reading itself,
with the material considered more a source of moral and intellectual
sustenance rather than a medium for directive guidance.

At the inception of its more modern development, bibliotherapy
was used mainly as an adjunct to psychoanalysis, either as a form
of projective assessment (Hartman, 1951; Lazarsfeld, 1949) or as an
aspect of psychotherapy in its own right. Shrodes (1949, 1960,
1961) and Slavson (1950) submitted the hypothesis, derived from
psychoanalytic theory, that the use of imaginative literature may
produce results similar to those of conventional analysis by virtue
of the presumed comparability of experiences during reading with

specific phases in psychoanalysis viz universalisation, identification, introjection, catharsis and insight. Thus, it was used in the context of group psychotherapy (Floch, 1958; Powell et al, 1952; Roman, 1957), with children (Cohoe, 1960), for stammerers (Emerick, 1966) and with schizophrenics (Mascarino and Goode, 1940). However the most obvious criticism is the total absence of empirical evidence to substantiate these claims for its effectiveness (Bry, 1942; Darling, 1957; Oathout, 1954; Peterson, 1935; Ryan, 1957).

For the last fifteen years, there has been a burgeoning interest particularly in clinical and educational psychology, in the development of a different type of bibliotherapy viz of directive 'self-help' or D.I.Y. treatment programmes, based mainly on behavioural principles. Many are 'non-prescription' treatment packages that may be totally self-administered or involve minimal professional consultation (Rosen, 1976a).

Such programmes may be designed to train the individual in the application of techniques such as systematic desensitisation (Baker, et al, 1973; Kahn and Baker, 1968) or relaxation (Rosen, 1976b) but the majority are problem orientated, the range being so wide that almost every main area of 'out-patient' behaviour therapy is represented. Examples include self-help booklets for weight reduction (Hagen, 1974; Hanson et al, 1976; Harris, 1969; Stuart and Davis, 1972); toilet training (Azrin and Foxx, 1974); phobic disorders Marshall et al, 1976; Mathews et al, 1977); study behaviour (Beneke and Harris, 1972); sexual dysfunction (Kass and Stauss, 1975; Lowe and Mikulas, 1975) and social skills (Fensterheim and Baer, 1975). The majority of such programmes are packaged as written guides, although most of the practical, ethical, methodological and clinical issues to be discussed here apply equally to those in audio or video tape forms. Indeed one may confidently predict that further advancement of video technology and marketing over the next decade will spotlight the clinical and commercial potential for a corresponding expansion of home-based self-help treatment programmes, thus reinforcing an ever greater need for adequate scrutiny of their validity (Rosen, 1976a).

The purpose of this paper is not to review, in detail, studies evaluating the efficacy of self-help behaviour therapy manuals, as this has been comprehensively covered elsewhere (Glasgow and Rosen, 1978). Instead, the main aim is to alert the prospective clinician in this field to particular methodological, practical, clinical and theoretical issues pertinent to behavioural self-help treatment research.

CONSIDERATIONS IN THE ASSESSMENT OF OUTCOME

The Need for Controlled Evaluation

Azrin (1977), in particular, has stressed a need for an appropriate emphasis on outcome research in applied psychology. There
seems little doubt that in many cases our readiness to talk about
and explain problems still vastly outstrips our ability to demonstrate adequately that we have an effective cure (Agras and Berkowitz, 1980). This is nowhere more apparent than in the enormous
growth of behavioural treatment innovations, including self-help
guides, which, despite their often intuitive, if not theoretical
appeal, typically lack empirical evidence for their validity. Perhaps of particular concern, in addition, is their increasing availability and apparent professional endorsement without even recognition of the importance of such evaluation.

Following an examination of the book review section of
"Behaviour Therapy" Journal, Rosen (1978) noted 4% (3/68) of the
full length reviews published in 1975-6 were concerned with self-
help programmes compared to a 17% rate for 1977. Although he con-
ceded that there was controversy concerning the best way of ensuring
consumer controls (Goldiamond, 1976; Rosen, 1977), he showed that
professional reviews which encompass statements of clinical efficacy,
as distinct from literary style, content or presentation, tend to
eschew the results of empirical analysis in favour of personal
opinion. This concern may be compounded by a comparable laxity of
attitude toward the production, marketing and distribution of these
guides without at present adequate controlled clinical trials (Rosen,
1976a). Outcome studies in any specialised field have their own
characteristic, though scarcely unique, problems. What factors then
should be given particular consideration in designing such research
in this field?

Cost-Effectiveness

Only rarely are cost-effectiveness indices accounted for in
the design and assessment of self-help outcome research (Glasgow
and Rosen, 1978). Yet one of the most obvious reasons for the
development of such programmes is the fact that they permit potentially considerable savings in therapist and patient time and that
effective treatments can be offered to a larger number of patients
(Bastien and Jacobs, 1974). Indeed when a self-administered programme is shown to be less effective than a conventional, but comparable therapist-administered approach, use of the former may still
be justified on the basis of superior cost-effectiveness. Rosen
(1976a) has argued, in addition, that if patients can be shown to
treat themselves effectively, then these treatments can usefully

serve as a standard against which more costly forms of treatment
might be compared. Thus, analysis of cost-effectiveness implies
comparison: often between treatments, or between different methods
of administration of the same treatment. While each of these research aims may seem equally valuable and intuitively reasonable, it
may be appropriate in this context, however, to remind the unwary of
the methodological constraints inherent in each practice; and in
particular the questionable validity of the former instance above
viz comparison between treatments of different theoretical or conceptual background, eg psychotherapy and self-help desensitisation.

Methodological Considerations in Treatment Comparison Designs

LoPiccolo (1977) reminds us that such basic two cell experimental designs were originally developed in agricultural evaluative
research in which fairly rigorous experimental control may be maintained over virtually all central independent variables. Such tight
control is clearly not possible in psychotherapy research and, even
with random assignment of subjects and independent ratings on reliable measures pre and post-treatments, a simple comparison between
disparate therapies may be of dubious validity. Following LoPiccolo
(1977), the need for caution is stressed for the following reasons:

Task Confounding. If the two treatments differ from each other
in more than one way, as implied above, then differential effects
may be essentially uninterpretable, at least with respect to the
identification of effective ingredients for change.

Patient Expectancy. Since patients attend clinics with certain
expectations about treatment and its effectiveness, confirmed and
disconfirmed expectancies may powerfully affect motivation in treatment which may then become the primary determinant of measured differences in treatment outcome.

Differential Expertise in Treatment. The therapist should be
equally expert in each procedure otherwise significant post-treatment
differences may be attributable to the quality of management. Two
experts assigned to their respective fields or a double cross-over
design, often introduced to overcome this potential problem, may
not however, offer the complete solution. In the former, treatment
type is confounded by the identity of the therapists and the latter
would demand an equal development and flexibility of treatment skills
not always possible to ensure.

Focus of Assessment. It is important that whatever is being
measured is not biased in favour of either treatment. This is frequently unavoidable, however, with theoretically distinct treatments with conceptually conflicting aims. In our example above,
it is obvious that loading the assessment battery with anxiety related measures or tests of ego strength and insight should tip the
scales in favour of whichever treatment the biased researcher wishes.

These issues do not imply that one should eschew any comparative investigation of treatments. On the contrary, the plea is only that care be observed in relation to the overall aims of the study. If they are basically practical rather than theoretical, or concerned more with treatment form rather than content, the group comparison design can be a useful strategy.

At this stage, a better design for the investigation of self-help procedures, and which obviates many of the above constraints (with the possible exception of patient expectancies), is one in which a self-administered programme is compared with its therapist-directed counterpart - indeed a design which focusses on treatment format rather than content.

Duration of Therapy and Behavioural Goal Attainment. In addition to treatment comparison, two other related factors are central to the study of cost-effectiveness: duration of therapy and behavioural goal attainment. Neither, however, is usually included in the evaluation of self-help programmes and this may be in part attributable to, or at least perpetuated by, the use of time-limited therapy - a regime which, in general, has been shown to be more effective and efficient than treatment conducted on a time-unlimited basis (McNair et al, 1963). For this reason, treatments of pre-arranged duration are to be preferred, but not, in this context, to the exclusion of the identification and possible attainment of the ultimate goals of treatment, since these provide a clinically relevant framework for assessing a treatment's cost-effectiveness.

Thus, behavioural targets may constitute predetermined criteria for discontinuing therapy prior to a pre-set maximum duration of therapy. Thus, it is suggested that care again be observed in comparisons of self-help with parallel therapist-directed approaches to ensure that data relating to goal attainment (eg numbers of patients achieving the goal and number of weeks to criterion) are available. This also implies, of course, that the ceiling duration established in time-limited therapy is not unrealistically rigorous. Any limit should have an appropriate bearing on normal clinical practice (ie should have external validity) and hopefully permit a comparison of treatments that is both methodologically sound and avoids obscuring clinical with statistical significance (Lick, 1973).

Confusion of the latter is a potential hazard with some time-limited studies which provide no information on goal attainment or "cure". Despite statistically significant within or between group differences, the central question of their clinical meaningfulness may be unclear or unknown. To the clinician, then, such confusion may seriously cloud a realistic appraisal of a therapy's potential clinical usefulness and, in addition, may be particularly relevant in relation to anxiety-mediated problems (eg clinical phobias) in which a highly resistant and maladaptive pattern of avoidance may be well established.

Consider, for example, a comparison of self-help and therapist-directed desensitisation in the treatment of a clinical phobia (eg agoraphobia) or sexual dysfunction in which anxiety may be a prominent feature (eg vaginismus). In the context of a graded hierarchical treatment model, based also on (avoidance) response prevention, the goal of therapy (eg entering crowded stores, or sexual intercourse) may in addition be the primary source of anxiety. One may then expect anxiety and avoidance to increase directly with proximity to this goal. In short, the last hierarchical step, ie the last stage of therapy, may take longer to achieve. Consequently, one may hypothesise that a therapist-directed approach may be more efficient (ie fewer sessions to criterion) thought not necessarily more effective (ie in terms of goal attainment per se) due to what is known about greater resistance of extinction of avoidance responses and the opportunity for closer patient supervision in the therapist-directed regime. If supported, such a finding may be particularly significant clinically and should therefore be considered in relation to the assessment of a treatment's cost-effectiveness. However, it is clear that too low a limit to the duration of treatment in such a time-limited design may totally vitiate a clinically relevant appraisal of a 'self-help' treatment's potential clinical effectiveness. The above example, of course, also illustrates the importance of theoretical validity in research and how the nature of a project's design should be tailored to the hypothesis being tested. The argument here then is that despite its being widely referred to in relation to bibliotherapy, the cost-effectiveness of self-help programmes in an area of which little is known at present. Consideration of the above issues in the design of comparative evaluative studies involving self-help and therapist-administered programmes should permit additional hypotheses, relating to this important area, to be tested.

Correlates of Outcome

Glasgow and Rosen (1978) assert that 'related to the efficiency and effectiveness of self-help manuals is the need for program developers to provide guidelines that assist potential consumers in determining the appropriateness of any given program' (p.4). Such guidelines may include information on those behavioural problems amenable or least responsive to a self-administered approach; the patient characteristics and other potential correlates of treatment outcome, such as instructional medium; degree of therapist involvement; or general intelligibility of the programmes.

However, this relates to perhaps the most fundamental question in psychotherapy research in general, for which there are still too few scientifically acceptable answers: 'what treatment, by whom, is more effective for this individual with that specific problem, under which set of circumstances?' (Paul, 1967, p.44). There is no reason to presume, therefore, that these issues with respect to such a specialised area such as bibliotherapy will be any more readily resolved.

Subject Characteristics. As yet, there is only limited information on subject or personality variables in behavioural self-help research apart from the incidental comment that subjects frequently vary in their motivation to regulate their own behaviour (Kanfer and Karoly, 1972; Marston and Feldman, 1972). Schallow (1975) on the other hand, using the social learning theory construct of locus and control (Rotter, 1966), tested the hypothesis that "internal" subjects (ie those perceiving their behaviour as principally under their own control as opposed to fate, chance, astrological sign etc) would evince greater motivation and, consequently, greater success at modifying their own behaviour, than those whose scores indicated an external locus of control. The sample comprised 45 undergraduates who undertook to modify a variety of selected "problem" behaviours, including smoking and overeating to more idiosyncratic behaviour, such as effeminate mannerisms and jealousy. From time-series analyses, 14 subjects were shown to produce significant positive changes in level and slope from pre to post-treatment. When these 14 most successful subjects were compared to the 14 least successful, the results confirmed the hypothesis that the most effective self-modifiers were significantly more internal by the Rotter I/E scale. Schallow (1975) claims that the more extreme scores on this scale may have potential predictive utility. However, self-modification in this study referred more to the subjects' application of the principles of contingency management (Watson and Tharp, 1972; Kanfer, 1971; Meichenbaum, 1977; Goldiamond, 1965) rather than adherence to a didactic and directive model as presented in an instructional written guide.

However, additional evidence broadly consistent with the above conclusions of a correlation between specific personality variables and outcome with self-directed behavioural treatment is provided by Repucci and Baker (1969). They found that subjects who showed the greatest improvement with self-directed desensitisation resembled Leary's autocratic personality (Leary, 1957). Thus, they were described as outgoing, energetic and well organised, perceiving themselves as powerful, competent and "in-charge". The similarity of the latter half of this description with that of Schallow's (1975) "internal" subjects seems fairly obvious. It is noteworthy too perhaps that Leary reports that those of autocratic personality typically drop out of conventional or traditional psychotherapy.

Baker et al (1973) in a controlled comparison of self-directed and therapist-directed desensitisation of acrophobia also provided evidence that of all Leary's traits (eight in all), the managerial-autocratic scale was the only predictor of outcome. The significant positive correlation, however, was observed for all treated subjects so that those scoring higher on a managerial/autocratic dimension and lower on self-effacing, masochistic and general anxiety tended to improve in both conditions. Moreover, they also showed that higher pre-treatment levels of acrophobia and avoidance, but lower

general anxiety, were associated directly with improvement. The
authors conclude by suggesting that individuals who described themselves as more phobic, introvert, and obsessive, tended to show less
improvement within the therapist-directed group where the therapist's
availability allowed such subjects to provoke digressions into verbal
interaction not required for desensitisation. 'On the other hand,
phobic subjects, who could differentiate their agoraphobia improved
more in the (self-directed) condition, which relies more heavily on
subjects ability to be attuned to his anxiety, to diagnose rough
spots in the treatment and to make modifications in his hierarchy
himself' (Baker et al, 1973, p.88). Clearly then there is a need
for an extension of some of these studies to encompass a wider range
of problems, of greater clinical relevance and severity, and involving techniques other than that of desensitisation . The implication
that certain personality dimensions may be associated with a differential response to self and therapist administered procedures
warrants closer examination.

   Problem Characteristics. With regard to problem characteristics
associated with outcome, Glasgow and Rosen (1978) have examined a
large number of studies purporting to demonstrate the effectiveness
of self-help programmes for an equally wide variety of problems and
the reader is directed to their review. To date, there would seem
to be limited information on the specific problem characteristics
associated with a relatively poor outcome with self-help procedures.
The issue is difficult to resolve, as inevitably an unfavourable
treatment response may be confounded by an infinite range of other
factors including compliance failure, sample attrition, inadequate
motivation and other variables not directly related to central
specific problem characteristics. There is some evidence in the
field of sex therapy, however, of a significant interaction between
form of therapy and type of dysfunction which has some bearing on
this specific issue (Dow, 1980). This study was, in part, designed
as a sequel to research by Mathews et al (1976) who reported a fairly
high degree of variability of response to a minimal contact "correspondence course" in the more clearly behavioural aspects of contemporary sex therapy (Masters and Johnson, 1970; Kaplan, 1974).
Dow (1980) showed that, for couples presenting with female sexual
unresponsiveness, a minimal contact self-help approach, based on a
modified Masters and Johnson approach, produced no significant improvement and was also significantly poorer on a wide range of measures than the same approach involving additional regular therapist
counselling.

   No comparable differential effect of these two approaches was
observed with respect to other categories of sexual dysfunction
(viz vaginismus, erectile impotence and premature ejaculation).
A possible reason for the difference may inhere in the fact that,
pre-treatment, the females with loss of libido also reported a
greater degree of more general marital maladjustment compared to

the complainants in the other problem groups. This evidence is consistent with the view of Mathews et al (1976) and McMullen and Rosen
(1979) that minimal contact treatment approaches may be of less benefit for those whose sexual problems are complicated by more general
interpersonal or communication difficulties. These findings, however, and their possible relevance for the self-help treatment of
problems other than sexual dysfunction still demand further investigation.

    Instructional Format and Form of Administration. Other aspects
of the use of self-help programmes which demand consideration with
respect to outcome are those of the instructional format (eg video
v written; single v multicomponent) and the form of administration
of self-help manuals (eg totally self-administered v minimal therapist contact). The former has received, as yet, scant attention
but the potential value of video taped self-instructional programmes
is immediately apparent in relation to sex therapy, or for illustra-
ting modelling treatments for obsessional-compulsive disorders and
phobias, or when training of the patient's family seems indicated.
There are few studies, as yet, which have compared the relative
merits of these media. McMullen and Rosen (1979) compared video
and written presentations of a self-administered programme for the
treatment of primary orgasmic dysfunction in both single and married
women (Heiman et al, 1976). A waiting list was also included. No
significant differences were observed between the video and written
forms, both of which were significantly more effective than the
waiting list control in terms of orgasmic frequency. Although the
authors claimed that this lack of difference between the formats
indicated that it was therefore the informational content which
was the effective component, such an interpretation can only be
tentative, as each medium of presentation may have been contributing
to change nondidactically, or in a way specific to itself.

    Glasgow and Rosen (1978) have already provided an extensive
review of clinical outcome research of self-help programmes. Many
of these studies involve a comparison of groups exposed to varying
levels of therapist contact. It is immediately clear that no one
specific form of administration is consistently associated with a
particular outcome, favourable or unfavourable, especially across
problem categories. However, at least within the field of weight
reduction and other areas of self-control a reasonably consistent
finding is that some degree of external control seems indicated.
Manuals or guides used under minimal contact or therapist-administered conditions seem to produce at least short-term gains but
long-term results are in general very discouraging (Bellack, 1975,
1976; Bellack et al, 1974; Hagen, 1974; Mahoney et al, 1973). The
results therefore suggest that external control at some level may
be necessary for the maintenance of self-control, and that the degree
of external control invoked may be less important than its presence
or absence per se (Bellack, 1976; Bellack et al, 1976; Mahoney, 1974;
Kanfer and Karoly, 1972).

Apart from its relation to self-control, the level of therapist contact may also be particularly relevant to treatment outcome in two other ways (a) in terms of patient compliance and remaining in treatment and (b) in terms of the maintenance of treatment gains.

Compliance with Treatment Regimes

Relevance to Self-Help Procedures. Treatment compliance is of particular relevance to the effective use of self-administered behavioural programmes for the following main reasons:

a)   In a guide designed to be used on a totally self-administered or even minimal contact basis, the need for compliance may be considered to be particularly important for its success, in view of the obvious constraints on evaluating progress, correcting misunderstandings, obtaining and providing feedback etc.

b)   The nature of certain problem categories for which self-help manuals have been designed impose even greater limitations on the therapist's control over the procedural aspects of treatment, for ethical and/or practical reasons (eg social, sexual and marital problems).

c)   Behaviour therapy, by definition, involves behavioural change and typically demands the patient's active co-operation and implementation of procedures on a "homework" basis. There is already a considerable amount of evidence to show that co-operation in therapy is less easily achieved when treatment demands active as opposed to passive involvement (Davis, 1967; Johannsen et al, 1966). Indeed 'a steep gradient has been demonstrated in which the compliance exhibited by patients who must acquire new habits, such as taking medications, is much greater than that exhibited by those who must alter old behaviours, such as dietary or vocational habits, which exceeds, in turn, that of those who must break personal habits, such as smoking or drinking or nonmedical use of drugs' (Haynes, 1976, p.31).

d)   Compliance has also been shown to be lower among patients with a psychiatric diagnosis than among those whose problems have been diagnosed as organic (Alpert, 1964; Atkinson, 1971; Carr and Wittenbaugh, 1968; Wilson and Enoch, 1967).

e)   A decline in compliance in direct relation to the length and. complexity of therapy has also been demonstrated (Bergman and Warner, 1963; Francis et al, 1969). Insofar as self-help approaches typically extend over weeks and months rather than days, consideration of compliance issues is again suggested.

f)   There is already evidence to suggest that at least one form of

failure to comply viz failure to remain in therapy is a problem
particularly marked in self-help programmes (Glasgow and Rosen,
1978). Moreover, adherence to treatment has been shown to be a
strong correlate of improvement with such programmes (Bellack et al,
1974; Rosen et al, 1976).

Failure to Comply - Extent of the Problem. As noted above, a
substantial drop out rate or failure to comply with treatment demands
are characteristic findings with the use of fear reduction manuals
(Clark, 1972; Marshall et al, 1976; Phillips et al, 1972; Rosen
et al, 1976, 1977); weight reduction programmes (Hanson et al, 1976;
Mahoney et al, 1973); study skills training (Beneke and Harris, 1972;
Harris and Ream, 1972); sex therapy (Zeiss, 1977) and 'in this
respect, self-administered programs may be similar to weight reduction programs, exercise regimes or other procedures that require
sustained self-directed efforts' (Zeiss, 1977, p.216). Glasgow and
Rosen (1978) conclude their review of fear-reduction manuals by
stating that 'although current self-help manuals benefit as many as
50% of participating subjects, an equally large percentage of subjects often fail to complete treatment' (p.6).

Many of the above studies observed significant drop out problems
with both minimum contact as well as strictly self-administered procedures but Marshall et al (1976), Zeiss (1977) and Bellack et al
(1974) reported that even minimal contact with a therapist may be
sufficient to reduce significantly this characteristic problem.
Failure to complete or comply with treatment is a complex issue still
poorly understood and, while level of therapist contact in itself
may facilitate continued attendance in some cases, its interaction
with other variables including type of problem, patient satisfaction
with treatment (Hagen, 1974) and many other correlates of compliance
is an important area for future research.

One need hardly justify the importance of adequate motivation,
compliance and subject maintenance in any discussion of treatment.
Its relevance in the context of limited personal therapist involvement is even more obvious. Especially significant is the fact that
there is already substantial consistent evidence that subjects' progress in treatment is highly correlated with post-treatment performance. "If they do it, they improve" may be an overstatement but
essentially not far from the truth and has been noted by Repucci and
Baker (1969) and Rosen et al (1976) with subclinical phobias;
Bellack et al (1974) with obese patients and Beneke and Harris (1972)
for studying skills. This observation has led to attempts to facilitate involvement in these programmes. Barrera and Rosen (1977)
studied the effects of a self-reward contingency contracting procedure to supplement self-administered desensitisation among snake
phobic undergraduates. The procedure did not help ensure compliance
and indeed those subjects encouraged to use the self-reward procedure
completed significantly fewer sessions than a comparable group not
using the self-reward technique.

Findings from a study by Hagen (1974) suggest on the other hand that phone calls reminding patients of their appointment may help and other untested suggestions to enhance compliance include recruiting the support of significant others (Barrera and Rosen, 1977; Baekeland and Lundwall, 1975); the use of refundable contingency deposits (commensurate with patient's income) and abbreviation and simplification of manuals (Zeiss, 1977; Barrera and Rosen, 1977). Some of these ideas have indeed been studied in relation to treatment compliance generally and will therefore be elaborated in the next section.

Compliance: Intelligibility and Recall of Medical Information

Of the many instructional features of a programme of potential relevance to treatment outcome - general intelligibility or readability may be one of the most important (Ley, 1972a). Yet it has been infrequently investigated (Arkell et al, 1976; Glasgow and Rosen, 1978), despite the fact that empirically validated measures of readability have been available for many years (Flesch, 1948; Fry, 1968; Klare, 1963).

The comprehensibility and readability of advice presented to a patient are important in this context insofar as they contribute to a cognitive hypotheses of compliance. This is based on the view that a patient's retention and comprehension of the medical information presented to him are directly related to his satisfaction with the doctor's communication and his compliance with the advice therein.

Thus in a series of studies starting in 1966 Ley and his colleagues first endeavoured to establish whether there were indeed problems of comprehension and recall of medical information and to determine the factors associated with them, before experimentally investigating the effects of enhanced understanding and recall on compliance. The first body of research produced the following main findings:

a)   In general, there is a surprising lack of elementary medical knowledge, as well as active misconceptions about basic bodily function among the lay population (Boyle, 1970; Roth et al, 1962; Spelman and Ley, 1966).

One may suspect that the same deficiencies of knowledge and mistaken beliefs would characterise the layman's understanding of those psychological problems covered by self-help guides. The relative absence of 'hard facts', perhaps an intolerance of ambiguity, and fears and folklore about psychopathology would presumably conspire to reinforce the myths and militate further against a reasonably accurate understanding of the area. For example, even medical undergraduates have been shown to have an alarmingly poor knowledge of central aspects of human sexuality (Lief, 1968).

b)   Patients tend to forget substantial amounts of information given
to them by their doctor. Medical out-patients have been shown to
forget about 40% of information within 10-80 minutes of its being
presented, a tendency unrelated to age or intelligence (Ley and
Spelman, 1965, 1967). Similarly, Ley et al (1973) found, among patients attending their general practitioner, that 50% of the statements given to them were forgotten within 5 minutes of the visit.
These findings, in themselves, are consistent with the use of written
guides, if only as aides memoires, but the order in which specific
types of information are presented also seems to be relevant. For
example, a strong primacy effect in the memory of medical information
has been demonstrated, and, secondly, patients recall more of the
information they believe to be most important (Ley, 1972b).

c)   A considerable amount of doctor/patient communication may be
largely unintelligible for much of the lay population.

    For example, Ley et al (1972) used Flesch's formula (1948) to
assess the readability of x-ray leaflets issued to patients in a
predominately working class area and found that the material would
be too difficult for a large proportion of the population for whom
it was intended. Similarly, only about 25% of the general population would be expected to comprehend a barium meal leaflet for patients (Wild and Evans, 1968) and an information leaflet provided
by a dental hospital (Lovius et al, 1973).

Readability of Self-Help Sex Therapy Manuals

    Despite the potential importance of a manual's readability and
the fact that it may be easily assessed, this aspect of the design
of self-help programmes has received scant attention. Dow (unpublished) again using Flesch's formula, examined the readability
of a selection of nine self-help guides for the treatment of sexual
dysfunction, five of which were designed and marketed for use on a
totally self-administered, 'non-prescription' basis* (see Table 1).
The remaining unpublished manuals were the focus of a separate
study (Dow, 1980). Mean reading ease (R.E.) scores, based on ten
100 word samples selected at random from each of the manuals were
then computed. From Table 2, it is clear that of those published
texts studied here, all are unsuitable for a majority (ie about 60%)
of the general population. (As Ley (1977) points out, however, the
figures should be interpreted cautiously, as the IQ levels are
simple linear equivalents of the comprehensibility percentiles and
do not take into account regression effects.) Of course the reading
ease of only a very restricted sample of published self-help manuals
have been examined here but there is perhaps already sufficient
evidence to suggest that it may be a largely ignored or at least
ill-considered aspect of their design. Given that the conscientious
therapist is motivated by clinical rather than purely commercial
interests, what evidence is there for the more far reaching implications of his text's intelligibility?

Table 1. Reading Ease (R.E.) Scores for Nine Self-Help
Guides for the Treatment of Sexual Dysfunction: Means
and SDs Based on Ten Random 100 Word Samples

Title	R.E. Mean	SD
*Sexual Awareness (McCarthy et al, 1975)	46.97	13.6
*For Yourself (Barbach, 1976)	49.79	17.8
*Treat Yourself to Sex (Brown and Faulder, 1977)	52.90	16.7
*Becoming Orgasmic (Heiman et al, 1976)	54.29	10.5
*Making Love (Raley, 1976)	56.80	11.7
Vaginismus (Dow, unpublished)	62.51	8.2
Premature Ejaculation (Dow, unpublished)	63.14	7.2
Erectile Impotence (Dow, unpublished)	64.44	6.7
Female Sexual Unresponsiveness (Dow, unpublished)	68.52	6.2

    Ley et al (1976), for example, studied the effects of increased
comprehension on compliance with an out-patient drug regime among
160 psychiatric patients, half of whom received anti-depressants,
the other half minor tranquillisers. Three leaflets of varying
degrees of readability – easy, moderate and difficult – were prepared to provide specific information about the treatment which
had previously been shown to be poorly understood. A 'no leaflet'
group was also included and the degree of compliance in all groups
was measured in terms of proportion of medication errors. The
results clearly supported the hypothesis, with the easy and moderately easy leaflets being associated with significantly fewer
medication errors, while the 'difficult' leaflet had no such effect.

Table 2. Interpretation of Reading Ease Scores
(from Ley, 1977, p.20)

Score	% who would understand	IQ required for comprehension
0- 30	4.5	126+
31- 50	24	111+
51- 60	40	104+
61- 70	75	90+
71- 80	80	87+
81- 90	86	84+
91-100	90	81+

Finally, in order to study the effects of differential recall
on compliance, Ley (1976) compared two leaflets of similar content
designed to encourage obese women volunteers to adhere to a low
carbohydrate diet. One leaflet (the control) was of moderate readability according to the Flesch formula, while the other (the experimental) was particularly easy and contained explicit categorisation and repetition of advice - variables shown to be associated
with increased recall (Ley, 1979). A significant between groups
difference was again observed, favouring the experimental group,
showing that clinically as well as statistically significant changes
can be produced by enhancing compliance with improved patient recall.

Recommendations

The fact that much of this research on patient compliance is of
direct relevance to the production and evaluation of behavioural
self-help programmes has received to date virtually no formal recognition by those involved in their design. On the other hand, failures to complete such programmes are frequently reported as indeed
is recognition of the practical constraints on the degree of therapist control of treatment procedure. The design of self-help booklets could therefore be improved by incorporating the following conclusions from Ley's research:

1.   In view of a primacy effect on retention, patients should, as
far as possible, be provided with instructions and advice at the
start of the information to be presented.

2.   The importance of instructions and advice should also be
stressed.

3.   Short words and sentences and the avoidance of jargon should
be observed.

4.   Explicit categorisation of information should be used where
possible.

5.   Advice or other important issues should be repeated.

6.   Advice should be as specific, concrete and detailed as possible.
                                                              (Ley, 1977)

MAINTENANCE OF TREATMENT GAINS

     Although therapist-directed procedures have been reported to
produce greater generalisation of effects (Marshall et al, 1976),
a frequent finding, among the relatively few studies with adequate
follow-up data, is a greater maintenance of treatment effects among
self-directed procedures, eg for agoraphobia (Mathew et al, 1976);
for snake phobia (Rosen et al, 1976); for acrophobia (Baker et al,
1973); for obesity (Hanson et al, 1976). Again this is of substantial theoretical and clinical significance and, in conjunction with
the problem of compliance noted above, highlights the importance of
ensuring that patients remain in treatment in its early stages.

     The maintenance of treatment-induced change has been a focus
of increasing clinical and theoretical interest over the last decade.
Research development in the field, however, has been relatively slow
to follow despite the obvious importance of assessing the generality
of such change: treatment which fails to generalise over time or
place is of dubious value, 'an exercise in futility' (Zielinski,
1978, p.353). For the purpose of this discussion, generalisation
will refer principally to the maintenance of behavioural change over
time rather than place, the former being for bibliotherapy (and for
many other behavioural treatments) the more critical issue, given
an increasing emphasis on therapy in the natural environment rather
than in the clinic alone eg sex therapy and other forms of 'instigation therapy' (Kanfer, 1979; Shelton, 1979; Zielinski, 1978).

     Historically, it is possible to understand the relative recency
of interest in the generality of treatment effects in terms of changing theoretical emphasis. As Kanfer (1979) points out, in the context of a psychoanalytic framework, detailed analysis of the maintenance of change was of limited relevance. If affective intra-
personal or cognitive change occurred, this was presumed to be a
function of a more pervasive and fundamental alteration in psychological processes which would permit the individual to cope more
adaptively with subsequent life stresses, irrespective of their precise nature or setting. Early behaviour therapists, too, were also
relatively unconcerned about generalisation of response change.

With their rejection of cognitive mediating variables and an emphasis
on operant conditioning, it focussed on the induction and maintenance
of overt behavioural change by environmental contingencies.   Generalisation was viewed as a passive phenomenon, which, like extinction, would be controlled not only by those stimuli specific to the
training situation but by members of the more general class of stimuli resembling those in treatment (Kanfer, 1979).   Stokes and Baer
(1977) summarised that view by asserting that 'generalisation was
something that happened, not something produced by a procedure specific to it' (p.349).

It was partly in response to the theoretical constraints of a
linear S - R model and the view that therapeutic effectiveness demands that behavioural change become, to some extent, independent
of exclusively external control that learning theorists expanded
their theories and treatment repertoire to encompass cognitive-
behavioural approaches.   Under this label is subsumed a range of
self-management strategies of which behavioural bibliotherapy may
be considered a part.

It is only relatively recently, however, that clinicians are
examining the value of bibliotherapy, in recognition of the problems
of relapse after behavioural treatment for certain problems (eg
Mathews et al, 1976).   In so doing, they are responding to the plea
of Baer et al (1968) that 'generalisation should be programmed,
rather than expected or lamented' (p.97).   Although, as noted earlier, many studies reported an increased maintenance or enhancement
of long-term treatment effects with self-directed regimes, it was
typically reported more as an incidental, and occasionally inconsistent finding (Donner, 1970) rather than as a product of prospective examination of specific hypotheses.   Yet, it may be argued that
it is with the latter approach that a more profitable understanding
and clarification of the role of self-directed programmes for temporal generality of treatment effects may be achieved.

One may predict that the use of self-help manuals would facilitate such generalisation in a number of (non-mutually exclusive)
ways:

a)   by a reduced dependence on external reinforcements and stimulus
control (Kanfer, 1971; Mahoney and Thoresen, 1974).

b)   given a characteristically strong directive and didactic element, they should provide an opportunity for learning general coping
strategies (Lazarus, 1976).

c)   by their contributing to an altered self-perception, based on
personal causal attribution of behavioural change.

Several researchers have interpreted their results, or been

prompted to use self-help procedures on the basis of the rationale
provided by the first two factors above, the effects of which have
been fairly well documented. The third, however, is an area which
awaits further detailed investigation in relation to bibliotherapy.

Attribution Theory and Self-Initiated Change

Bandura (1977) developed the view that different treatments may
exert their effects through a common cognitive mechanism of 'self-
efficacy'. This model is based on the notion that a person's experience of personal mastery - the conviction that he has been responsible for producing a desired change - serves to reinforce coping
behaviour and enhance efforts to resolve difficulties. The factors
believed to influence self-efficacy include information about particular personal achievements and their effects, feedback from others,
and from one's own physiological arousal. Bandura asserts that a
treatment approach which enhances an expectation of self-efficacy
should in turn facilitate the development of relatively enduring
behavioural and attitude change. This theoretical formulation is
essentially, then, an extension of attribution theory which contains
similar implications for sustained treatment gains at follow-up
(Kopel and Arkowitz, 1975). In short, it is argued that perceiving
a change in one's behaviour as primarily caused by oneself as opposed
to extrinsic controlling factors leads to new self-inferences which,
in turn, cut across the locus and time of initial behavioural change.
These hypotheses also bear similarities to those derived from cognitive dissonance theory (Festinger, 1957) and the relative persis-
tence of attitude and behaviour change which occurs only insofar as
freedom of choice or insufficient external justification for such
changes are perceived (Brehm and Cohen, 1962).

The research literature is replete with evidence consistent with
the above hypotheses. Thus, Davison (1968) showed that patients who
were involved in their own planning of treatment were more likely
to maintain therapy gains over time. Secord and Backman (1964) also
reported an increase in self-control skills acquired by patients who
perceived themselves as the principal agent of change. Additional
empirical support is also provided by Bandura et al (1975) who,
using snake phobic volunteers, compared participant modelling alone
with participant modelling and 'self-directed performance' which
permitted the subjects to practise independently any of the activities conducted earlier under the therapist's direct guidance. This
latter phase then was designed to increase feelings of personal efficacy. The group given the additional self-directed phase was further divided into two subgroups in which one was exposed only to the
original phobic object (a boa constrictor) used in the modelling
phase and the other to the same boa and an unfamiliar snake. Although all groups showed significant improvement as measured by
avoidance tests, the self-directed treatments effected greater gen-

eralised changes at post-test and at follow-up. Of relevance here
was the finding that those who were given the self-mastery treatment
showed greater snake anxiety reduction, which also generalised beyond
the original phobic situation, and higher ratings of self-competency.
It was concluded that the results lent support to the prediction that
self-directed treatment led to successful transfer effects, in part
due to the enhancement of self-adequacy and the acquisition of general coping skills.

A similar study by Bandura et al (1977) compared the relative
efficacy of a modelling procedure which included progressively more
active patient involvement and initiative with the same modelling
technique allowing only passive observation. The latter, it was
predicted would produce lower self-efficacy expectations, less improvement and less generalisation. These hypotheses were supported
and self-report measures of efficacy expectations were also shown to
correlate highly with outcome, irrespective of treatment form.

Research in this area, however, has not unequivocally supported
Bandura's theory (eg O'Brien and Kelley, 1980; Smith and Coleman,
1977) which nevertheless remains one of the few amenable to further
empirical evaluation and has application to the field of self-directed therapy in general. It is not enough to presume increased temporal generality of treatment change with any self-directed programme
and it is hoped that the further development and design of written,
audio and video self-help programmes will take account of the results
of future examination of the above theories. Based on the above
and related hypotheses, design and administrative changes are already suggested.

RECOMMENDATIONS FOR FUTURE RESEARCH

One may hypothesise that behavioural treatment guides may be
improved as follows:

1.   By incorporating regular 'feedback' and self-monitoring procedures. Self-assessment in itself has been shown to produce behavioural change (Kanfer, 1975; Kazdin, 1974; Nelson, 1977) by encouraging skills central to more general self-diagnostic and self-correct-
ive processes. They would also be consistent with the notion of
self-mastery largely dependent on performance feedback, as described
above.

2.   By introducing self-help manuals only towards the end of a
therapist-directed programme. Initial involvement of a therapist
may help inhibit patient 'drop-out' (Marshall et al, 1976; O'Brien
and Kelley, 1980), permit the use of a participant modelling procedure, help prevent maladaptive avoidance and allow closer supervision of inherently stressful procedures eg flooding and response

prevention. The subsequent introduction of a self-directed programme
may then lead to more of its potential benefits being fully realised.

3.   By encouraging patients to practise or overlearn those skills
or activities most clearly associated with an experience of self-
mastery. One may expect that these will be the tasks perceived
initially to be the most difficult (eg those close to the top of a
behavioural hierarchy) and involving greater clinical and personally
relevant change, rather than milder threats (Smith and Coleman,
1977).

CONCLUSIONS

    For a variety of reasons, including commercial, clinical and
theoretical, there has been increasing interest over the past decade
in particular, among both the 'consumer' and the 'supplier', in the
use of self-administered behavioural programmes. That a behavioural
psychology should share in this growth industry of manuals, kits and
tapes is readily understandable in terms of a 'D.I.Y.' Zeitgeist, a
ready market, a theoretical framework based on behavioural self-control in its broadest sense, and a health service which may be primed
to consider issues of cost-effectiveness. Whatever the reasons, the
need for careful evaluation and preparation of any non-prescription
'over-the-counter' programme is readily apparent. The processes
and the effective parameters of behavioural self-help programmes
have in general not been adequately investigated.

    The main aim of this chapter has been to focus on the more
practical aspects of planning research in this area rather than to
encompass the numerous methodological inadequacies of existing research with self-management procedures. For example, the reliability
of self-recorded behaviours and the questionable practice of relying
exclusively on the honesty and accuracy of subjects' 'self-reports'
(Mahoney, 1972) is not dealt with here. Moreover, there is also a
need for prospective researchers in this field to distinguish carefully between the different ways of administering a self-directed
programme particularly with respect to the degree of therapist contact and control (Glasgow and Rosen, 1978). Booklets may be (a)
totally self-administered, and constitute the sole basis for treatment or (b) predominately self-administered, with supplementary
minimal therapist contact usually in the form of weekly 'phone calls,
postal correspondence or infrequent personal meetings or (c) therapist-administered, in which manuals either supplement conventional
therapist-directed help or are the focus of discussion and elabora-
tion during regular meetings. This distinction may seem obvious but
it is frequently overlooked in reviews of a programme's general
effectiveness, when disparity exists between the conditions under
which it was tested and its intended use. The relationship between
level of therapist contact and the long term efficacy of certain
programmes for particular problems (eg weight reduction and smoking)
already seems likely to be a crucial one.

Widely documented in the self-help literature, though rarely studied, are problems of compliance, and dropping out of therapy. It is suggested here that simple fundamental questions relating to a programme's design and particularly its comprehensibility should be asked first before necessarily renouncing the whole concept of self-management in the light of a poor response. Equally surprising perhaps has been the paucity of information concerning the relative cost-effectiveness of our methods of treatment, as well as the limited number of studies examining specific hypotheses relating to self-management and maintenance of behavioural change over time.

While this is not intended to be an exhaustive review of the potential problems in the implementation and study of self-help procedures, it has hopefully offered for consideration several areas which may facilitate further research inquiry into what is certainly one of the most promising and demanding developments in clinical research.

ACKNOWLEDGEMENT

The author would like to acknowledge the kind permission of Pergamon Press for the reproduction of Table 2.

REFERENCES

Agras, W.S., and Berkowitz, R., 1980, Clinical research in behaviour therapy: Halfway there?, Beh. Ther., 11:472-487.

Alpert, J.J., 1964, Broken appointments, Pediatrics, 34:127-132.

Arkell, R.N., Kubo, H.R., and Meunier, C.P., 1976, Readability and parental behaviour modification literature, Beh. Ther., 7: 265-266.

Atkinson, R.M., 1971, AMA and AWOL discharges: a six year comparative study, Hosp. Comm. Psychiat., 22:293-296.

Azrin, N.H., 1977, A strategy for applied research - Learning based but outcome orientated, Amer. Psychol., Feb., pp.140-149.

Azrin, N.H., and Foxx, R.M., 1974, "Toilet Training in Less Than a Day," Simon & Schuster, New York.

Baekeland, F., and Lundwall, L., 1975, Dropping out of treatment: a critical review, Psychol. Bull., 82:738-783.

Baer, D.M., Wolf, M.M., and Risley, T.R., 1968, Some current dimensions of applied behaviour analysis, J. App. Beh. Anal., 1:91-97.

Baker, B.L., Cohen, D.C., and Saunders, J.T., 1973, Self-directed desensitisation for acrophobia, Beh. Res. & Ther., 11:79-89.

Bandura, A., 1977, "Social Learning Theory," Prentice-Hall, Englewood Cliffs, New Jersey.

Bandura, A., Adams, N.E., and Beyer, J., 1977, Cognitive processes mediating behavioural change, J. Pers. & Soc. Psychol., 35: 125-139.

Bandura, A., Jeffery, R.W., and Gajdos, E., 1975, Generalising change through participant modelling with self-directed mastery, Beh. Res. & Ther., 13:141-152.

Barbach, L.G., 1976, "For Yourself: The Fulfilment of Female Sexuality," Anchor Press/Doubleday, New York.

Barrera, M. Jr., and Rosen, G.M., 1977, Detrimental effects of a self-reward contracting program on subjects' involvement in self-administered desensitisation, J. Cons. & Clin. Psychol., 45:1180-1181.

Bastien, S., and Jacobs, A., 1974, An experimental study of the effectiveness of written communication as a form of psychotherapy, J. Cons. & Clin. Psychol., 42(1):151.

Bellack, A.S., 1975, Behaviour therapy for weight reduction: an evaluative review, Addictive Behs., 1:73-82.

Bellack, A.S., 1976, A comparison of self-reinforcement and self-monitoring in a weight reduction program, Beh. Ther., 7:68-75.

Bellack, A.S., Glanz, L., and Simon, R., 1976, Self-reinforcement style and covert imagery in the treatment of obesity, J. Cons. & Clin. Psychol., 44:490-491.

Bellack, A.S., Schwarts, J., and Rozensty, R.H., 1974, The contribution of external control to self-control in a weight reduction program, J. Beh. Ther. & Exp. Psychiat., 5:245-249.

Beneke, W.M., and Harris, M.B., 1972, Teaching self-control of study behaviour, Beh. Res. & Ther., 10:35-41.

Bergman, A.B., and Werner, R.J., 1963, Failure of children to receive penicillin by mouth, New Eng. J. Med., 268:1334-1338.

Boyle, C.M., 1970, Differences between doctors' and patients' interpretations of some common medical terms, B.M.J., 2:286-289.

Brehm, J.W., and Cohen, A.R., 1962, "Explorations in Cognitive Dissonance," Wiley, New York.

Brown, P., and Faulder, C., 1977, "Treat Yourself to Sex - A Guide for Good Loving," Dent & Sons Ltd., London.

Bry, I., 1942, Medical aspects of literature, Bull. Med. Libr. Assoc., 30:252-266.

Carr, J.E., and Wittenbaugh, J.A., 1968, Volunteer and non-volunteer characteristics in an out-patient population, J. Abn. Psychol., 73:16-17.

Clark, F., 1973, Self-administered desensitisation, Beh. Res. & Ther., 11:335-338.

Cohoe, E., 1960, Bibliotherapy for socially maladjusted children, Nat. Educ. Assoc. J., 49:34.

Darling, R.L., 1957, Mental hygiene and books. Bibliotherapy as used with children and adolescents, Wilson Libr. Bull., 32: 293-296.

Davis, M.S., 1967, Predicting non-compliant behaviour, J. Health & Soc. Beh., 8:265-271.

Davison, G., 1968, Systematic desensitisation as a counter conditioning process, J. Abn. Psychol., 73:91-99.

Donner, L., 1970, Automated group desensitisation - a follow-up report, Beh. Res. & Ther., 8:241-247.

Dow, M.G.T., 1980, A comparative evaluation of 'self-help' and conventional Masters and Johnson treatments for sexual dysfunction. Paper presented at Brit. Psychol. Soc. Ann. Conf., March, 1980, University of Aberdeen.

Emerick, L.L., 1966, Bibliotherapy for stutterers: Four case histories, Quart. J. Speech, 52:74.

Fensterheim, H., and Baer, J.L., 1975, "Don't Say Yes When You Want to Say No: How Assertiveness Training Can Change Your Life," Dell, New York.

Festinger, L., 1957, "A Theory of Cognitive Dissonance," Harper & Row, New York.

Flesch, R., 1948, A new readability yardstick, J. App. Psychol., 32:221-233.

Floch, M., 1958, Bibliotherapy and the library, The Bookmark, Dec. 1958, 18:57-59.

Francis, V., Korsch, B.M., and Morris, M.J., 1969, Gaps in doctor-patient communication, New Eng. J. Med., 280:535-540.

Fry, E.B., 1968, A readability formula that saves time, J. of Reading, 11:513-516, 575-578 (April).

Glasgow, R.E., and Rosen, G.M., 1978, Behavioural bibliotherapy: a review of self-help behaviour therapy manuals, Psychol. Bull., 85(1):1-23.

Goldiamond, I., 1965, Self-control procedures in personal behaviour problems, Psychol. Rep., 17:851-868.

Goldiamond, I., 1976, Singling out self-administered behaviour therapies for professional overview: a comment on Rosen, Amer. Psychol., 31:142-147.

Hagen, R.L., 1974, Group therapy vs. bibliotherapy in weight reduction, Beh. Ther., 5:222-234.

Hanson, R.W., Borden, B.L., Hall, S.M., and Hall, R.G., 1976, Use of programmed instruction in teaching self-management skills to overweight adults, Beh. Ther., 7:366-373.

Harris, M.B., 1969, Self-directed program for weight control: a pilot study, J. Abn. Psychol., 74:263-270.

Harris, M.B., and Ream, F., 1972, A program to improve study habits of high-school students, Psychol. in the Schools, 9:325-330.

Hartman, E.A., 1951, "Imaginative Literature as a Projective Technique: A Study in Bibliotherapy," Unpublished Ph.D. dissertation, Stanford University.

Haynes, R.B., 1976, A critical review of the "determinants" of patient compliance with therapeutic regimens, in: "Compliance With Therapeutic Regimens," D.L. Sackett & R.B. Haynes, eds., John Hopkins University Press, New York, pp.26-39.

Heiman, J., LoPiccolo, L., and LoPiccolo, J., 1976, "Becoming Orgasmic: A Sexual Growth Program for Women," Prentice-Hall, New Jersey.

Johannsen, W.J., Hellmuth, G.A., and Sorauf, T., 1966, On accepting medical recommendations, Arch. Envir. Health, 12:63-69.

Kahn, M., and Baker, B., 1968, Desensitisation with minimal therapist contact, J. Abn. Psychol., 73:198-200.

Kanfer, F.H., 1971, The maintenance of behaviour by self-generated stimuli and reinforcement, in: "The Psychology of Private Events," A. Jacobs & L.B. Sachs, eds., Academic Press, New York.

Kanfer, F.H., 1975, Self-management methods, in: "Helping People Change: A Textbook of Methods," F.H. Kanfer & A.P. Goldstein, eds., Pergamon, New York.

Kanfer, F.H., 1979, Self-management and strategies and tactics, in: "Maximising Treatment Gains - Transfer Enhancement in Psychotherapy," A.P. Goldstein & F.H. Kanfer, eds., Academic Press, London, pp.185-224.

Kanfer, F.H., and Karoly, P., 1972, Self-control: a behaviouristic excursion into the lion's den, Beh. Ther., 3:398-416.

Kaplan, H.S., 1974, "The New Sex Therapy," Baillière Tindall, London.

Kass, D.J., and Stauss, F., 1975, "Sex Therapy at Home," Simon & Schuster, New York.

Kazdin, A.E., 1974, Self-monitoring and behaviour change, in: "Self-control: Power to the Person," M.J. Mahoney & C.E. Thoresen, eds., Brooks/Cole, Monterey, California.

Klare, G.R., 1963, "The Measurement of Readability," Iowa State University Press, Iowa.

Kopel, S., and Arkowitz, H., 1975, The role of attribution and self-perception in behaviour change: Implications for behaviour therapy, Genet. Psychol. Monogs., 92:175-212.

Lazarsfeld, S., 1949, The use of fiction in psychotherapy, Amer. J. Psychother., 3:26-33, January 1949.

Lazarus, A.A., 1976, "Multimodal Behavior Therapy," Springer Publishing, New York.

Leary, T., 1957, "Interpersonal Diagnosis of Personality," Ronald Press, New York.

Ley, P., 1972a, Comprehension, memory and the success of communication with the patient, J. Instit. Health Educ., 10:23-29.

Ley, P., 1972b, Primacy, rated importance and recall of medical information, J. Health & Soc. Beh., 13:311-317.

Ley, P., 1976, Toward better doctor-patient communications. Contributions from social and experimental psychology, in: "Communications in Medicine," A.E. Bennet, ed., Oxford University Press, London for the Nuffield Provincial Hospitals Trust.

Ley, P., 1977, Psychological studies of doctor-patient communication, in: "Contributions to Medical Psychology, Vol. 1," S. Rachman, ed., Pergamon Press, Oxford, Chap. 2, pp.9-42.

Ley, P., 1979, Memory for medical information, Brit. J. Soc. & Clin. Psychol., 18:245-255.

Ley, P., Bradshaw, P.W., Eaves, D.E., and Walker, C.M., 1973, A method of increasing patients' recall of information presented to them, Psychol. Med., 3:217-220.

Ley, P., Goldman, M., Bradshaw, P.W., Kincey, J.A., and Walker, C.M., 1972, The comprehensibility of some x-ray leaflets, J. Instit. Health Educ., 10:47-55.

Ley, P., Jain, V.K., and Skilbeck, C.E., 1976, A method for decreasing
    patients' medication errors, Psychol. Med., 6:599-601.
Ley, P., and Spelman, M.S., 1965, Communications in an out-patient
    setting, Brit. J. Soc. & Clin. Psychol., 4:114-116.
Ley, P., and Spelman, M.S., 1967, "Communicating With The Patient,"
    Staples Press, London.
Lick, J.R., 1973, Statistical vs. clinical significance in research
    on the outcome of psychotherapy, Int. J. Ment. Health, 2:26-37.
Lief, H.I., 1968, Sex education of medical students and doctors,
    Chap. 2, pp.19-33, in: "Human Sexuality in Medical Education
    and Practice," Clarke E. Vincent, ed., Charles C. Thomas,
    Springfield, Illinois.
LoPiccolo, J., 1977, Methodological issues in research on treatment
    of sexual dysfunction. Paper presented for NIMH Conf. on
    methodology in research on human sexuality, Washington D.C.
Lovius, J., Lovius, B.B.J., and Ley, P., 1973, Comprehensibility of
    the literature given to patients at a dental hospital,
    J. Publ. Health Dent., 33:23-26.
Lowe, J.C., and Mikulas, W.L., 1975, Use of written material in
    learning self-control of premature ejaculation, Psychol. Rep.,
    37:295-298.
Mahoney, M.J., 1972, Research issues in self-management, Beh. Ther.,
    3:45-63.
Mahoney, M.J., 1974, Self-reward and self-monitoring techniques for
    weight control, Beh. Ther., 5:48-57.
Mahoney, M.J., Moura, N.G.M., and Wade, T.C., 1973, Relative efficacy
    of self-reward, self-punishment, and self-monitoring techniques
    for weight loss, J. Cons. & Clin. Psychol., 40:404-407.
Mahoney, M.J., and Thoresen, C.E., 1974, "Self-Control: Power to
    the Person," Brooks/Cole, Monterey, California.
Marshall, W.L., Presse, L., and Andrews, W.R., 1976, A self-admin-
    istered program for public speaking anxiety, Beh. Res. & Ther.,
    14:33-40.
Marston, A.R., and Feldman, S.F., 1972, Toward the use of self-
    control in behaviour modification, J. Cons. & Clin. Psychol.,
    39:329-433.
Mascarino, E., and Goode, D., 1940, Reading as a psychological aid
    in the hypoglycemic treatment of schizophrenia, Med. Bull.
    Vet. Admin., 117:61.
Masters, W.H., and Johnson, V.E., 1970, "Human Sexual Inadequacy,"
    Little Brown, Boston.
Mathews, A., Bancroft, J., Whitehead, A., Hackmann, A., Julier, D.,
    Bancroft, J., Gath, D., and Shaw, P., 1976, The behavioural
    treatment of sexual inadequacy: a comparative study, Beh. Res.
    & Ther., 14:427-436.
Mathews, A., Teasdale, J., Munby, M., Johnston, D., and Shaw, P.,
    1977, A home-based treatment program for agoraphobia, Beh.
    Ther., 8:915-924.
McCarthy, B.W., Ryan, M., and Johnson, F., 1975, "Sexual Awareness:
    A Practical Approach," Scrimshaw Press, San Francisco.

McMullen, S., and Rosen, R.C., 1979, Self-administered masturbation
    training in the treatment of primary orgasmic dysfunction,
    J. Cons. & Clin. Psychol., 47(5):912-918.
McNair, D.M., Lorr, M., and Callahan, D.M., 1963, Patient and
    therapist influences on quitting psychotherapy, J. Consult.
    Psychol., 27:10-17.
Meichenbaum, D., 1977, "Cognitive-Behavior Modification: An In-
    tegrative Approach," Plenum Press, New York.
Melamed, B., and Lang, P.J., 1967, Study of the automated de-
    sensitisation of fear. Paper read at the meeting of the Mid-
    western Psychol. Assoc., Chicago.
Nelson, R.O., 1977, Methodological issues in assessment via self-
    monitoring, in: "Behavioral Assessment: New Directions in
    Clinical Psychology," J.D. Cone & N.P. Hawkins, eds., Brunner/
    Mazel, New York.
Oathout, M.C., 1954, Books and mental patients, Libr. J., 79:405-410,
    (March 1).
O'Brien, T.P., and Kelly, J.E., 1980, A comparison of self-directed
    and therapist-directed practice for fear reduction, Beh. Res. &
    Ther., 18:573-579.
Peterson, M.C., 1935, The hospital library in relation to psychiatric
    research, Trans. Amer. Hosp. Assoc., 37:608-614.
Phillips, R.E., Johnson, G.D., and Geyer, A., 1972, Self-administered
    systematic desensitisation, Beh. Res. & Ther., 10:93-96.
Powell, J.W., Stone, A.R., and Frank, J.D., 1952, Group reading and
    group therapy: a concurrent test, Psychiat., 15:33-51.
Raley, P.E., 1976, "Making Love: How to be Your Own Sex Therapist,"
    Dial Press, New York.
Repucci, N.D., and Baker, B.L., 1969, Self-desensitisation: implica-
    tions for treatment and teaching, in: "Advances in Behaviour
    Therapy, 1968," R.D. Rubin & C.M. Franks, eds., Academic Press,
    London.
Roman, M., 1957, "Reaching Delinquents Through Reading,"
    Charles C. Thomas, Springfield, Illinois.
Rosen, G.M., 1976a, The development and use of non-prescription
    behaviour therapies, Amer. Psychol., 31:139-141.
Rosen, G.M., 1976b, A manual for self-administered progressive
    relaxation, in: "Practical Psychology," J.P. Flanders, ed.,
    Harper & Row, New York.
Rosen, G.M., 1977, Non-prescription behaviour therapies and other
    self-help treatments: a reply to Goldiamond, Amer. Psychol.,
    32:178-179.
Rosen, G.M., 1978, Suggestions for an editorial policy on the review
    of self-help treatment books, Beh. Ther., 9:960.
Rosen, G.M., Glasgow, R.E., and Barrera, M. Jr., 1976, A controlled
    study to assess the clinical efficacy of totally self-admin-
    istered systematic desensitisation, J. Cons. & Clin. Psychol.,
    44:208-217.

Rosen, G.M., Glasgow R.E., and Barrera, M. Jr., 1977, A two-year
    follow-up on systematic desensitisation with data pertaining to
    the external validity of laboratory fear assessment, J. Cons. &
    Clin. Psychol., 45:1188-1189.
Roth, P.M., Caron, M.S., Ort, R.S., Berger, D.G., Albee, G.W., and
    Streeter, G.A., 1962, Patients' beliefs about peptic ulcer and
    its treatment, Ann. Int. Med., 56:72-80.
Rotter, J.B., 1966, Generalised expectancies for internal versus
    external control of reinforcement, Psychol. Monogs., 80:
    (1, whole No. 609).
Ryan, M.J., 1957, Bibliotherapy and psychiatry: changing concepts
    1937-1957, Spec. Librs., 48:197-199.
Schallow, J.R., 1975, Locus of control and success at self-modifica-
    tion, Beh. Ther., 6:667-671.
Schneck, J.M., 1944, Studies in bibliotherapy in a neuropsychiatric
    hospital, Amer. J. Phys. Med., 8:316-323.
Secord, P.F., and Backman, C.W., 1964, "Social Psychology,"
    McGraw-Hill, New York.
Shelton, J.L., 1979, Instigation therapy: using therapeutic homework
    to promote treatment gains, in: "Maximising Treatment Gains -
    Transfer Enhancement in Psychotherapy," A.P. Goldstein &
    F.H. Kanfer, eds., Academic Press, London.
Shrodes, C., 1949, "Bibliotherapy: A Theoretical and Clinical-
    Experimental Study," Unpublished Ph.D. dissertation,
    University of California.
Shrodes, C., 1960, Bibliotherapy: an application of psychoanalytic
    theory, Amer. Imago, 17:311-319.
Shrodes, C., 1961, The dynamics of reading: implications for biblio-
    therapy, Etc., 18:21-33.
Slavson, S.R., 1950, "Analytic Group Psychotherapy With Children,
    Adolescents & Adults," Columbia University Press, New York.
Smith, G.P., and Coleman, R.E., 1977, Processes underlying general-
    isation through participant modelling with self-directed
    practice, Beh. Res. & Ther., 15:204-206.
Spelman, M.S., and Ley, P., 1966, Knowledge of lung cancer and
    smoking habits, Brit. J. Soc. & Clin. Psychol., 5:207-210.
Stokes, T.F., and Baer, D.M., 1977, An implicit technology of
    generalisation, J. App. Beh. Anal., 10:349-367.
Stuart, R.B., and Davis, B., 1972, "Slim Chance in a Fat World:
    Behavioural Control of Obesity," Research Press, Champaign,
    Illinois.
Tews, R.M., 1970, Progress in bibliotherapy, in: "Advances in
    Librarianship (Vol I)," M.J. Voigt, ed., Academic Press,
    New York, pp.171-188.
Watson, D.L., and Tharp, R.G., 1972, "Self-Directed Behaviour:
    Self-Modification for Personal Adjustment," Brooks/Cole,
    Monterey, California.
Wild, A.A., and Evans, S.J., 1968, The patient and the x-ray
    department, B.M.J., 2:607-609.

Wilson, J.D., and Enoch, M.D., 1967, Estimation of drug rejection
    by schizophrenic in-patients, with analysis of clinical factors,
    Brit. J. Psychiat., 113:209-211.
Zeiss, R.A., 1977, "Self-administered Treatment for Premature
    Ejaculation: A Controlled Investigation," Unpublished Ph.D.
    dissertation, University of Oregon.
Zielinski, J.J., 1978, Maintenance of therapeutic gains: issues,
    problems and implementation, Prof. Psychol., 9(2):353-360.

CARDIAC REHABILITATION – AN EDINBURGH EXPERIENCE WITH

IMPLICATIONS FOR CLINICAL PSYCHOLOGY

Nicola A Stuckey   Senior Clinical Psychologist

Rehabilitation Unit
Astley Ainslie Hospital
Edinburgh, Scotland

INTRODUCTION

A Background to the Association Between the Heart and Psychology

The heart has had historic associations with the psyche for a long time. The heart is still considered to be the seat of emotions as reflected by expressions such as: "He really took what I said to heart" and "Let's have a heart to heart chat". In recent years, the role of stress has received much attention in terms of its place as a primary risk factor in the genesis of heart disease. This research has concentrated on two main areas: life events and Type A personality.

The life events literature has examined using standardised scales, the number of stressful life events experienced and the degree of upset to the individual caused by the particular event in cardiac patients. Such studies have been carried out retrospectively (Theorell and Rahe, 1971), and as twin studies (De Faire, 1975), to control for genetic factors. The results of this work are very interesting and suggest some association between life events and heart disease, although other authors have demonstrated a clear relationship between stressful life events and subsequent morbidity, (Rahe and Arthur, 1978). However, cardiac patients once they have experienced a heart attack, readily look for preceding stresses as an explanation for their illness.

Type A personality is a concept first investigated by Rosenman et al (1975) and subsequently taken up by Jenkins. The concept gained credibility when a prospective study of several thousand

individuals showed that those who went on to have heart attacks were
able to be differentiated on a measure of Type A or B personality.
The Type A individual is time-pressured, striving, ambitious and
determined, while the Type B individual is more easy going and
relaxed. Assessment of Type A personality can only be by structured
interview carried out by an interviewer trained by Rosenman and
Friedman. Jenkins has recently developed a rather complex scale for
this purpose (Jenkins, 1979). While high associations have been
demonstrated between heart disease and measures of Type A, it is a
somewhat tenuous concept which may be specific to a North American
culture and not apply to others. It may well be measuring something
important, but at present the measures indicate a strong bias
towards the white collar, Anglo-Saxon male. There are dangers in
accepting a package wholesale and applying it in such a complex
area as aetiology of heart disease where the eventual answer will
undoubtedly be multi-factorial.

Outcome of Patients Following Heart Attack or Myocardial Infarction (MI)

    Another major area of psychological research in recent years
has been the investigation of sequelae of a heart attack in terms
of personal and social cost. A heart attack very often comes out
of the blue and still has connotations of invalidism for many people.
Public opinion has not yet caught up with the positive changes in
medical policies to expectations following a heart attack. Many
individuals cope well and readjust to everyday life with little
difficulty. Others do not find this process so easy.

    Assessment of outcome depends on who is making the assessment.
The physician is rightly concerned with physical measures such as:
survival, ECG changes, angiography findings, left ventricular
function and symptoms of angina and breathlessness. The patient
will also be concerned about survival, residual symptoms and the
state of his heart, but may place more emphasis on factors such as
ability to resume work, social and sporting activities, ability to
alter habits such as smoking and diet, ability to maintain a
positive self-image and resume family and married life.

    Lamm and Dorrosiev (1978) cite data from the WHO Myocardial
Infarction Community Registers, where only 40% of survivors had
returned to full activity at 12 months post-MI. Cay et al (1973)
found 66% of patients with a first MI working at 4 months and only
one third of these patients working as hard as prior to admission.
These findings were virtually identical at 12 months' follow-up.
While residual physical symptoms were related to ability to work,
only 44% of patients with angina encountered work problems.
Patients showing emotional upset at 4 months post-MI were
significantly more likely to have encountered work difficulties than
those not upset (p<.001).

Anxiety and depression have been noted in post-MI patients by several authors lasting longer than would be considered an appropriate response. Cay et al (1972) found emotional upset in 61% of first MI patients while in the ward, 51% at 4 months and 56% at one year. Stern et al (1977) found 70% of those depressed immediately post-MI remained so throughout follow-up, failing to return to work and/or sexual function. Mayou et al (1978) have reported significantly higher levels of anxiety and depression amongst spouses when compared with patients.

This brief review of outcome studies indicates that in general those who do not cope well with having had an MI continue to have difficulty in adjustment and this difficulty is correlated with problems in returning to work and leisure activities ($p < .01$, Cay et al, 1973). Presence of emotional upset is also independent of severity of infarct (Stern et al, 1976; Cay et al, 1973).

CONTRIBUTION OF REHABILITATION

Rehabilitation programmes for patients following a heart attack have begun to be offered in many parts of the world. These programmes have been initiated for a variety of reasons: the shift of emphasis in medical thinking that a heart attack should not necessarily preclude an individual from exercising and returning to a virtually normal life; heart disease is an epidemic in the Western world and the social cost of unemployment and psychological morbidity is an unnecessarily high price to pay; patient demand for a better quality of life; and perhaps also the fact that some cardiologists have taken up jogging!

Rehabilitation programmes vary greatly in their components and their aims. They fall, however, into three basic categories.

Physical Training Programmes. This is usually a relatively high intensity exercise programme lasting 12 months or longer, with a view to significantly improving cardiac function and exercise ability. Outcome is measured largely in terms of prevention of death and reinfarction. To date this has not been unequivocally demonstrated.

Educational and/or Counselling Programmes. Such programmes aim to modify risk factors such as smoking and weight and to advise on exercise. This may be done individually or in groups where other issues relating to recovery and adjustment are discussed. Spouses are frequently included. Timing is usually during admission and early convalescence. Group content is not psychotherapy but information and education. A randomised controlled trial by Naismith et al (1979) reported significantly earlier return to work and more social independence in the rehabilitation group.

Combined Exercise and Educational Programmes. The exercise
component to these programmes is aimed at giving patients confidence
in their ability to resume activities, teach a sensible approach to
exercise and help establish safe limits which are often higher than
patients set themselves. The educational component is as described
above. Improving mortality and reinfarction rates is not a specific
aim of such programmes. They usually last during admission and the
following 2-3 months.

Naughton (1978) has demonstrated a significant increase in
physical work capacity (uncontrolled). Improved emotional state,
return to work, and confidence has been reported by Prosser et al,
(1978), Kavanagh et al (1975) and Naughton (1978).

Britain has been slow to adopt any such rehabilitation schemes
although WHO is currently conducting a multi-centre European trial,
and comprehensive programmes are offered in many places in Canada
eg Dr Kavanagh's unit in Toronto, and in the USA. Wholesale
application of a rehabilitation programme may, however, not be
appropriate as many patients make a satisfactory recovery from their
MI. The question of selecting patients for rehabilitation poses
the problem of predicting which individual, when in hospital, is
"at risk" of finding difficulty in resuming normal life.

Predicting Outcome

Various predictive factors have been identified by authors
which could be used to select patients for rehabilitation.
Significantly high levels of anxiety and/or depression while in the
ward (Cay et al, 1973; Kavanagh et al, 1975; Philip et al, 1980),
severity of infarct (Philip et al, 1980), existing employment
problems (Schiller and Baker, 1976), demographic factors (Garrity,
1973), and strength of personality resources (Philip et al, 1980).
This is by no means an exhaustive list, and outcome is likely to be
determined by multiple factors so any prediction must be made on the
basis of a variety of measures. Physical factors such as symptoms
of angina and breathlessness, general cardiac state and additional
complications, undoubtedly play their part in determining outcome.
However, it would appear from the evidence available that much
weight must be placed on psychological and social factors.

EDINBURGH CARDIAC REHABILITATION PROGRAMME

The number of patients passing through the Coronary Care Unit
(CCU) of the Royal Infirmary of Edinburgh (RIE) with a myocardial
infarction each year is approximately 480. In light of these large
numbers and the increasing interest in rehabilitation, a pilot
cardiac rehabilitation service was initiated between the RIE and

the rehabilitation unit of the Astley Ainslie Hospital (AAH), Edinburgh. Some caution was expressed by the physicians at the outset about the effect of such a programme. Reservations were expressed about the value of exercise, and also that psychological or social work presence might induce unnecessary introspection and iatrogenic anxiety. However, agreement was reached that a pilot service should be set up, using the existing staff and facilities of the two hospitals, and an evaluative study to be initiated at some point in the future.

Operation of the Service

Patients to be included in the service were limited to 55 years and under, male and female, who were transferred to eight of the twelve medical wards after leaving the CCU of RIE. The service was to be operated on two levels, all patients included in the rehabilitation programme while in-patients in RIE, and a proportion of these patients to attend an exercise-based rehabilitation programme at AAH approximately 6 weeks post-MI.

Royal Infirmary Rehabilitation Programme (see Table 1). The physiotherapist is the first person to make contact with patients in the CCU and continues to see them in the medical ward. She gives simple mobilising exercises, increases level of activity during their stay, and gives specific advice on exercise when home. This is done with consultation with ward medical and nursing staff.

A structured interview is carried out by the clinical psycho-logist (NAS) when the patient has been in the medical ward for about four days. This timing is to ensure that the patient's medical condition has settled. This interview covers information that might provide an indication of the individual's future outcome in social and psychological terms, eg work record, type of employment, response to previous and present illness, social and financial problems and emotional upset. This was assessed by means of clinical ratings and the Delusions Symptoms Sign Inventory (DSSI) (Foulds and Bedford, 1975).

Patients and spouses are given the opportunity to attend a discussion meeting while in the ward, run by the psychologist, cardiac social worker and nursing staff. Concern was expressed initially that such a meeting might serve to raise anxieties of patients as "a little knowledge can be a dangerous thing". The emphasis of this meeting was very definitely not psychotherapeutic but practical discussion of risk factors in relation to heart disease and how patients should modify these - eg smoking, diet, etc. Information on what constitutes a heart attack and angina is covered, using as a basis the information booklet which all patients receive. Other 'do's and don'ts' as consequences of a heart attack are also discussed.

Table 1. RIE Rehabilitation Programme – Male and Female
          MI Patients Aged 55 and Under

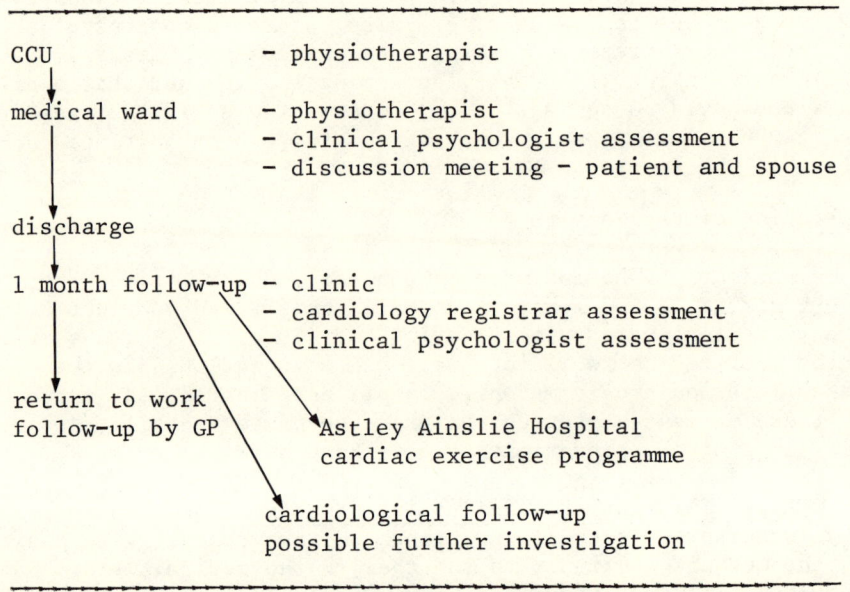

Patients are then discharged and reviewed one month later by a
cardiology registrar when they are also given an exercise tolerance
test. This assesses how the heart performs under exercise and the
degree to which the heart has recovered. The clinical psychologist
makes a further assessment at this review of activity level since
discharge, confidence to exercise, employment problems, social
problems, emotional state and understanding about their physical
condition.

At this point all patients are given the opportunity to attend
the Astley Ainslie Hospital cardiac rehabilitation programme unless
there are any medical contra-indications. For the first year of the
service, fewer people attended the AAH programme as criteria for
selection were used, but this is now not the case. Some patients
do not wish to take up the offer and are discharged to the care of
their general medical practitioner (GP) and to return to work,
although approximately half the patients have attended AAH during
1980 (see Table 2).

Astley Ainslie Hospital Rehabilitation Programme (see Table 3).
Patients participating in this programme following their review
appointment, attend three mornings a week (9-11.30 am) for approximately 4 weeks. The class is based round an exercise programme
involving a warm-up, exercise circuit, period on the bicycle
ergometer and walking practice on a treadmill. The amount of

Table 2. Numbers Through Cardiac Rehabilitation Programme –
MI's Aged 55 and Under

	1979	1980 (Jan–Aug)
Total no in rehab programme (RIE)	130	91
No referred to AAH at 6 weeks	29 (22%)	44 (48%)
Did not attend	2	3
Did not complete programme	1	1

exercise each patient does is determined by the guidelines set down
following the exercise tolerance test at RIE, and by pulse rate and
general appearance in the class. This class is run by physio-
therapists with medical and nursing cover. The aim of the exercise
is not high training, but teaching each individual their correct pace
and where their limitations lie which are often much higher than they
think.

All patients are taught relaxation exercises appropriate to
their cardiac condition and a tape is played at the end of each
class. Many opportunities exist for individual discussion with the
clinical psychologist or other staff members. A discussion meeting

Table 3. AAH Rehabilitation Programme

Time	– 3 mornings weekly for an average of 4 weeks
Programme	– exercise class run by physiotherapist, medical and nursing cover provided, with one consultant responsible
	Relaxation
	Individual discussion and group meetings with clinical psychologist
	Dietician optional swimming class relatives domestic activities simulated work weekly case conference

on subjects such as risk factors, return to work, social activities etc is frequently held by the clinical psychologist and nursing staff Relatives are always invited to come and discuss progress and any other issues with the staff.

Patients are usually expected to return to work at the finish of the class and liaison is made with the GP about this, also with the employer where appropriate. For some patients work activities are simulated in the class in order to increase the individual's confidence in his ability. The Disablement Resettlement Officer is available if necessary. Domestic activities can also be practised with the occupational therapy department and where families are over-protective, this can often be of great benefit. The Dietician attends weekly for advice on weight loss and there is a weekly swimming group at the local pool where a member of nursing staff is present.

The benefits that patients receive from this programme are difficult to quantify. They undoubtedly gain in knowledge of the correct way to exercise and how to translate this learning into everyday activities. Many take up new activities such as swimming and golf. Their general fitness is improved and many patients have stopped smoking and lost weight. The most obvious gain to the observer is the increase in confidence to go about their everyday life and activities and improved sense of wellbeing. These, however, are difficult qualities to measure objectively.

Clinical Problems

The above gives only a very brief outline of the operation of this programme and in establishing a rehabilitation service many problems occurred. Various points from our experience may serve as a cautionary tale for others embarking on a similar venture, particularly for clinical psychologists wishing to work in a new field.

Anxieties and concerns expressed by medical and nursing staff in RIE about the introduction of a new service had to be taken seriously. Previous studies of cardiac rehabilitation had mixed results dependent on the kind of programme being offered. Some of the outcome measures did not relate to physical and medical factors as they were aiming to improve quality of life rather than survival and cardiac symptoms. Some of these studies were uncontrolled and thus the cause of improvement was not clear.

A psychologist is rarely involved with acute medical care and a clear picture of skills available and the potential role within treatment is unlikely to be held by existing staff. A common view is that a psychologist would only deal with patients who were psychiatrically disturbed or that he/she might stir up thoughts and anxieties within "normal" patients by delving too deeply and trying some sort of psychotherapy on them. Neither of these approaches is appropriate, not least as medical patients themselves are suspicious of why they are seeing a psychologist.

In view of the above comments, it was very important for this programme that rehabilitation was carried out with good liaison with the medical and nursing team involved with the patient. They have been dealing with post-MI patients for many years and frequently do not have the time to add the aspects to patient care which rehabilitation can provide.

The patients themselves are tired and still quite shaky in the early stages following a heart attack. It is not appropriate to ask them questions which require much concentration and do not appear to relate to their present condition. Thus any approach which smacks of psychotherapy, or an interview which goes on too long, or where very personal questions are asked in an open medical ward, is not appropriate. Timing and location of interviews had to fit in with ward routine.

A further problem encountered was that of frequent staff changes. Eight medical wards were covered by the scheme all with staff liable to change. Junior medical staff rotated every 3 or 6 months, while nursing staff also moved occasionally, to say nothing of changes due to shifts etc. The number of patients being transferred from CCU per month was approximately 13, and they would go to whichever ward was receiving that day. It was thus possible for a ward not to have contact with the rehabilitation team for some time and in that time for staff changes to take place. This would mean ensuring again that all staff were aware of the existence of the scheme and what was involved. Thus there was a need for frequent information meetings and liaison with staff in order to ensure continuity.

Staffing of the rehabilitation service was achieved by tacking on these duties to existing posts. This meant that it inevitably took second place when other matters became a priority. This became a particular problem when the cardiology registrar was having difficulty in covering his own duties regardless of an extra rehabilitation clinic, and brought about a temporary hiatus in follow-up. When any pilot service is initiated, it cannot be expected that all necessary staffing will be covered by the creation of new posts. It is essential, however, that responsibility for continuity of any service operating within a large acute hospital is taken by one consultant, for there are many points at which breakdown can occur before anyone has noticed difficulties. It is also important that all consultants feel that responsibility is being taken centrally by one person, where access to patients under their care is being sought.

Future Developments

The literature to date and the experience of running a pilot cardiac rehabilitation service in Edinburgh has clearly demonstrated the need for a service of some sort for patients following a heart attack. The present rehabilitation programme, while at times appearing tenuous due to staffing problems, is relatively rich with resources of staff and equipment. Not every district general hospital will have access to a psychologist for assessment of cardiac patients who might benefit from rehabilitation, or perhaps to physio-therapists who have the necessary expertise. It should, however, be possible to tease out the important components to such a programme in terms of (a) which type of patient is likely to gain from rehabilitation, ie selection of an "at risk" group; (b) what patients gain from a rehabilitation programme, ie evaluation with appropriate outcome measures.

It is intended that an evaluation will be carried out of the current cardiac rehabilitation programme using research staff in the near future. The important areas will be further development of measures for selection of patients and measures of outcome. Concepts such as confidence and morale appear very woolly and soft to outside observers. What is needed is a breakdown of such outcome variables into something which can be measured and is sensitive to change. Such areas of measurement are not peculiar to cardiac rehabilitation and have equal importance in other areas of rehabilitation and recovery from illness and surgery.

Methodological Problems

Introduction of any new service should include some element of evaluation. As stated earlier, the aims of this rehabilitation programme and expected benefits lie in qualitative rather than quantitative areas ie increased morale and confidence rather than reduction of symptoms and recurrence rate of heart attacks. In view of these aims the problem of finding objective measures which are valid, reliable and acceptable to physicians presents itself.

How outcome is measured depends upon the stance from which the problem is viewed. The physician has objective measures such as ECG recordings, cardiothoracic ratio, blood lipids, coronary angiograms, survival, reinfarction, to name a few. However, these are not the main areas which this cardiac rehabilitation programme aimed to induce change. Some acceptable measures exist for quanti-fying the presence of anxiety and depression, weight loss, cessation of smoking, and exercise tolerance. However, acceptable measurement of improved morale, increased confidence, ability to perform work and leisure activities, return to normality of family and married life, is not so easy to achieve. Psychologists should certainly

have the expertise and skills to develop new and adapt existing
measures for the purpose, but this is not the whole answer. Such
measures may be somewhat cumbersome, have low sensitivity to change
and above all not seem relevant to physicians who may not assess
outcome in these terms. The task of development of such measures
is an important one if any intervention with medical or surgical
patients of a social or psychological nature is to gain credibility.

A more specific problem of measurement is which anxiety and
depression scales are appropriate. Cardiac and other patients will
not tolerate lengthy questionnaires or those including psychiatric
items, at a time when they still feel unwell and their concentration
is limited. A measure suitable and acceptable to the population
being studied must be sought, and scales such as the MMPI are not
appropriate.

The prevalence of heart disease is such that it would be
impossible to provide a rehabilitation service for everyone
experiencing a heart attack. The literature clearly suggests that
some individuals remain unable to resume much of their previous
life following an MI for reasons which appear largely independent
of their physical state. If a rehabilitation service is to be
offered to a selected group of patients, one must be able to select
on the basis of prediction of future problems in adaptation. Much
clinical data is already available on predictive factors and it
should also be possible to devise a method of measurement and
prediction of those patients "at risk". The current Edinburgh
rehabilitation programme hopes to go on to do this, once it is
possible to make follow-up assessments of patients who have not
participated in the exercise rehabilitation programme.

IMPLICATIONS FOR CLINICAL PSYCHOLOGY

Psychology has had associations with heart disease for some
time as outlined earlier. The role of a clinical psychologist has
been both clinical and research in this particular programme.
Involvement in the clinical aspects of the work has proved essential
to gaining a grasp of the complexity of the picture of response of
individuals to a heart attack and to go on to use this knowledge for
development of appropriate measures. It is, however, by no means
essential that a psychologist can be the only person qualified to
carry out all these clinical tasks. It could as well be done by a
cardiac nurse or social worker who had the right degree of interest
and training. In fact, such personnel are much more commonly
involved in cardiac programmes in USA, Australia and New Zealand.

The model of treatment on which this rehabilitation programme
is based, is equally applicable to other conditions such as gastric
ulcer, amputees, surgery, hip replacements and others. An assess-

ment of the individual's personality resources, previous history of coping ability, emotional state, employment and social factors all combine to influence eventual outcome and adaptation to ill-health.

Clinical psychologists are now moving towards working with a different group of patients such as those with medical and surgical problems from those seen traditionally. Any such involvement should take into account the fact that many fantasies and uncertainties exist about the potential contribution of clinical psychology amongst those who are unfamiliar with the profession. Memories are long and care should be taken not to prejudice attitudes towards psychologists' involvement in areas of work which will undoubtedly prove fruitful in the future. The experience of the Edinburgh cardiac rehabilitation programme indicates that there is a critical factor in determining the success of such a project. Where a team of staff from various professional backgrounds and interests are working in a large acute hospital, it is essential that one consultant takes overall responsibility for the management and clinical liaison of such a project. Without this backing, any such project will have many difficulties.

This cardiac rehabilitation programme has had equally valuable and important contributions from each team member. Clinical psychology has much to offer both in clinical skills and development of methods of measurement. These are the tools of the trade and where it is important to evaluate any new service, psychology should have a key role to play.

Cardiac rehabilitation is a fascinating and rewarding area of work where one is constantly learning and uncovering new areas of interest. The services available in the UK are limited and the more that evaluation of such programmes can be put into practice, the more the future quality of life for those experiencing a heart attack should be improved.

REFERENCES

Cay, E.L., Vetter, N., Philip, A.E., and Dugard, P., 1972, Psychological status during recovery from an acute heart attack, J. Psychosom. Res., 16:425.
Cay, E.L., Vetter, N., Philip, A.E., and Dugard, P., 1973, Return to work after a heart attack, J. Psychosom. Res., 16:231.
De Faire, U., 1975, Life change patterns prior to death in ischaemic heart disease: a study on death – discordant twins, J. Psychosom. Res., 19:273.
Foulds, G.A., and Bedford, A., 1975, Hierarchy of classes of personal illness, Psychol. Med., 5:181-192.
Garrity, T.F., 1973, Vocational adjustment after first myocardial infarction, Soc. Sci. Med., 7:705.

Jenkins, C.D., Zyzanski, S.J., and Rosenman, R.H., 1979, "Jenkins
    Activity Survey, Form C," Psychological Corporation, New York.
Kavanagh, T., Shephard, R.J., Tuck, J.A., and Qureshi, S., 1975,
    Depression following myocardial infarction, Can. Med. Assoc. J.,
    113:23.
Lamm, G., and Dorrosiev, D.L., 1978, WHO collaborative study on
    rehabilitation of and comprehensive secondary prevention with
    patients after acute MI, Advances in Cardiology, 24:179-186.
Mayou, R.A., Foster, A., and Williamson, B., 1978, Psychological
    and social effects of myocardial infarction on wives, B.M.J.,
    1:699.
Naismith, L., Robinson, J., Shaw, G., and MacIntyre, M., 1979,
    Psychological rehabilitation after myocardial infarction,
    B.M.J., 17 Feb, p.439.
Naughton, J., 1978, The national exercise and heart disease project,
    Cardiology, 63:352.
Prosser, G., Carson, P., Gelson, A., Tucker, H., Neophytou, M.,
    Phillips, R., and Simpson, R., 1978, Assessing the psychological
    effects of an exercise training programme for patients following
    myocardial infarction, Brit. J. Med. Psych., 51:95.
Rahe, R.H., and Arthur, R.J., 1978, Life change and illness studies:
    past history and future directions, J. Human Stress, March, 3.
Rosenman, R.H., Brand, R.J., Jenkins, C.D., Friedman, M., Straus, R.,
    and Wurm, M., Coronary heart disease in the western collaborat-
    ive group study - a final follow-up experience of 8½ years,
    J. Amer. Med. Assoc., 233:872.(1975)
Schiller, E., and Baker, J., 1976, Return to work after myocardial
    infarction - evaluation of planned rehabilitation and of a
    predictive rating scale, Med. J. Aust., 1:859.
Stern, M.J., Pascale, L., and McLoone, J.B., 1976, Psychosocial
    adaptation following an acute myocardial infarction, J. Chron.
    Dis., 29:513.
Stern, M.J., Pascale, L., and Ackerman, A., 1977, Life adjustment
    post-MI: determining predictive variables, Arch. Int. Med.,
    137:1680.
Theorell, T., and Rahe, RH., 1971, Psychosocial factors and myo-
    cardial infarction. I. An in-patient study in Sweden,
    J. Psychosom. Res., 15:25.

THE PSYCHOLOGICAL TREATMENT OF PRIMARY DYSMENORRHOEA

Brian Sheffield

Area Department of Clinical Psychology
Hope Hospital
Salford, England

Ana M Gomez

University of Manchester
England

INTRODUCTION

Primary dysmenorrhoea was first reported in the medical literature by B.T. Frank (1931). Dalton (1969) differentiated primary dysmenorrhoea into two distinct syndromes: congestive and spasmodic dysmenorrhoea described in detail in Tasto and Insel (1977). Chesney and Tasto (1975) devised the Menstrual Symptom Questionnaire to distinguish these symptom clusters. Dalton (1969) also suggested that the menstrual discomfort of spasmodic dysmenorrhoea might be related to muscular contractions, while the menstrual discomfort of congestive dysmenorrhoea might result from water retention and ischaemia. As yet no agreement has been reached concerning either the aetiology of the condition or its treatment. The physiological basis and psychological treatment now will be reviewed.

Incidence

Estimates of the incidence of dysmenorrhoea vary widely, but there seems little doubt that dysmenorrhoea has a significant impact on the life of many women. Absenteeism due to sickness occurs significantly more frequently during the four days of the premenstruum and the days of menstruation. Estimates of the number of

women requiring absences from work due to dysmenorrhoea range from
3% to 10% (Ylikorkala and Dawwood, 1978; Berjsjo, 1979). The
academic work of schoolgirls is allegedly affected by menstruation
(Dalton, 1961, 1968), and school absenteeism is reported as high
during menstruation (Widholm, 1979). Dalton (1961) has also
indicated that the crime rate in women increased during the paramenstruum and menstruation. Of acute admissions to psychiatric
wards, 46% are admitted in menstruation and the paramenstruum
(Dalton, 1969, 1977; Kramp, 1968). Glass (1971) suggested that the
number of suicidal attempts was three times higher during the paramenstruum than at other times.

Authors have also suggested that there is some disruption of
family life during the paramenstruum and menstruation, for example,
Coppen and Kessel (1963), suggested there was a 21% reduction in
daily activities as menstruation approached and Dalton (1967)
suggested that menstruation in the mother played a part in children's
illnesses.

Aetiology

Physiological Basis. Frank (1931) suggested the aetiology was
due to the continued circulation of an excessive amount of female
sex hormones in the blood producing in some people cardiovascular
disturbance but in others definite psychic disturbance and nervous-
ness. Green and Dalton (1953) first used the term premenstrual
syndrome proposing as a possible aetiology an abnormal oestradiol/
progesterone ratio and pointing out the importance of the symptom
of water retention. Later investigators such as Reeves (1971) agree
on the possible role of electrolyte imbalance and weight gain. The
hypothesis postulated at the time was a change in sodium metabolism
which occurs to a slight extent in healthy women and to an exagg-
erated extent in sufferers from the premenstrual syndrome. The
rhythm of this change seems to be controlled by the level of
oestradiol in the tissues and this, in its turn, to be under the
partial control of progesterone. Excessive water retention may
therefore be present even with a fairly low level of oestradiol if
progesterone is entirely lacking; or absent with a very high level
of oestradiol if progesterone is present in adequate quantities.
Dalton (1961) defined premenstrual tension as mood changes, headaches, tiredness, bloatedness or mastitis during the premenstruum
and dysmenorrhoea as pain during menstruation. She later presented
a wide range of symptomatology including psychological and somatic
problems and established the possibility of two different entities,
the premenstrual syndrome and dysmenorrhoea (Dalton, 1964). The
possible aetiological sites proposed are the hypothalamus-pituitary
system and adrenal glands. In the latter, the adrenal cortex may
have a relationship to symptomatology. The two different types of
dysmenorrhoea: congestive and spasmodic proposed by Dalton (1969),

are still believed to be caused by different levels of circulating
ovarian hormones, oestrogen and progesterone. It was believed that
many, but not all, symptoms are characterised by water retention and
accumulation of cellular fluids. In the premenstrual syndrome the
psychological symptoms of tension, irritability, depression and
lethargy are thought to be due to sodium retention and potassium
depletion.

Other physiological theories include the inherent hyper-
contractivity of the uterus (Ylikorkala and Dawwood, 1978; Filler
and Warner, 1970) and increased prostaglandin production (Lundstrom,
1976; Ylikorkala and Dawwood, 1978).

Psychodynamic. Other aetiological theories include myth and
taboo, sociological and cultural influences and psychological
variables. Psychoanalytic theories regard as an important aetiological factor that "increased heterosexual desire revives Oedipal
regression" (Ylikorkala and Dawwood, 1978).

This revival of infantile fantasies is important in the disorder
(Horney, 1933). The guilt feelings are directed towards the mother
(Edwards, 1950; Wengraf, 1964) and they constitute suppressed
material which may be reached, yet the repressed material can be
difficult to get at and there may be symptom substitution. Other
factors in the disorder are: the rejection of the feminine role
(Israel, 1938; Edwards, 1950; Berry and McGuire, 1972); the first
menstrual period (Edwards, 1950; Wengraf, 1944); psychosexual
immaturity (Edwards, 1950); neuroticism (Wengraf, 1944) and the
failure to conceive resulting in the "weeping uterus" (Ylikorkala
and Dawwood, 1978).

Theoretical Approaches to Treatment

Psychoanalytical. Psychoanalysis, combined with hypnosis was
used as a treatment method by Kroger and Freed (1943). Five cases
were treated successfully, using age regression and hypno-analysis.
A further four cases were treated by hypnosis, suggestions being
made that the next menses would be free from pain and discomfort,
and all cases were reported permanently cured. Hypnosis has been
found to bring about a complete cessation of dysmenorrhoeic cramps
in a great many cases (Wengraf, 1944). Leckie (1964) used hypnotherapy on 25 dysmenorrhoeic subjects. During 30 minute sessions
the patient is hypnotised and it is suggested that menstruation is
a normal physiological process, that some blood congestion is
present but that it is the expectance and anxiety which causes the
pain by tightening the womb's neck. If the patient relaxes no
discomfort will be felt. She is also reminded of her health,
matureness and happiness and it is stressed that her following
periods will be normal and regular. Of the 25 cases, 20 (80%) were

apparently cured; 17 of these, by direct suggestion with follow-ups
from 6 months to 2 years. The other 3 cases, in which direct suggestion was not successful, were treated with depth therapy (age
regression, abreaction, dream therapy) and were found to be a
manifestation of deeper problems. Five cases (20%) are reported as
failures. It is argued that in these cases there was little motivation and/or an aggressive attitude. No symptom substitution was
found, the patient was either cured or retained the symptom and
judged as a failure. It was suggested that the gynaecologist should
be trained in hypnotherapy because of the close bond with the
patient.

    Psychosomatic. Psychosomatic approaches to the problem have
been tried by Fortin et al (1958) and Hunter and Rolf (1943). Hunter
and Rolf do not argue that the disorder has a psychodynamic origin
but rather that it is initiated and developed by physiological
changes. This process of sensory conditioning gives rise to a
neurosis and the patient's pain threshold is reduced. Four cases
were reported to be treated successfully: 2 treated by narco-
suggestion, and 1 by hypnosis and oestrogen. In the fourth case a
subject with no symptomatology underwent hypnosis and it was suggested that her next period would be extremely painful. Symptoms of
dysmenorrhoea were induced, this being suggestive that the disorder
is a result of physiological change. The authors concluded that
one method (surgical, medical, suggestion, placebo, hypnosis) is
as effective as another. Fortin et al (1958) views dysmenorrhoea as
a psychosomatic effect mediated through the autonomic nervous system.
25 dysmenorrhoeic subjects and 20 normal subjects were used in a
controlled study. 7 psychiatric interviews were carried out to
study psychological variables, fluid retention was compared in both
groups and a diuretic was given to the experimental group. No
significant differences were found between the groups as to fluid
retention nor between treated and untreated subjects. In the
psychiatric findings, 18 subjects of the experimental group showed
improvement in tension states and physical symptoms, 8 showed no
improvement and 3 became worse. From this group, 13 subjects
received the premenstrual diuretic; of these 9 improved, 2 showed
no improvement and 2 became worse. In this group a negative reaction
to menarche was found, resentment towards menstruation, unhealthy
sexual attitudes, family incidence of premenstrual tension and
trends towards depression and self-depreciation. The control group
showed no changes, except in one case in which premenstrual tension
was developed when traumatic material was revealed by the subject.
In general, this group showed greater acceptance of the female role
and no feelings of resentment or shame towards menstruation. It
was concluded that many patients suffering from premenstrual tension
are amenable to psychotherapy.

    Gill (1943) suggested that menstruation appears to be aston-
ishingly susceptible to psychological influences and it is perhaps

the ease with which the process can be influenced which accounts
both for the frequency of menstrual distress and the facility with
which menstruation is influenced by hypnosis and superficial
psychological explanation. Suggested examples are the cessation
of menstruation due to psychological factors such as "false pregnancy" or prolonged bleeding to avoid sexual intercourse (Novak and
Hanvik, 1929).

Israel (1938) implied that an anxiety neurosis about menstruation could develop by suggestion such as in the case of girls
influenced by their mothers, family and friends. The pain is a
result and even if an organic cause is found, there always exists
a "complex psychogenic overlay".

In trying to establish the relationship between the incidence
of premenstrual tension syndrome between normal and neurotic patients
Rees (1953) found a higher incidence in the latter group. However,
when comparing within the normal group with and without the syndrome,
no significant difference was found in personality, stability or
neurosis. It was concluded that neurosis is not sufficient to
account for the premenstrual syndrome. However, a positive correlation was established between the rating of neurotic constitution
and rating of premenstrual tension. Subjects with severe premenstrual tension have significantly higher incidence of maladjustment and the greater predisposition to breakdown the more intense
the premenstrual syndrome. "The condition cannot be dismissed as
neurotic or primarily psychogenic" and is seen as a complex psycho-
physical state determined by a variety of factors; physiological,
constitutional and psychological.

Psychometric. In another study, Coppen and Kessel (1963), in
which 50 English women were given the Maudsley Personality Inventory
and a questionnaire with the symptomatology of menstrual problems,
there was no significant correlation found between dysmenorrhoea
and neuroticism. However, premenstrual symptoms such as headaches,
sweating and reduction of activity during menstruation were significantly correlated with neuroticism and also correlated with premenstrual irritability, tension and depression. The authors conclude
"Dysmenorrhoea is not correlated with neuroticism and extraversion.
This survey provides no evidence to justify dysmenorrhoea as being
regarded as a psychosomatic condition or one that calls for
psychological treatment".

It has also been reported that menstrual problems are more
common among women being diagnosed as suffering from emotional
illness. Personality factors and attitudes towards menstruation
were studied by Levitt and Lubin (1967). A menstrual history and
Menstrual Attitude Inventory were given to 190 subjects and correlated with the frequency of psychosomatic complaints taken from
the Students Health Service Record. Of 25 intercorrelations between

personality variables and 3 menstrual indices computed, 14 reached
significance. Results showed psychosomatic and menstrual complaints
to be modestly correlated and a general tendency of women who have
psychosomatic problems to have menstrual disturbances. Those
students with unfavourable attitudes have more frequent and intense
menstrual complaints, have unwholesome attitudes toward menstruation
and a tendency to be emotionally unstable. No correlation was found
between menstrual attitude and psychosomatic complaints. It has
also been reported that women with the premenstrual syndrome show
more psychiatric symptomatology than those without it (Glass, 1971).

Treatment by Behavioural Methods

Primary Dysmenorrhoea and Anxiety Reduction Techniques. Mullen
(1968) reviewed evidence of the effectiveness of behaviour therapy
in psychophysiological sexual reactions. He described the treatment
of a 31 year old woman who had suffered from dysmenorrhoea for 21
years. The patient had undergone medical and physical treatment as
well as hypnotherapy with no improvement. She was an only child,
with an unhappy home life but a reasonably compatible marriage and
normal interpersonal relationships. The dysmenorrhoea was associated
with anxiety attacks which she suffered about 14 days before the
menses. She also was reported to become anxious at the sight of
pregnant women. The treatment used was a process of reconditioning
through systematic desensitisation (SD) aided by relaxation training
and a relearning procedure. Two hierarchies were constructed: one
concerned with the patient's behaviour related to menstruation and
the other related to pregnancy. The treatment lasted a period of
6 months with 16 visits, 2-3 items of the hierarchy being desen-
sitised per session. By the sixth visit the patient had completed
the first 16/22 items of the menstruation hierarchy. She reported
a change of attitude towards menstruation and very little pain and
discomfort with the period for the first time in years. On the
twelfth visit the subject had mastered all the items on both
hierarchies with no anxiety but some pain remained during menstruation. The last 4 items of the hierarchy were completed to prevent
spontaneous recovery and she was asked to practise relaxation training at home while manipulating or wearing a sanitary napkin. During
the last visit, the patient reported her last 2 periods to be free
from pain and had a carefree attitude towards menstruation. A
6 month follow-up showed that her improvement remained and no symptom
substitution was found. It was hypothesised that the patient
rejected the feminine role and used dysmenorrhoea as a means of
obtaining attention during childhood, and later was used to attract
attention from her husband to avoid undesirable chores.

Another study using SD was undertaken some years later by
Mullen (1971) treating successfully 5 college students with
dysmenorrhoea. The experimental and control groups were tested

before and after the study on the Symptom Rating Scale and a significant reduction in symptomatology in the experimental group was
reported.

Tasto and Chesney (1974) used other behavioural techniques in
the treatment of primary dysmenorrhoea. Tasto and Chesney (1974)
treated 7 female students suffering from primary dysmenorrhoea by
group muscle relaxation training and imagery associated with pain
reduction during menstruation. They argued that the development of
individual hierarchies and sessions used by Mullen (1971) were too
complex and time consuming. They hypothesised that a state of muscle
relaxation could be paired with imagery associated with pain during
menstruation, and the imagery could gain cue properties so as to
invoke muscle relaxation and so reduce pain due to muscle tension.
The subjects completed the Symptom Rating Scale and a Menstrual
Anxiety Scale (Mullen, 1971) on 3 occasions. The first occasion was
10 weeks before treatment, the second immediately before treatment
and finally after 2 menstrual periods following the end of treatment.
Treatment lasted 4 weeks each of 5 group sessions. The first 2
sessions were used to teach relaxation procedures, in the third
session imagery was paired with neutral scenes, and in the last 2
sessions imagery associated with menstrual pain reduction was paired
with deep muscle relaxation. Subjects practised relaxation at home
until the last scales were administered. There were no significant
differences between the first two administrations, indicating that
the passage of time produced no amelioration of the symptomatology.
After treatment, significant differences were found on all scales.
It was concluded that behaviour therapy is effective in the treatment
of primary dysmenorrhoea for college students, "the fact that this
treatment was successful without hierarchies is important because
it indicates that subjects can be treated quickly, in a group, with
minimal therapist-patient contact" (Tasto and Chesney, 1974). It
was noted, however, that not all subjects responded to treatment,
which might relate to Dalton's theory (1969) of the existence of two
types of dysmenorrhoea.

Spasmodic and Congestive Dysmenorrhoea and Anxiety Reduction
Techniques. Chesney and Tasto (1975) suggested that behaviour
therapy and muscle relaxation might be a more effective treatment
of spasmodic rather than congestive dysmenorrhoea. 69 female
volunteers were used in the study. The Menstrual Symptom
Questionnaire (MSQ) (Chesney and Tasto, 1975) was used to differentiate the subjects into the congestive and spasmodic groups, and
the Symptom Severity Scale (SSS) developed by Mullen (1971) was
used to assess the degree of symptomatology before and after treatment. A total of 6 groups were formed by a 2 (congestive versus
spasmodic) X 3 (behaviour therapy versus pseudo treatment versus
waiting list) factorial design. The treatment period was 5 weeks
with 40 minute sessions each week. In the behaviour therapy group
a standard relaxation procedure was taught during the first two

sessions. In the third session the relaxation was paired with
neutral imagery and in the fourth and fifth sessions the relaxation
was paired with imagery associated with the onset of menstruation.
After these 5 weeks the subjects were asked to keep practising at
home until the SSS was administered again. The pseudo-treatment
group also had weekly sessions which consisted of a self-directed
group discussion which included topics such as causes of
dysmenorrhoea, symptomatology, etc. The control group, which
consisted of a waiting list was sent letters asking them to wait
until treatment was available since, due to the large number of
patients, it was not possible to provide treatment at that time.
Two months after treatment was over, all the subjects were asked to
take the SSS. The major clinical finding was that behaviour therapy
with scenes, not necessarily in the form of hierarchies, was highly
effective with spasmodic dysmenorrhoea but did not necessarily have
a positive effect on congestive dysmenorrhoea. The pseudo-treatment
and control groups reported no significant decrease in symptoms.
The authors concluded that any change in the pseudo-treatment and
the congestive/behaviour modification groups was due to the group
treatment experiences and/or therapist contact, whereas in the
spasmodic dysmenorrhoea/behaviour modification group the change was
accounted for by the behavioural treatment.

     The results of this study support those of Mullen (1968, 1971)
and Tasto and Chesney (1974). It is argued that the greater reduction in symptomatology found by Mullen (1971) may have been due to
variations between the two studies. A possible explanation is that
the difference is not due to the use of hierarchies but to the
types of scenes used by Chesney and Tasto (1975) (menstrual pain
reduction rather than onset of menstruation), and/or sample
characteristics (more subjects with certain type of dysmenorrhoea).
In this study (Chesney and Tasto, 1975), the scenes used were
associated with the onset of menstruation as compared to the previous
study (Tasto and Chesney, 1974). It is thought that this might
account for the difference in effectiveness in both types of
dysmenorrhoea, since the imagery is more appropriate for spasmodic
dysmenorrhoea. However, since no reduction was found on the SSS
items characteristic of spasmodic dysmenorrhoea in the congestive
dysmenorrhoea group subjects, it was concluded that "the imagery
was probably not solely responsible for the differential effectiveness of the behaviour modification treatment" (Chesney and Tasto,
1975). It can, then, be concluded that behaviour modification is
effective in reducing the symptomatology of women suffering from
spasmodic dysmenorrhoea but not those with congestive dysmenorrhoea.
The authors point out the limitations of the study as to generalisation of results due to subjects' characteristics. Further study is
advised on the treatment method and in the use of the MSQ as a
diagnostic device.

Biofeedback. Adler and Adler (1979) reported that 5 patients receiving temperature feedback for migraine headaches spontaneously described the disappearance of symptoms of dysmenorrhoea. Tubbs and Carnahan (1976) reported on an uncontrolled study of 10 subjects who received EMG and temperature feedback. 40% showed dramatic improvement and a further 20% moderate improvement. Type of dysmenorrhoea was not reported. Sedlaceck and Heczey (1977) reported on the successful treatment of 3 subjects using 3-site training of frontalis EMG, temperature feedback for hand and vaginal temperature. Type of dysmenorrhoea was not reported. The use of temperature feedback was also reported in a case-study, eg Dietvoist and Osborne (1978). The subject had not responded to hormone therapy and analgesics. She was classified as suffering from spasmodic dysmenorrhoea and received training in autogenic phrases as well as the temperature feedback. Heczey (1977) reported on the use of autogenic training and vaginal temperature feedback in 44 college women suffering from primary dysmenorrhoea. The students were divided into 4 groups: (a) no training control (CO); (b) group autogenic training (GT); (c) individual autogenic training (IT); (d) relaxation and vaginal temperature feedback (BT). The improvement rates reported were 92% for (BT), 76% (IT), 64% (GT) and no improvement in the control group.

DISCUSSION

The available evidence does suggest that some forms of dysmenorrhoea may be helped by a variety of psychological interventions. However, many important questions have still to be answered. The level of methodological rigour in the studies reported has so far been generally low, often indeed being rather anecdotal. A common element in all the successful approaches so far reported is relaxation of one sort or another. This may be the important component in the SD studies. Possibly the biofeedback studies are also merely reflecting an indirect approach to relaxation. It is necessary to determine whether some simple form of relaxation training would be as effective as biofeedback assisted relaxation training. Also whether EMG or temperature training is more effective and whether there is any indication between mode of treatment and type of dysmenorrhoea, indeed, whether the congestive type is amenable to improvement by any behavioural techniques. It is also not clear whether vaginal temperature training offers any decisive advantage over hand-warming.

The authors are currently conducting a study to answer some of these questions. The design includes 4 groups of patients diagnosed as suffering from primary dysmenorrhoea and each group balanced for spasmodic and congestive type. The control group will have baseline measures taken and then not be seen for the period of treatment covered by the other groups. A second group will receive relaxation

training and will be attached to monitoring equipment but will
receive no feedback. The other two groups will receive either hand-
warming feedback or frontalis EMG feedback in addition to relaxtion
training. The full data from this study are not yet available, but
early indications are that either of the two biofeedback packages
are effective in spasmodic dysmenorrhoea, in line with previous
findings.

CONCLUSION

Clearly, although many questions are unresolved at the present
time, there is sufficient encouragement from the literature to
suggest that a behavioural approach to the problem of primary
dysmenorrhoea is likely to prove fruitful. It seems likely that
behavioural methods could be applied in a primary care or occupational health setting, and group methods may be effective, which
raises the possibility of offering help with relatively small
disruption of the patient's life. There seems little doubt that
this is an area which should be regarded as a high priority for
further research.

REFERENCES

Adler, C.S., and Adler, S.M., 1979, Biofeedback and psychosomatic
    disorders, in: "Biofeedback: Principles and Practice for
    Clinicians," J.V. Basmajian, ed., The Williams & Wilkins Co.,
    Baltimore.
Berjsjo, P., 1979, Sociometric implications of dysmenorrhoea,
    Acta Obstet. Gynaec. Scand. Suppl., 87:67-68.
Berry, C., and McGuire, F.L., 1972, Menstrual distress and acceptance
    of sex role, Amer. J. Obstet. & Gynaec., 114, Nov.
Chesney, H.A., and Tasto, D.L., 1975, The effectiveness of behaviour
    modification and spasmodic and congestive dysmenorrhoea,
    Beh. Res. & Ther., 13:240-253.
Coppen, A., and Kessel, N., 1963, Menstruation and personality,
    Brit. J. Psychiat., 109:711-721.
Dalton, K., 1961, Menstruation and crime, B.M.J., 2:1752.
Dalton, K., 1964, "The Premenstrual Syndrome," William Heinemann
    Medical Books Ltd., London.
Dalton, K., 1969, "The Menstrual Cycle," Penguin Books Ltd.,
    Harmondsworth, Middlesex.
Dalton, K., 1977, "The Premenstrual Syndrome and Progesterone
    Therapy," William Heinemann Medical Books Ltd., London.
Dietvoist, T.F., and Osborne, D., 1978, Biofeedback assisted
    relaxation training for primary dysmenorrhoea: a case study,
    Biofeedback and Self-Regulation, 3:301-305.
Edwards, J.A., 1950, Psychological implications of dysmenorrhoea
    and the menopause, Med. J. Aust., 1:178-181.

Filler, W.D., and Warner, C.H., 1970, Dysmenorrhoea and its therapy: a uterine contractility study, Amer. J. Obstet. & Gynaec., 106:104.

Fortin, J.N., Wittkower, C.D., and Kalz, F., 1958, A psychosomatic approach to the menstrual-tension syndrome: a preliminary report, Can. Med. Assoc. J., 79:Dec 15.

Frank, B.T., 1931, The hormonal causes of premenstrual tension, Arch. Neurol. & Psychiat., 26:1053-1057.

Gill, M.M., 1943, Functional disturbances of menstruation, Bull. Menninger Clinic, 7:6.

Glass, D., 1971, Psychiatric emergency related to the menstrual cycle, Amer. J. Psychiat., 128:6.

Green, R., and Dalton, K., 1953, The premenstrual syndrome, B.M.J., 1:1007.

Heczey, M.D., 1977, "Effects of Biofeedback and Autogenic Training on Menstrual Experiences, Relationships Among Anxiety, Locus of Control and Dysmenorrhoea," Unpublished Ph.D. Dissertation, The City University of New York.

Horney, K., 1933, Psychogenic factors in functional female disorders, Amer. J. Obstet. & Gynaec., 25:694.

Hunter, W.R., and Rolf, B.B., 1943, The psychosomatic aspect of dysmenorrhoea. A sensory conditioning process, J. Obstet. & Gynaec., 53:123.

Israel, S.L., 1938, J. Amer. Med. Assoc., 110:1721.

Kramp, J., 1968, Studies on the premenstrual syndrome in relation to psychiatry, Acta Psychol. Scand. Suppl., 203.

Kroger, W.S., and Freed, S.C., 1943, The psychosomatic treatment of functional dysmenorrhoea by hypnosis, Amer. J. Obstet. & Gynaec., 46:817.

Leckie, H.F., 1964, Hypnotherapy in gynaecological disorder, Int. J. Clin. & Exp. Hypn., 12(3):121-146.

Levitt, E.E., and Lubin, B., 1967, Some personality factors associated with menstrual complaints and menstrual attitudes, J. Psychosom. Res., 11:267-270.

Lundstrom, V., Green, K., and Wigrist, N., 1976, Prostaglandins, Indomethacin and dysmenorrhoea, Prostaglandins, 11(5):893.

Mullen, F.C., 1968, The treatment of a case of dysmenorrhoea by behaviour therapy technique, J. Nerv. & Ment. Dis., 147:371-376.

Mullen, F.C., 1971, Treatment of dysmenorrhoea by professional and student behaviour. Proceedings of the Fifth Annual Meeting of the Assoc. for the Advancement of Behaviour Therapy, Washington D.C.

Novak, J., and Hanvik, H., 1929, Uterus blutingen psychogenen Urspungs, Zentralbe. f. Gynak., 53:2977.

Rees, L., 1953, Psychosomatic aspects of the premenstrual tension syndrome, J. Ment. Sci., 99:62.

Reeves, B.D., Harris, J.E., and McClin, T.W., 1971, Premenstrual tension, symptoms and weight changes related to potassium therapy, Amer. J. Obstet. & Gynaec., 109(7)1036-1041.

Sedlaceck, D., and Heczey, M., 1977, A specific biofeedback
    treatment for dysmenorrhoea, Biofeedback and Self-Regulation,
    2(3):294.
Tasto, D.P., and Chesney, M.A., 1974, Muscle relaxation treatment
    for primary dysmenorrhoea, Beh. Ther., 5:668-672.
Tasto, D., and Insel, P.M., 1977, The premenstrual and menstrual
    syndromes: a psychological approach, in: "Contributions to
    Medical Psychology," Vol. 1, S. Rachman, ed., Pergamon Press,
    Oxford.
Tubbs, W., and Carnahan, C., 1976, Clinical biofeedback for primary
    dysmenorrhoea: a pilot study. Proc. Biofeedback Res. Soc.,
    Colorado Springs.
Wengraf, P., 1944, Psychodynamic and therapeutic aspects of
    functional dysmenorrhoea, Amer. J. Obstet. & Gynaec.,
    48(19):475.
Widholm, O., 1977, Dysmenorrhoea during adolescence, Acta Obstet. &
    Gynaec. Scand. Suppl., 87:61-66.
Ylikorkala, O., and Dawwood, M.V., 1978, New concepts in
    dysmenorrhoea, Amer. J. Obstet. & Gynaec., 130:833.

PSYCHOPHYSIOLOGICAL APPROACHES TO THE CLASSIFICATION AND TREATMENT

OF HEADACHE

Clive Reading   Principal Psychologist

Manchester Area Health Authority (Teaching)

The experience of headache is so common and the symptom pattern so varied, that establishing the prevalence of headache in general and of headache syndromes in particular is methodologically very difficult. Waters (1975) reviewed the epidemiology of migraine in adults and concluded that migraine may not be a separate entity but may be an extreme in a continuous spectrum of headache. The three main features of migraine - unilateral headache, the warning prior to attacks and nausea and/or vomiting - were reported to be extremely common in the general population, and occurred together no more frequently than would be expected on a chance basis. In view of the widespread occurrence of headache, and the widely held belief that a large proportion of headaches are the result of stressful stimulation combined with predisposing psychological and physiological characteristics (Bakal, 1975), it is somewhat surprising that only recently have there been attempts to objectively investigate psychological, behavioural and psychophysiological correlates of headache and its treatment. In a review of biopsychological aspects of migraine and muscle-contraction headache Bakal (1975) suggested that the aetiological factors are largely psychophysiologically based, and that a variety of psychological and behavioural techniques are effective in the teatment of headache. The most important of these treatment procedures will be discussed in this review, and it will be apparent that effective treatment procedures are being developed. Demonstrating the therapeutic impact of such treatments is not, however, the only procedure necessary for their validation. Psychological, psychophysiological and behavioural approaches to the treatment of headache must also identify aetiological factors upon which the treatment programmes are based, and must then demonstrate a specific effect of treatment upon the postulated aetiological factors.

231

Following a review of psychological and psychophysiological
aspects of headache, and of currently practised psychological,
behavioural and psychophysiological treatments in this chapter, two
experimental studies of headache will be reported in Chapter 13.
The first is a psychophysiological investigation of patients with
chronic headache, and the second a comparison of three forms of
biofeedback treatment for chronic headache. Experimental studies
of headache face the major problem of defining the patient group
involved, and it is of interest therefore to discuss the classification of headache in some detail.

THE CLASSIFICATION OF HEADACHE

The Ad Hoc Committee on Classification of Headache (1962) draw
a clear distinction between "Muscle-Contraction Headache" and
"Vascular Headache of the Migraine Type". The former were described
by the Ad Hoc Committee as: "Ache or sensation of tightness, pressure
or constriction, widely varied in intensity, frequency, and duration,
sometimes long-lasting, and commonly sub-occipital. It is associated
with sustained contraction of skeletal muscles ....".

Vascular headaches were described by the Ad Hoc Committee as:
"Recurrent attacks of headache, widely varied in intensity,
frequency, and duration. The attacks are commonly unilateral in
onset; are usually associated with anorexia and, sometimes, with
nausea and vomiting; in some are preceded by, or associated with,
conspicuous sensory, motor, and mood disturbances; and are often
familial. Evidence supports the view that cranial artery distention
and dilation are importantly implicated in the painful phase ....".

Although the Ad Hoc Committee recognised a category of
"Combined Headache: Vascular and Muscle-Contraction", there is no
doubt that "Vascular" and "Muscle-Contraction" headaches were
regarded as separate entities with distinct symptomatologies and
aetiologies.

The assumed vascular aetiology of migraine, proposed by Wolff
and his associates (Graham and Wolff, 1938; Schumacher and Wolff,
1941), was reiterated by O'Brien (1973) when reviewing the haemodynamics of migraine. O'Brien concluded that all attacks of
migraine are biphasic in relation to the blood flow changes:
"The prodrome of migraine is associated with generalised cerebral
vasoconstriction though the degree of this vasoconstriction is
closely associated with, but is probably not the cause of, prodromal
and specific aura symptoms; both may be linked to an unidentified
third factor. This phase occurs in all attacks of migraine and may
be asymptomatic .... the headache stage is associated with
vasodilation of both cerebral and non-cerebral cranial vessels".

Empirical investigations have given little support to the distinction drawn by the Ad Hoc Committee between vascular and muscle-contraction headache, either in terms of symptomatology (Ziegler et al, 1972; Bakal and Kaganov, 1979; Waters 1975), or psychophysiologically (Bakal and Kaganov, 1977), but support instead a continuum model (Philips, 1978; Bakal and Kaganov, 1979). There has been considerable recent interest in psychophysiological approaches to the classification and treatment of headache, largely as a consequence of biofeedback and other relaxation-based or behavioural approaches to treatment. Such treatments include training headache patients to exercise voluntary control over extracranial vascular activity (Friar and Beatty, 1976), a procedure based directly on the vascular model of migraine, and also the more indirect biofeedback approach of hand temperature training (Sargent et al, 1973). The rationale for the latter technique has not been adequately stated, although Morley (1977) regarded the central assumption of the temperature feedback studies as the conceptualisation of migraine as a general vasomotor disorder, reduction of hand temperature during migraine attacks being a consequence of increased sympathetic tone, with the latter being also responsible for extracranial vascular changes associated with the pain of migraine. Sargent et al (1973) also considered training in hand temperature control to be effective as a treatment for migraine through a process of "general relaxation of sympathetic out-flow". The reason for selecting hand temperature as an indicator of sympathetic activity rather than, say, skin conductance, is not made clear. The possible use of non-vascular measures of sympathetic activity is referred to by Werbach and Sandweiss (1978) who suggested that "any method which reduces sympathetic activity may be useful as an aborting technique for migraine".

Biofeedback treatment of "muscle-contraction" or "tension" headaches has concentrated on the reduction of frontalis EMG activity (Budzynski et al, 1973), reflecting the assumed aetiology of such headaches. However, in the case of both "muscle-contraction" and "vascular" headaches, the development of biofeedback approaches to treatment, and the use of psychophysiological monitoring procedures during the assessment and treatment of headaches, has led to a reappraisal of the classification of headaches, and to the possibility of developing a psychophysiological basis for both classification and treatment.

Psychophysiological Studies of Headache

Although early studies of biofeedback treatment of headache were consistent with the system of classifying headaches proposed by the Ad Hoc Committee on Classification of Headache (1962), ie, "vascular" headaches were treated by trained control of vasomotor activity, and "muscle-contraction" headaches were treated by

frontalis EMG training, it has usually been apparent that neither
vascular (migraine) nor muscle-contraction (tension) headaches were
considered to be associated with a single psychophysiological abnormality. Sargent et al (1973) refer to vascular abnormalities
during both migraine and tension headaches, and suggest that both
disorders might be ameliorated by regulation of blood flow. Bakal
and Kaganov (1977) reported that muscle tension levels were raised
during both migraine and tension headaches, and that frontalis EMG
training was equally effective for both groups of patients. The
question arises, therefore, whether psychophysiological differences
can be found between "vascular" and "muscle-contraction" headaches
and between headache-prone and headache-free individuals.

   Vasomotor Activity in Headache. The haemodynamics of migraine
as summarised by O'Brien (1973) were referred to earlier. Edmeads
(1979) also reviewed the vascular theory of migraine and concluded
that measurements of regional cerebral blood flow (rCBF) demonstrate
"clear-cut changes in the cerebral circulation in migraine and in
cluster headaches". There was considered to be a reasonable consensus of rCBF changes in vascular headaches. These changes are a
decreased rCBF during the migraine aura followed by an increased
rCBF during the headache phase. The latter increase in rCBF was
considered to outlast the headache by up to two days. Extracranial
blood-flow increases during the headache and subsides when the headache clears. Edmeads considered the headache to be a consequence of
increased extracranial blood-flow, with the increased cerebral blood-
flow a mere sideshow. Sakai and Meyer (1979) tested cerebral
vasomotor responsiveness to 5% CO_2 or 100% O_2 inhalation or to hyper-
ventilation in groups of patients with migraine, cluster or muscle-
contraction headaches and also on a non-headache healthy control
group. Abnormal cerebrovascular activity was found during the headache and headache-free interval in patients with vascular headaches.
The authors also present evidence for "two different types of abnormality in cerebral vascular receptor sites .... which make it
possible to differentiate migraine from cluster headache". Patients
with muscle-contraction headache showed normal cerebral vasomotor
responsiveness. In contrast, Martin and Mathews (1978), who reported
that inhaling a vasodilator made tension headaches worse on 43% of
occasions, concluded that tension headaches are associated with
cranial vasodilation, and suggested that differences between tension
and migraine headaches "may be largely in terms of severity rather
than psychological mechanism". A vasomotor component to muscle-
contraction headache was also emphasised in reviews by Haynes (1981)
and Cohen (1978). Haynes proposed a psychophysiological model of
muscle-contraction headache incorporating both vasomotor and muscle-
contraction elements with localised vasoconstriction exacerbating
pain associated with muscle-contraction by diminishing the blood
supply to muscles already experiencing an oxygen deficit and symptoms
of muscle fatigue. Cohen reviewed psychophysiological studies of
both migraine and muscle-contraction headache and concluded that

vasoconstriction of the scalp arteries is important in both types of
headache, and that headache sufferers respond to innocuous stimuli
with vasoconstriction of the temporal artery. Headache-free subjects
were hypothesised to show vasodilation to the same stimuli.

It has been suggested that the abnormality in cranial vascular
activity in migraineurs is part of a general vasomotor dysfunction,
a proposal reviewed recently by Morley (1977). Morley cited experiments supporting this contention (Appenzeller et al, 1963;
Downey and Frewin, 1972; Elliot et al, 1973) and others failing to
do so (French et al, 1967; Hockaday et al, 1967). Morley criticised
the methodologies employed in the majority of these experiments, but
nevertheless concluded that "migrainous individuals do not differ
substantially from normals in their vasomotor reflexes to sustained
body heating when in a non-headache state". He left open the
question of whether stimuli other than body heating, eg stimuli which
produce orienting responses, produce different responses in
migraineurs and normals. Since the behavioural and biofeedback
approaches to the treatment of headache assume that attacks may be
triggered by environmental events perceived as stressful (Mitchell
and Mitchell, 1971), sustained body-heating may not be the most
interesting stimulus from a psychophysiological standpoint. Price
and Clarke (1979) compared the digital vasomotor responses of
migraineurs and normal controls, using a classical conditioning
paradigm with a 90dB white noise as UCS. Migraineurs did not show
differential conditioning of digital pulse volume, whereas the
controls showed conditioned vasoconstriction to the CS. Price and
Tursky (1976) studied the digital and extracranial vasomotor
responses of 40 migraineurs and 40 normal controls to a single
session of either (1) digital blood volume feedback, (2) false feedback, (3) a relaxation tape, or (4) a neutral tape. Normal subjects
produced vasodilation over time, regardless of treatment condition,
whereas migraine subjects tended to constrict or not to change over
time. High positive correlations were found between digital and
extracranial blood volume change. Bakal and Kaganov (1977) compared
the responses of 10 migraine patients, 10 muscle-contraction patients,
and 10 headache-free controls to a series of 10 trials of 80dB white
noise of 0.5 second duration. For both headache groups pulse
velocity in the superficial temporal arteries decreased, while the
controls increased pulse velocity in the same circumstance. The
experiments of Price and Clarke (1979), Price and Tursky (1976) and
Bakal and Kaganov (1977), which used very different stimuli of a
"psychological" nature, all provide evidence of differences in
vasomotor function in headache patients and headache-free controls.

Autonomic Nervous System Instability in Headache. If as seems
to be suggested by the evidence, persons prone to migraine and/or
muscle-contraction headaches show a general vasomotor dysfunction,
is this to be regarded as a unique and fundamental psychophysiological abnormality characterising such patients, or is it

merely one manifestation of a general instability of the ANS? There appears to be a commonly held belief that migraineurs differ from non-migraine sufferers in ANS function (Price and Clarke, 1979). This assumption seems to be based mainly on evidence of differences in vasomotor function between migraineurs and normal controls (Price and Tursky, 1976; Bakal and Kaganov, 1977; Price and Clarke, 1979). The assumption of an instability in the ANS clearly underlies behavioural and biofeedback approaches to the treatment of headache. Sargent et al (1973) provided a rationale for the use of autogenic-feedback training that conceptualised migraine as a stress-related syndrome, with the somatic response of dysfunction of vascular behaviour in the head related to intense sympathetic dysfunction. An increase in hand skin temperature was used as an index of voluntary control of the sympathetic component of the ANS. Mitchell and Mitchell (1971) regarded migraine reduction "as a function of increased ability to control emotional reactivity, that is, reduced sympathetic nervous system activity to events perceived as stressful in the environment". Stroebel and Glueck (1976) suggest that biofeedback training in hand temperature control may abort migraine during the prodromal phase by preventing the increased sympathetic outflow from reaching a rebound threshold, implying that any method of decreasing sympathetic activity may be useful for aborting migraine. Bakal (1975), reviewing the physiochemical basis of migraine, concluded that this disorder is associated with excessive cranial vascular responsivity and ANS instability, though elsewhere in the review Bakal stated that there was no research suggesting that high levels of sympathetic nervous system activity characterise headache sufferers. Indirect evidence that migraine headaches are associated with increased sympathetic outflow comes from Sovak et al (1978), who compared responses of supraorbital, superficial temporal, and digital arterial beds and the heart rate in 5 normal and 10 migraine subjects during volitional hand temperature increase. In both normal subjects and clinically improved migraineurs, but not unimproved migraineurs, bradycardia occurred, reflecting a general decrease of tonic sympathetic outflow. Sovak et al argue against the specificity of the volition-induced finger temperature increase, but regard it as an indication of a general decrease of the tonic sympathetic outflow. It seems, therefore, that experiments comparing migraineurs with headache-free controls offer at least some support to the widespread assumption that migraine headaches are associated with a general instability in the nervous system, rather than a specific deficit in vasomotor control. However, experiments providing support for the role of a general ANS instability in the development of migraine (eg Price and Tursky, 1976), invariably include no information regarding non-headache anxiety-related symptoms present in either the headache patients or the normal control group. A description of the psychophysiological abnormalities uniquely associated with headache cannot be based with any confidence on comparisons of groups of subjects who may differ significantly in terms of general levels of anxiety and neurotic symptomatology.

EMG Abnormalities in Headache. A sustained increase in tension
levels in the muscles of the scalp and neck is a commonly assumed
aetiological factor in muscle-contraction headache (Martin, 1972;
Bakal, 1975), although it is usually acknowledged that extracranial
vasoconstriction is an additional aetiological factor (Dalessio,
1972; Cohen, 1978). Elevated scalp and neck muscle tension levels
have also been reported in migraine patients, leading to the
suggestion that muscular tightness is a predisposing factor for both
classes of headache (Bakal and Kaganov, 1977). The latter authors
compared frontalis and neck EMG levels in patients diagnosed as
migraine or muscle-contraction headache sufferers with a headache-
free control group. Frontalis EMG was significantly higher in
migraine patients than in muscle-contraction patients, who were not
significantly different to the controls in this respect. Migraine
and muscle-contraction patients did not differ in neck EMG levels,
and the combined headache group had a significantly higher neck EMG
level than the controls. The absence of significantly elevated
frontalis EMG levels in the patients studied by Bakal and Kaganov
is not typical of the muscle-contraction headache literature however,
since there have been other studies where increased frontalis EMG
activity has been reported for this group of patients (Philips,
1977). Recent reviews by Philips (1978) and Haynes (1981) have both
referred to the inconsistent results obtained when groups of headache
patients have been compared to headache-free controls, though both
authors concluded that frontalis EMG levels appear to be elevated in
muscle-contraction headache patients as a group, though Philips is
careful to point out that tension headaches are not associated with
sustained increases in muscle tension in all cases. Bakal and
Kaganov (1979) investigated the symptom characteristics of chronic
and non-chronic headache sufferers and found that the musculo-
skeletal symptoms of neck pain, top-of-head pain, forehead pains,
and feelings of tightness and pressure were, together with nausea,
the best predictors of problem or chronic headache. Pozniak-
Patewicz (1976) reported increased neck and temporalis EMG levels
in both tension and migraine headache patients, when compared with
a headache-free control group. For the headache patients EMG levels
were higher during headaches than during headache-free intervals,
and were higher in migraine than tension headache patients. The
increased muscular activity was interpreted by Pozniak-Patewicz as
a consequence rather than a cause of headache.

In summary, despite inconsistent results, it seems that headache
patients as a group have higher levels of tension in the muscles of
the head and neck, particularly in the frontalis muscles, and that
more severe or chronic headaches are associated with particularly
high EMG levels. Differences between groups of headache patients
and headache-free controls seem to be present both during headaches
and in headache-free intervals. Inconsistent results from different
laboratories may reflect differences in diagnostic criteria,
differences in experimental procedures, and, as emphasised by

van Boxtel and van der Ven (1978) differences in EMG recording technique. A further difficulty in assessing the aetiological significance of raised EMG levels in headache patients is the absence,
in psychophysiological comparisons of headache patients with headache-free controls, of information regarding anxiety-related symptoms
other than headache in the experimental and control groups.

Conclusions

It is difficult to differentiate muscle-contraction (tension)
headaches and vascular (migraine) headaches, either on the basis of
symptomatology or psychophysiologically, and differences that have
been found have been quantitative rather than qualitative. A more
appropriate description model may be the severity/chronicity continuum model (Bakal and Kaganov, 1977; Philips, 1978; Martin and
Mathews, 1978; Bakal and Kaganov, 1979) which assumes similar
physiological or psychobiological processes underlying all headaches
previously classified as "tension" or "migraine". The continuum
model acknowledges both musculo-skeletal and vascular aetiological
mechanisms, and psychophysiological comparisons of headache-prone
and headache-free subjects offer some support for the involvement
of these mechanisms. It should be noted, however, that such comparisons have not controlled for differences between headache
patients and headache-free subjects with regard to general levels of
neurotic symptomatology. We cannot, therefore, exclude the
possibility that the groups of headache patients studied have included many patients with a broad range of anxiety-related symptoms,
and that it is with the latter that the reported psychophysiological
abnormalities are associated.

A recent study by Harper and Steger (1978) supports the association between elevated frontalis EMG levels and neurotic symptomatology other than headache. Correlations between frontalis EMG and
subjective reports of pain in a group of 33 female patients with
chronic muscle-contraction headache were non-significant. Significant correlations were reported between frontalis EMG and measures
of physical distress and emotional illness. Abnormalities of peripheral vasomotor activity in headache patients may similarly be associated with high levels of anxiety rather than with a predisposition
to headaches as such. Indeed, peripheral pulse volume has been
reported to be a more reliable measure of anxiety than heart rate,
which is the more common index (Bloom et al, 1976). The aetiological significance of extracranial vascular responses has been
established (Sakai and Meyer, 1979), but the reported general
autonomic nervous system, vasomotor and musculo-skeletal correlates
of chronic headache require further investigation.

PSYCHOLOGICAL ASPECTS OF HEADACHE

Personality Type

As noted by Philips (1976), there is a widespread clinical
agreement on the personality characteristics of headache sufferers.
For example, Alpers and Mancall (1971), while recognising that not
all sufferers can be so defined, considered the migraine personality
to comprise the following characteristics: "Childhood shyness,
obedience, neatness, and reliability, and stubborn inflexibility in
certain circumstances; adult perfectionism, ambitiousness, in-
elasticity, tension, resentment, repetitiousness, efficiency, poise,
and social grace. The result is an obsessive-compulsive type of
personality structure in which two trends are noted: (a) a need for
love and approval and (b) the inability to recognise anger or to
handle it properly in the individual himself. In essence, the
migraine sufferer develops headache against a background of an
obsessive-compulsive personality, with feelings of inadequacy,
tendencies to perfectionism and rigidity and excessive conscientious-
ness and numerous frustrations, extending far back into childhood.
No treatment of migraine is successful without a serious investigation of the personality factors involved".

There have been very few objective studies of the personality
of migraine sufferers. Henryk-Gutt and Rees (1973) investigated
some of the personality traits that have been reported clinically in
migraine patients. They found increased EPI 'N' scores and increased
anxiety in female migraine patients, and increased hostility scores
on the Buss-Durkee scale for classic migraine subjects and the female
migraine patients attending a clinic. They were unable to confirm
that migraine subjects are especially obsessional or ambitious.
Philips (1976) analysed Eysenck Personality Questionnaire scores for
a group of migraine sufferers selected from a community sample without reference to headache complaints, and found that they were in-
distinguishable from standardisation sample norms on measures of
Neuroticism, Extraversion, and Psychoticism. Philips argued that
views of the personality of headache sufferers have been formed on
the basis of only those sufferers who seek treatment, this latter
group not necessarily being representative of headache sufferers
in general. Henryk-Gutt and Rees (1973) also compared past and
present emotional stress in migraine and control subjects and found
no difference, although migraine subjects reported more subjective
symptoms of emotional distress. The authors concluded that migraine
patients are predisposed, by constitutional and not by environmental
factors, to experience greater reactions to stress than control
subjects. Pearce (1977) reviewed the role of psychological factors
in migraine and concluded that there is no consistent personality
type, and that psychological factors are important, but are secondary
rather than precipitating aetiological agents. The migraine person-

ality described by Alpers and Mancall is not supported by the available evidence, and there is no clear evidence that personality
structure as such is important in the causation of migraine. Bakal
(1975) suggested that a more appropriate research strategy involves
identifying the reactions of headache subjects to situations
associated with the onset of headaches. Psychophysiological investigations of such response stereotypy in migraine patients have
been discussed earlier, and represent a more useful line of enquiry
than attempts to describe a "migraine personality".

Psychological Approaches to Treatment

   General Behavioural Approaches. The treatment of migraine by
psychological/behavioural procedures assumes the existence of
modifiable abnormalities in migraine patients, either in terms of
personality characteristics or in terms of patterns of reactivity
in certain situations or classes of situations. Mitchell and
Mitchell (1971) based their programmed behaviour therapy upon a
conceptualisation of migraine reduction as: "..... a function of
increased ability to control emotional reactivity that is, reduced
sympathetic nervous system activity to events perceived as stressful in the environment".

   A treatment package of relaxation training, systematic desensitisation, and assertive training had been previously found to
be effective (Mitchell, 1969). An attempt was then made (Mitchell
and Mitchell, 1971) to test the relative effectiveness of the component techniques comprising the combined desensitisation package.
Results indicated that the combined programme was superior to single-
model approaches, only 7.4% of patients being "unimproved", with
22.2% "headache free" and 70.4% "substantially improved". The
"relaxation application" and "systematic desensitisation" groups were
not significantly different to the no-treatment controls. The
relaxation application group reported some reduction in migraine
frequency, while the desensitisation group reported a "somewhat
greater" reduction in frequency and duration, although these changes
did not reach statistical significance (the numbers in each group
were however rather small, ranging from three to seven).

   Programmed behaviour therapy is time-consuming and therapist-
intensive and, more recently (Mitchell and White, 1976, 1977)
attempts have been made to apply training in behavioural self-
management to the problem of migraine. Mitchell and White (1977)
used a "dismantling" strategy with a group of 12 subjects to determine the effects of each phase of a four stage behavioural self-
management package. The four phases were self-recording, self-
monitoring, and two degrees of "skill-acquisition". The latter
involved self-control techniques of physical and mental relaxation,
self-desensitisation and self-change techniques. Neither self-

recording nor self-monitoring produced a significant reduction in headache frequency. Significant improvement did occur as a result of the "skill acquisition" procedures, the greatest improvement taking place in subjects who received both stages of the self-control phase. Mitchell and White (1977) speculate that behavioural self-management will prove superior to either symptom-oriented or therapist dominated intervention since the former: "....... provides the individual with both a strategy and the tools necessary to cope with the unexpected crises of everyday life".

Discussing the rationale for the behavioural approach to migraine treatment, Mitchell and Mitchell (1971) reported that the environmental life-style of their patients could in almost all cases be categorised as: "defensive with characteristic anxiety-hostility interaction patterns. Situationally-anxious, achievement oriented, perfectionistic, over-controlled and routine-regimented behaviour patterns were seen as supporting evidence for such a description. It is probable that during periods of perceived threat where the consequences of the threat are uncertain (increased ego-involvement) the migraine susceptible individual becomes increasingly defensive behaviourally, and anxious and hostile emotionally, resulting in the placement of more emphasis upon establishing routine even when inappropriate to changed circumstances. Defensive behaviour was operantly (sic) defined as "uncertainty-reactive behaviour"."

It is not made clear upon what evidence this detailed and contentious description of the migraine personality is based. Furthermore, Mitchell and Mitchell do not demonstrate that following treatment the personality pattern/environmental life-style described above altered substantially, evidence for which is necessary before it can be concluded that the treatment programme produced clinical improvement via the mechanisms proposed. In fact, despite the encouraging clinical results, we must conclude that the assumptions upon which the behavioural treatments reported by Mitchell and Mitchell (1971) and Mitchell and White (1977) are based, are speculative and without objective support. Indeed, the studies of Henryk-Gutt and Rees (1973) and Philips (1976) contradict them.

Relaxation Procedures. Several studies have investigated the effectiveness of relaxation training in the treatment of migraine. As previously reported, Mitchell and Mitchell (1971) found that a modified version of Jacobson's progressive relaxation was not significantly better than a no-treatment control condition. However, the number of subjects was small (7 in the relaxation group, 3 in the control group) and there were only 3 relaxation training sessions plus instructions to practise relaxation for three ten-minute sessions each day. There is no data on whether subjects actually became more relaxed, or indeed whether they practised the training at home as requested. Thus, although these results are not encouraging the investigation was not sufficiently thorough to be conclusive.

Hay and Madders (1971) conducted an uncontrolled assessment of relaxation therapy in the treatment of migraine, basing their approach on the assumption that migraine sufferers exhibit a "chronic state of arousal", as evidenced by: "..... their facial expressions, posture and behaviour".

The treatment involved group relaxation training (based on Jacobson) with "informal group discussion". Of 115 patients registered for the course 69 (60%) reported a decrease in frequency, severity or duration of attacks. Unfortunately, no control group was included, evidence that patients had learned to relax is absent, and headache information was recorded only before and after treatment rather than on a daily basis.

Benson et al (1974) assessed the value of the relaxation response, as elicited through transcendental meditation, in the treatment of 17 migraine patients. Each patient kept a daily record of the severity of headaches and any medication. There was a pre-treatment baseline period of one to three months. Of the 17 patients, only 3 experienced statistically significant reduction in headache units per month, although a further 2 had a non-significant trend of decreasing headache. The authors conclude that relaxation training through transcendental meditation is of limited usefulness in the therapy of migraine.

Hypnosis and Autohypnosis.   Relaxation procedures based on hypnosis and autohypnosis have been used in the treatment of migraine, with encouraging results. Anderson et al (1975) randomly allocated 47 migraine patients to either hypnotherapy (with autohypnosis) or prochlorperazine treatment. The hypnosis group received "at least" 6 sessions of hypnosis during which attention was directed to the cranial arteries and the suggestion made that they remain "smaller" and "more normal". For the hypnotherapy group there was a signif-icant reduction in the median number of attacks per month and the number of patients experiencing Grade 4 (blinding and totally in-capacitating) attacks. 43.5% reported complete remission. For the drug control group there was no significant treatment effect. The groups were not controlled for therapist attention and no objective record of headache attacks was kept, patients merely reporting to the therapist at monthly intervals.

Graham (1975) reported the successful use of hypnosis in two controlled case studies. Subjects kept daily records of headache activity, and there was a one-month pre-treatment baseline period. Each subject received 5 sessions of hypnosis and self-hypnosis, suggestions of increasing hand warmth being made. Subjects were required to practise the hand-warming technique daily, and to implement it on the first appearance of prodromal signs. Both subjects were headache-free at follow-up (9 months and 12 months), although the author notes that the frequency of pre-headache

phenomena had not altered, supporting the specificity of the treatment effects. The rationale given for the treatment is based on the
temperature biofeedback studies, and in fact Graham's hypnotherapy
treatment of migraine is similar to the temperature training treatment to be described later, although of course a different procedure
is used for producing voluntary increases in finger temperature.

Biofeedback Treatment of Headache

The most widely used forms of biofeedback training for the
treatment of chronic headache are finger temperature, training where
patients attempt to produce voluntary increases in finger temperature,
and frontalis EMG biofeedback, where patients attempt to reduce
levels of frontalis EMG activity. Although as discussed earlier,
psychophysiological and symptomatological differences between so-
called muscle-contraction and vascular headaches are quantitative
rather than qualitative, finger temperature training has been used
mainly with patients diagnosed as migraine headache sufferers, with
frontalis EMG biofeedback being a widely used treatment for patients
diagnosed as muscle-contraction headache sufferers. In both cases
there have been numerous studies demonstrating substantial clinical
improvement, although as has been noted in recent reviews, (Diamond
et al, 1978; Budzynski, 1978) the relative contributions of the component parts of the biofeedback package have not been fully
established. In addition, it has yet to be adequately demonstrated
that the use of temperature and EMG biofeedback for so-called vascular and muscle-contraction headache respectively, is appropriate
either in terms of therapeutic response or in terms of the psychophysiological rationale for treatment.

Less widely reported biofeedback training procedures used as a
treatment for chronic headache include extracranial vascular feedback (Friar and Beatty, 1976), alpha EEG feedback (Andreychuk and
Skriver, 1975) and skin conductance feedback (Werbach and Sandweiss,
1978). In the first two of these, the procedures are more technically difficult than either frontalis EMG or finger temperature
biofeedback, and the reported clinical improvements were substantially less than those typically reported with EMG and temperature
biofeedback. In the report of skin conductance feedback by
Werbach and Sandweiss, patients also received EMG and temperature
feedback, abdominal breathing techniques, modified progressive
muscle relaxation, meditative mantras, and autogenic phrases. The
specific contribution made by skin conductance feedback cannot therefore be ascertained.

The rationale for biofeedback treatment of chronic headache is
unclear. For the less intense, so-called muscle-contraction headache, the use of frontalis EMG biofeedback is based on the assumption
that these headaches are associated with increased frontalis EMG

levels. As pointed out by Philips (1977), a sustained increase in
frontalis EMG levels is not found in all such patients, and Harper
and Steger (1978) found that frontalis EMG levels were unrelated to
pain measures. For the more intense, migrainous headaches, the
rationale for biofeedback treatment is even less clear, and several
possible therapeutic models have been suggested.

Vasomotor Control. The first model assumes that migraine is a
disorder of vasomotor control, and that digital temperature training
aborts attacks by producing cranial vasodilation, thus preventing
the process of cranial vasoconstriction and increased sympathetic
outflow from reaching a rebound threshold (Stroebel and Glueck,
1976). The frequency of attacks is further reduced by alterations
in the abnormal patterns of physiological responsivity and response
stereotypy presumed to underlie the disorder. Evidence for this
model is far from convincing. Whilst there is some evidence for a
vasomotor dysfunction in migraine, the nature of any changes in
cranial vascular activity accompanying voluntary regulation of
digital temperature remains unclear. Although it has been reported
that subjects trained in voluntary hand-warming show a reduction in
headache activity, whereas subjects trained in voluntary hand-cooling
apparently do not (Turin and Johnson, 1976), Largen et al (1978)
found no rCBF differentiation under hand-warming and hand-cooling
conditions. In addition, it has not been established that training
in voluntary hand-warming modifies the peripheral vasomotor response
to stress. Rickles et al (1979) found no differences in vasomotor
stress responses before and after temperature biofeedback training.
Stoffer et al (1979) also reported that the acquisition of voluntary
temperature control did not reduce the stress response to thermal
pain. Even more damaging to this explanation of biofeedback treatment of migraine by digital temperature training is the finding that
voluntary hand-warming and clinical improvement appear to be unrelated (Mathew et al, 1979; Werbach and Sandweiss, 1978; Lake et al,
1979; Kewman and Roberts, 1980). Indeed, evidence for a consistent
temperature training effect is lacking (Lake et al, 1979) and it
seems possible that migraine patients may respond particularly
poorly to temperature training procedures (Price and Tursky, 1976).

Psychobiological Mediation. A second model assumes that chronic
headache is associated with several predisposing psychobiological
factors, with increased frontalis EMG levels and abnormal vasomotor
activity being central features and with the vascular component
increasing with the more intense and more chronic headache problems
(Bakal and Kaganov, 1979; Philips, 1977). It has been reported that
frontalis EMG biofeedback is equally effective in the treatment of
muscle-contraction and migraine headache (Bakal and Kaganov, 1977).
Since this model assumes that similar psychobiological processes
mediate both the predisposition to headache and the actual headache
attacks, there is the implication that temperature and frontalis
EMG biofeedback abort headaches by normalising the physiological

abnormalities associated with attacks, and reduce the frequency of
attacks by modifying the psychobiological predisposing mechanisms.
We would therefore expect improvement in headache occurrence to be
related to success on the biofeedback training procedures. As discussed earlier, this appears not to be so. In addition, Rickles
et al (1979) found no evidence of changed responsivity or modified
physiological response patterns following frontalis EMG and finger
temperature biofeedback.

   Biochemical Basis of Biofeedback. A third suggestion is that
biofeedback produces clinical improvement by either general relaxation or by a combination of relaxation and non-specific demand
characteristics. The latter was suggested by Largen et al (1978).
Mathew et al (1979) proposed that by producing relaxation, biofeedback aborts migraine by preventing increases in MAO activity and
consequent acceleration of serotonin activity. They point out that
MAOIs are effective in treating migraine. Again the apparent lack
of a consistent correlation between clinical improvement and training success is not supportive of such a model, although a recent
report by Sovak et al (1978) did provide evidence of a general decrease of the sympathetic tonic outflow in improved, but not unimproved, migraineurs, leading the authors to conclude that biofeedback has a clinical effect via a process of general relaxation.

   The three models discussed above represent attempts to provide
a psychophysiological rationale for the use of finger temperature
and frontalis EMG biofeedback in the treatment of chronic headache.
These two biofeedback approaches are the most widely reported,
although as discussed earlier, other biofeedback approaches have been
reported. Friar and Beatty (1976) investigated the effect of
training vasoconstriction in the extracranial arteries involved in
migraine headache. The rationale for this approach was that biofeedback would reduce the extracranial vasodilation associated with
the pain of migraine. This contrasts with the model of finger
temperature control discussed earlier, where it is assumed that
training involves producing extracranial vasodilation during the
early stages of headache attacks.

   Two experimental investigations of headache are described in
the next chapter.

REFERENCES

Ad Hoc Committee on Classification of Headache, 1962, Classification
     of headache, J. Amer. Med. Assoc., 179:717-718.
Alpers, B.J., and Mancall, E.L., 1971, "Clinical Neurology,"
     F.A. Davis & Co., Philadelphia.
Anderson, J.A.D., Basker, M.A., and Dalton, R., 1975, Migraine and
     hypnotherapy, Int. J. Clin & Exp. Hypn., 23:48-58.

Andreychuk, T., and Skriver, C., 1975, Hypnosis and biofeedback in the treatment of migraine headache, Int. J. Clin. & Exp. Hypn., 23:172-183.

Appenzeller, O., Davison, K., and Marshall, J., 1963, Reflex vasomotor abnormalities in the hands of migrainous subjects, J. Neurol. Neurosurg. & Psychiat., 26:447-450.

Bakal, D.A., 1975, Headache: a biopsychological perspective, Psychol. Bull., 62:369-382.

Bakal, D.A., and Kaganov, J.A., 1977, Muscle contraction and migraine headache: psychophysiologic comparison, Headache, 17:208-215.

Bakal, D.A., and Kaganov, J.A., 1979, Symptom characteristics of chronic and non-chronic headache sufferers, Headache, 19: 285-289.

Benson, H., Klemchuk, H.P., and Graham, J.R., 1974, The usefulness of the relaxation response in the therapy of headache, Headache, 14:49-52.

Bloom, L.J., Houston, B.K., and Burish, T.G., 1976, An evaluation of finger pulse volume as a psychophysiological measure of anxiety, Psychophysiol., 13:40-42.

Budzynski, T.H., Stoyva, J.M., Adler, C.S., and Mullaney, D.J., 1973, EMG biofeedback and tension headache: a controlled outcome study, Psychosom. Med., 35:484-496.

Budzynski, T.H., 1978, Biofeedback in the treatment of muscle-contraction (tension) headache, Biofeedback & Self-Regulation, 3:409-434.

Cohen, M.J., 1978, Psychophysiological studies of headache: is there similarity between migraine and muscle contraction headaches?, Headache, 18:189-196.

Dalessio, D.J., 1972, "Wolff's Headache and Other Head Pain," Oxford University Press, New York.

Diamond, S., Diamond-Falk, J., and De Veno, T., 1978, Biofeedback in the treatment of vascular headache, Biofeedback & Self-Regulation, 3:385-408.

Downey, J.A., and Frewin, D.B., 1972, Vascular responses in the hands of patients suffering from migraine, J. Neurol. Neurosurg. & Psychiat., 35:258-263.

Edmeads, J., 1979, Vascular headaches and the cranial circulation - another look, Headache, 19:127-132.

Elliot, K., Frewin, D.B., and Downey, J.A., 1973, Reflex vasomotor responses in hands of patients suffering from migraine, Headache, 13:188-196.

French, E.B., Lassers, B.W., and Desai, M.G., 1967, Reflex vasomotor responses in the hands of migrainous subjects, J. Neurol. Neurosurg. & Psychiat., 30:276-278.

Friar, L.R., and Beatty, J., 1976, Migraine: management by trained control of vasoconstriction, J. Cons. & Clin. Psychol., 44: 46-53.

Graham, G.W., 1975, Hypnotic treatment for migraine headaches, Int. J. Clin. & Exp. Hypn., 23:165-171.

Graham, J.R., and Wolff, H.G., 1938, Mechanism of migraine headache and action of ergotamine tartrate, Arch. Neurol. & Psychiat., 39:737-763.

Harper, R.G., and Steger, J.C., 1978, Psychological correlates of frontalis EMG and pain in tension headache, Headache, Sept., pp.215-218.

Hay, K.M., and Madders, J., 1971, Migraine treated by relaxation therapy, J. Roy. Coll. Gen. Pract., 21:664-669.

Haynes, S.N., 1981, Muscle-contraction headache: a psychophysiolog-ical perspective of etiology and treatment, in: "Psychosomatic Disorders: A Psychophysiological Approach to Etiology and Treatment," S.N. Haynes & L.R. Gannon, eds., Wiley, 1981 in press, London and New York.

Henryk-Gutt, R., and Rees, W.L., 1973, Psychological aspects of migraine, J. Psychosom. Res., 17:141-153.

Hockaday, J.M., Macmillan, A.L., and Whitty, C.W.M., 1967, Vasomotor reflex response in idiopathic and hormone dependent migraine, Lancet, 1:1023-1026.

Kewman, D., and Roberts, A.H., 1980, Skin temperature biofeedback and migraine headaches: a double-blind study, Biofeedback & Self-Regulation, 5:327-345.

Lake, A., Rainey, J., and Papsdorf, J.D., 1979, Biofeedback and rational-emotive therapy in the management of migraine head-ache, J. App. Beh. Anal., 12:127-140.

Largen, J.W., Mathew, R.J., Dobbins, K., Meyer, J.S., and Claghorn, J.L., 1978, Skin temperature self-regulation and non-invasive regional cerebral blood flow, Headache, 8:203-210.

Martin, M.J., 1972, Muscle-contraction headache, Psychosom., 13: 16-19.

Martin, P.R., and Mathews, A.M., 1978, Tension headaches: psycho-physiological investigation and treatment, J. Psychosom. Res., 22:389-399.

Mathew, R.C., Kralik, P., and Claghorn, J.L., 1979, Biochemical basis for biofeedback treatment of migraine: a hypothesis, Headache, 19:290-293.

Mitchell, K.R., 1969, The treatment of migraine: an exploratory application of time-limited behaviour therapy, Technol., 14:50-55.

Mitchell, K.R., and Mitchell, D.M., 1971, Migraine: an exploratory treatment application of programmed behaviour therapy tech-niques, J. Psychosom. Res., 15:137-157.

Mitchell, K.R., and White, R.G., 1976, The control of migraine headache by behavioural self-management: a controlled case study, Headache, 16:178-184.

Mitchell, K.R., and White, R.G., 1977, Behavioural self-management: an application to the problem of migraine headaches, Beh. Ther., 8:213-221.

Morley, S., 1977, Migraine: a generalised vasomotor dysfunction? A critical review of evidence, Headache, 17:71-74.

O'Brien, M.D., 1973, The haemodynamics of migraine - a review, Headache, 12:160-162.

Pearce, J., 1977, Migraine: a psychosomatic disorder, Headache, 17:125-128.

Philips, C., 1976, Headache and personality, J. Psychosom. Res., 20:535-542.

Philips, C., 1977, A psychological analysis of tension headache, in: "Contributions to Medical Psychology, Vol. I," S. Rachman, ed., Pergamon Press, Oxford.

Philips, C., 1978, Tension headache: theoretical problems, Beh. Res. & Ther., 16:249-261.

Pozniak-Patewicz, E., 1976, "Cephalgic" spasm of head and neck muscles, Headache, 15:261-266.

Price, K.P., and Clarke, L.K., 1979, Classical conditioning of digital pulse volume in migraineurs and normal controls, Headache, 19:328-332.

Price, K.P., and Turskey, B., 1976, Vascular reactivity of migraineurs and non-migraineurs: a comparison of responses to self-control procedures, Headache, 16:210-217.

Rickles, W.H., Cohen, M.J., McArthur, D.L., and Grove, R.N., 1979, Physiological response stereotypy in migraine headache is not modified by biofeedback training. Paper presented at the 10th Annual Meeting of the Biofeedback Soc. of Amer., San Diego, California, Feb. 1979.

Sakai, F., and Meyer, J.S., 1979, Abnormal cerebrovascular reactivity in patients with migraine and cluster headache, Headache, 19:257-266.

Sargent, J.D., Walters, E.D., and Green, E.E., 1973, Psychosomatic self-regulation of migraine headaches, in: "Biofeedback: Behavioural Medicine," L. Birk, ed., Grune & Stratton, New York, pp.55-68.

Schumacher, G.A., and Wolff, H.G., 1941, Experimental studies on headache, Arch. Neurol. & Psychiat., 45:199-214.

Sovak, M., Kunzel, M., Sternbach, R.A., and Dalessio, D.J., 1978, Is volitional manipulation of hemodynamics a valid rationale for biofeedback therapy of migraine?, Headache, 18:197-202.

Stoffer, G.R., Jensen, J.A.S., and Nesset, B.L., 1979, Effects of contingent versus yoked temperature feedback on voluntary temperature control and cold stress tolerance, Biofeedback & Self-Regulation, 4:51-61.

Stroebel, C.F., and Glueck, B.C., 1976, Psychophysiological rationale for the application of biofeedback in the alleviation of pain, in: "Pain," M. Weisenberg & B. Tursky, eds., Plenum Press, New York.

Turin, A., and Johnson, W.G., 1976, Biofeedback therapy for migraine headaches, Arch. Gen. Psychiat., 33:517-519.

Van Boxtel, A., and van der Ven, J.R., 1978, Differential EMG activity in subjects with muscle contraction headaches related to mental effort, Headache, 17:233-237.

Waters, W.E., 1975, Review of the epidemiology of migraine in
     adults, Danish Med. Bull., 22:86-88.
Werbach, M.R., and Sandweiss, J.H., 1978, Peripheral temperatures of
     migraineurs undergoing relaxation training, Headache, 18:
     211-214.
Ziegler, D.K., Hassanein, R., and Hassanein, K., 1972, Headache
     syndromes suggested by factor analysis of symptom variables in
     a headache prone population, J. Chron. Dis., pp.353-363.

EXPERIMENTAL INVESTIGATIONS OF PSYCHOPHYSIOLOGICAL BASIS OF

HEADACHE AND ITS TREATMENT USING BIOFEEDBACK

Clive Reading   Principal Psychologist

Manchester Area Health Authority (Teaching)

Studies using biofeedback in the treatment of headache are
reviewed in the previous chapter.

EXPERIMENT 1

The purpose of this experiment was a psychophysiological comparison of chronic headache patients and headache-free anxious
patients, in order to investigate suggestions that chronic headache
is associated with abnormalities in control of vasomotor activity,
elevated frontalis EMG levels, and increased sympathetic nervous
system activity. An anxiety control group was included, in preference to the more frequently reported "normal" control group, so that
any observed differences between the groups could be attributed to
the predisposition to headache rather than to the presence of non-
headache neurotic symptomatology. Resting levels of frontalis EMG,
finger temperature, skin conductance, and heart rate were compared
for the two groups before and after a series of taxing procedures.

METHOD

Subjects

The experimental (ie headache) group subjects were 7 female and
5 male chronic headache sufferers, referred for biofeedback treatment
of their headaches, and who had been diagnosed as migraine sufferers
by the referring neurologist or general practitioner. The mean age
of the group was 37.0 (SD 12.6). The minimum headache history was

251

2 years and subjects were experiencing a mean of 29.5 (SD 27) hours
of headache each week. In all cases headaches were associated with
nausea and/or vomiting.

The control (ie anxiety-state) group subjects were 7 female and
5 male patients referred for behavioural treatment of general anxiety
states. The mean age of the group was 37.6 (SD 12.6) years. The
control patients had no history of migraine or frequent or severe
tension headaches. No patient in either group had previously received relaxation training or been exposed to a biofeedback or
psychophysiology laboratory. Patients were not asked to reduce
medication prior to the assessment session. Three neurotic control
group patients had taken medication within 24 hours. One subject
had taken Anafranil the previous day, one had taken Equanil the
previous night, and one had taken Valium and Anafranil. Within the
headache group, 9 of the 12 had taken medication within 24 hours.
Three had taken vasoconstrictor drugs, one had taken prophylactic
drugs, and eight had taken analgesics. Clearly it is not possible
to discount drug effects on the obtained results, although Price
and Clarke (1979) found no difference in the psychophysiological
reactivity of prophylactic and vasoconstrictor drug users, and
Werbach and Sandweiss (1978) reported that the correlation between
ergot use and initial finger temperature approached zero.

Apparatus and Measurements

Self-Report Measures. The Eysenck Personality Questionnaire
(Eysenck and Eysenck, 1975) and the SCL-90 (Derogatis et al, 1973)
were completed by all 24 subjects so that the headache and anxiety
patients could be compared for levels of neuroticism and neurotic
symptomatology.

Electrophysiological Measures. Frontalis EMG in the range
100-200 Hz was monitored by an A1700 Feedback Myograph (Autogenic
Systems Inc., Berkeley, California), with a bipolar placement of
silver/silver chloride electrodes. The contact medium was Spectra
360 Electrode Gel (Parker Laboratories Inc., New Jersey).

Skin conductance was measured by an A3400 Feedback Dermograph,
with Beckman silver/silver chloride electrodes. The contact medium
was Johnson & Johnson KY Jelly. The area of contact for each of
the two active electrodes was 1 cm^2. Conductance was measured by
the application of a constant AC voltage. Active electrodes were
placed on the middle phalanges of the first and second fingers of
the right hand.

Hand temperature was recorded from the middle phalange of the
little finger of the right hand, using an A2000 Feedback Thermometer
with research grade thermistor.

Heart rate was monitored by a modified San-ei Pulsemeter, with
a Type E-107 photoelectric plethysmogram pulse-rate pick-up attached
to the right hand thumb. The output signal was amplified by a
Devices Instruments Ltd 3461 DC Amplifier and converted to a DC
voltage proportional to heart rate by a Devices 4520 Ratemeter. The
heart rate, frontalis EMG, skin conductance, and finger temperature
signals were each converted to mean values as described in the
following section. Also monitored, but not included in the present
analysis, were left hand finger temperature, respiration rate, and
forehead blood volume pulse.

Procedure

The single psychophysiological assessment session took place
in a dimly-lit, sound-attenuated laboratory, with the temperature
maintained at approximately $70^{o}F$. The subject was seated in a comfortable relaxation chair. Upon entering the room each subject was
informed of the purpose of the session and the measures to be used.
A standardised description of the session, and the sequence of events,
was given. The EMG and skin conductance electrode placement sites
were prepared by rubbing with Sterets H injection swabs, and the
electrodes attached. The thermistor and pulse pick-up were secured
with micropore tape. The experimenter then left the room. Following
an adaptation period of 10 minutes, physiological recording took
place for two 5 minute periods during one of which the subjects were
asked to try and become as mentally and physically relaxed as possible (relaxation instruction 1), and during the other of which subjects were asked to sit comfortably but without trying to become
deeply relaxed (baseline period). One half of the subjects in each
group received the relaxation period instruction before the baseline
period instruction, with the reverse order of presentation for the
remaining subjects. There then followed a series of five taxing
procedures, presented in balanced order. There were mental arith-
metic (subtracting 12 serially from 978), 90 dB white noise, a word
recognition test, and two memory tests. Each procedure involved a
two-minute pre-stimulus phase and a two-minute recovery phase. Each
test was two-minutes in duration, and was separated from the next
test by a two-minute interval during which the subject was informed
that physiological measures were not being taken. Each test therefore occupied approximately 8 minutes, and the time taken for the
completion of all five tests was 45 minutes. Following the tests
subjects were again asked to relax as deeply as they could for 5
minutes, following which the experimenter re-entered the subject-
room and electrodes were removed. The physiological data to be
reported here concerns only the initial and final relaxation periods,
plus the initial baseline period, each of these periods being 5
minutes in duration. Mean values were obtained for EMG, skin
conductance, hand temperature and heart rate for each of the three
phases of five-minutes' duration. Data reduction was accomplished

by an Autogen Systems Inc. A5600 Data Aquisition Centre and P5000
alpha/numeric printer.

Data Analysis

Electrophysiological Measures. Between-group comparisons of
frontalis EMG, skin conductance, finger temperature, and heart rate,
were made for each of the three periods (baseline, initial relaxation, final relaxation). The analysis was by independent t-tests.
Within-group comparisons were also made, using dependent t-tests,
between the baseline and initial relaxation periods and between the
initial and final relaxation periods. Mean EMG for each five-minute
period is expressed as microvolts integral average (bandpass 100-200
Hz). Mean skin conductance level (SCL) is expressed as micromhos
per cm^2x2. Temperature is expressed in ^{o}F, and heart rate as beats-
per-minute. Physiological levels during the initial (ie pre-stress)
relaxation (R1) and baseline (B) periods were used to compare resting
psychophysiological activity in the headache and anxiety patients,
with the second (ie post-stress) relaxation (R2) period revealing
any differential responses of the two groups of patients to prolonged
exposure to taxing conditions.

Self-Report Measures. A comparison of the headache and anxiety
patients was made using independent t-tests for each of the following
self-report items.

1)   E.P.Q. "Neuroticism" sub-scale score (EPQ/N).

2)   E.P.Q. "Extraversion" sub-scale score (EPQ/E).

3)   The total number of SCL-90 items receiving a positive rating
(SCL/PST).

4)   The mean distress rating given to positively rated SCL-90
items (SCL/PSDL).

The above sub-scales permit a comparison of the two groups in terms
of their overall symptomatology and symptom distress levels.

RESULTS

Self-Report Measures

No significant differences between the groups were found on
measures of extraversion, neuroticism, total number of positively
rated symptoms, or the mean distress levels reported for the
positively rated symptoms (see Table 1).

Table 1.   Self-Report Measures

		EPQ E-Scale	EPQ N-Scale	SCL-90 PST	SCL-90 PSDL
Headache Group	$\overline{X}$	9.16	17.00	50.41	2.06
(N=12)	SD	5.02	3.97	21.83	0.75
Anxiety Group	$\overline{X}$	11.16	16.58	44.33	1.81
(N=12)	SD	4.46	3.28	21.01	0.55

Physiological Measures

Frontalis EMG. Mean frontalis EMG levels for the two groups during the three phases of the experimental session are shown in Table 2. There were no significant differences between the groups during pre-stress baseline, pre-stress relaxation or post-stress relaxation. Within the headache group frontalis EMG was significantly lower during pre-stress relaxation than during pre-stress baseline ($p < 0.001$), demonstrating that the instruction to relax was associated with a decrease in frontalis EMG activity. No significant difference was found between pre-stress and post-stress frontalis EMG levels for the headache patients. The results for the anxiety group were as for the headache group. Frontalis EMG was significantly lower during pre-stress relaxation than during pre-

Table 2.   Frontalis EMG

		Pre-stress Baseline (B)	Pre-stress Relaxation (R1)	Post-stress Relaxation (R2)
Headache Group	$\overline{X}$	4.64	2.64	2.86
(N=12)	SD	1.63	1.30	1.10
Anxiety Group	$\overline{X}$	5.22	3.10	3.41
(N=12)	SD	2.72	1.43	1.14

stress baseline (p < 0.02). No significant difference was found
between pre-stress and post-stress frontalis EMG levels for the
anxious patients.

Finger Temperature. Finger temperatures expressed in ^{o}F for
the two groups during pre-stress baseline, pre-stress relaxation and
post-stress relaxation are shown in Table 3. There were no significant differences between the groups during any of the three phases
of the session. Within the headache group, finger temperature was
not significantly different during the pre-stress baseline and pre-
stress relaxation phases, but was significantly lower during post-
stress relaxation than during pre-stress relaxation (p < 0.01).
Exposure to the 45 minute duration stress-induction procedure was
associated with a significant decrease in finger temperature for the
headache group patients. Within the anxiety group, finger temperature was not significantly different during the pre-stress baseline and pre-stress relaxation phases, nor during the pre-stress and
post-stress relaxation phases. For this group of patients exposure
to the stress tests was not associated with a decrease in finger
temperature.

Skin Conductance Level. Skin conductance levels for the two
groups of patients are shown in Table 4. There were no significant
differences between the groups during any of the three phases. There
were no significant differences between the pre-stress baseline and
pre-stress relaxation skin conductance levels for either group of
patients. There were significant increases on skin conductance
levels from pre-stress to post-stress relaxation for both headache
(p < 0.02) and anxiety (p < 0.01) group patients.

Heart Rate. Mean heart rate was lower in the headache group
than the anxiety group during all three session phases (Table 5),

Table 3. Finger Temperature

		Pre-stress Baseline (B)	Pre-stress Relaxation (R1)	Post-stress Relaxation (R2)
Headache Group	$\overline{X}$	87.10	87.44	82.81
(N=12)	SD	8.60	8.05	7.41
Anxiety Group	$\overline{X}$	82.31	82.86	82.94
(N=12)	SD	10.53	10.47	10.09

Table 4. Skin Conductance Level

		Pre-stress Baseline (B)	Pre-stress Relaxation (R1)	Post-stress Relaxation (R2)
Headache Group	$\overline{X}$	5.46	5.40	6.35
(N=12)	SD	1.96	1.96	2.15
Anxiety Group	$\overline{X}$	8.53	8.03	9.89
(N=12)	SD	6.16	5.20	6.59

though the difference achieved statistical significance only during the pre-stress relaxation phase ($p < 0.02$). Within the anxiety group mean heart rates during the baseline and pre-stress relaxation phases were not significantly different. Heart rate decreased from pre-stress to post-stress relaxation within the anxiety group, but this decrease was not statistically significant. Within the headache group heart rate decreased significantly from pre-stress relaxation to post-stress relaxation ($p < 0.02$), and was significantly lower during pre-stress relaxation than during pre-stress baseline ($p < 0.05$).

Table 5. Heart Rate

		Pre-stress Baseline (B)	Pre-stress Relaxation (R1)	Post-stress Relaxation (R2)
Headache Group	$\overline{X}$	71.17	69.52	66.29
(N=12)	SD	13.36	13.58	13.43
Anxiety Group	$\overline{X}$	80.00	80.56	76.37
(N=12)	SD	11.76	10.24	12.66

DISCUSSION

　　Bakal and Kaganov (1979) have suggested that heightened muscle
activity may be a major component of the predisposition to headache.
The same authors (Bakal and Kaganov, 1977) reported higher frontalis
EMG levels in migraine patients than in headache-free controls, and
also showed that frontalis EMG biofeedback is an effective treatment
for migraine.

　　The results of the present study suggest that when the control
group is matched with the headache patients for overall levels of
neurotic symptomatology, no association between elevated frontalis
EMG levels and the predisposition to headache is found. Levels of
frontalis EMG in the headache patients and the headache-free neurotic
patients were similar, both before and after a series of taxing
procedures. There were no significant differences between the groups
in levels of skin conductance before and after the stress tests, both
groups showing significant skin conductance level increases from pre-
stress to post-stress. Heart rate differences between the groups
were found, and achieved statistical significance during the pre-
stress relaxation phase. The implication of this finding is unclear,
although if heart rate is viewed as an index of somatic activity
(Obrist et al, 1972), it is possible that the observed difference in
heart rate between the groups indicates higher bodily muscle tension
levels in the anxiety group patients. The significant decrease in
finger temperature for the migraine patients, but not for the anxiety
group patients, during the course of the session, confirms previous
reports of abnormal digital vascular responses in migraine patients.
Price and Tursky (1976), for example, reported a similar vasoconstriction over time in migraine patients. Unlike previous studies
however, the current experiment has demonstrated that this effect is
not attributable to elevated levels of general anxiety in the headache patients.

EXPERIMENT 2

　　The purpose of this experiment was to investigate the suggestion
that chronic headache will respond to biofeedback treatment based
either on frontalis EMG or peripheral vasomotor activity (Bakal and
Kaganov, 1977) or on any measure of sympathetic activity (Stroebel
and Glueck, 1976; Sovak et al, 1978). If, has been suggested,
chronic headache is associated with abnormal levels of frontalis
EMG, abnormal peripheral vasomotor activity, and increased sympathetic activity, then biofeedback treatment of headache using frontalis
EMG feedback, hand temperature feedback and skin conductance level
feedback should be equally effective. The demonstration of a specific biofeedback effect can only be assumed, however, if an association
between symptom reduction and the presence of a training effect can
be demonstrated. In addition to the effect of the three biofeedback

procedures on the occurrence of headaches, the experiment was also
designed to determine the physiological specificity or generality
of feedback. If feedback has a training effect specific to the
physiological feedback function involved then, for example, temperature increases should be greater during temperature feedback
than during frontalis EMG feedback and vice versa. If the training
effect is achieved as part of a general relaxation response, then
changes in frontalis EMG, skin conductance and hand temperature,
should be independent of the physiological feedback function.

METHOD

Subjects

     15 female and 9 male chronic headache patients were included in
the study. All had been referred for biofeedback treatment and had
been diagnosed as migraine sufferers by the referring neurologist or
general practitioner. The mean age of the group was 41.4 (SD 12.8)
years. Patients were experiencing a mean of 31.5 (SD 24.8) hours of
headache in the five weeks prior to the start of treatment, and had
a minimum headache history of 2 years. The mean frequencies per week
for mild, moderate and severe headaches were 2.16 (SD 1.28), 1.44
(SD 1.23), and 0.77 (SD 0.86) respectively. The definitions of mild,
moderate and severe headaches will be discussed shortly.

Design: Apparatus and Measurements

     Self-Report Measures. A headache diary was completed daily by
all subjects during the course of the study. The diary included
headache frequency, duration and severity. A 3-point grading of
mild, moderate and severe headaches was used. A mild headache was
defined as one where the pain of the headache did not interfere with
daily activities. A moderate headache was defined as a headache
where the pain interfered with concentration and everyday activities,
and a severe headache was defined as a complete disruption of everyday activities (eg it is necessary to lie down or go to bed).

     At the start of the study subjects completed a 40 item headache
symptom checklist, recording the occurrence of symptoms commonly
reported by patients with a chronic headache problem. The checklist
includes items usually associated with muscle-contraction headache,
in addition to items considered to indicate a vascular headache.
In addition to providing a description of the headache symptoms
reported by each subject, the checklist also enabled a total headache symptom score to be given. The checklist was included in the
study not only to enable a description of the headache patient
sample, but also so that any association between symptoms, symptom

Table 6. Number of Patients Reporting the Presence of Headache
Symptom Checklist Items Before or During Headaches

SYMPTOM	N	SYMPTOM	N
1. Spots or dark patches before the eyes	12	21. Dizziness	10
2. Nausea	17	22. Palpitations	9
3. Vomiting	11	23. Vertigo (giddiness and disorientation)	7
4. Weakness in an arm or leg	7	24. Depression	19
5. Difficulty in speaking	4	25. Diarrhoea	8
6. Double vision	8	26. A tight feeling around the head	20
7. The pain starting on only one side of the head	20	27. Cold hands or feet	11
8. A pain over the eye	21	28. Feeling irritable	21
9. A stuffy nose	10	29. Sweating a lot	11
10. Watery eyes	9	30. Shivering	15
11. Neck pains	18	31. Feeling hot	17
12. Nervousness	14	32. A feeling of pressure inside the head	22
13. Fainting or feeling faint	8	33. A burning sensation inside the eye	9
14. Scalp tenderness	15	34. A feeling of "fuzziness" in the head	16
15. Blind spots or partial loss of vision	7	35. Loss of appetite	16
16. Avoiding bright lights	18	36. Facial swelling	6
17. Buzzing, singing, hissing or roaring in the ears	12	37. A constant dull ache in the head	21
18. A churning feeling in the stomach	16	38. A throbbing pain in the head	22
19. A "dimming" of vision or not being able to see things clearly	12	39. A feeling of unusual well-being	6
20. Flashing lights	7	40. A pain over the heart	3

frequencies and success of treatment could be assessed. The 40 items
of the headache symptom checklist, and the number of subjects
reporting the presence of each symptom are shown in Table 6.

Electrophysiological Measures. Frontalis EMG, skin conductance
level, and finger temperature were measured as in Experiment 1. Data
reduction was again accomplished by an Autogenic Systems Inc. A5600
Data Aquisition Centre, which in this case provided mean EMG, SCL
and finger temperature values for each of the four ten-minute periods
of the treatment sessions. Also monitored, but not included in the
present analysis, were left hand finger temperature, respiration
rate, heart rate, and forehead blood volume pulse.

Feedback Display. An identical visual feedback display was used for feedback of frontalis EMG, SCL and finger temperature. A remote diamond light display, connected to a modified Autogen Systems Inc. Light Feedback Centre provided subjects with continuous analogue feedback. The diamond light display comprised a series of 20 red l.e.d.s forming a diamond shape 6 cm high and 6 cm wide. At a given time only one l.e.d. was activated, and continuous movement of the light in either direction around the diamond provided the feedback information. When switched to monitor skin conductance level or frontalis EMG, movement in an anti-clockwise direction was required, corresponding to decreases in SCL and EMG, and therefore indicating relaxation. For temperature feedback, subjects were required to produce movement of the light in a clockwise direction, indicating a relaxation response associated with increasing finger temperature. In addition to the continuous analogue feedback provided by the diamond light display, subjects received intermittent digital feedback from an Autogen A5100 Digital Integrator. At intervals of one minute the digital display informed the subject of the mean EMG, SCL or finger temperature obtained during that minute. Subjects in the EMG and SCL groups were told that successful movement of the diamond light in an anti-clockwise direction would lead to lower numbers being displayed each minute. Subjects in the temperature group were told that movement of the diamond light in a clockwise direction would lead to higher numbers being displayed each minute.

Procedure

Subjects kept a record of headache occurrence for 5 weeks before the start of treatment, for 5 weeks during treatment, and for a further 5 weeks after treatment. Each subject attended for 10 treatment sessions. The laboratory setting was as described in Experiment 1. Subjects were allocated to the EMG, SCL or finger temperature (TEMP) treatment groups prior to the first treatment session. Following the attachment of electrodes at the start of the first session subjects were given a lengthy, standardised description of the nature and purpose of the feedback, and the structure of the session was divided into four ten-minute phases. The first was an adaptation or stabilisation phase during which the subject was asked to sit comfortably but without making any effort to achieve deep mental or physical relaxation. No feedback was given during this phase. The second and fourth phases were feedback phases during which subjects attempted to control the feedback display. The third phase was a comparison phase without feedback and with instructions as for the adaptation phase. At the start of each feedback phase during all 10 sessions the subject was given a brief, recorded reminder of the feedback task. Subjects were asked to keep their eyes open during the whole session.

Data Analysis

   Headache Data. Comparisons between groups and across the 15
weeks were carried out by analysis of variance (ANOVAs) with repeated
measures, applied to total hours of headache per week, total number
of headaches per week, and number of mild, moderate and severe headaches per week.

   Physiological Data. Comparisons between groups, across sessions
and between phases (stabilisation, first feedback, comparison, second
feedback) within sessions were carried out by ANOVAs with repeated
measures, applied to session phase means for EMG, TEMP and SCL.

RESULTS

Headache Data

   There was significant weeks effect for number of hours of
headache per week (p < .017), total number of headaches per week
(p < 0.001), number of severe headaches per week (p < 0.02) and number
of moderate headaches per week (p < 0.03). The effect for the number
of mild headaches per week approached significance (p < 0.17). There
was no significant groups X weeks effect. The number of patients
showing a reduction in the number of hours of headache per week of
at least 30% was 12 (50%). The mean number of headaches per week
for all subjects during the 15 week programme are shown in Fig 1.

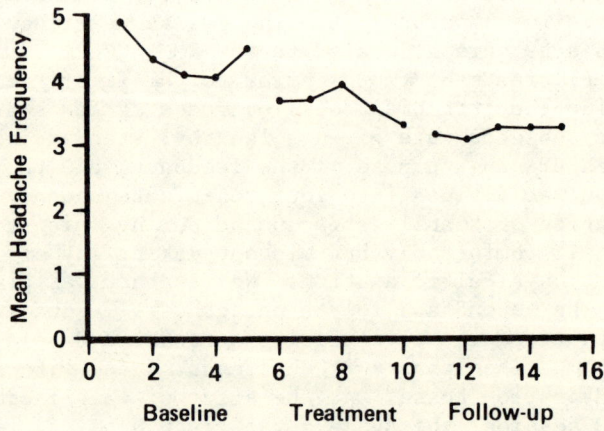

Fig. 1. Mean headache frequency during each
treatment phase.

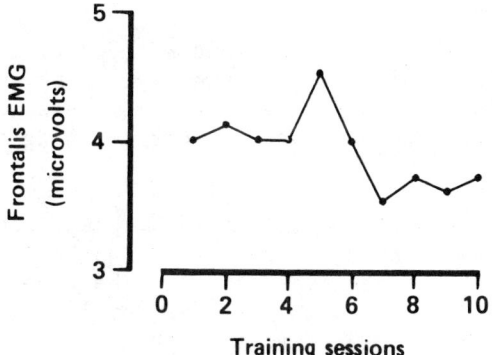

Fig. 2.   Frontalis EMG training session means.

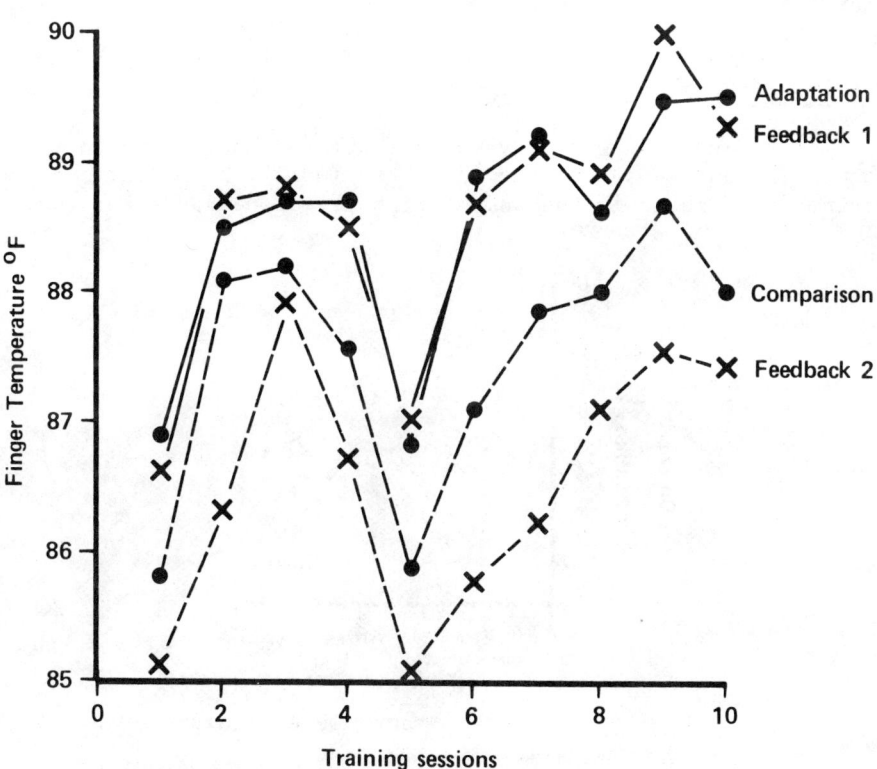

Fig. 3.   Finger temperature training session effects.

Physiological Data

There was a significant sessions effect for frontalis EMG
(p < 0.007) but no significant treatment group or session phase effects
and no significant interaction effect. Mean sessional frontalis EMG
levels for all subjects combined, across training sessions, are shown
in Fig 2.

The sessions effect for finger temperature approached significance, (p < 0.114). There was no significant treatment group effect,
and no significant interaction effects. There was a significant
phase effect (p < 0.001) within sessions for finger temperature, resulting from a temperature decrease within sessions. Fig 3. shows
mean finger temperature for all subjects for the four phases within
sessions.

The sessions effect for skin conductance level approached significance (p < 0.124). The treatment group, session phase, and interaction effects were not significant. Fig 4. shows mean skin conductance levels for all subjects combined for the 10 treatment sessions, with the skin conductance levels combined for the four phases
within sessions.

Training Effects, Headache Symptomatology and Outcome

The 24 subjects were divided into those showing the most improvement (N=12) and those showing the least (N=12), as measured by the
percentage decrease in the number of hours of headache each week

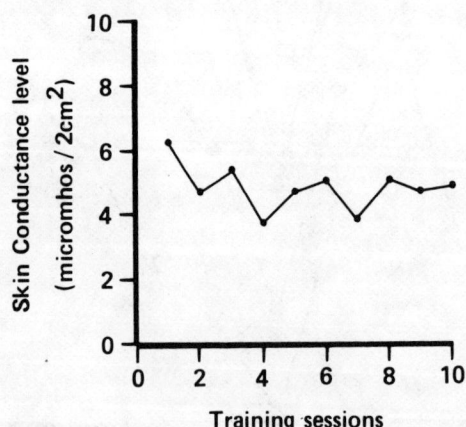

Fig. 4. Skin conductance level training session means.

post-treatment compared to pre-treatment. A significant difference between the most and least improved subjects was found for the total number of items on the headache symptom checklist receiving a positive rating (t=2.26, p < 0.05). The obtained scores are shown in Table 7.

The most and least improved subjects were also compared for each headache symptom checklist item. The frequency with which the two groups positively rated each item were analysed by the Fisher Exact Probability Test. No item was positively associated with a good outcome, and only one item was associated with a poor response to treatment, namely the presence of nausea (p < 0.007). All other headache symptoms occurred with similar frequencies in the most and least improved subjects.

The groups of most and least improved subjects were also compared on a number of criteria of successful biofeedback training, in a similar manner to Kewman and Roberts (1980). Comparisons were made between the two feedback phases and the comparison (no-feedback) phase for each session for each subject. The criteria included in this analysis were: frontalis EMG, skin conductance level, and finger temperature absolute values during feedback for the final three training sessions; the total number of occasions on which mean EMG and mean SCL were lower, and mean TEMP was higher, during first and second feedback phases compared to the no-feedback comparison phase (maximum score per subject = 60); the total number of occasions (maximum = 20) when, for each subject, the feedback function (ie EMG, TEMP or SCL) had a mean value lower (for EMG and SCL) or higher (for the TEMP group) under feedback compared to no-feedback conditions. Correlations between improvement in headaches and these estimates of successful training were all small and non-significant. A comparison, using independent t-tests, of the most and least improved subjects on each training criterion also revealed no statistically significant differences.

Table 7. Total Headache Symptom
Checklist Scores

	Mean	SD
Most Improved	18.3	5.1
Least Improved	23.7	6.3

Discussion

There was a significant clinical effect on the number of headaches and the number of hours of headache reported by the patients
in this study, although only half of the patients improved by 30% or
more. Fig 1. seems to suggest that improvement was occurring during
the pre-treatment self-monitoring phase. The role of non-specific
treatment effects is also suggested by the lack of association between
clinical outcome and training success. A good outcome was associated
with fewer initial headache symptoms and the absence of nausea.
Clinical outcome was independent of feedback group, and in fact there
was no evidence of a specific physiological training effect. There
were no differences between the groups on measures of frontalis EMG,
skin conductance level, and finger temperature. There was no difference between feedback and no-feedback phases, and the only significant within-sessions effect was for finger temperature, which decreased within sessions. Fig 3. shows that finger temperature during
the first feedback phase remained stable, and during some sessions
increased very slightly, relative to the adaptation phase, but then
decreased during the comparison and second feedback phases. Across
training sessions frontalis EMG decreased significantly, and there
were non-significant trends toward a temperature increase and a skin
conductance level decrease over sessions. Although the physiological
changes over sessions were consistent with an improved ability to
relax, there is no evidence that this was a consequence of biofeedback. The temperature decrease within training sessions is consistent with the results of the first experiment, and with the report
by Price and Tursky (1976), who found that migraine patients tended
to vasoconstrict over time, whereas normal controls tended to vaso-
dilate over time within training sessions.

Summary and Conclusions. Psychophysiological and symptomatological studies of headache do not support a categorical classification system. Headache phenomena are best understood on the basis
of a severity continuum, with no clear point at which "normal" headache ends and chronic "tension" or "migraine" headache begins
(Waters, 1975; Philips, 1978; Bakal and Kaganov, 1979). It seems
probable that the more severe headaches involve greater abnormalities
of cerebrovascular reactivity (Sakai and Meyer, 1979). There is no
clear support for predisposing personality features in headache
sufferers as a group, although reactions to being a headache sufferer may be related to personality. Philips (1976) found that high
medication use was associated with high Neuroticism and Extraversion
scores on the Eysenck Personality Questionnaire. It seems that
headache patients are not representative of headache sufferers as
a group (Waters, 1975; Philips, 1976), and that predisposing psychological features identified clinically in the former group do not
characterise the broader group of headache sufferers. A similar
methodological difficulty exists when trying to identify predisposing psychophysiological features. A number of studies have com-

pared headache patients and headache-free controls psychophysiologically and have reported systematic differences between the groups
in scalp and neck muscle tension levels, vasomotor reactivity, and
general autonomic arousal and reactivity levels. Generalising from
these groups of headache patients to headache sufferers as a whole,
and reaching conclusions about predisposing psychophysiological
features, without controlling for overall levels of neurotic symptomatology may result in misleading conclusions. In the first experiment reported here, a group of chronic headache patients were compared with a group of headache-free anxious patients. The two groups
had similar overall levels of neurotic symptomatology and obtained
similar scores on the Neuroticism scale of the Eysenck Personality
Questionnaire. Following exposure to a series of taxing procedures
the headache patients' group had shown a significant decrease in
finger temperature, whereas the control group had not. This experiment offers some support for the presence of a specific vasomotor
dysfunction in severe chronic headache patients.

The treatment of chronic headache by psychological, behavioural
or psychophysiological procedures should be evaluated against three
main criteria. Firstly the processes assumed to mediate the predisposition to and/or the occurrence of headache attacks should be
specified, and it should be demonstrated that the treatment programme is based upon the adopted model of headache occurrence.
Secondly, the treatment should be shown to be clinically effective,
and to have a specific therapeutic action. Thirdly, it should be
shown that successful treatment is associated with alterations to
the pathological processes postulated to underlie the predisposition
to headache and/or the occurrence of headache attacks. The behavioural treatment programme developed by Mitchell and Mitchell (1971),
and discussed earlier, was apparently clinically effective. However,
the treatment rationale is not supported by evidence and Mitchell
and Mitchell did not demonstrate that successful treatment was associated with alterations to the abnormal personality patterns/environ-
mental lifestyles postulated as aetiological factors.

Biofeedback approaches to treatment are also without a convincing rationale, and have not been shown to have a specific therapeutic effect. In a double-blind trial of temperature feedback
training Kewman and Roberts (1980) found no specific training effect.
Lake et al (1979) compared frontalis EMG biofeedback, temperature
biofeedback with and without rational emotive therapy, and a waiting
list control group. There was a significant clinical effect but no
difference between the groups, and improvement was not related to
the training effect or to home practice of relaxation. In the present experimental report (Experiment 2) it was also found that clinical outcome was unrelated to the biofeedback training effect. A
specific biofeedback treatment effect has not been adequately demonstrated. Furthermore the changes in physiological reactivity that
by implication should result from biofeedback training have not been

demonstrated. Rickles et al (1979) found no differences in vasomotor stress responses before and after temperature biofeedback
training, and Stoffer et al (1979) reported that the acquisition of
voluntary temperature control did not reduce the stress response to
thermal pain.

The rationale for biofeedback treatment of chronic headache,
by either frontalis EMG or temperature training, has not been validated, or even clearly stated. Psychophysiological differences
between headache patients and headache-free subjects are difficult
to interpret, because of methodological shortcomings. There is
evidence of abnormal vasomotor responsivity and response stereotypy
in migrainous headache patients (Price and Clarke, 1979; Cohen et
al, 1978), and the first experiment reported here also found evidence of abnormal vasomotor responsivity in a group of migraine
patients. It seems, however that migraine patients may be particularly poor at acquiring the hand-warming skill (Price and Tursky,
1976), and it has been reported that there is no differential effect
on regional cerebral blood flow with hand-warming and hand-cooling
procedures (Largen et al, 1978).

It has been suggested that any relaxation procedure which reduces sympathetic outflow will be effective on the treatment of
migraine, by preventing the increased sympathetic activity from
reaching a "rebound threshold" (Stroebel and Glueck, 1976; Sovak et
al, 1978). The implication here is that a sustained increase in
physiological activity is of aetiological significance in chronic
headache. Psychophysiological studies of headache have concentrated
on reactions to short duration stimuli, and have paid little attention to the effects of sustained arousal increases and possible
differences in physiological recovery rates following exposure to
stressors. The suggestion that treatment procedures incorporating
relaxation training are effective as a consequence of interrupting
prolonged states of increased sympathetic outflow, implies that the
effective treatment components will be: (1) Training in the recognition of states of increased physiological arousal and (2) Applying
relaxation techniques to prevent prolonged increases in physiological arousal. Biofeedback procedures have paid little attention to
the recognition of states of physiological over-arousal. Interest-
ingly, Gainer (1978) reported the successful use of temperature
discrimination training in a migraine patient who had previously
failed to respond to orthodox temperature biofeedback training. It
is possible that the absence of any significant association between
clinical outcome and laboratory biofeedback training effects is a
consequence of a definition of training success that excludes improved physiological awareness. Without increased awareness of
physiological changes that could lead to a headache attack, the appropriate and effective use of applied relaxation procedures is
made much more difficult. However, until the therapeutic components
and clinical efficacy have been clarified, biofeedback treatment of

headache should be regarded as a clinical research procedure, rather than as a routine treatment.

Evidence of abnormal peripheral vasomotor activity in chronic (migraine) headache was obtained in Experiment 1, but Experiment 2 did not demonstrate that any of the three biofeedback procedures included were effective in inducing peripheral vasodilation in these patients. On the contrary, mean finger temperature decreased during the biofeedback sessions. It is possible that the use of mean temperature values for the four phases within training sessions disguised differing temperature trends within feedback and no-feedback phases. Nevertheless, it is difficult to avoid the conclusion that, for chronic headache patients such as those included in Experiment 2, the instruction to apply the biofeedback relaxation technique is unlikely to consistently result in an increase in finger temperature.

ACKNOWLEDGEMENT

I would like to thank Brian Faragher for his contribution to the statistical analyses.

REFERENCES

Bakal, D.A., and Kaganov, J.A., 1977, Muscle contraction and migraine headache: psychophysiologic comparison, Headache, 17:208-215.

Bakal, D.A., and Kaganov, J.A., 1979, Symptom characteristics of chronic and non-chronic headache sufferers, Headache, 19: 285-289.

Cohen, M.J., Rickles, W.H., and McArthur, D.L., 1978, Evidence for physiological response stereotypy in migraine headache, Psychosom. Med., 40:344-354.

Derogatis, L.R., Lipman, R.S., and Covi, L., 1973, SCL-90: an outpatient psychiatric rating scale - preliminary report, Psychopharm. Bull., 9:13-27.

Eysenck, H.J., and Eysenck, S.B.G., 1975, "Manual of the Eysenck Personality Questionnaire," Hodder & Stoughton, London.

Gainer, J.C., 1978, Temperature discrimination training in the biofeedback treatment of migraine headache, J. Beh. Ther. & Exp. Psychiat., 9:185-188.

Kewman, D., and Roberts, A.H., 1980, Skin temperature biofeedback and migraine headaches: a double-blind study, Biofeedback & Self-Regulation, 5:327-345.

Lake, A., Rainey, J., and Papsdorf, J.D., 1979, Biofeedback and rational-emotive therapy in the management of migraine headache, J. App. Beh. Anal., 12:127-140.

Largen, J.W., Mathew, R.J., Dobbins, K., Meyer, J.S., and Claghorn, J.L., 1978, Skin temperature self-regulation and noninvasive regional cerebral blood flow, Headache, 8:203-210.

Mitchell, K.R., and Mitchell, D.M., 1971, Migraine: an exploratory
    treatment application of programmed behaviour therapy tech-
    niques, J. Psychosom. Res., 15:137-157.
Obrist, P.A., Sutterer, J.R., and Howard, J.L., 1972, Preparatory
    cardiac changes: a psychobiological approach, in: "Classical
    Conditioning II: Current Theory and Research," A.H. Black &
    W.F. Prokasy, eds., Appleton-Century-Crofts, New York,
    pp.312-340.
Philips, C., 1976, Headache and personality, J. Psychosom. Res.,
    20:535-542.
Philips, C., 1978, Tension headache: theoretical problems, Beh. Res.
    & Ther., 16:249-261.
Price, K.P., and Clarke, L.K., 1979, Classical conditioning of
    digital pulse volume in migraineurs and normal controls,
    Headache, 19:328-332.
Price, K.P., and Tursky, B., 1976, Vascular reactivity of migrain-
    eurs and non-migraineurs: a comparison of responses to self-
    control procedures, Headache, 16:210-217.
Rickles, W.H., Cohen, M.J., McArthur, D.L., and Grove, R.N., 1979,
    Physiological response stereotypy in migraine headache is not
    modified by biofeedback training. Paper presented at the
    10th Annual Meeting of the Biofeedback Soc. of Amer., San Diego,
    California, Feb. 1979.
Sakai, F., and Meyer, J.S., 1979, Abnormal cerebrovascular reactivity
    in patients with migraine and cluster headache, Headache,
    19:257-266.
Sovak, M., Kunzel, M., Sternbach, R.A., and Dalessio, D.J., 1978,
    Is volitional manipulation of hemodynamics a valid rationale
    for biofeedback therapy of migraine?, Headache, 18:197-202.
Stoffer, G.R., Jensen, J.A.S., and Nesset, B.L., 1979, Effects of
    contingent versus yoked temperature feedback on voluntary
    temperature control and cold stress tolerance, Biofeedback &
    Self-Regulation, 4:51-61.
Stroebel, C.F., and Glueck, B.C., 1976, Psychophysiological rationale
    for the application of biofeedback in the alleviation of pain,
    in: "Pain," M. Weisenberg & B. Tursky, eds., Plenum Press,
    New York.
Waters, W.E., 1975, Review of the epidemiology of migraine in adults,
    Danish Med. Bull., 22:86-88.
Werbach, M.R., and Sandweiss, J.H., 1978, Peripheral temperatures
    of migraineurs undergoing relaxation training, Headache,
    18:211-214.

METHODOLOGICAL APPROACHES TO BEHAVIOR MODIFICATION WITH LONG-STAY

PSYCHIATRIC PATIENTS

William R Lindsay

Psychology Department
Monklands District General Hospital
Airdrie, Scotland

INTRODUCTION

This section contains contributions in behaviour modification with long-stay psychiatric patients, who represent the core of patients showing the most intractable symptoms, requiring long periods of hospitalisation or repeated hospitalisations. These patients typically present a long-standing aetiology and poor prognosis (Zigler and Phillips, 1960, 1961, 1962), severe psychotic symptoms often stabilised by long periods of drug treatment (Matson, 1980), and poor social adjustment and current social status (Kant, 1948; Murray and Cohen, 1959). Matson (1980) points out that as a greater emphasis is put on Community Care of the psychiatrically ill patient, and total hospital numbers are reduced, so a greater proportion of hospital beds are occupied by this "hard core" of chronic patients.

The main treatments for these patients is the administration of anti-psychotic or phenothiazine drugs. Hersen and Bellack (1976), when considering the most effective ways of dealing with psychotic symptomatology, state that "at this point there can be little doubt that phenothiazines are the treatment of choice for controlling schizophrenic symptomatology............ However, despite the impressive reconstitutive and maintenance roles of the phenothiazines it is obvious that they are not able to remediate basic behavioural deficits" (p.10). They go on to argue for the inclusion, in the therapeutic regime, of behavioural treatments aimed at remediating skill deficits.

The behavioural approaches used with this group of patients can be split in to three basic categories: the Reinforcement and Motivational approach; the Skill Acquisition approach, and the

271

approach which employs Situational and Environmental manipulations. By grouping treatments in this way it is not implied that therapists have confined themselves to one or another. Some treatments combine two or three of these approaches to behaviour change. However, therapists have tended to emphasise aspects of their treatment consistent with the above categorisation and the following short review of methodologies will follow those categories of approach.

The Reinforcement and Motivational Approach

This is the most comprehensively researched model, although it is by no means fully understood. The whole area is well served with excellent reviews (Carlson et al, 1972; Kazdin and Bootzin, 1972; Kazdin, 1973; Lieberman, 1972; Kazdin, 1979; Matson, 1980) and its most formal and widespread application is the token economy. The following paper by Fraser et al is part of a large series of studies (Fraser, 1976; Fraser, 1978; Fraser et al, 1981; Fraser et al, 1981, in press) which attempts to look closely at the parameters surrounding the approach.

The token economy is a system based within an institution whereby certain patient behaviours are selected for their desirability. Behaviours commonly selected are self-care activities, such as, dressing, washing and shaving and domestic living activities, such as, keeping one's living area tidy and washing dishes. The target behaviours selected for each patient will be appropriate to him and the level at which he is expected to fulfil them will again be appropriately judged. Patients are then reinforced for emitting these behaviours with tokens which are exchangeable for goods, outings, privileges, ward luxuries etc.

The system is apparently simple, but is far more complicated in practice. Earlier reviewers tended to conceptualise the token economy as a relatively simple reinforcement system (Carlson et al, 1972; Krasner, 1968). However, more recently it is becoming clear that they are complicated social, psychological and economic systems (Stoffelmayer et al, 1973; Gripp and Magaro, 1974; Winkler, 1972).

A study by Schaffer and Martin (1966) serves as an example. They reported a behaviour therapy for apathy in hospitalized schizophrenics. They defined apathy as a lack of personal hygiene (patient does not care about himself), a lack of social interaction (patient has no interest in other people), and a lack of adequate work performance and considered it a major problem in hospitalised schizophrenics. The emission of these behaviours by a patient was reinforced by the nursing staff with both tokens and social reinforcement. The result of these procedures was that apathy, including lack of social interaction, decreased in the group of experimental patients, while in a control group there was no change in the level of apathy recorded.

Psychotic behaviour has also been treated in this way. In a now classic study Ayllon and Haughton (1964) reported that deviant patient speech could be controlled by contingent reinforcement. In the context of a large behavioural study they focused on the psychotic and psychosomatic verbal behaviour of three patients. The reinforcers used to manipulate these responses were attention, approval and tangible reinforcement. They first increased the occurrence of deviant verbalisations by giving reinforcement contingent on the target response and then decreased deviant verbalisations by contingent withdrawal of reinforcement. This demonstrated that psychotic delusional verbalisations could be increased or decreased depending on the consequences of the behaviour. This treatment has been replicated by Barton (1972, 1973) and Wincze et al (1972). The chapter by Fraser et al in this volume outlines other examples of these methods.

An essential aspect of the reinforcement and motivational approach is the assumption that a patient is able to carry out the various self-help, work etc behaviours and the reason for not doing so is that the reinforcement and motivational contingencies are so arranged that the patient is either prevented from behaving or not encouraged to do so. Alternatively it is assumed that the reinforcement contingencies are maintaining the patient's abnormal or deviant behaviours.

The Skill Acquisition Approach

Here it is not necessarily assumed that the desired behaviours are within the patient's behavioural repertoire and so various methods of teaching and training are employed to develop and encourage these behaviours. The techniques most often used are modelling, rehearsal, roleplay, prompting, shaping, and reinforcing behaviour. The most common example of this technique is social skills training in which target behaviours are split into simpler more easily trained units. Therefore, social behaviour is presented as skills of voice volume, tone, gaze direction, facial expression, gesturing etc. The training methods mentioned above are then used to promote these behaviours in patients with skill deficits. Various aspects of social skills training are outlined in a later chapter by the present author.

Similarly several authors have reinstated speech in mute patients using a skill acquisition model (Isaacs et al, 1960; Fraser et al, 1981). Here the methods of prompting and shaping are used to bring verbal noises under control; they are then shaped through to vowel sounds and then to audible words. Self-help skills have also been trained using these methods of breaking behaviours down into smaller units and then teaching them to patients with specific deficits (Lloyd and Able, 1970).

Situational and Environmental Manipulation

Finally there are those approaches which employ situational and environmental manipulation to alter behaviour. One of the most striking examples of this approach is a study by Zarlock (1966) demonstrating very forcibly the effect that environmental cues and controlling stimuli have on the verbal and symptom behaviour of psychiatric in-patients. By changing the furniture and props in the same room, he found radical changes in behaviour. He had four environmental stimulus settings corresponding to four different conditions - Recreational, Occupational, Social and Medical. He found that when the room was a medical environment (nurses with white coats present, attendants with uniforms, hard chairs placed in a circle etc) bizarre behaviour and delusional utterances increased dramatically over the other conditions. On the other hand when the room was a social or recreational environment (couches, easy-chairs, reading material, table-tennis etc) schizophrenic reactions decreased and social interaction increased correspondingly over the medical condition. He concluded that "schizophrenic patients ..... appeared to be sensitive to the rules of conduct implied in each of the environmental conditions and demonstrated an ability to behave in accordance with these rules". Stated another way, we could say that psychiatric patients respond to the controlling stimuli in these different settings. The different environmental contingencies produce different behaviour from the patients. Behaviour which would be classed as inappropriate and abnormal in ordinary circumstances become appropriate because of the controlling stimuli in the medical environment.

Studies in this section by Lindsay, Taylor and Turvey et al illustrate different aspects of this approach, the essential features of which have been used in psychiatric settings for decades. Hays (1974) writes that some of the most important improvements in patients' behaviour came about through environmental changes in the 19th century. In France Pinel produced behavioural and psychological improvements in patients after positive changes in their asylum environment. The "open door" policy and the reforms in the regime of psychiatric hospitals produced considerable improvements in patients' psychotic behaviour and increased discharge rates. This thesis proposes that the reason why patients behave as they do is because the Institution demands this sort of behaviour from them. Consequently apathy, lack of interest, aggressive outbursts, poor eating and working habits etc are seen as resulting from demands of the system. It would be predicted that if the environment were to change then these behaviours would change accordingly.

A strength of this approach is that since behaviour is being established by situational conditions which will be relatively permanent, it may be easier to maintain behaviour after therapeutic changes have been instigated. This issue of maintenance and trans-

fer of behavioural improvements has dogged behaviour therapists for
some time (O'Leary and Drabman, 1971; Liberman, 1972; Kazdin, 1975;
Stokes and Baer, 1977). A major weakness of the approach is that
it is less able to take account of individual differences in patients'
initial level of ability, since the methods are of necessity situationally based and not based on treatment for individual patients.
In her paper, Taylor looks at the effects of changing the environment
on a most embarrassing problem with these patients, ie messy eating.
Turvey et al view the area from a novèl perspective investigating
the effects of different activities on patients' social behaviours.
The final paper is an assessment of patients' social skill across
situations. The main conclusion to be drawn is that long-stay
patients seem to be differentially responsive in different situations.
Behaviour and skills which they show in one environment may not be
evident in another and conversely behaviour which is increased or
encouraged in a therapeutic situation may not transfer to another
situation. This issue has been viewed as a lack of generalisation,
and also (at least for social skills) as a lacking in flexibility
of responding to different situations (Trower, 1980).

Finally and perhaps the most important point to be made about
this section concerns the operations of assessing change during
treatment. Reliable observation and measurement of clearly defined
responses is a fundamental tenet of the behavioural approach.
The third paper in this section by Lindsay deals with this important
consideration which cuts across the whole field of behaviour
modification.

REFERENCES

Ayllon, T., and Haughton, E., 1964, Modification of symptomatic
    verbal behaviour of mental patients, Beh. Res. & Ther.,
    2:87-97.
Barton, E.S., 1972, Operant conditioning of social speech in the
    severely subnormal and the use of different reinforces,
    Brit. J. Soc. & Clin. Psychol., 11:387-396.
Barton, E.S., 1973, Operant conditioning of appropriate and in-
    appropriate speech in the profoundly retarded, J. Ment. Def.
    Res., 17:183-191.
Carlson, C., Hersen, M., and Eisler, R., 1972, Token economy
    programmes in the treatment of hospitalised adult schizo-
    phrenics, J. Nerv. & Ment. Dis., 115:192-204.
Fraser, D., 1976, An integrated system of behavioural assessment,
    Beh. Mod., 9:17-30.
Fraser, D., 1978, Critical variables in token economy systems: a
    review of the literature and a description of current research,
    Beh. Psychother., 6:46-55.

Fraser, D., Anderson, J., and Grime, J., 1981, An analysis of the
    progressive development of vocal responses in a mute schizo-
    phrenic patient, Beh. Psychother., 9:2-12.
Fraser, D., Black, D., and Cockram, L., 1981, An examination of the
    effectiveness of instructional training and response cost
    procedure in controlling the inappropriate behaviour of male
    schizophrenic patients, Beh. Psychother., 9: to be published.
Gripp, R.F., and Magaro, P.A., 1974, The token economy programme in
    the psychiatric hospital: a review and analysis, Beh. Res. &
    Ther., 12:205-228.
Hays, P., 1971, "New Horizons in Psychiatry," Penguin Books Ltd.,
    Harmondsworth, Middlesex.
Hersen, M., and Bellack, A., 1976, Social skills training for chronic
    psychiatric patients: rational, research findings, and future
    directions, Comp. Psychiat., 17:559-580.
Isaacs, W., Thomas, J., and Goldiamond, I., 1960, Application of
    of operant conditioning to reinstate verbal behaviour in
    psychotics, J. Speech & Hear. Disord., 25:8-12.
Kant, O., 1948, Clinical investigation of simple schizophrenia,
    Psychiat. Quart., 22:141-151.
Kazdin, A.E., 1973, Methodological and assessment considerations in
    evaluating reinforcement programmes in applied settings,
    J. App. Beh. Anal., 6:517-531.
Kazdin, A.E., 1975, Recent advances in token economy research, in:
    "Progress in Behaviour Modification, Volume 1," M. Hersen,
    I. Eisler, & P. Miller, eds., Academic Press, New York.
Kazdin, A.E., 1977, "The Token Economy: A Review and Evaluation,"
    Plenum Press, New York.
Kazdin, A.E., and Bootzin, R.R., 1972, The token economy: an
    evaluative review, J. App. Beh. Anal., 5:343-372.
Kazdin, A.E., 1979, The application of operant techniques in treat-
    ment, rehabilitation and education, in: "Handbook of Psycho-
    therapy and Behaviour Change," A. Bergen & S.L. Garfield, eds.,
    Wiley, New York.
Krasner, L., 1968, Assessment of token economy programmes in
    psychiatric hospitals, in: "The Role of Learning in Psycho-
    therapy," Symposium CIBA.
Liberman, R.P., 1972, Behaviour modification of schizophrenics -
    a review, Schiz. Bull., 6:37-48.
Lloyd, K.E., and Able, L., 1970, Performance on a token economy
    psychiatric ward: a two year summary, Beh. Res. & Ther., 8:1-9.
Matson, J., 1980, Behaviour modification procedures for training
    chronically institutionalised schizophrenics, in: "Progress
    and Behaviour Modification - Volume 9," M. Hersen, R. Eisler,
    & P. Miller, eds., Academic Press, New York.
Murray, E.J., and Cohen, M., 1959, Mental illness, milieu therapy
    and social organisation in ward groups, J. Abn. & Soc. Psychol.,
    58:48-54.
O'Leary, K.D., and Drabman, D., 1971, Token reinforcement programmes
    in the classroom, Psychol. Bull., 75:379-398.

Schaffer, H., and Martin, P., 1966, Behaviour therapy for apathy of hospitalised schizophrenics, Psychol. Rep., 19:1147-1158.

Stokes, T., and Baer, D.M., 1977, An implicit technology of generalisation, J. App. Beh. Anal., 10:349.

Stoffelmayer, B.E., Faulkner, G.A., and Mitchell, W.S., 1973, "The Rehabilitation of Chronic Hospitalised Patients - A Comparative Study of Operant Conditioning Methods and Social Therapy Techniques," Report to the Scottish Home and Health Department.

Trower, P., 1980, Situational analysis of the components and processes of behaviour of socially skilled and unskilled patients, J. Cons. & Clin. Psychol., 48:327-339.

Winkler, R.C., 1972, A theory of equilibrium in token economies, J. Abn. Psychol., 79:169-173.

Wincze, J., Leitenberg, H., and Agras, W.S., 1972, The effect of token reinforcement and feedback on the delusional verbal behaviour of chronic paranoid schizophrenics, J. App. Beh. Anal., 5:247-262.

Zarlock, S.P., 1966, Social expectations, language, and schizophrenia, J. Human. Psychol., 6:68-74.

Zigler, E., and Phillips, L., 1960, Social effectiveness and symptomatic behaviours, J. Abn. & Soc. Psychol., 61:231-238.

Zigler, E., and Phillips, L., 1961, Social competence and outcome in psychiatric disorder, J. Abn. & Soc. Psychol., 63:264-271.

Zigler, E., and Phillips, L., 1962, Social competence and the process - reactive distinction in psychopathology, J. Abn. & Soc. Psychol., 65:215-222.

THE COMPARATIVE EFFECTIVENESS OF INSTRUCTIONS, VERBAL REINFORCEMENT
AND TOKENS IN TEACHING SELF-HELP SKILLS TO LONG-TERM SCHIZOPHRENIC
PATIENTS

Douglas Fraser, David Black, Linda Cockram
and Joanne Grimes

Royal Dundee Liff Hospital
Dundee, Scotland

INTRODUCTION

In a series of studies conducted in 1965 and 1968, Ayllon and
Azrin demonstrated the importance of token reinforcement in maintaining job performance on and off the ward in a group of female chronic
schizophrenic patients. They showed that the token contingencies
were effective in altering voluntary job performances by manipulating the number of tokens that could be earned.

Several other studies have demonstrated the effectiveness of
token reinforcement in promoting the development of independent
functioning within the hospital setting: Allen and Magaro (1971);
Chase (1970); Ellsworth (1969); Gericke (1965); Hersen et al (1972);
Lloyd and Garlington (1968); McReynolds and Coleman (1972) and
Steffy et al (1969). What these studies have in common, however,
is that they fail to examine the relationship between the variables
comprising the token economy system and the degree and nature of
the changes shown by their patient groups.

Studies by Heap et al (1970) and a substantial body of largely
unpublished work by Fernandez (1971, 1974, 1976, 1978) have attempted
some control over the variables whose effects in isolation had
hitherto been largely unexamined in token economy systems. These
studies used a sequential design in which variables (including
checking, verbal reinforcement and token delivery) were added
cumulatively in order to study their effects on the patients' behaviour. Heap et al, concluded that the contingent token plus verbal
reinforcement contingency was superior to verbal reinforcement
alone. The major finding, in this context, from Fernandez' work
suggested that while significant changes can be brought about by

279

using instructions alone, the majority of target behaviours show
most change when instructions are combined with prompting and verbal
reinforcements.

However, the cumulative effect of the treatment programme is not
controlled for in these sequential designs, ie it is not demonstrated
whether continuing to apply one variable, eg instructions, over a
lengthy period of time would have the same effect as applying several
variables sequentially over the same period of time. This also
highlights the problem, evident in these studies, that when treatment phases are of relatively short durtation there is the possibility of facilitatory or inhibitory carry-over from one treatment
phase to the next (Poulton and Freeman, 1966).

Baker et al (1974) used a sequential design for their pilot
study and concluded that contingent tokens were not the critical
therapeutic agent. Their main study (Hall et al, 1977) tried to
clarify the problems mentioned above by using three matched groups
of patients, one group receiving contingent tokens, one receiving
non-contingent tokens and a group which remained in their own ward
whose response would control for the passage of time alone. Treatment phases were reasonably long in this study. Both experimental
groups improved similarly during the study while the control group
deteriorated slightly.

One further, largely unresolved problem, is that of identifying
the specific component of token presentation which is effective.
Some studies (eg Lloyd and Garlington, 1968) have compared the
effectiveness of contingent versus non-contingent tokens but failed
to control for the additional social interaction and reinforcement
which is available during contingent token presentation.

It is suggested that these problems could be, to some extent,
overcome by studying two groups of patients within the framework of
a multiple baseline design (Risley and Wolf, 1972; Kazdin, 1973b)
and with careful analysis of variables. The details of such a
study, carried out by the authors and a team of nursing staff, are
presented below.

THE STUDY

Experimental Procedures

The study which was carried out in Ward 6A, Royal Dundee Liff
Hospital, was designed to investigate the increments, if any, of
token reinforcement over verbal reinforcement as it seemed plausible
that a token reinforcement regime only achieves its results through
the increased social reinforcement which it effects.

Variables Under Investigation. It was decided to focus investigations upon the following variables which emerged from the studies reviewed above as likely contributors to the changes shown in token economy programmes:

1.   Use of instructions – the process of detailing verbally and by written notes the behaviours which the patient is expected to display and those which he is expected to refrain from displaying.

2.   Verbal reinforcement – the expression of social approval consequent upon the emission of a desired response by the patient.

3.   Presentation of valueless token – the contingent presentation of tokens which have no exchange value in order to assess their role in facilitating the delivery of verbal reinforcement.

4.   Presentation of exchangeable tokens – the contingent presentation of tokens which are claimed to derive their reinforcing power from their association with intrinsically reinforcing stimuli (the back-up reinforcers). It has been argued that tokens act as generalised conditioned reinforcers from the responses which precede their delivery and as discriminative stimuli which signal the availability of reinforcement (Kelleher and Gollub, 1962).

Subjects. Ten male schizophrenic patients ranging in age from 30 to 58 years and each with over 2 years continuous stay in hospital since last admission were selected, on the basis of two main measures and a variety of additional criteria, for removal from their original wards to Ward 6A, a behaviour modification research unit.

The measures used were an early version of the Target Behaviour Rating Scales (TBRS) (Fraser, 1976a) and the original version of the Ward Behaviour Rating Scales (WBRS) (Wing, 1961). The selection criteria were as follows: a clear and uncomplicated diagnosis of schizophrenia; a minimum length of stay of 2 years since last admission; male patients under 60 years of age with no history of organic pathology. A total of 18 patients fulfilling these criteria were assessed by means of the TBRS and the WBRS. The 10 patients who achieved the poorest combined scores on these measures were transferred to Ward 6A in November 1975.

One patient died shortly after transfer leaving 9 patients who were split into two groups following a baseline period of assessment of 20 weeks in duration.

Data on the age and length of stay of the 9 patients who took part in the study are presented in Table 1. The fact that Group B was composed of younger patients with a shorter average length of stay than patients in Group A was thought to be of little significance in view of the fact that the groups were, following selection, closely matched on several separate measures of performance.

Table 1. Age and Length of Stay in Hospital of Patients Transferred to Research Unit

	Patient	Age	Length of Stay (since last admission)
Group A	a	50	27 years 2 months
	b	51	27 years 1 month
	c	50	3 years 10 months
	d	44	15 years 4 months
		$\overline{X}$ = 48.75 years	$\overline{X}$ = 18 years 4 months
Group B	a	44	21 years 7 months
	b	31	8 years 5 months
	c	37	10 years 5 months
	d	47	24 years 7 months
	e	30	4 years 10 months
		$\overline{X}$ = 37.8 years	$\overline{X}$ = 13 years 11 months

The aim of the part of the study described here was to encourage independent functioning in the ward dining room.

Measurement Techniques

The main measure used was Form 2 of the TBRS (Fraser, 1976a, 1976b). The TBRS has been specifically designed for use in contingency management programmes. They are designed to measure the degree of independence shown by patients in the performance of self-care and self-help skills.

Reliability. An early version of the TBRS (Fraser, 1976a) was submitted to an item by item analysis of the correlation between two observers independently rating the performance of the 10 patients. Items demonstrating a low level of agreement between observers (Spearman's rho = .564, Siegel, 1956) were revised or dropped from the scales altogether. This led to the construction of three separate TBRS forms (Fraser, 1976b) all of which were found to demonstrate acceptably high levels of agreement between independent observers (Spearman's rho = .60).

Method and Design

Following a lengthy baseline of 20 weeks in order to allow for the effects of environmental change (Higgs, 1970; Zlotowski and Cohen, 1965; De Vries, 1968) the patients were split into two groups matched in terms of work performance, social behaviour and inappropriate behaviour.

During the baseline period the newly transferred staff were merely instructed to continue using the techniques for managing behaviour which they had employed in their former wards. For six of the seven staff concerned the wards from which they had been recruited were entirely non-behavioural in orientation.

A sequential design similar to that employed by Fernandez (1974) was then applied within the framework of a multiple baseline design. The use of this mixed design largely rules out the possibility of a failure to observe facilitatory or inhibitory carry-over from one stage to the next as, for the first 16 weeks, contingencies were added cumulatively to one set of behaviours in one of the groups (Group A) whilst the first contingency to be introduced was applied continuously to the patients in the other group (Group B) for the entire 16 week period. This also provides a control for the passage of time. Ideally, in a multiple baseline design, each behaviour should change only when it is exposed to the treatment variable and not before. This serves as a powerful demonstration that the treatment variable introduced accounts for the specific changes in behaviour which may be observed (Hersen and Barlow, 1976).

RESULTS

In the interests of brevity the results of this study are presented in terms of group mean scores. Although the use of grouped data has long been in disfavour in behaviour modification research, there has recently been a relaxing of this attitude heralded by Kazdin's (1973b) article in which he argued that the use of grouped data is appropriate in studies which attempt to isolate the critical variables in treatment procedure. A further justification for the use of grouped data in the present study is that careful inspection of the raw data reveals that group trends, in the main, reflect individual patterns of change, and also that there were no 'non-responders' among the subjects, ie all subjects showed some improvement during the course of the study.

Arranging Table Settings for Breakfast

The performance of this item of behaviour consisted of arranging the crockery, cutlery and table settings on the table in time for breakfast.

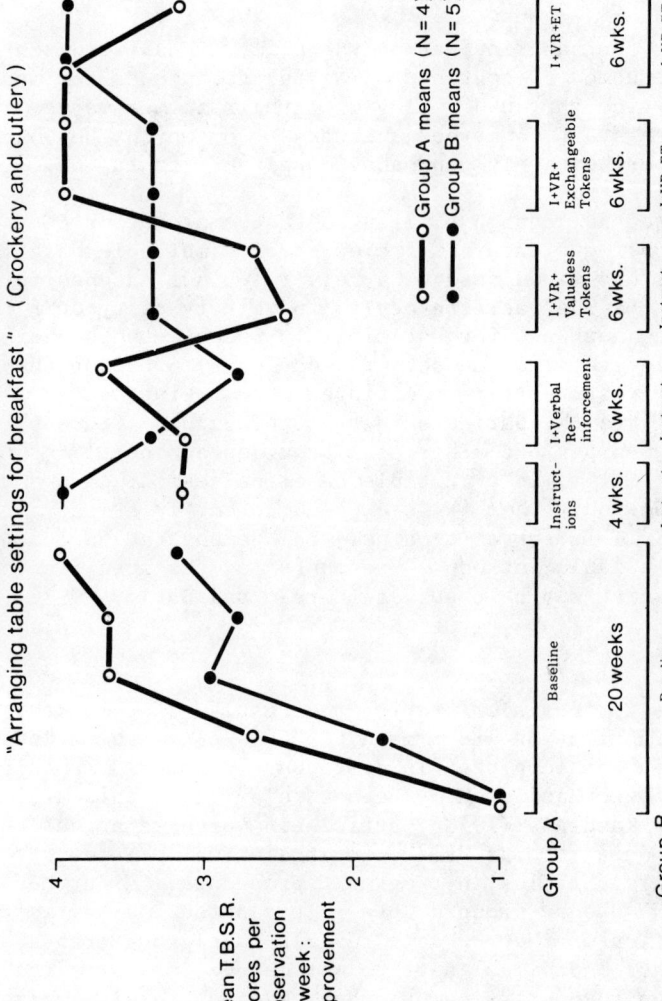

Fig. 1. Arranging table settings for breakfast.

In Fig 1. data on the ordinate indicate the level of performance of patients on this item of behaviour with higher scores signifying increasing independence in functioning. Data on the absissa indicate the length of each successive stage and the contingencies operating within each stage for each of the 2 groups.

The following abbreviations are used in discussing the contingencies:

I = Instructions
VR = Verbal Reinforcement
VT = Valueless Tokens
ET = Exchangeable Tokens

Both groups showed steady and substantial rises in performance to near ceiling levels during the 20 week baseline period.

Group A showed a decline under the I contingency, a rise during the I + VR contingency and a further decline during the I + VR + VT contingency. Performance at or near ceiling levels was re-established and maintained during the two final ET stages.

Group B rose to ceiling levels of performance under the I contingency but a decline and levelling off in performance was noted with the continued application of this contingency. Stability of performance was carried into the first stage of application of the ET contingency. In the second stage performance was again raised to ceiling levels.

Arranging Table for Lunch

The performance of this item of behaviour consisted of setting bread, jam, butter, milk, sugar, salt, pepper, sauce and a jug of juice on the table (Fig 2.).

Group A showed a fairly substantial rise in performance over the baseline period. This was continued to near ceiling levels during the I stage but an initial decline was noted in the I + VR stages. Gradual but continued improvement was shown in the I + VR + VT phase but the implementation of the ET contingency led to an initial decline. Continued application of the ET contingency raised performance again to ceiling levels.

Group B showed a steep rise in performance to near ceiling levels mid-way throughout baseline but this was not maintained. The I contingency had little effect upon performance during the first 2 stages of its application. The introduction of ET led to an initial decline but continued application again raised performance to near ceiling levels.

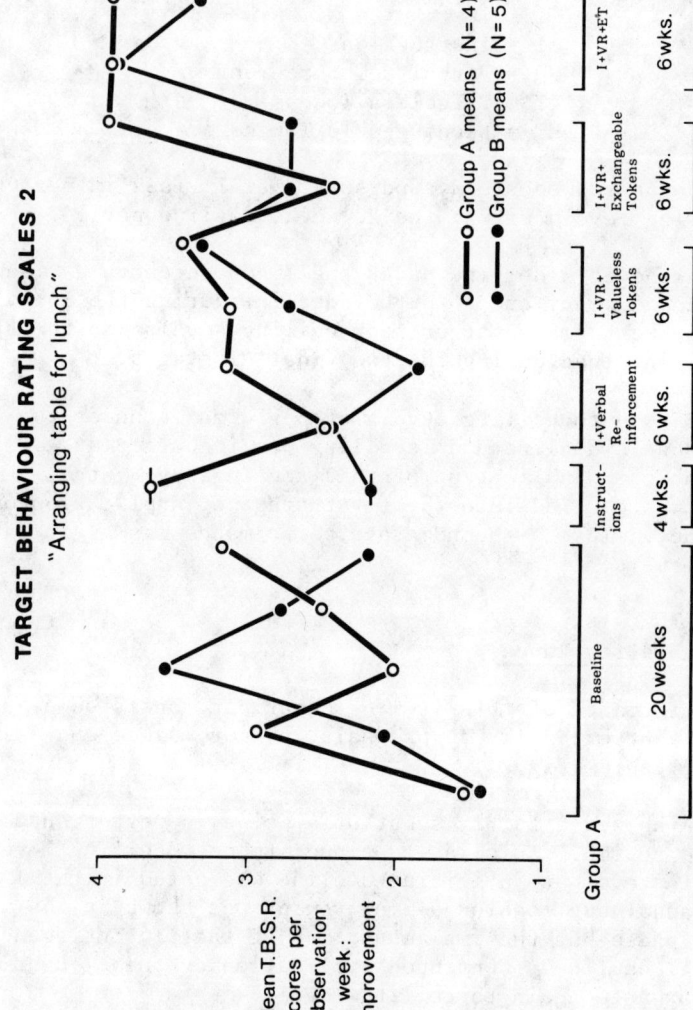

Fig. 2. Arranging table for lunch.

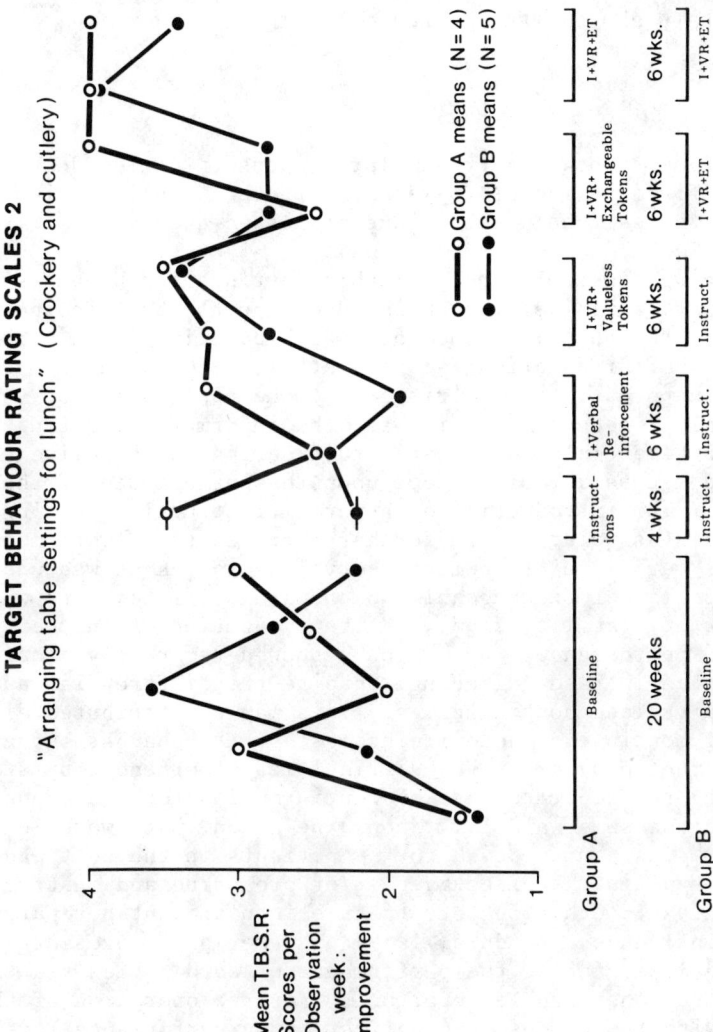

Fig. 3. Arranging table settings for lunch.

Arranging Table Settings for Lunch

The performance of this item consisted of arranging the crockery, cutlery and table settings on the table for lunch (Fig 3.).

The performance of Groups A and B on this set of behaviours was practically identical to their performance of the behaviours discussed immediately above with reference to Fig 2.

DISCUSSION

Both groups showed very similar response profiles despite the fact that, for a period of 16 weeks, different contingencies were applied to the self-help behaviours discussed above.

Arranging the table and the table settings for breakfast and for lunch was fairly well established during the baseline period. This illustrates the importance of length baseline as in other studies of shorter duration (eg Heap et al, 1970) such changes might have been inappropriately attributed to the application of various experimental procedures. As it was, the informal "prompting and praising" regime employed by ward staff during the baseline appears to have had a considerable effect upon the performance of these behaviours. The introduction of a formal instruction contingency was generally associated with further increments in performance but the role of verbal reinforcement and valueless tokens was unclear. The introduction of exchangeable token was associated more with the achievement of stability than with the production of further increments in performance. Both groups showed remarkably close correspondence in rates of change despite the differential application of the various contingencies. This may be attributed either to one type of contingency determining most of the changes shown (most likely instructions) or to the difficulties experienced by staff in implementing two separate sets of contingencies for two groups of patients in the same ward. It should be noted that "work in the dining room" was a novel task to the patients in the unit and this may partly explain the effectiveness of prompting and instructions in this context. Other factors to take into account here are modelling influences (Bandura, 1969) and peer group pressures; the groups were mixed during the performance of ward duties and there was therefore considerable opportunity for the operation of these variables with their consequent effects upon performance levels.

Implications

Two main points emerge from this study:

1)   The importance of a lengthy baseline period in studies which

involve long-term patients in changes in the ward environment and in relationships with new members of staff. The effects of these variables have been well documented by Higgs (1970), Zlotowski and Cohen (1965) and De Vries (1968). In the present study the baseline period proved to be the time of the greatest change when viewed of both rapidity and magnitude of change. A shorter baseline period would, no doubt, have led to the confounding of "environmental change" effects and treatment effects.

2)   The effectiveness of the component variables of the token economy when used in isolation was most in evidence in the case of instruction. This finding is encouraging in two ways. Firstly, it suggests that the difficult and often costly business of establishing a token economy may not be required in order to achieve an acceptable level of control over the behaviour of long-term schizophrenic patients. Secondly, it suggests that these patients (or some of them) may be responsive to social variables and may not necessarily require to be motivated by elaborate incentive schemes. Indeed Fraser (1978) has demonstrated that a wide range of inappropriate behaviours characteristically displayed by long-term patients can be controlled very effectively by the application of a systematic programme of instructional training.

We already know that token economies work (Kazdin, 1977), what we need to discover is how they work in order that we may establish the necessary and sufficient conditions for behavioural change.

ACKNOWLEDGEMENTS

The authors are grateful to Dr H.C. Fowlie, Mr A.E. Lerpinier, Dr F. McPherson and Dr A.S. Presly for facilitating the implementation of this programme of research. The development of the programme was stimulated by the work of Dr J. Fernandez, who also provided us with a great deal of valuable advice and information. We should like to acknowledge the diligent efforts of the following members of staff of the behaviour modification research unit: J. Barclay, A. Ford, A. McLean, L. Phillips, P. Short and J. Weir. We are also grateful to Dr J. Aungle, the ward's Senior Registrar.

REFERENCES

Allen, D.J., and Magaro, P.S., 1971, Measures of change in token
    economy programmes, Beh. Res. & Ther., 9:311-318.
Ayllon, T., and Azrin, N.H., 1965, The measurement and reinforcement
    of behaviour of psychotics, J. Exp. Anal. Beh., 8:357-383.
Ayllon, T., and Azrin, N.H., 1968, "The Token Economy: A Motivational
    System for Therapy and Rehabilitation," Appleton-Century-Crofts,
    New York.

Baker, R., Hall, J.N., and Hutchinson, K., 1974, A token economy
    project with chronic schizophrenic patients, Brit. J. Psychiat.,
    124:367-384.
Bandura, A., 1969, "Principles of Behaviour Modification," Holt,
    Rinehart & Winston, New York.
Chase, J.D., 1970, "Token Economy Programme in the Veterans
    Administration," Unpublished manuscript, V.A. Department of
    Medicine and Surgery, Washington, D.C.
De Vries, D.L., 1968, Effects of environmental change and of
    participation on the behaviour of mental patients, J. Cons. &
    Clin. Psychol., 32:532-536.
Ellesworth, J.R., 1969, Reinforcement therapy with chronic patients,
    Hosp. & Comm. Psychiat., 20:36-38.
Fernandez, J., 1971, The token economy: a learning environment,
    Paper presented at the Third International Symposium on Social
    Psychiatry, Slantchev Bryag, Bulgaria.
Fernandez, J., 1974, Variables which contribute towards the
    behavioural improvement shown by subjects in token programmes,
    Paper presented at the Fourth Annual Conference of the
    European Association for Behaviour Therapy, London.
Fernandez, J., 1976, Token economies and contingency management
    practices, Invited workshop conducted at St. Brendan's Hospital,
    Dublin.
Fernandez, J., 1978, Token economies: will the controlling variables
    stand up and be counted? Paper presented at the Annual
    Conference of the British Association for Behaviour Therapy,
    Stirling, Scotland.
Fraser, D., 1976a, An integrated system of behavioural assessment
    and reinforcer allocation for use in token economies, Beh. Mod.,
    Issue No. 9:17-30.
Fraser, D., 1976b, "The Revised Target Behaviour Rating Scales,"
    Unpublished manuscript.
Fraser, D., 1978, The role of instructions and response cost
    procedures in controlling the inappropriate behaviour of long-
    term patients, Paper presented at the Annual Conference of
    the British Association for Behavioural Psychotherapy, Stirling,
    Scotland.
Gericke, O.L., 1965, Practical use of operant conditioning procedures
    in a mental hospital, Psychiat. Stud. & Projs, 3:2-10.
Hall, J.N., Baker, R.D., and Hutchinson, K., 1977, A controlled
    evaluation of token economy procedures with chronic schiz-
    ophrenic patients, Beh. Res. & Ther., 15:261-283.
Heap, R.F., Bobitt, W.D., Moore, C.H., and Hord, J.E., 1970,
    Behaviour-milieu therapy with chronic neuropsychiatric patients,
    J. Abn. Psychol., 76:349-354.
Hersen, M., and Barlow, D.H., 1976, "Single Case Experimental
    Designs: Strategies for Studying Behaviour Change," Pergamon,
    New York.

Hersen, M., Eisler, R.M., Smith, B.S., and Agras, W.S., 1972, A token
    reinforcement ward for young psychiatric patients, Amer. J.
    Psychiat., 129:142-147.

Higgs, W.J., 1970, Effects of gross environmental change upon
    behaviour of schizophrenics: a cautionary note, J. Abn. Psychol.,
    76:421-422.

Kazdin, A.E., 1973b, Methodological and assessment considerations in
    evaluating reinforcement programs in applied settings,
    J. App. Beh. Anal., 6:517-531.

Kazdin, A.E., 1977, "The Token Economy: A Review and Evaluation,"
    Plenum Press, New York.

Kelleher, R.T., and Gollub, L.R., 1962, A review of positive
    conditioned reinforcement, J. Exp. Anal. Beh., 5:543-597.

Lloyd, K.E., and Garlington, W.L., 1968, Weekly variations in
    performance on a token economy psychiatric ward, Beh. Res. &
    Ther., 6:407-410.

McReynolds, W.T., and Coleman, J., 1972, Token economy: patient and
    staff changes, Beh. Res. & Ther., 10:29-34.

Poulton, E.C., and Freeman, P.R., 1966, Unwanted Asymmetrical
    transfer effects with balanced experimental designs,
    Psychol. Bull., 66:1-8.

Risley, T.R., and Wolf, M.M., 1972, Strategies for analysing behav-
    ioural change over time, in: "Life-Span Developmental Psychol-
    ogy," J. Nesselroade & H. Reese, eds., Academic Press, New York.

Siegel, S., 1956, "Non-Parametric Statistics for the Behavioural
    Sciences," McGraw-Hill, New York.

Steffy, R.A., Hart, J., Crow, M., Torney, D., and Marlett, N., 1969,
    Operant behaviour modification techniques applied to severely
    regressed and aggressive patients, Can. Psychiat. Assoc. J.,
    14:59-67.

Wing, J.K., 1961, A simple and reliable subclassification of chronic
    schizophrenia, J. Ment. Sci., 107:862-875.

Zlotowski, M., and Cohen, D., 1965, Effects of environmental change
    upon behaviour of hospitalised schizophrenic patients,
    Paper presented at Annual Meeting of the Eastern Psychological
    Association, Atlantic City, New Jersey.

THE EFFECT OF CHANGED SITUATION, ATTENTION AND TRAINING ON THE

MEALTIME BEHAVIOR OF LONG-STAY PSYCHIATRIC PATIENTS

Valerie A Taylor

Psychology Department
Leverndale Hospital
Glasgow, Scotland

INTRODUCTION

Among the more deteriorated group of long-stay psychiatric patients, problematic mealtime behaviours are frequently identified and often result in restriction of access to outings or holidays and many contribute to lessening relative-patient contact. Modification of these behaviours could, therefore, have considerable advantages for the patient.

Paden et al (1974) advise that an overall token economy supplemented by one-to-one training, is a more useful approach with the low functioning patients who usually exhibit this set of problems.

Most of the work on mealtime behaviour has been carried out with mentally defective populations. Richman et al (1980) review the work in this field and conclude that most programmes concentrate either on the acquisition of self-feeding skills, or on procedures for motivating continued performance of skills previously acquired. Some studies (Nelson et al, 1975; O'Brien and Azrin, 1972; O'Brien et al, 1972) have, however, combined shaping new skills, suppressing improper eating by punishment, and maintenance procedures for ensuring continuation of proper eating skills. Variations on such programmes include frequent "mini-meal" training sessions (Azrin and Armstrong, 1973) and the use of simulated food during training (Richman et al, 1980).

Proper eating habits have been included as target behaviour in various modification programmes for long-stay psychiatric patients (Coleman and McReynolds, 1972; Goreham and Green, 1970; Lloyd and Abel, 1970; Lloyd and Garlington, 1968; Steffy et al, 1969).

293

The problems of mealtime behaviour with deteriorated long-stay psychiatric patients may be somewhat different from those of mental defectives, in that one would assume that although satisfactory eating behaviours may not at present be in evidence, the behaviours may well be in the patient's repertoire of behaviour. It therefore seemed necessary to include in a programme designed to improve the mealtime behaviour of this group of patients, procedures both for acquisition (or reinstatement) of skills, as well as for maintenance of appropriate eating, once established.

The purpose of the present study was to compare the relative effectiveness of two slightly different methods for training eating skills (O'Brien and Azrin, 1972) with non-specific prompting, the current practice during mealtimes in many hospital settings.

MATERIAL AND METHODS

Subjects

Twelve male, long-term psychiatric in-patients, whose eating was considered unacceptable, were ranked according to their frequency of eating errors during baseline observations and split into groups above and below the mean in the numbers of eating errors. Two each from the high and low frequency groups were then randomly assigned to each of the three groups.

Research Design

The research design is summarised in Fig 1.

(A) During the observation phase in the ward, the patients were observed seated at table along with 3 other patients. No interventions other than the presence of an observer occurred.

(B) All 12 patients were taken in groups of 4 to a cafe in the centre of Aberdeen to eat lunch. They were accompanied by a nurse and by an observer both of whom sat at a separate table, apart from the patients. No special instructions about table manners were given and no interventions made during the meal. (The purpose of the observations in the cafe was to assess the degree of generalisation of treatment effects from the ward treatment setting).

(C) During the individual training, no observation took place as there seemed little sense in counting the frequency of a set of behaviours which was sampled over the period during which these procedures took place.

Group 1	Observed in ward 5 days	Observed in cafe 5 days	Individual training in side room of ward 2 days	Maintenance (a) in ward 9 or 11 days +	Observed in ward 3 days	Observed in cafe 3 days
Group 2	Observed in ward 5 days	Observed in cafe 4 days *	Individual training in side room of ward 2 days	Maintenance (b) in ward 9 or 11 days +	Observed in ward 3 days	Observed in cafe 3 days
Group 3	Observed in ward 5 days	Observed in cafe 5 days	Attention in ward 13 days		Observed 3 days	Observed 3 days

* One day missed due to observer illness. + Only 2 patients could be trained at one time.

Fig. 1. Design of study.

Phases D and E were procedurally identical to phases A and B respectively in order to assess treatment and generalisation effects.

Observational Method

Each of the 4 patients was observed sequentially for 5 seconds so that three 5-second periods were sampled every minute during the meal while food was in front of the patient. About 40 observational samples on average were collected per patient.

During each 5-second period, 5 categories of error were noted as present or absent. The categories were:-

1. Dribbling.

2. Using fingers where not appropriate.

3. Using the wrong cutlery.

4. Position at table or position of plate on table (when markedly abnormal).

5. Picking up a plate to eat, other than tilting soup plate.

Prior to the study, the inter-observer reliability was assessed. An observational sample of 5 seconds was deemed "agreed" if all categories of error were agreed as present or absent. The reliability estimate was taken as the number of "agreed" samples in one lunch time observation session, and was expressed as a percentage of the total number of 5-second periods during which food was available.

The overall figure for inter-rater agreement was 89%. While, in retrospect, further analysis of reliability should have been undertaken (Turvey et al, this volume), given the detailed coding instructions worked out initially, and the relatively "gross" nature of the behaviours involved, there is no reason to suspect that the categories were unreliable in fact.

Procedure

Group 1 The method followed that described by O'Brien and Azrin (1972) and involved two sessions of intensive one-to-one training with the main emphasis on obtaining the first correct response using repeated prompts with manual guidance as necessary. Where possible, mistakes were prevented by the therapist interposing his arm between the patient's hand and mouth. Correct responses, once achieved, were reinforced by praise and, of course, by access to the food. A detailed description of the method is provided by O'Brien and Azrin (1972).

This individual training took place out of the ward dining room, but for later sessions patients returned to eat in the ward. During this maintenance phase, the patients continued to eat under supervision at a table for four. At the beginning of each course they were prompted to eat properly, ie to use correct cutlery, not to use fingers etc. They were then praised intermittently for appropriate eating while minor errors were ignored. The first gross error led to a warning while subsequent errors occasioned the removal of food for 30 seconds.

Group 2   The procedure differed from the above only in the maintenance phase where the patients received only the verbal prompting prior to each course and the 30 second 'time-out' period with the removal of food as described above.

Group 3   This group remained at a table for four in the ward dining room under the supervision of a nurse who gave non-specific instructions which in practice involved fairly unsystematic verbal prompting and criticism without any individual training.

The specific hypotheses investigated were as follows:-

1.   There would be no difference in errors in any group between the two initial observational phases.

2.   All three groups would display significantly few errors at the end of the treatment phase than during either of the baseline phases.

3.   Groups 1 and 2 would improve significantly more than Group 3.

4.   During both follow-ups, Group 1 would deteriorate less than Group 2 (owing to the intermittent social reinforcement received only by Group 1).

RESULTS

Since differences in mutual level of error were taken into account in the allocation to groups (see above) it was decided to combine results within each group. The individual coding categories were combined to give an overall measure of eating competence and in order to control for variation in time actually spent eating during different meals, the number of time intervals during which an error was made was compared with total possible number of such 'error periods'. The dependent variable for each group is thus the mean percentage of possible error periods during which an error was actually observed. Since statistically there were insufficient data for an analysis of trend (Box and Jenkins, 1970); and since the problem of serial dependency made analysis of variance across phases somewhat problematic, it was decided following Parsonson and Baer

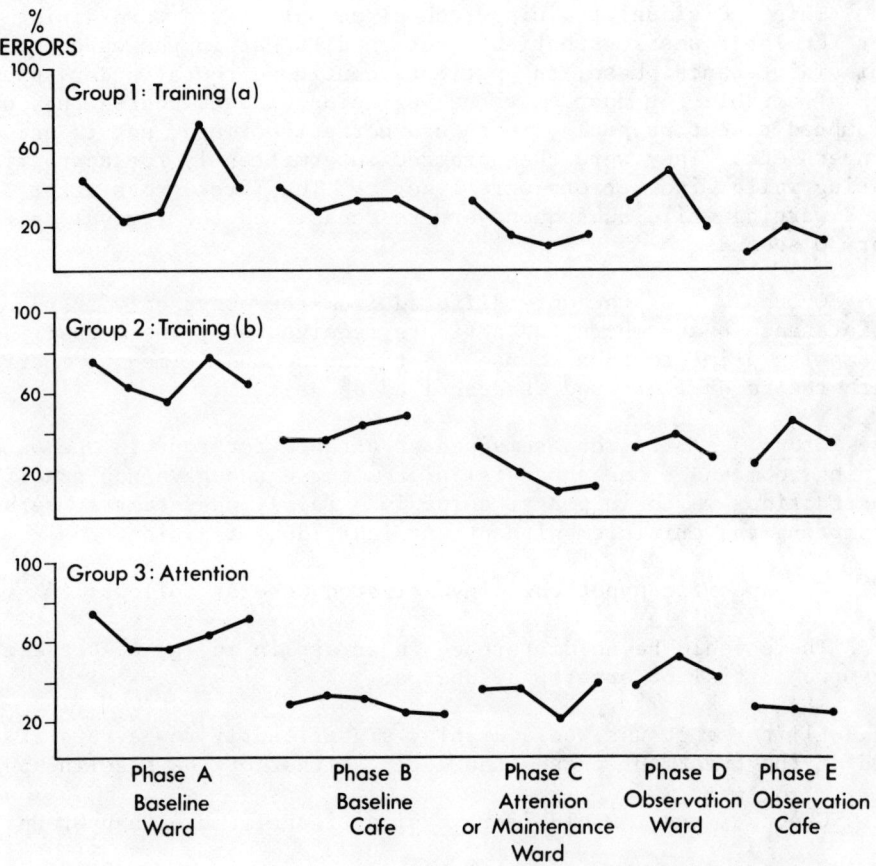

Fig. 2.   Results of study.

(1978) to simply present the results graphically for visual inspection. The results for the three groups across the five phases of study are shown in Fig 2.

1.   As far as the first hypothesis is concerned, the data clearly indicate a difference (especially for Groups 2 and 3) between the two baseline phases and so the hypothesis is not supported.

2.   Each group shows fewer errors at the end of the treatment phase (C) than at the end of the baseline in the ward (A). Group 1 shows a slight improvement while for Group 3, the non-specific attention phase (C) if anything produced a decrease in the accuracy in comparison with the cafe baseline (B).

3.   The follow-up findings are unclear. If the two ward observation phases are compared (A and D), Group 2 shows a maintained decrease in

errors, but Groups 3 and 1 less so. However as already mentioned, the change is explained by change between baseline phases A and B. Only Group 1 shows any evidence of improvement between the two cafe phases (B and E).

4.   Groups 1 and 2 showed an almost identical proportion of errors during the treatment phase (C). Both groups showed relapse on the second ward observation phase (D), but Group 1 showed much less relapse between treatment phase (C) and second cafe observations phase (E).

DISCUSSION

    The greatest improvements in the present study seem to be caused more by environmental effects rather than treatment effects. The changes in eating behaviour are explicable only to a slight extent in terms of acquisition, maintenance and generalisation of skills resulting from the specific treatment procedures used. The patients all demonstrated that they possessed the skills to eat more appropriately and that their eating behaviours were at least partly under the control of the stimulus conditions.

    The research design was organised to control for the effects of treatments and as such was unable to control for the surprising effects found in all three groups. Therefore it is not possible to exclude a simple historical explanation between phases A and B. The inclusion of a second ward observation phase after the cafe observation phase would have perhaps clarified the interpretation, but practical arrangements precluded changing the research design at that stage.

    The aims of treatment are frequently twofold - to change behaviour in the treatment setting and also to help the patient transfer these improvements in behavioural problems to other relevant settings.

    The present study poses a procedural warning in that when improvements in behaviour are seen to generalise to new situations they may be erroneously attributed to generalisations of treatment effects. In fact the change found may be partly or wholly due to the effects of the new environment which causes improvements in behaviour. Therefore researchers should be aware that changes may be an artefact of the environmental control of behaviour and may not be due to generalisation. It may be that generalisation effects found in previous studies have similarly been at least partly explicable by behaviour changes elicited, since it is unusual for the generalisation situation to be assessed prior to the treatment or experimental phase. If the observation in the cafe had not been carried out prior to treatment the behaviour changes would certainly have been interpreted as resulting from the treatment phase.

Implications

The commonly hypothesised gradual erosion of skills and behaviours over prolonged periods of hospitalisation, referred to as "Institutionalisation" (Barton, 1959; Wing and Brown, 1970) may be explained as well by change in the situational demands for a particular set of behaviours as by the effect of low levels of stimulation on a pre-existing disease process. It cannot be assumed, therefore, that the set of behaviours exhibited in a ward setting is more than part of a wider set of behaviours under different stimulus control. Using a patient's performance in a ward setting may lead to an underestimation of his behavioural potential eg as far as rehabilitation is concerned.

Finally, the assumption that all the behaviours required for life outside hospital need to be taught or retaught may be inaccurate. While long-stay psychiatric patients have undoubted handicaps which will limit their functioning to different extents, rehabilitation as well as providing opportunity for learning new skills and behaviours, needs also to concentrate on modifying pre-existing environments or finding new environments which provide the necessary stimulus conditions for the range of behaviours deemed necessary for as full and satisfying a life as possible.

REFERENCES

Azrin, N.H., and Armstrong, P.M., 1973, The "Mini-meal" - a method for teaching eating skills to the profoundly retarded, Ment. Retard., 11:9-13.
Barton, R., 1959, "Institutional Neurosis," John Wright & Sons, Bristol.
Box, G.E.P., and Jenkins, G.M., 1970, "Time Series Analysis: Forecasting and Control," Holden-Day, San Francisco.
Coleman, J., and McReynolds, W., 1972, Token economy: patient and staff changes, Beh. Res. & Ther., 10:29-34.
Goreham, D., and Green, L., 1970, A set of operant conditioning techniques on the chronic schizophrenic, Psychol. Rep., 27:223-234.
Lloyd, K.E., and Abel, L., 1970, Performance on a token economy psychiatric ward: a two-year summary, Beh. Res. & Ther., 8:1-9.
Lloyd, K.E., and Garlington, D., 1968, Weekly variations and performance on a token economy psychiatric ward, Beh. Res. & Ther., 6:407-410.
Nelson, G.L., Cone, S.D., and Hanson, C.R., 1975, Training correct utensil use in retarded children - modelling versus physical guidance, Amer. J. Ment. Defec., 76:68-75.
O'Brien, F., and Azrin, N.H., 1972, Developing proper mealtime behaviours of the institutionalised retardate, J. App. Beh. Anal., 5(4):389-399.

O'Brien, F., Bugle, C., and Azrin, N.H., 1972, Training and maintaining a retarded child's proper eating, J. App. Beh. Anal., 5:67-72.

Paden, R.C., Himelstein, H.C., and Paul, G.L., 1974, Videotape versus verbal feedback in the modification of meal behaviour of chronic mental patients, J. Cons. & Clin. Psychol., 42(4):623.

Parsonson, B.S., and Baer, D.M., 1978, The analysis and presentation of graphic data, in: "Single Subject Research: Strategies for Evaluating Change," T.R. Kratochwill, ed., Academic Press, New York.

Richman, J.S., Sonderby, T., and Khan, J.U., 1980, Prerequisite versus in vivo acquisition of self-feeding skill, Beh. Res. & Ther., 18(4):327-337.

Steffy, R.A., Hart, J., Craw, M., Torney, D., and Marlett, N., 1969, Operant behaviour modification technique applied to a ward of severely regressed and aggressive patients, Can. Psychiat. Assoc. J., 14:59-67.

Wing, J.K., and Brown, G.W., 1970, "Institutionalism and Schizophrenia," Cambridge University Press, London.

REACTIVITY TO THE PRESENCE OF OBSERVERS IN A NATURAL SOCIAL SETTING

William R Lindsay

Psychology Department
Monklands District General Hospital
Airdrie, Scotland

For many clinicians one attraction of the behaviour therapies
has been their emphasis on reliable observation as a primary source
of data about the nature of problems and the course of treatment.
Therefore, changes which occur after treatment are often measured
by observation rather than through subjective reports from the patient or judged impressions of the therapist. The main strength of
observation as a technique to assess change is that the public
nature of the data source enables measures of change to be checked
for their reliability. Because of the importance of direct observation for behaviour therapy there has been a growing interest in the
processes of observation, (Nelson and Hayes, 1979) and the effect it
has on the people being observed. It is well recognised that the
very act of observing people can change their behaviour (Johnson
and Bolstad, 1973) and indeed monitoring can be a therapeutic process
in itself (Nelson, 1977).

This experiment looks at the effects of observing people on
their verbal and social behaviour, and also investigates these
effects over time as subjects become more used to observers being
present.

One of the first people to make reliable observations of verbal
behaviour was Chapple (1942, 1953). He developed a machine which
measured verbal behaviour and interaction during the interview called
the 'interaction chronograph'. This was simply a paper tape moving
at a constant speed and two keys. Whenever an individual in the
interview talked, an observer pressed the key assigned to that
person, for the duration of the speech, and this produced a visual
representation of the speech patterns during the interview. By this
it was possible to measure the length of a person's actions,
silences and interruptions.

Chapple's pioneering work was immensely important. Not only did he provide a tool for systematic study of the interview focusing on verbal behaviour, but also demonstrated that social and verbal behaviour could be profitably considered as a dependent variable. More sophisticated versions of the interaction chronograph have been employed by later researchers (Matarazzo and Saslow, 1961; Weins et al, 1966).

Kendon (1963) used the interaction chronograph to study normal conversation. He compared subjects' performances during a standard interview with coffee break chat and compared intimates' conversations with strangers' conversation. From the point of view of the present study, the importance of Kendon's work is that it indicated that the patterns of verbal behaviour during conversation could be reliably recorded. From this type of analysis data can be collected about the length of utterance, silences, and interruptions as well as temporal aspects of the sequences of behaviour.

With the advent of more reliable recording techniques, other aspects of social interaction have recently been investigated. For example, the use of video recordings allowed Rutter and Stephenson (1972a, 1972b) to take reliable measures of the amount of time spent in eye contact and averted gaze, using schizophrenic and depressed patients as subjects. Argyle and Kendon (1967) and Argyle (1975) report several studies indicating how people with different types of relationship differ in various aspects of non-verbal communication, eg eye contact, proximity and body movement.

It should be remembered that most of the foregoing studies have been conducted in an experimental environment. This is very often far removed from the natural environment in which the social behaviours which are being investigated normally occur. For example, in the Rutter and Stephenson studies, a camera was pointed almost directly into the eyes of the patient, only five feet away from him, during an interview. It is possible that there would have been considerable reaction to this experimental set-up, especially since the procedure consisted of one short interview and patients were unlikely to have had long enough to habituate to the setting.

While work such as that of Chapple provided the orientation and basis of approach for this type of analysis, others have developed more encompassing observation codes. In observational studies of aggressive children, Rauch et al (1959) and Rauch et al (1960) analysed several aspects of the child's social behaviour over time and the cross settings. They were able to show changes of cross settings, changes after treatment and were further able to point out differences in different children's responsiveness to treatment. This work was pioneering, but it lacked certain requirements of objectivity and reliability. Following from Rauch et al, G.R. Patterson and his co-workers have conducted a lengthy series of

studies on the deviant social behaviour of aggressive children.
Their work is squarely based on reliable observations of the child's
social behaviour. He has conducted several studies which describe
and analyse the naturally occurring sequences of behaviour as recorded
by his observation code (Patterson and Reid, 1970; Patterson and
Cobb, 1971; Patterson, 1974, 1975) and several studies which investigate the changes in observed behaviour after interventions
(Patterson and Brodsky, 1966; Patterson et al, 1967; Patterson,
1974). All the studies have used direct observation as their key
measures.

    One major strength of these observations is that they are of
naturally occurring social behaviour. Observations consist of the
person who emits the behaviour, the behaviour emitted, the people
who reacted to that behaviour and the behaviours with which they
reacted. By this method they record the continuous sequence of
behaviour. The percentage agreement in recording between trained
observers was between 52% and 97% with an average of 85%. Percentage
agreement is calculated by the number of agreed observations over a
number of agreements plus disagreements. Therefore, the code is a
reliable measure of the subtle, and complex social interaction in
the family. Patterson has shown it to be a powerful tool in the
systematic description of behaviour, assessment of the problem
situation and in planning treatment strategies.

    The work done by Patterson has been followed up and extended by
a number of researchers (Johnson and Lobitz, 1974; Lewinsohn and
Atwood, 1969; Lewinsohn et al, 1970). It is through the work of
Lewinsohn and his research team that the methods were extended into
the field of adult social behaviour. The observation code which he
uses (Lewinsohn, 1971) is a derivative of the code used by Patterson.
Observations are confined to verbal behaviour. Like Patterson he
finds it meaningful and useful to distinguish between behaviours
emitted and those elicited. The terms used are "actions" and
"reactions". Actions are distinguished from reactions in that they
precede reactions. Furthermore actions are considered to be emitted
and reactions elicited, ie actions are not obviously directly
contingent on other utterances, whereas reactions occur in response
to an emitted utterance.

    Libet and Lewinsohn (1973) report the reliability of the coding
system, using Spearman-Brown reliability coefficients. These ranged
from excellent (.995) to fair (.634). These codes produced by
Patterson and Lewinsohn were used in the present study as models
from which to develop an observation code for recording normal
conversation. Their particularly strong features are that they can
deal with naturally occurring social behaviour, they enable the
ongoing interaction to be categorised and also to be recorded tem-
porally. The observer can also record which participant is emitting
which behaviour.

PROBLEMS IN THE USE OF NATURALISTIC OBSERVATION

There are of course many pitfalls when one uses observation as
a primary source of data. While it was proven to be an essential
source of data, with many strengths (Goldfried and Kent, 1972), it
is not without its weaknesses. In a review paper Lipinski and
Nelson (1974) divide the problems into three main categories:
procedural problems in observations, potential observer bias and the
reactive nature of "being observed".

Procedural Problems in Observation

Included in this category is the loss of information which
occurs when one uses a code. Firstly, a decision must be made as to
the behaviours coded and this decision will exclude a whole range of
behaviour. The present author chose verbal behaviour as the most
appropriate information to gather, but by doing so excluded many
other aspects of social interaction, eg gaze, gesturing, body movement etc. Since it records continuous sequences of behaviour the
present code is able to derive information on length of utterance,
length of silences etc, as well as amount of each behaviour and
patterning of behaviour recorded.

Another important procedural problem is the reliability of the
data recorded. Since a substantial agreement between observers is
a prerequisite for a sound study, most studies employ two observers
for a fair percentage of the observations and calculate the agreement between them. The most common method for calculating reliability is to derive a percentage from the number of agreed observations
over the number of agreements plus disagreements. This is used by
Patterson and his co-workers. Where the target behaviour occurs
with a low frequency, eg observing verbal behaviour with a socially
withdrawn patient, reliability can be spuriously high because of
the large number of no behaviour agreements made by observers.
Therefore, in these cases reliability should only be checked using
cells where behaviour has been recorded. More recently Cohen's
kappa has been recommended as a preferable statistic to percentage
agreement (Fleiss et al, 1969) since it takes account of chance
agreements. In the present study Cohen's kappa was used, with
Fleiss's recalculation of the significance levels.

Potential Observer Bias

This source of error is tapped by the amount of agreement or
disagreement between trained observers. As we have noted, when
there is good agreement between observers then we can assume a high
degree of reliability in the observations being taken. However, a
number of variables can give rise to low reliability and this is
seen to indicate the fact that one of the observers has a bias in

some direction not shared by the other. Once source of bias was documented by Reid (1970) when he found a marked drop in reliability from overt to covert assessment. When observers were not told, and did not realise that they were being assessed by another observer then reliability dropped considerably. This was due to observers being biased in favour of the procedural interventions and recording deviant behaviour accordingly. To assess this during an experiment some researchers have included covert reliability checks during the course of the observations and have found that the problem is perhaps not as great as Reid first imagined (Herbert et al, 1973). A further method of overcoming this bias is to keep the observers ignorant as regards the nature of the experiment (Johnson and Lobitz, 1974; Johnson and Bolstad, 1975). The nature of the present observational study overcomes the point in some respects. To the extent that the study is exploratory and no hypotheses were made, the possibility of a bias in favour of the hypothesis is ruled out. Furthermore the observers were aware of such an influence and were at pains to ensure that it did not affect the recording of social behaviours.

Several other sources of bias have been found in observational studies. O'Leary et al (1975) allowed the observers a knowledge of the experimental hypothesis and gave them feedback about observations which supported these hypotheses. This procedure resulted in observers producing data which was in line with the experimental hypothesis made. Therefore, a knowledge of the experiment can bias the observations that are made. Cooper et al (1974) point to another source of invalid data in a powerful critique of direct observation. They point out that "high agreement between observers may not mean that they eliminated their bias; they may simply all have been trained to have the same bias".

This and other criticisms have been answered by Richer (1974) and Hutt (1974). The present author agrees with some of the arguments advanced by Richer (1974): "when observing, a person does not commit himself to explicit hypothesis beforehand ..... an observer tries to be as disciplined as possible ..... he tries not to make obvious unnecessary assumptions ..... the important point about observing natural phenomena is that the observer tries to interfere as little as possible" (pp.500-501).

The main point about these arguments is that the observer should acquaint himself with the possible sources of bias in his recording. As far as possible formal steps should be taken to ensure that the procedural problems, reaction to the observer and observer bias can be overcome or measured to determine the extent of the error. However, in the present author's experience it is seldom possible to cover every possible error source with a formal counter procedure. Therefore, sometimes the best one can do is to be aware of the possible influences and guard against them trying "to be as disciplined as possible".

Reactive Nature of the Observation Process

It cannot be assumed that the observer in a situation is a neutral stimulus who merely records the ongoing process, but does not influence it or interact with it. This is probably the most important consideration in the present study since the subjects (factory workers and non-medical personnel) are not used to having observers in an otherwise familiar situation and have not asked for assistance or interest in their social interaction. Patterson and Harris (1968) reported that the behaviours recorded when an observer was present were different from those obtained when no observer was present. Soskin and John (1963) investigated the speech of a couple in relation to situations and events, by attaching to them a microphone which they carried around all day. They found most subjects' references to being observed disappeared after one or two days, indicating habituation to observers occurs quite rapidly. However, this has not been empirically tested.

Intuitively it may seem that certain methods of observation are more intrusive than others. However, studies have shown that this is not always the case. Johnson and Bolstad (1975) found no differences in family interaction when there were observers present and when there was only audio equipment present (presumed to be less obtrusive). Kent et al (1979) found no significant distortion in the data recorded by three different techniques - observation in vivo, via a mirror and via television.

Reactivity to being observed is not always considered a problem in the treatment of patients. Mercatoris and Craighead (1974) found that teachers showed more interest in their pupils when they knew their behaviour was being observed. Similar effects have been found when people record and monitor their own behaviour. Burg et al (1979) found that when nursing staff recorded their interaction with patients, this interaction increased considerably without any detriment to other nursing duties. Nelson (1977) reviews a number of studies which have found a positive therapeutic effect from patient's self-monitoring, including reports of hallucinations, hair pulling, lip biting, alcohol and drug abuse and insomnia. However, she does note that improvements in symptomatology during self-monitoring are not universally reported.

PRESENT STUDY

The present study on reactivity to observers is part of a larger piece of research (Lindsay, 1981) in which the conversation of several non-patient groups was recorded in an attempt to establish goals for social skills training. For the present paper the conversations of two groups were analysed to ascertain the extent to which reactivity to the observer changed over time. By looking

at changes in behaviour recorded over time, we can get a measure of
how much initial reactivity there was, what the format took and how
quickly it subsided.

Method

Two groups of people served as subjects. One group of 4 members
of the non-medical hospital staff - a porter, a carpark attendant
and two cleaners. The second group was of 3 women workers in a
factory in Aberdeen.

Setting. Group 1 was observed in a small room in the hospital
during their morning tea-break. Group 2 was observed in the factory
canteen, again during morning tea-break.

The Observation Code. The code used to observe conversation
was developed on the basis of codes used by Patterson and his co-
workers and Lewinsohn and his co-workers. It is fully explained by
Lindsay (1977, 1981). Observations were of the ongoing interaction,
or lack of it, and are confined to verbal behaviour. Four observations were taken every 30 seconds.

As with the two codes mentioned above, verbal behaviour was
split into actions and reactions. Actions were considered to be
emitted and not obviously contingent on another utterance, while
reactions were considered to be elicited and made in response to
another subject's actions. The subjects in the group were each
assigned a number. Typically an observation would consist of the
subject number, in the action emitted by him, followed by the numbers
of the subjects who reacted to the action and the verbal behaviour
with which they reacted.

Reaction categories of behaviour analysed in the present study
were silence, actions which were observed within one observation
cell (1 cell), actions which lasted more than one observation cell
(> 1 cell) and question asking. The reaction categories were
reaction of silence, a single word (W), more than one word (IN),
interruptions (INT) and question answering. Reliability data was
derived for 44% of the observations taken in Group 1. This amounts
to 2,112 observations altogether. Because the categories within
the actions and those within the reactions are each mutually exclusive, Cohen's kappa was derived in a single computation for all
observations of actions and in one computation for all observations
of reactions (Bartko and Carpenter, 1976). Percentage agreement
for each action and reaction was also completed. The reliability
data can be seen in Table 1.

Table 1 shows the action and reaction categories for which
reliability was completed. Percentage agreement and Cohen's kappa

Table 1.   Reliability Data

	% Agreement	Kappa
Action		
Silence	84	
1 cell	82	
> 1 cell	78	.69
Question asking	86	
Reaction		
Silence	87	
W	82	
IN	88	.63
INT	63	
Question answering	98	

are also inserted. As can be seen percentage agreement ranges from 78% to 98%. One notable exception is the percentage agreement for "interrupts" (INT) which is 63%. While this would normally be considered unacceptable it should be noted that this category accounts for only 6% of their observed reactions overall and for none of the reactions in the present analysis of data. The main actions and reactions of 1 cell, > 1 cell, W, Silence and IN account for over 80% of all observations and show acceptable percentage agreement. The results for kappa are again acceptable and show significant levels of inter-observer agreement.

Results

The graphs in Fig 1. show the number of "no interaction" or silent cells recorded in each 2 minutes of observation during each day. The maximum number of cells in each 2 minutes was 16.

The graphs showing data for Group 1 show that at the beginning of the observations on day 1 large amounts of silence were recorded and this dropped to lower levels of silence towards the end of the 15 minute period. On day 2 we see a recurrence of the high amounts of silence at the beginning of the session, again decreasing as the session progressed. The same pattern is seen in days 3 and 4 and to a lesser extent in day 5. On day 6 the amount of silence recorded at the beginning of the session is no greater than the low levels throughout the session. This pattern of low silence levels remains consistent for the rest of the experiment, through day 17 (chosen randomly), to the final day (day 35).

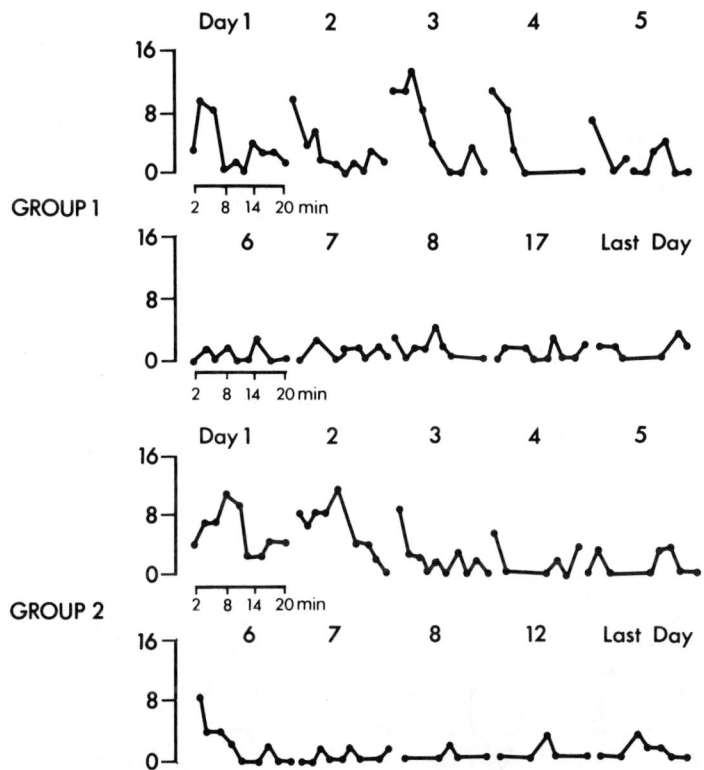

Fig. 1. No. of cells in which Silence was Recorded during each Session.

This pattern was generally replicated by Group 2. On day 1 the amount of silence increased until the 8th minute and then decreased. On days 2, 3 and 4 larger amounts of silence were recorded initially and these decreased progressively earlier in the session. On day 5 this pattern disappeared altogether. However, the relatively large amount of silence recurs at the beginning of day 6 (a Monday), falling to lower levels as the session progresses and remaining stable and low until the end of the experiment.

The data show very clearly that subjects' initial reactions to being observed was to inhibit verbal behaviour. However, even

Table 2. The Percentage of Cells in which Each Action was Emitted by Subjects, During Different Phases of Observation

	Overall			1st 5 Mins. Week 1			2nd 15 Mins. Week 1			1st 5 Mins. Week 2		
	1 cell	>1 cell	Q	1 cell	>1 cell	Q	1 cell	>1 cell	Q	1 cell	>1 cell	Q
Group 1												
Subject 1	53	34	13	100	0	0	73	22	5	64	27	9
Subject 2	38	53	9	68	29	3	41	48	11	37	58	5
Subject 3	62	32	6	82	14	4	75	21	4	57	36	7
Subject 4	43	43	14	100	0	0	79	18	3	53	37	10
Group 2												
Subject 5	17	78	5	74	21	5	48	48	4	25	71	4
Subject 6	33	54	13	99	0	1	50	39	11	35	51	14
Subject 7	44	42	14	86	8	6	68	23	9	51	37	12

after as short a time as 10 minutes of observation there is some
lessening of reactivity and the high levels of silence began to
reduce. Despite this habituation to observers during the previous
session data from the next session show a recurrence of the reactivity which was present initially. This had been replicated by
Group 2.

The levels of silence indicate that considerable reaction to
the observer has taken place. Table 2 shows an analysis of the
verbal behaviour which did occur during the early stages of observation. Scores for all 7 subjects in both groups have been inserted.
Each section of the table shows the percentage of observations which
were recorded in one cell (1 cell), in more than one cell (>1 cell)
and the percentage of questions (Q). The first section shows the
results over the whole study (30 days for Group 1 and 24 days for
Group 2). These are given so that the data derived from the early
observation sessions can be compared. The second section shows
data from the first 5 minutes of each session during week one. The
third section shows data from the second 15 minutes of each session
during week one. The last section shows data from the first 5
minutes of session in the second week.

It can be clearly seen that speech which was emitted during
the first 5 minutes of week one was markedly different from the
overall data. There is a predominance of one cell utterances,
whereas over the whole study this is not the case. This difference
in one cell utterances is significant at t < .001, using a matched
pair t-test (t = 7.4). Therefore, not only do subjects react by
reducing their quantity of speech as in Fig 1, but frequency of
behaviours with which they do interact has markedly changed with far
fewer longer utterances and far more shorter utterances.

The second part of the table shows that in the second 15 minutes
of week one frequencies of behaviours become less discrepant from
the overall results. However, the differences in one cell utterances
remain significant (p = .002, t = 4.9). Therefore, although the
data from Fig 1. and the data from Table 2 show some habituation to
observers present, the patterns of speech remains significantly
distorted when compared with the overall results.

By the first 5 minutes of week two (the last section of Table 2)
considerable habituation has occurred and the percentage of one cell
utterances is no longer significantly different from the overall
results (t = 1.83, not significant). Therefore, it appears that by
week two reactivity to the observer has subsided sufficiently for
the differences between observed behaviour and the overall scores
to be non-significant.

Given the lower levels of speech which did occur during the
first 5 minutes of sessions during week one, it makes little sense

Table 3.   Reactions to 1 Cell Actions in the First
Five Minutes of Sessions During Week One

	Silence	W	IN	INT
Group 1	54	10	36	
Group 2	49	8	43	
Overall	10.9	10	65.2	6.9

to compare statistically between the reactions to utterances in this period and similar data from the overall study.   Therefore, Table 3 will be merely described.   Since the predominant action during this period of observation was a one cell action, only the reactions to this utterance have been inserted.

Again the reactions to one cell utterances are different from the corresponding reactions in the overall results.   There is a far greater preponderance of silence given in reaction to utterances and a lower percentage of IN responses.   This is a further indication of reactivity to the observer.

Discussion

On every index of conversation in the present study, subjects have shown considerable reaction to observers being present.   The contribution of this study is that it shows the patterns of reactivity over time and further shows that some indices of reactivity persist longer than others.

Firstly, during week one the amounts of silence are greater than in later sessions.   Subjects showed lower levels of silence as each session progressed and this indicates that some habituation may have been occurring even after only 10 minutes of observation. However, at the start of the next session there was a recurrence of the high levels of silence indicating that subjects did not continue their habituation through to the next day.

Apart from looking at levels of silence this paper also presents data on frequencies and patterns of speech which occurred during the early part of the observations.   Taken together the first 5 minutes of each session in week one show considerably deviant patterns from the overall data,   the main differences being a much larger percentage of short 1 cell utterances and a larger percentage of silence in reaction to those utterances.

   This pattern continues with a lessened but still significant frequency into the latter part of these sessions. Therefore, although the amount of silence has reduced, the frequencies and patterns of verbal behaviour which occur remain discrepant from the overall study. Certainly, the results show that while some aspects of reactivity may subside a more subtle and detailed analysis indicates that considerable reactivity to observers remained. By the second week the patterns of behaviour seem to be not significantly different from the patterns overall.

IMPLICATIONS

   For the applied psychologist the importance of this data is plain. Let us assume that a child, patient, couple or a family have been observed in a previous session and the observer feels that subjects have habituated sufficiently to being observed. One cannot assume that data collected in the early stages of the next observation session are not influenced by a recurrence of the subject's reactivity. Indeed this study would suggest that data collected at the end of the first session may be less influenced by reactivity than data taken at the beginning of the second session. It was not until the 5th or 6th session of recording that silence reduced to levels seen during the subsequent weeks of observation, although it should be noted that the observation sessions reported were short. It may be a more time saving strategy to increase the length of each session enabling the therapist to use the latter part rather than conduct a longer series of short observation sessions.

   The results on the speech itself would suggest that while behaviour may seem to have reverted to normal because there are no longer lapses in speech or the like, this may not be the case. The patterns of behaviour remain deviant in the latter part of the sessions, even although the amount of silence reduced. Perhaps observers should remain aware of this source of error in the data, even over long programmes of recording and monitoring.

ACKNOWLEDGEMENT

   For the period during which this research was conducted the author was in receipt of a Medical Research Council Grant.

REFERENCES

Argyle, M., 1975, "Bodily Communication," Methuen & Co. Ltd., London.
Argyle, M., and Kendon, A., 1967, The experimental analysis of
     social performance, in: "Advances in Experimental Social
     Psychology," Vol. 3, L. Berkowitz, ed., Academic Press,
     New York.

Bartko, J.J., and Carpenter, W.T. Jnr., 1976, On the methods and
    theory of rehability, J. Nerv. & Ment. Dis., 163:307-317.
Burg, M., Reid, D., and Lattimore, J., 1979, Use of a self recording
    and supervision programme to change institutional staff
    behaviour, J. App. Beh. Anal., 12:363-375.
Chapple, E., 1942, The measurement of inter-personal behaviour,
    Transactions of the New York Academy of Sciences, 4:222-233.
Chapple, E., 1953, The standard experimental interview as used in
    interaction chronograph investigations, Human Organisation,
    12:23-32.
Cooper, E.S., Costello, A., Dougals, S., Ingleby, D., and Turner, R.,
    1974, Direct observation, Bull. Brit. Psychol. Soc., 27:3-7.
Fleiss, J.L., Cohen, J., and Everitt, B.S., 1969, Large sample
    standard errors of kappa and weighted kappa, Psychol. Bull.,
    72:323-327.
Goldfried, M.R., and Kent, R., 1972, Traditional and behavioural
    personality assessment. A comparison of methodological and
    theoretical assumptions, Psychol. Bull., 77:409-420.
Herbert, E.W., Pinkston, E., Hayden, M., Sajwaj, T., Pinkston, S.,
    Cordua, G., and Jackson, C., 1973, Adverse effects of
    differential parental attention, J. App. Beh. Anal., 6:15-30.
Hutt, C., 1974, Critique of direct observation by Cooper et al,
    Bull. Brit. Psychol. Soc., 27:503-504.
Johnson, S.M., and Bolstad, O.D., 1973, Methodological issues in
    naturalistic observation: some problems and solutions for field
    research, in: "Behaviour Change: Methodology, Concepts and
    Practice," L.A. Hamerlynck, L.C. Hendry & E.J. Mash, eds.,
    Illinois Research Press, Campaign.
Johnson, S.M., and Bolstad, O.D., 1975, Reactivity to home observa-
    tions: a comparison of audio recorded behaviour with observers
    present or absent, J. App. Beh. Anal., 8:181-186.
Johnson, S.M., and Lobitz, G., 1974, Parental manipulation of child
    behaviour in home observations, J. App. Beh. Anal., 7:23-32.
Kent, R.N., O'Leary, K.D., Dietz, A., and Diament, C., 1979,
    Comparison of observational recordings in vivo via mirror and
    via television, J. App. Beh. Anal., 12:517-522.
Kendon, A., 1963, "Temporal Aspects of the Social Performance in
    Two Person Encounters," Ph.D. thesis, Oxford University.
Lewinsohn, P., 1971, "Manual of Instructions for the Behaviour
    Ratings Used for the Observation of Interpersonal Behaviour,"
    Unpublished manuscript.
Lewinsohn, P., and Atwood, G., 1969, Depression: a clinical-research
    approach, Psychother. Theory Res. & Prac., 1969, 6:166-171.
Lewinsohn, P., Weinstein, M.S., and Alper, T.A., 1970, A behav-
    iourally orientated approach to the group treatment of persons
    with depression, J. Clin. Psychol., 26:525-532.
Libet, J.N., and Lewinsohn, P., 1973, The concept of social skill
    with special reference to the behaviour of depressed persons,
    J. Cons. & Clin. Psychol., 40:304-311

Lindsay, W.R., 1977, "The Analysis and Training of Social Skills
    with Particular Reference to Long-stay Psychiatric Patients,"
    Unpublished Ph.D. thesis, University of Aberdeen.
Lindsay, W.R., 1981, Some normative goals for conversation training,
    Beh. Psychother., in press.
Lipinski, D., and Nelson, R., 1974, Problems in the use of natural-
    istic observation as a means of behavioural assessment,
    Beh. Ther., 5:341-351.
Matarazzo, J., and Saslow, G., 1961, Differences in interview inter-
    action behaviour among normal and deviant groups, in:
    "Conformity and Deviation," Berg & Bass, eds., Harper Row,
    New York.
Mercatoris, M., and Craighead, E., 1974, The effects of non-
    participant observation on teacher-pupil classroom behaviour,
    J. Educ. Psychol., 66:512-519.
Nelson, R.O., 1977, Assessment and therapeutic functions of self-
    monitoring, in: "Progress in Behaviour Modification," Vol. 4,
    M. Hersen, R. Eisler & P. Miller, eds., Academic Press,
    New York.
Nelson, R.O., and Hayes, S., 1979, The nature of behavioural assess-
    ment: a commentary, J. App. Beh. Anal., 12:491-500.
O'Leary, K.D., Kent, R., and Kanowitz, J., 1975, Shaping data
    collection congruent with experimental hypothesis,
    J. App. Beh. Anal., 8:33-52.
Patterson, G.R., 1974, Stimulus control in natural settings, in:
    "Determinants and Origins of Aggressive Behaviour," De Wit &
    Hartup, eds., Mouton Press, The Hague.
Patterson, G.R., 1975, A basis for identifying stimuli which control
    behaviours in natural settings, Child Dev., 45(2):900-911.
Patterson, G.R., and Brodsky, G., 1966, A behaviour modification
    programme for a child with multiple problem behaviours,
    J. Child Psychol. & Psychiat., 7:277-295
Patterson, G.R., and Cobb, J.A., 1971, "Manual for Coding of Family
    Interactions, 6th Revision," M.A.P.S. document number 01234.
Patterson, G.R., and Harris, A., 1968, Some methodological
    considerations for observation procedures, Paper presented at
    the Amer. Psychol. Assoc. Ann. Conv., San Francisco.
Patterson, G.R., McNeal, S., Hawkins, N., and Phelps, R., 1967,
    Re-programming the social environment, J. Child Psychol. &
    Psychiat., 8:181-195.
Patterson, G.R., and Reid, J., 1970, Reciprocity and coercion: two
    facets of social symptoms, in: "Behaviour Modification in
    Clinical Psychology," Neuringer & Michael, eds., Appleton-
    Century-Crofts, New York.
Rauch, H., Dittman, A., and Taylor, T., 1959, Person, setting and
    change in the social interaction, Hum. Rel., 12:361-378.
Rauch, H., Farbman, I., and Llewllyn, L., 1960, Person, setting and
    change in social interaction - a normative control study,
    Hum. Rel., 13:305-332.

Reid, J.B., 1970, Reliability and assessment of observation data: a possible methodological problem, Child Dev., 41:1143-1150.

Richer, J.N., 1974, Direct observation: a reply to Cooper et al, Bull. Brit. Psychol. Soc., 27:500-502.

Rutter, D.R., and Stephenson, G.M., 1972a, Visual interaction in a group of schizophrenic and depressed patients, Brit. J. Soc. & Clin. Psychol., 11, 1:57-65.

Rutter, D.R., and Stephenson, G.M., 1972b, Visual interaction in a group of schizophrenic and depressed patients: a follow-up study, Brit. J. Soc. & Clin. Psychol., 11, 4:410-411.

Soskin, W., and John, V., 1963, The study of spontaneous talk, in: "The Stream of Behaviour," R. Barker, ed., Appleton-Century-Crofts, New York.

Weins, A., Saslow, G., and Matarazzo, J., 1966, Speech interruption behaviour during interviews, Psychother. Theory Res. & Prac., 3:153-158.

THE EFFECT OF SOCIAL ACTIVITY ON THE SPEECH OF CHRONIC

SCHIZOPHRENIC PATIENTS

Anthony A Turvey

Psychology Department
Royal Dundee Liff Hospital
Dundee, Scotland

Chris J Main

Psychology Department
Gartnavel Royal Hospital
Glasgow, Scotland

Douglas Montgomery   Charge Nurse

Craig Dunain Hospital
Inverness, Scotland

INTRODUCTION

The use of activity in the treatment of psychiatric patients has a long history (Ozarin, 1954), and is central to industrial, occupational and some psychological approaches (Watts, 1976; MacDonald et al, 1972; Paul and Lentz, 1977). There have been many explanations for the way activity may influence chronic schizophrenics' social behaviour, such as by group pressure inducing conformity (Tillotson, 1939), by influencing the expectations of both staff and patients (Paul and Lentz, 1977), by structuring patterns of stimulation (Wing, 1978), or by reducing institutionalisation (Barton, 1959). There is little clear evidence, however, to show precisely how these procedures operate, or indeed whether they operate at all.

Historically, social activity therapy can be seen as a development of two related but distinct therapeutic approaches: the therapeutic community and milieu therapy. In the therapeutic community (Jones, 1952; Brown and Peddar, 1979), change is thought to

result from the improvement of staff-patient relationships, and from
increased participation by the patients themselves in their treatment. Studies have shown (Fairweather, 1964; Saunders et al, 1962)
that discharge rates in therapeutic communities were better than for
controls, but at follow-up there was found to be no difference
between the therapeutic community and traditional psychiatric care.
Furthermore, the extent to which all the ingredients of the therapeutic community are necessary is unclear, as it has been shown
(Ellsworth, 1964) that simple encouragement to staff to increase
their interaction with patients is highly effective. Milieu or
'total push' (Tillotson, 1939) approaches aim simply to provide
stimulation through activity and have met with some success
(Ellsworth, 1968). In their review, Paul and Lentz (1977) concluded
that milieu approaches seemed to be superior to traditional hospital
care although several flaws in research designs such as non-independ-
ent assessments, the use of administrative measures (such as
discharge rates) as an indirect measure of behaviour change, and the
failure to evaluate specific components of the treatment package,
preclude unequivocal acceptance of the results.

    The general findings of loss of initial success at follow-up
may be a consequence of inappropriate initial discharge, increased
stress in the community (Vaughan and Leff, 1976; Leff et al, 1973)
or the failure of the treatment effects to generalise across
settings. This poor generalisation suggests that the treatments
were not causing global changes in the patients' behaviour, but were
situationally specific in their effects. This finding has important
implications for the extent to which treatment effects may be
expected to generalise to and be maintained in other settings.
Ellsworth (1968), for example, found a low readmission rate after a
30 month activity programme and this may have been a consequence of
the similarity of the hospital to the sheltered care facilities to
which the patients were discharged.

    Token economies have also been used to promote social inter-
action (Bennet and Maley, 1973; Baker, 1971; Stahl et al, 1974;
Doty, 1975; Tracey et al, 1974). Their general effectiveness and
the variables of importance have been reviewed in detail elsewhere
(Kazdin, 1977; Fraser, 1978, 1981; Fernandez, 1978) and will not be
discussed here. Of relevance here, however, are three studies
comparing token economies with social activity programmes.

    In the Leeds project, Baker et al (1974) found that contingent
tokens led to little improvement on an activity programme, but the
type of design used precluded effective analysis of the additional
variables (Hersen and Barlow, 1976; Fraser, 1981). Hall et al
(1977) found no difference between contingent and non-contingent
tokens although the treatments (which both included social activities) were both superior to custodial care. Stoffelmayr et al
(1973, 1979) again compared social activity with a token economy

and with traditional care. Unfortunately, differences in the
statistical methods in the two reports make interpretation of the
results difficult. Thus, while both the activity programmes were
better than traditional care, they differed between themselves and
the precise importance of differences in researched involvement and
in the type of activity used is unclear. Furthermore, the extent
to which the token economy programme was superior to the better
activity programme is unclear from the results. In the third study
(Paul and Lentz, 1977) an extremely well controlled comparison of a
token economy, a general activity programme and traditional hospital
care, the token economy was found to be generally superior to both
the activity programme and the traditional hospital care, with little
difference between latter approaches.

      In general then, these comparative studies would appear to
indicate that while token economies are usually effective, the
findings concerning activity therapy are less clear cut. It seems
important, therefore, to attempt an evaluation of the effective
ingredients of social activity programmes and identify variables
influencing their effectiveness. Taylor (1974) compared a social
activity programme lasting one year with traditional care on groups
of chronic schizophrenic patients who had been hospitalised for at
least 20 years. Although there was no overall difference between
groups, an analysis of individual results showed clear cut changes
among some individuals, suggesting that treatment effects may
interact with patient characteristics (Mischel, 1973; Paul and
Lentz, 1977). Again, while little difference was found between
activity and non-activity periods for the grouped data, idiosyncratic
changes in individual patients support the notion of situation-
specific effects. Differences in patient behaviour was found across
five activities (art, pottery, discussions, table-games and industrial therapy). Games elicited most patient-initiated speech;
discussions, art and games produced most patient-therapist interaction, while pottery and industrial therapy were generally poor
at promoting speech. While this study supports the hypothesis of
a differential effect of different activities on speech, the small
sample size and the variation in the environments in which the
activities were carried out, limit the conclusions which can be
drawn. (The study reported below is essentially a more controlled
replication of this study).

      Much of the early work on activity therapy simply assumed that
general changes in behaviour had occurred. Several studies (Taylor,
1974; Robertson, 1979; Powell et al, 1979), however, have shown
that this is not the case. Behaviour change more often occurs under
the specific stimulus control of the treatment setting and
generalisation "must be programmed ..... rather than lamented"
(Baer et al, 1968). Such a view is consistent with experimental
evidence from social skills training studies (Shepard, 1977;
Goldsmith and McFall, 1975; Lindsay, 1980; Matson et al, 1980;

Hersen and Bellack, 1976; Marzillier and Winter, 1978).

This specificity has implications for the assessment, and for the goals of activity treatments. While an activity programme may change patients' behaviour, this may not automatically generalise to other activities, therapists or settings. Where extensive change is desired, additional procedures may be necessary (Stokes and Baer, 1977; Marholin, 1976). While it is inappropriate, therefore, to attempt the evaluation of activity programmes as a "package", the investigation of the specific variables involved would seem important to enable optimal decisions about the use of such programmes to be made.

A number of variables meriting consideration are listed below:-

1.   Reinforcement during activity, whether intrinsic eg winning a game, or extrinsic eg social approval, material rewards or tokens.

2.   Characteristics of the physical setting (Somner and Ross, 1958).

3.   Distance between patients (Polsky and Chance, 1979a).

4.   Overall treatment regime (Marriotto and Paul, 1975).

5.   Staff-patient ratio and proximity (Sanson-Fisher et al, 1979).

6.   Demand for co-operation or interaction during the activity.

7.   Level of patient skill and amount of staff training necessary.

8.   Usefulness of activity in providing topics of conversation.

9.   Necessity for speech and manual activity.

10. Length of session.

The above list is clearly far from exhaustive, but illustrates at least some of the important features in the assessment of activities. In the present study, it was decided to examine the influence of four different activities on patient speech. The specific activities were chosen to represent a high demand for speech, a high demand for manual activity and two levels of co-operative interaction. The activities were similar to those used in a previous study (Taylor, 1974) to enable comparison with its findings; the activities were already being used as part of the ward activity programme (and so the experiment had direct clinical relevance); and being frequently used activities in occupational therapy, the results could be fairly easily replicated in other settings.

PRESENT STUDY

The effect of four different activities on the patients' speech was studied. The activities were:

a)   Crafts - patients worked individually weaving the seats of wooden stools. Patient interaction was not required. This activity represented a low demand for speech and a high demand for manual activity.

b)   Discussion - this represented a high demand for speech (particularly therapist-patient interaction) with no manual activity.

c)   Cards - the game 'knockout whist' was played. This was thought to have a high demand for group interaction eg deciding on the dealer and on who had won the game, although it was possible for one of the participants to spend time out of the game.

d)   Dominoes - a simple game of dominoes was played. It was thought that less verbal interaction than for the card game would be necessary in order to complete the activity eg for most rounds there would be a clear winner and there was no need to decide trumps. (Both games were similar in that each round was separated by an interval when the cards or dominoes were redistributed. Such periods provided opportunity for conversation.)

The general hypothesis was that differences would be found in the amount of speech observed across activities.

The specific hypotheses were:

1.   The total speech of therapists and patients (combined) would vary across activities.

2.   The total speech of patients would vary across activities.

3(a) Patient-to-patient speech would differ across activities.

 (b) Patient-to-therapist speech would differ across activities.

 (c) Patient-to-group speech would differ across activities.

4.   The amount of conversational speech (ie speech unrelated to the particular activity) would differ across activities.

Observational Method

The method used was similar to that of Taylor (1974) and is shown in Fig 1. For the 3 members of each session (therapist and

Time Intervals (15 seconds)

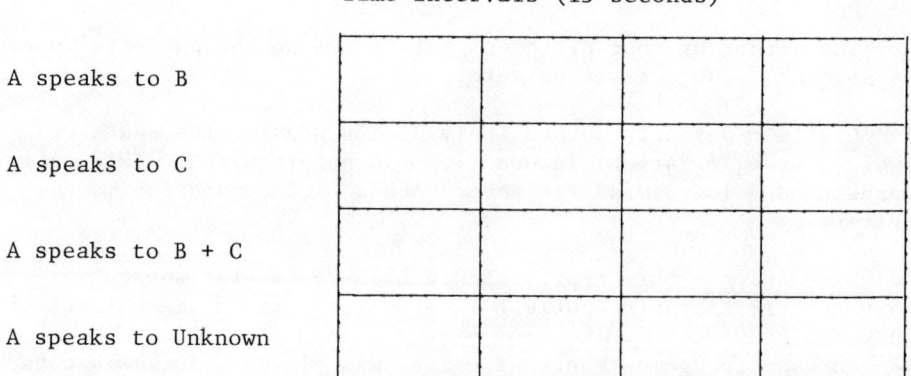

A speaks to B

A speaks to C

A speaks to B + C

A speaks to Unknown

Fig. 1.   Observational method

2 patients), there were four possible directions of interaction.
Speech could be recorded in all of these directions during any 15
second interval giving a total of 12 possible utterances. The
"utterance" did not have to last the complete time period. The
method used was partial interval sampling (Powell et al, 1977).
The utterances were coded as follows:-

     c - conversational speech, unrelated to current activity.

     g - speech related to activity engaged in.

     It has been shown (Powell et al, 1979) that using this method
and time interval, there is little measurement error.

Training of Observers

     A video of the triads (therapist and 2 patients) engaged in
these activities was compiled. The main observer ran live pilot
groups to test the observational code and format of the experimental
session. He then further trained observational accuracy using the
videotape. Kendall's Coefficient of Concordance, W (Siegel, 1956)
was then used to assess inter- and intra-rater agreement. As the
data were analysed non-parametrically, a test measuring observer
agreement using rank order (Kendall's W) was considered most
appropriate. The choice of appropriate statistical tests in such
circumstances is discussed in more detail elsewhere (Hollenbeck,
1978; Bartko and Carpenter, 1976; Mitchell, 1979). After ten trials
with the videotape, intra-rater agreement was considered satisfactory
(W = 0.92) and the main study was initiated.

     A second observer was trained to use the videotape, although

Table 1. Overall Observer Agreement

	Craft	Dominoes	Cards	Discussion	Mean
W =	0.939	0.954	0.922	0.943	0.939

(all significant at $p < 0.05$)

practical circumstances made it impossible to complete this training prior to the start of the main study. Each training session consisted of two viewings of the videotape by both observers, thus permitting the assessment of both inter- and intra-rater agreement. This method was used to control for possible decay in the accuracy of the main observer during the study (Hollenbeck, 1978). After six videotape sessions and one live practice session, inter-rater agreement was considered satisfactory ($W = 0.92$), suggesting that the videotape training had successfully generalised (Eisler et al, 1973).

Four reliability sessions were then completed (one for each activity) with subject pairs randomly chosen. Agreement was assessed by dividing each reliability session into three equal time periods and then totalling the observations within these periods to give a sample size of 12 items. High observer agreement was found over all directions and categories of utterance combined. The results are shown in Table 1. Good observer agreement ($p < 0.05$) was found for 13 of the 16 variables studied with less than significant agreement ($p < 0.10$) found for the other three measures.

The study took place in a male long-stay ward of a district psychiatric hospital. Behaviourally based training programmes had been implemented on the ward for about 15 months. The activities used frequently took place on the ward and the study was carried out where most of the group activities normally took place.

Subjects

Of the total 33 patients which comprised the ward complement, 12 patients fulfilled the inclusion criteria for the study. The criteria were:-

1.   Diagnosis of chronic schizophrenia.

2.   Hospitalised continuously for at least 5 years.

Table 2. Subject Details

	Mean age (years)	Mean time since first admission (years)	Mean length of last hospitalisation (years)	Mean P.I.P. Seclusiveness Score Rater I Rater II		Mean Overall Interaction Rank
All patients	56.2	27.4	19.5	19.7	26.7	
High Interactors	54.8	28.0	15.4	15.2	21.0	3.2
Low Interactors	57.6	26.8	23.6	24.2	32.4	7.8

3.   Not involved in activities outside the ward at the times for the study.

4.   Not considered too disturbed to participate.

5.   Willing to take part.

6.   Little likelihood of change in medication, transfer or discharge during the duration of the study.

From this pool of 12 patients, five pairs were randomly chosen. All patients were on long acting phenothiazines. The patients were assigned 'High' or 'Low' Interactor status (to allow for the evaluation of activity X subject interactions) by totalling their utterances over all sessions. Within each pair, the patient who had spoken more was labelled 'High'. This method is similar to that used by Polsky and Chance (1979a).

Subject details are shown in Table 2. The mean age of patients was 56.2 years, with no difference between the groups (t = 0.43, df = 8, NS).

The two senior nurses on the ward independently rated the patients on the Psychotic Inpatient Profile (Lorr and Vestre, 1969). Although their ratings were highly correlated (r = 0.79, p<0.001), the second rater rated the patients as being significantly more withdrawn overall (t = 3.39, p<0.01).

The patients had been divided into high or low interactor status on the basis of their total utterances within pairs. These totals were ranked across all patients to give an Overall Interactional Score and patients labelled 'High' within each pair did indeed prove to be higher interactors on the overall ratings (Mann-Whitney U = 1, p = 0.008), one-tailed). Finally, the seclusiveness scores were ranked and compared with the overall interactional ranks. For both raters, seclusiveness scores correlated significantly with the interactional ranks (Rater I : rs = 0.76, p<0.01; Rater II : rs = 0.57, p<0.05).

To conclude, the two groups did not differ in age or hospitalisation. Those labelled 'High' spoke more than those labelled 'Low' and the ward seclusivness ratings were highly correlated with interactional rankings suggesting that the speech observed in the study was representative of the patients' speech on the wards.

The division of subjects into high and low interactor status (Polsky and Chance, 1979a) was thus validated by the differences between the groups on overall interaction ranking and on seclusiveness.

Table 3a. Significant Differences Across Activities

	Dependent Variables	Combined Patients	High Interactors	Low Interactors
Line 1	Total speech Patient + Therapist	DOM + CARDS + DISC > CRAFT	—	—
Line 2	Patients' total speech	DISC + DOM > CRAFT	No difference	DOM + DISC > CRAFT

Table 3b. Significant Differences Across Activities

	Combined Patients	High Interactors	Low Interactors
Line 3 Patient-to-therapist speech	DISC + CRAFT > DOM + CARDS	DISC + CRAFT > DOM + CARDS	CRAFT > DOM + CARDS DISC > CARDS
Line 4 Patient-to-patient speech	No difference	DOM + CARDS > CRAFT + DISC	No difference
Line 5 Patient-to-group speech	DOM > DISC + CRAFT	DOM + CARDS > CRAFT + DISC	No difference
Line 6 Conversational speech	DISC > CRAFT + DOM + CARDS	DISC > CRAFT + DOM + CARDS	DISC > DOM /+ CARDS

KEY: DOM = DOMINOES,   DISC = DISCUSSIONS

1. Where an activity is not listed it did not differ significantly from the other three activities.

Table 4. Utterances of Therapist and Patients Combined and Patient Groups

	Craft	Dominoes	Cards	Discussion	Overall	Reliability (W)
Therapist and Patients Combined						
Mean	185.6	246.2	251.6	296	244.8	0.95
Range	159-212	228-275	211-289	270-323	-	-
*% (mean)	12.9	17.1	17.4	20.5	17	
Patient Groups						
Total						
Mean	74	121.2	110.6	154	114.9	0.941
**% (mean)	39.6	48.6	42.8	51.9	45.7	
High Interactors						
Mean	51.8	75.6	66	86.6	70	0.961
**% (mean)	27.9	30.2	25.2	29.3	28.1	
Low Interactors						
Mean	22.2	45.6	44.6	67.4	44.9	0.971
**% (mean)	11.7	18.4	17.7	22.7	17.6	

* % = Percentage of total observation cells
** % = Percentage of total speech observed (patients and therapists combined)

Experimental Procedure

Each session lasted 30 minutes. The therapist and pair of
patients sat around a table with the therapist facing the observer
(who was eight to ten feet away). The five pairs of patients were
seen in a random order. During the session, the therapist was
instructed to try to promote as much speech as possible and attempt
to keep the activity going. The patients received coffee and
cigarettes during the groups and were thanked for attending.

The therapist and observers were experienced in the running of
behaviour programmes and were well known to the patients.

RESULTS

The results were analysed non-parametrically using the Friedman
Two-way Analysis of variance (Siegel, 1956). Where a significant
difference was found among activities, the randomisation test for
matched pairs (Siegel, 1956) was used to find where the difference
lay. A summary of the significant results are displayed in Table 3.

Order of Session

No significant order effect was found across activities
(chi^2 = 2.04, p < 0.1), or across pairs (chi^2 = 4.8, p < 0.1). The
repeated measures design therefore successfully balanced any possible
order effect over activities and subjects.

Total Utterances - Therapist and Patients Combined

Good observer agreement (W = 0.95) was obtained for this
variable. The average number of utterances (244.8) observed in each
session represents 17% of the possible observations. Although this
may not appear a high figure, it should be remembered that there
were a possible 12 different speech items which could be recorded
in any time period, and so this figure represents a mean of 2.04
utterances per 15 second time period (with a range in means of
1.54 to 2.46 over activities). The data are shown in Table 4.

A significant difference across activities was found
(chi^2 = 11.88, p < 0.01). Paired comparison of activities showed
that Craft elicited less total speech than any other activity
(p = 0.06) (with an n = 5, this represents the largest value possible
for a significance level). The results are included in line 1,
Table 3a and displayed graphically in Fig. 2.

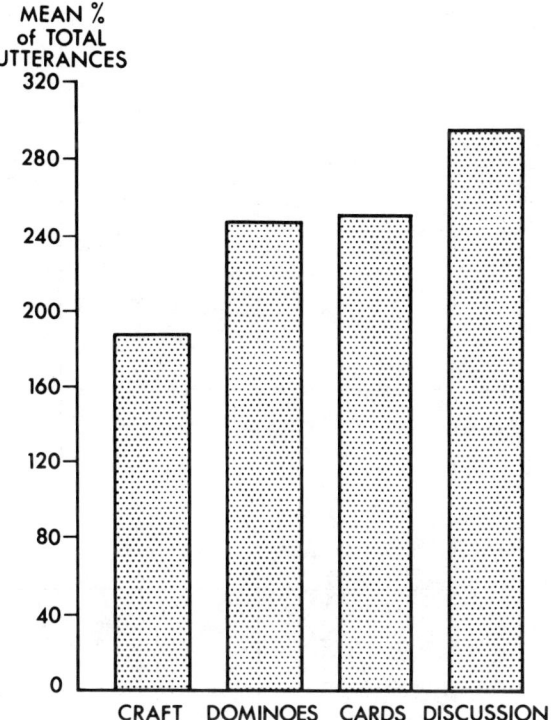

Fig. 2. Therapist and Patients Speech Combined

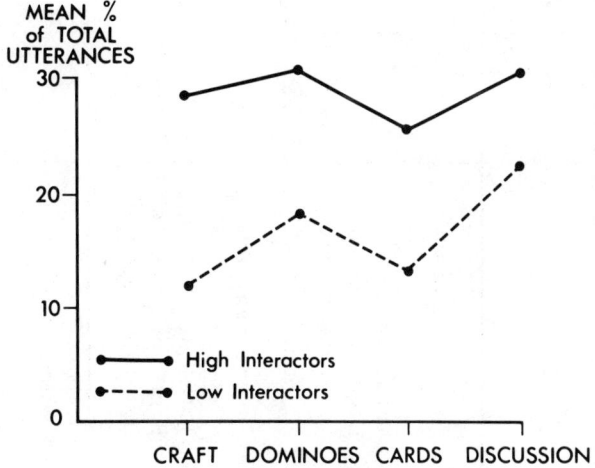

Fig. 3. Therapist and Patients Speech Combined

Table 5. Directions of Patient Utterances (as mean percentage of total patient utterances)

DIRECTION	ACTIVITY					
	Craft	Dominoes	Cards	Discussion	Overall	Reliability (W)
Patient-to-Therapist						
Total Group	90.7	58.8	63.8	90.0	75.8	0.98**
High Interactors	88.6	59.0	66.6	90.3	74.1	0.96***
Low Interactors	95.1	62.8	63.5	89.8	77.8	0.99***
Patient-to-Patient						
Total Group	2.6	17.0	9.4	7.5	9.1	0.98**
High Interactors	3.3	15.8	10.9	6.9	9.2	0.97**
Low Interactors	1.7	13.9	7.1	8.1	7.7	0.89**
Patient-to-Group						
Total Group	4.6	17.4	15.7	0.9	9.7	0.85*
High Interactors	5.8	20.9	14.7	1.1	10.6	0.90**
Low Interactors	1.9	12.9	16.8	0.8	8.1	0.86*

(* $p < 0.1$, ** $p < 0.05$)

Total Utterances - Patients

Again, satisfactory observer agreement was found for the total patient group (W = 0.94); for high interactors (W = 0.96); and for low interactors (W = 0.97). Overall, the patients emitted less than half the utterances observed, with the high interactors speaking more than low interactors in all activities (whether considered as raw scores or as percentage of total speech). Since a difference in total speech has been found, the analysis was carried out in a percentage scores to control for this difference.

For all patients, the activities differed slightly (chi^2 = 9.24, p < 0.05) and patients spoke more in Dominoes and Discussion than in Craft (p = 0.06). The results are shown in line 2, Table 3a and displayed in Fig 3.

The speech of the high and low interactors was then analysed separately. For high interactors, there was no difference across activities (chi^2 = 1.62 NS), but for the low interactors there was again a difference (chi^2 = 8.76, p < 0.05) with Discussion and Dominoes both superior to Craft. Again this result is illustrated in line 2, Table 3a.

Direction of Speech

This data is analysed in terms of the percentage of total patient speech. Overall patient-to-therapist interaction accounted for approximately 75% of utterances observed, while patient-to-patient and patient-to-group utterances, each accounted for less than 10%.

Patient-to-Therapist Speech. All measures produced high observer agreement (Table 5). High and low interactors contributed a similar percentage of speech towards the therapist. There were differences across activities for the combined group (chi^2 = 12.6, p < 0.01), for high interactors (chi^2 = 13.08, p < 0.01) and for low interactors (chi^2 = 10.18, p < 0.05). The significant comparisons are highlighted in line 3, Table 3b and results are shown in Fig 4.

Patient-to-Patient Speech. The results are shown in Table 5 and in Fig 5. There was no difference across activities for either the total group (chi^2 = 7.8 NS) or the low interactors (chi^2 = 3.3 NS), but for the high interactors a significant difference was found (chi^2 = 10.68, p < 0.05). As seen in line 4, Table 3b, comparison tests indicated that Craft elicited less patient-to-patient speech than any other activity.

Patient-to-Group Speech. The results are shown in Table 5 and Fig 6. There a lower level of agreement between observers reflects

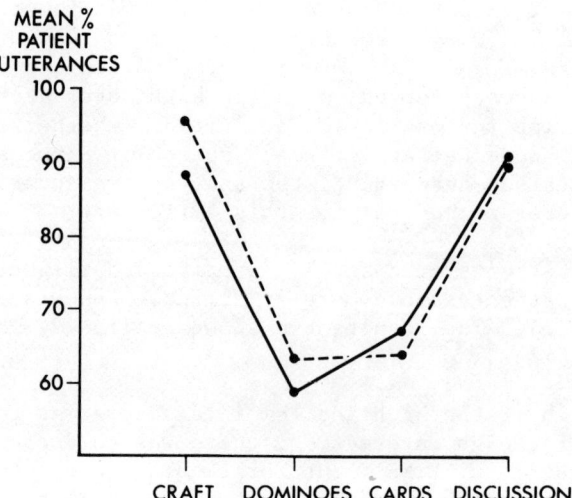

Fig. 4. Patient to Therapist Speech

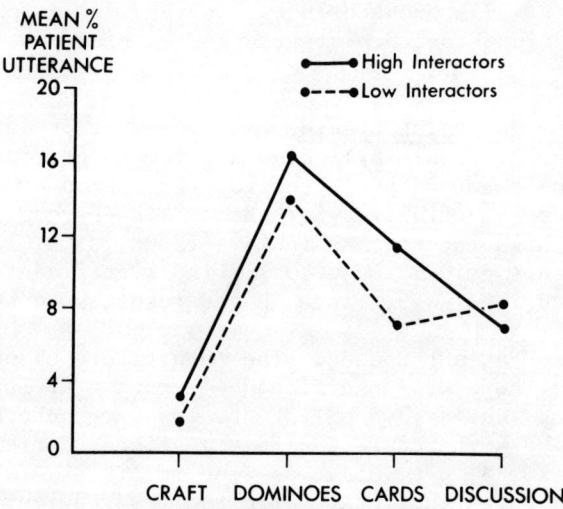

Fig. 5. Patient to Patient Speech

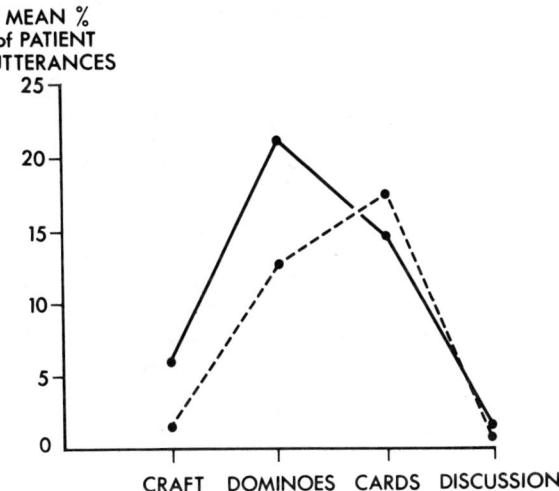

Fig. 6. Patient to Group Speech

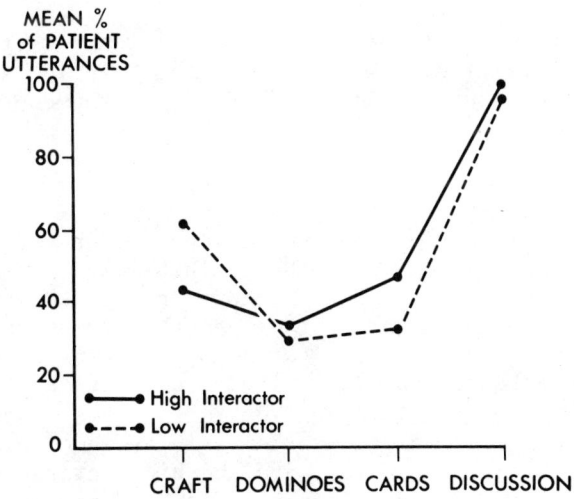

Fig. 7. Conversational Speech

difficulty in identifying such speech accurately. Both the percentage
scores for the total group (chi² = 15.18, p< 0.01) and for the high
interactors (chi² = 9.6, p< 0.05) varied across activities although
there was no difference with the low interactors (chi² = 3.3 NS).
Again comparison tests were used to elicit the differences and the
results are shown in line 5, Table 3b. As can be seen Dominoes
elicited a lower percentage of speech than Craft and Discussion for
the combined patients, while Craft and Discussion elicited a greater
percentage of speech than Cards and Dominoes for the high interactors.

Conversational Utterances

     Differences in general conversation (ie speech not directly
related to the ongoing activity) were next examined. The results
are shown in Table 6 and Fig 7. Utterances were totalled over all
directions of speech and satisfactory observer agreement was found
for this category. Although the low interactors spoke less than
the high interactors conversationally, this represented a similar
proportion of their speech with the exception of the Craft activity
where the percentage for the low interactors is much greater.
Statistically, there was a difference across activities for the
total group (chi² = 10.68, p< 0.05), for the high interactors
(chi² = 9.0, p< 0.05) and for the low interactors (chi² = 13.02,
p< 0.01). Discussion produced significantly more general conversation than the other activities for all comparisons. The results are
again summarised in line 6, Table 3b.

DISCUSSION

     On all five variables selected significant differences in the
order of activities was found between high and low interacting
patients. The results will be discussed in the context of each
activity.

Craft

     Overall this activity elicited less speech (for patients and
therapist combined) than any other. This was especially true for
low interactors who contributed a lower percentage of speech on this
activity than on any other. It may be that the relatively complex
nature of the activity necessitated more concentration and this
particularly affected the more withdrawn patients.

     The independent nature of the activity made no demand on
patient-to-patient interaction and the high interactors spoke mainly
to the therapist. Conversation comprised a similar percentage of
their speech as it did in the two games. The low interactors,
however, directed more of their speech to the therapist here than
in the games.

Table 6. Conversational Utterances (total over all directions as percentage of patient utterances)

Patient Group	Craft	Dominoes	Cards	Discussion	Overall	Reliability (W)
Total Group	48.6	29.9	32.6	99.2	52.6	0.89*
High Interactors	44.6	32.8	34.7	99	52.8	.091**
Low Interactors	59.2	29.9	30.5	98.9	54.6	0.96**

(* p < 0.1, ** p < 0.05)

It can be concluded therefore that the complexity of the activity appeared to reduce the speech in the whole group (but particularly
with the more withdrawn patients) and that lack of inherent demand
for patient-to-patient interaction led to a low proportion of such
speech from high interactors. Overall, this activity seems to have
little value in promoting speech among patients or with the therapist.

The Two Games: Cards and Dominoes

It had been predicted that the card game would promote more
interaction than the dominoes, but in fact any difference favoured
dominoes. The games elicited as much total speech as did the
discussion group and there was no difference between the games in the
percentage of patient speech.

For the high interactors both games promoted more patient-to-
patient speech than did the craft and both games elicited more
patient-to-group speech than craft or discussion group. Since
conversation comprised a similar proportion of speech as did the
craft, the increase in high interactors' speech to the low interactors and to the group was not just related to games but also non-
game related, ie conversational. Only high interactors responded
to the increased demands for patient-to-patient and patient-to-
group speech demonstrating an interaction between subject characteristics and activity. Co-operative games appear to have useful
therapeutic effects, therefore, particularly for less withdrawn
patients.

Discussion Groups

Although discussion elicited more speech than any other activity it was significantly superior only to craft. The proportion of
high interactor speech did not differ from other activities and
discussion was as good as games at eliciting speech from the low
interactors. This suggests that being placed in a setting with a
high demand for speech did not adversely affect any of the patients.
Conversely the high demand did not produce significantly more speech
than cards.

More of the speech was directed towards the therapist here than
in the games for all subjects. The conversation category had been
intended to measure speech not directly related to the activity,
but as no manual activity was involved, most of the speech was
rated as conversational.

There was no evidence that the clear demand for speech adversely
affected either high or low interactors. Most speech was directed
towards the therapist and so although the therapist was able to

promote a high level of interaction, he was not able to increase the proportion of patient-to-patient speech. Thus, while discussion groups will appear to have value in promoting patient-to-therapist speech, additional procedures may be necessary if increased patient-to-patient interaction is the target of intervention.

Three variables (total patient speech; patient-to-patient speech and patient-to-patient therapist speech) can be compared to Taylor's (1974) study. The order of activities found here differed on each variable - changes in observational method and analysis, in group size or subject differences all may account for the different results. Here discussion groups elicited more patient speech than in her study.

CONCLUSIONS

The effect of the activities on speech was specific and inter-acted with subject characteristics. This supports an interactional explanation (Paul and Lentz, 1977; Bowers, 1973; Mischel, 1973) of social behaviour and demonstrates the importance of a separate analysis of the effect of each activity. Insensitivity of global evaluation may account for some of the variation in utility of activity programmes reported. Indeed from the literature, it is sometimes impossible to determine the nature of the specific activity involved in the programme.

The actual effects of the activities in this study differed from those predicted a priori and from Taylor's study (Taylor, 1974). Possible reasons for this have been discussed above. It is clear that any programme using activities should be monitored carefully to ensure that it is achieving the expected behaviour change: direct observational methods can provide accurate information about these effects (Sackett, 1978).

As far as choice of activities is concerned, three factors of importance emerged from this study: the complexity of the activity, the inherent demands for interaction, and the amount of manual activity involved.

In this study, a complex activity with no demand for patient-to-patient interaction and a high level of manual activity was poor at promoting speech, particularly for the more withdrawn patients. In fact, this type of activity appears to be of little use in a socialisation programme. On the other hand, higher demands for patient-to-group interaction affected the behaviour of the less withdrawn patients. For the more withdrawn patients, more direct procedures (Bennet and Maley, 1973) where the contingencies are clearly specified (Mitchell, 1978) might be more useful.

Relatively high levels of speech (particularly patient-to-therapist speech) were found in the discussion groups. But while the therapist may be able to increase patients' conversation directed towards himself (eg through social approval) it would appear more difficult to stimulate patient-to-patient speech without more explicit training methods.

There was no evidence in this study that small discussion groups with an experienced, known therapist were unacceptable to these patients. Since all these patients, however, were already involved in the ward socialisation programme, it is possible that such groups may be more stressful for patients beginning treatment and activities with lower demands or verbal skills, such as games, may be more appropriate initially. A longitudinal study of the usefulness, and acceptability of different activities would provide an interesting continuation of this cross-sectional study.

Less withdrawn patients were more responsive to differences in demands for interaction. This finding is in accord with other studies (Moos, 1968; Marriotto and Paul, 1975) which found that the behaviour of lower functioning patients was less situationally specific.

The possible combination of activities with social skills training aimed at specific behavioural deficits should be explored. Activity groups may provide appropriate stimulus conditions for eliciting newly learned behaviours outside the treatment setting thus enabling generalisation (Stokes and Baer, 1977; Shepard, 1979). Such activities might be more selected through analysis of their relationships with target behaviours (eg eye contact, response latency or speech initiation) in a social skills training programme.

The possible harmful effects of over-stimulation (Wing, 1978; Venables and Wing, 1962), however, should be assessed in any activity programme. The effects of spacing and duration of activity sessions must also be considered, as satiation effects of social stimulation have been demonstrated (Mitchell, 1978).

In conclusion, this study provides strong evidence for a highly specific situational effect of activities on social interaction with chronic schizophrenic in-patients. This effect may explain in part the previous somewhat equivocal results of social activity programmes. With attention to subject characteristics and the selection of appropriate activities, the small group would seem to represent a therapeutic milieu, acceptable to patients, within which deficits in social communication can be identified and ameliorated.

REFERENCES

Baer, D., Wolf, M., and Risley, T., 1968, Some current dimensions of
    applied behaviour analysis, J. App. Beh. Anal., 1:91
Baker, R., 1971, The use of operant conditioning to reinstate speech
    in a mute schizophrenic, Beh. Res. & Ther., 9:329.
Baker, R., Hall, J.N., and Hutchinson, K., 1974, A token economy
    project with chronic schizophrenic patients, Brit. J. Psychiat.,
    124:367.
Bartko, J., and Carpenter, W., 1976, On the methods and theory of
    reliability, J. Nerv. & Ment. Dis., 163:307.
Barton, R., 1959, "Institutional Neurosis," John Wright and Sons,
    Bristol.
Bennett, P., and Maley, R., 1973, Modification of interactive
    behaviours in chronic mental patients, J. App. Beh. Anal.,
    6:609.
Bowers, J., 1973, Situationism in psychology - an analysis and
    critique, Psychol. Rev., 80:307.
Brown, D., and Peddar, J., 1979, "Introduction to Psychotherapy,"
    Tavistock, London.
Doty, D.W., 1975, Role playing and incentives in the modification
    of the social interactions of chronic psychiatric patients,
    cited in Kazdin (1977), p.91.
Eisler, R., Hersen, M., and Agras, W., 1973, Videotape: a method
    for the controlled observation of non-verbal interpersonal
    behaviour, Beh. Ther., 4:420.
Ellsworth, R.B., 1964, The psychiatric aide as rehabilitation
    therapist, cited in Paul and Lentz (1977).
Ellsworth, R.B., 1968, Non-professionals in psychiatric rehabilita-
    tion, cited in Watts (1976).
Fairweather, G., ed., 1964, Social psychology in treating mental
    illness: an experimental approach, cited in Watts (1976).
Fernandez, J., 1978, Critical variables in token economy systems:
    a review of the literature and description of current research,
    Beh. Psychother., Vol. 6.
Fraser, D., 1978, Critical variables in token economy systems: a
    review of the literature and description of current research,
    Beh. Psychother., 6:46.
Fraser, D., 1981, Chapter in this volume.
Goldsmith, J., and McFall, R., 1975, Development and evaluation of
    an interpersonal skill training programme for psychiatric
    patients, J. Abn. Psychol., 84(1):51.
Hall, J.N., Baker, R., and Hutchinson, K., 1977, A controlled
    evaluation of token economy procedures with chronic
    schizophrenic patients, Beh. Res. & Ther., 15:261.
Hersen, M., and Barlow, D., 1976, "Single Case Experimental Designs:
    Strategies for Studying Behaving Change," Pergamon, New York.

Hersen, M., and Bellack, A.S., 1976, Social skills training for chronic psychiatric patients: rationale, research findings and future directions, Comp. Psychiat., 17:559.

Hollenbeck, A.R., 1978, Problems of reliability in observational research, Chapter 5 in Sackett (1978).

Jones, M., 1952, "Social Psychiatry: A Study of Therapeutic Communities," Tavistock, London.

Kazdin, A.E., and Bootzin, R., 1973, The token economy: an examination of issues, in: "Advances in Behaviour Therapy," Vol. 4, B. Rubin & J. Brady, eds., Academic Press, New York.

Kazdin, A.E., 1977, "The Token Economy: A Review and Evaluation," Plenum, New York.

Leff, J., Hirsch, S., Gainds, R., Rohole, P., and Stevens, B., 1973., Life events and maintenance therapy in schizophrenic relapse, Brit. J. Psychiat., 123:659.

Lindsay, W.R., 1980, The training and generalisation of conversation behaviour in psychiatric in-patients: a controlled study employing multiple measures across settings, Brit. J. Soc. & Clin. Psychol., 19:85.

Lorr, M., and Vestre, N., 1969, The psychotic inpatient profile: a nurse observation scale, J. Clin. Psychol., 25:137.

MacDonald, E., MacCane, G., and Mirrey, L., 1972, "Occupational Therapy in Rehabilitation," 3rd Ed., Ballier, Tindale & Cassell, London.

Marholin, D, II., Siegel, L.J., and Philips, D., 1976, Treatment and transfer: a search for empirical procedures, in: Progress in Behaviour Modification," Vol. 4., M. Hersen, R. Eisler & P. Miller, eds., Academic Press, New York.

Mariotto, M., and Paul, G.L., 1975, Persons versus situations in the real life functioning of chronically institutionalised mental patients, J. Abn. Psychol., 84:483.

Marzillier, J., and Winter, K., 1978, Success and failure in social skills training: individual differences, Beh. Res. & Ther., 16:67.

Matson, J., Zeiss, A., Zeiss, R., and Bowman, W., 1980, A comparison of social skills training and contingent attention to improve behavioural deficits of chronic psychiatric patients, Brit. J. Soc. & Clin. Psychol., 19:57.

Mischel, W., 1973, Toward a cognitive social learning reconceptualisation of personality, Psychol. Rev., 80:252.

Mitchell, S., 1979, Inter-observer agreement, reliability and generalisability of data collected in observational studies, Psychol. Bull., 86(2):376.

Mitchell, W.S., 1978, Contingency learning in chronic schizophrenics and its relevance to the social maturation deficits, Brit. J. Med. Psychol., 51(4):357.

Moos, R.H., 1968, Situational analysis of a therapeutic community milieu, J. Abn. Psychol., 73:49.

Ozarin, L.D., 1954, Moral treatment and the mental hospital, Amer. J. Psychiat., 111:371.

Paul, G., and Lentz., R.J., 1977, "Psychosocial Treatment of Chronic
    Mental Patients: Milieu Versus Social Learning Programmes,"
    Harvard University Press, Mass., USA.
Polsky, R., and Chance, M., 1979a, An ehtological perspective on
    social behaviour in long-stay hospitalised psychiatric patients.,
    J. Nerv. & Ment. Dis., 167(11):658.
Powell, J., Martindale, B., Kulp, S., Martindale, A., and Bowman, R.,
    1977, Taking a closer look: time sampling and measurement error,
    J. App. Beh. Anal., 10:325.
Powell, L., Felie, D., Jenkins, J., and Lunt, B., 1979, Increasing
    engagement in a home for the elderly by providing an indoor
    gardening activity, Beh. Res. & Ther., 17(2):127.
Robertson, I., 1979, Increasing engagement of adult psychiatric
    patients in a day hospital, Beh. Psychother., 7(2):25.
Sackett, G., ed., 1978, "Observing Behaviour, Data Collection and
    Analysis Methods, " Vol. 2, University Park Press, Baltimore.
Saunders, R., Weinman, B., Smith, A., Kenny, J., and Fitzgerald, B.,
    1962, Social treatment of the male chronic mental patient,
    cited in Paul and Lentz (1977).
Sanson-Fisher, R.W., Poole, A.D., and Thompson, V., 1979, Behaviour
    patterns within a general hospital psychiatric unit: an
    observational study, Beh. Res. & Ther., 17(4):317.
Shepard, G., 1977, Social skills training: the generalisation
    problem, Beh. Ther., 8:1008-1009.
Shepard, G., 1979, The implementation of social skills training in
    institutional settings. Paper presented at "Social Skills
    Training in Practice", MIND Conf., London.
Siegel, S., 1956, "Non-parametric Statistics for the Behavioural
    Sciences," McGraw-Hill, KogaKusha Co. Ltd., Tokyo.
Somner, R., and Ross, H., 1958, Social interaction in a geriatric
    ward, Int. J. Soc. Psychiat., 4:128.
Stahl, J.R., Thomson, L.E., Leitenber, H., and Hasagi, J.E., 1974,
    Establishment of praise as a conditioned reinforcer in socially
    unresponsive psychiatric patients, J. Abn. Psychol., 83(5):488.
Stoffelmayr, B., Faulkener, G., and Mitchell, W., 1973, The
    rehabilitation of chronic hospitalised patients by means of
    operant conditioning methods. Final report to the Scottish
    Home and Health Department.
Stoffelmayr, B., Faulkener, G., and Mitchell, W., 1979, The compar-
    ison of token economy and social therapy in the treatment of
    hard core schizophrenic patients, Europ. J. Beh. Anal. & Mod.,
    3:3.
Stokes, T., and Baer, D.M., 1977, An implicit technology of
    generalisation, J. App. Beh. Anal., 10:349.
Taylor, V., 1974, "A Behavioural Analysis of Activity Group Therapy
    with 'Hard Core' Chronic Schizophrenics," Unpublished PhD,
    Aberdeen.
Tillotson, K.J., 1939, The practice of the total push method in the
    treatment of chronic schizophrenics, Amer. J. Psychol., 95:1205.

Tracey, E., Briddell, D., and Wilson, G., 1974, Generalisation of verbal conditioning to verbal and non-verbal behaviour: group therapy with chronic psychiatric patients, cited in Kazdin (1977), p.92.

Vaughan, C., and Leff, J., 1976, Influence of family and social factors on the course of psychiatric illness, Brit. J. Psychiat., 129:125.

Venables, P., and Wing, J.K., 1962, Levels of arousal and the sub-classification of schizophrenia, Arch. Gen. Psychiat., 7:114.

Watts, F.N., 1976, Social treatments, Chapter 21 in Eysenck, H.J., and Wilson, G.D., "A Textbook of Human Psychology," M.T.P., England.

Wing, J.K., 1978, ed., "Schizophrenia: Towards a New Synthesis," Academic Press, London.

A SITUATIONAL ANALYSIS OF SOCIAL BEHAVIOR IN LONG-STAY PSYCHIATRIC

PATIENTS

William R Lindsay

Psychology Department
Monklands District General Hospital
Airdrie, Scotland

INTRODUCTION

Reports of Social Skills Training (SST) have appeared with increasing frequency in the last 10 to 15 years. The techniques have
now been used with a wide variety of patient groups including
psychiatric in-patients (Hersen and Bellack, 1976), psychiatric out-
patients (Argyle et al, 1974), alcoholics (Foy et al, 1976), adolescents (Lindsay et al, 1979) and children (Frosh and Callias, 1980).
Several reviewers have documented this rapid growth and the application of SST to these several patient groups, (Hersen and Bellack)
1976; Marzillier, 1978; Hersen, 1979; Trower, 1979). In assessing
the effectiveness of SST, three aspects have usually been considered;
improvements in social behaviour within the treatment setting, generalisation of improvement from the treatment setting to other important situations of the patient's life, and the maintenance of
these changes after treatment has finished. It is not the purpose
of this introduction to cover information which has already been
done extensively elsewhere. This short review will outline some
of the shortcomings in the effectiveness of SST in order to make a
case for helping the patient to use the skills he already possesses
in a greater variety of settings, rather than training individuals
in relative isolation of their social surroundings.

Improvements Within Treatment

There now seems reasonable evidence that the social skills of
psychiatric patients can be enhanced through a programme of SST.
A long list of studies reviewed comprehensively by the above authors
attests to this conclusion. Marzillier (1978, p.124) writes that

345

"experimental evidence from studies in both psychiatric patients and
volunteer subjects indicates that skills training can produce positive changes in social behaviour in the short-term". He does point
out, however, that some studies report only limited improvement in
social behaviour. Hersen (1979) concludes in relation to SST that
"a relatively effective methodology has been devised to deal with
severely disturbed psychiatric patients whose medication is controlling psychotic symptomatology". More recent studies such as
Marzillier and Winter (1978), Lindsay (1980), and Matson et al (1980)
have provided further evidence supporting the conclusion that, within
treatment, the social skills of patients can be improved and that
this improvement is not due to non-specific treatment effects or the
passage of time.

Generalisation of Improvement

The second index of effectiveness for SST is generalisation of
improvements to the patient's own social environment, and the evidence here is more equivocal. Bellack (1979, p.97) reports that
"there is no evidence that increasing eye contact, voice volume, or
the like actually affects marital interaction, dating frequency,
level of depression, or any other clinically meaningful set of behaviours". In essence he is saying that there is no evidence that
a package of social skills training or improvements in the various
social behaviours during treatment affects the more general aspects
of a patient's social life.

One problem with many studies which do show generalisation of
improvement is that the generalisation may not be clinically relevant
for two main reasons. Firstly, many studies in social skills and
assertion training have been done on college students. While the
principles of SST remain the same, it should be noted that it may
prove a more intractable problem to improve the social behaviour of
psychiatric patients (Mahoney, 1977). Secondly, when generalisation
has been shown to occur it is often from role played settings used
in the treatment to new role played scenes. These role played
generalisation scenes may be considerably different from the patient's real social world.

Some studies published in the early 1970s reported poor results
on generalisation tasks (eg Hersen et al, 1974; McFall and Lilliesand,
1971; Thorpe, 1975), and Hersen and Bellack (1976) write that "Baer,
Wolf, and Risley's (1968) dictum that 'generalisation should be
programmed rather than expected or lamented' has essentially been
ignored in the social skills training literature". However, studies
published more recently have provided more encouraging results.
Shepherd (1978) writes that a revised programme of SST promoted
significant amounts of generalisation, whereas he had not found
evidence of generalisation of skills in a previous study (Shepherd,

1977). To do this he organised homework tasks and "in vivo" treatment sessions so that patients could practise their newly acquired
social behaviours in the settings where they would usually interact.
Lindsay (1980) used similar principles to generalise social behaviour
from treatment to the ward setting with psychiatric in-patients.
In this study homework tasks were given to patients to complete before
each session and several treatment sessions were conducted in the
setting to which behaviour was to generalise. Matson et al (1980)
have also reported generalisation of social skill to the ward situation.

     In the Shepherd and Lindsay studies the common elements of home-
work tasks and "in vivo" training sessions seemed to promote generalisation. The important part about these studies is that they take
account of the patients' normal social surroundings. Certainly,
more research is needed in the area of generalisation, but these
reports indicate some optimism for therapists attempting to promote
generalisation of social behaviours into the patient's real social
world. In this respect Trower (1980) has mentioned the distinction
between components and processes of social interaction. He feels
that therapists should focus more on the processes of social interaction, teaching patients the ability to be flexible and vary their
social interaction depending on the demands of the situations, thereby promoting generalisation through internal rather than external
control.

Maintenance of Change

     For SST to be effective improvements should maintain after the
treatment has finished. Marzillier (1978) writes that the issues
of maintenance and generalisation should be priorities for research
in the area. Several authors have reported poor maintenance of behaviour, months or even weeks after treatment has finished (Serber
and Nelson, 1971; Goldsmith and McFall, 1975; Lindsay et al, 1976).
On the other hand Marzillier et al (1976) found that, after SST,
gains made by patients had maintained at 6 months' follow-up.

     In one of the longest follow-up studies Longin and Rooney (1975)
found maintenance of assertion skills in a psychiatric population
2 years after the cessation of treatment. More recently Matson
et al (1980) found that improvements in social behaviour of psychiatric in-patients maintained extremely well 4 weeks after treatment.
At an 8 week follow-up after treatment, Lindsay (1980) assessed
maintenance of social behaviour in terms of both the frequency of
interaction on the ward and the quality of patients' social skills.
It was found that while increased frequency of interaction did not
maintain at post-treatment levels, the social skill improvements
which patients had shown were maintained at follow-up. Therefore,
items of speech quality, non-verbal interaction and length of speech
maintained at post-treatment levels.

There remains a need for developments in the areas of generalisation and maintenance of social behaviour. It is important to have
this effective methodology since it has been found that a large
proportion of psychiatric patients evidence social inadequacy. This
has been reported at between 7% (Curran et al, 1980) and 16% (Bryant
et al, 1976). The present study on psychiatric in-patients investigates an aspect of these various issues by assessing social behaviour across the situations and relating the relevance of this approach
to patients' general social lives.

PRESENT STUDY

One of the major strengths of behaviour modification is its
emphasis on the initial specification and measurement of the problem
to be dealt with and the need for adequate knowledge about the
assessment of behavioural deficit is of paramount importance. In
cases where the target behaviour is assessed, treated and a programme evaluated all in one setting, and it is only relevant to that
single setting, there is perhaps less need to consider the problem
of determinants of behaviour across situations. However, if the
target behaviour is a response deficit in social competence then it
is necessary to consider to what extent the patients' difficulties
are evident across various settings.

Evidence has been available for some time indicating that aspects of social behaviour are situationally specific (eg Hartshorne
and May, 1928 on moral behaviour) and Mischel (1968) argues that
environmental determinants play an important part in understanding
behaviour. Eisler et al (1975) investigated the issue of situational
specificity with reference to assertion. They found that the stimulus characteristics of the situation were important in eliciting
assertive responses. Males tended to be more assertive with females
than with other males and unfamiliar individuals tended to elicit
more assertion than familiar ones. They conclude that "in general,
the results support a stimulus specific theory of assertiveness".
Trower (1980), in a study of skilled and unskilled psychiatric patients, has found a situational component with respect to certain
social skills, notably speech and aspects of gaze. The present experiment looks at the variability of social behaviour in high sociable and low sociable subjects in relation to the stimulus dimensions of familiarity and unfamiliarity.

Method

Subjects. Twenty long-stay psychiatric patients served as subjects. They were chosen from 62 patients according to their scores
on the seclusiveness scales on the psychotic in-patient profile
(Lorr and Vestre, 1969). The 10 patients who scored highest on the

PIP seclusiveness scale were included as a group of withdrawn, "low sociable" (LS) patients. The 10 least seclusive patients were included as a "high sociable" (HS) group.

Procedure. Patient's social behaviour was recorded in three standard situations:

1. Videotaped recordings of the patient talking to a male nurse whom he had known for some 2 years, ie, this member of staff knew the patient and was quite familiar to him. These tapes were filmed in a side room on the ward under standard conditions.

2. Audiotaped recordings of the patient talking to a male nurse who had been on the ward for only 2 weeks. Therefore, the patients were not very familiar with this person. These recordings were made unobtrusively and the conversation took place as they would in the ongoing activity on the ward. The nurse sat down beside the patient and after a few minutes switched on the taperecorder and began the conversation.

3. Audiotaped recordings of the patient talking to a male nurse whom he had known over 2 years.

On all occasions the member of staff covered a standard interview during which he introduced several topics in the following order, using the statements below:

"This is awful/fair/lovely weather we are having",
"What have you been doing with yourself lately?",
"What is it that you are working at just now?",
"Were you watching TV last night?",
"Did you have a good weekend?",
"Have you anything planned for this weekend?".

The nurse was also encouraged to use topical news items for making conversation. The recordings lasted 5-12 minutes each depending on how quickly the schedule was covered. All interviews were conducted over a 2 week period and although conditions were not balanced the results do not indicate any practice effects.

The films were rated on the social skills rating scale developed by Lindsay (in press). The items on which subjects were rated were volume, tone, clarity, pitch, length of utterance, amount of interest in the other person, amount of interest in self, and general social skill. Development of the rating scale and full reliability data are reported elsewhere (Lindsay, in press).

Each item was arranged along a 7 point semantic differential from too much of the behaviour through appropriate (the mid-point) to too little of the behaviour eg in the case of volume from far

too loud to far too quiet. The only exception to this was general
social skill which was rated on a 7 point scale from extremely easy
to talk to, to extremely difficult to talk to. Agreement between
observers in the present study was 82%. Where disagreements did
occur on the initial ratings short discussions were held between
raters and an agreed rating arrived at.

Ward observations were also made of patients amount and type
of social interaction using a code developed and used by Lindsay
(1977) and Lindsay (1980). This code measures total amount of social
behaviour and breaks this into short exchanges, longer exchanges,
initiated by the patient or by others. When testing for the reliability in this code (Lindsay, 1977) agreement between trained
observers was found to be between 92% and 100%. The data used in
the current analysis was simply the presence or absence of speech.
These observations were highly reliable with a Cohen's kappa coefficient of .90. Patients were observed for 4 hours during four
consecutive lunch breaks.

Results

Table 1 indicates the large discrepancy between the HS and LS
groups in terms of the total amount of social interaction engaged
in during observations over four consecutive lunch hours.

The HS group spent 32% of their time in social interaction
while the LS group spent only 3.9% in social interaction and most
of this was short exchanges initiated by the staff to the patient.
This difference is significant ($p < .001$) using an independent groups
t-test.

Tables 2 to 6 show the group ratings for audiotaped and videotaped interviews. The mid-point on the semantic differentials rating
scale was given a score of zero indicating appropriate behaviour on
that item, ie no social deviancy. As the ratings became more extreme
in either direction scores of 1, 2 and 3 were given with 3 being the

Table 1. Percentage of Observations in which Patients
          Engaged in Conversation During Lunch Breaks

	HS	LS
% Observation of interaction	32.	3.9
% Observation of silence	68.	96.1

Table 2. Audio: Unfamiliar

	HS v.	LS	P
Volume	2	22	<.002
Tone	4	21	<.002
Clarity	4	26	<.002
Pitch	4	6	NS
Length	0	27	<.002
Others	8	27	<.002
Self	12	29	<.002
General	22	69	<.002

Key to conditions in Tables 2 and 3

Audio - audiotaped interview.
Video - videotaped interview.
Unfamiliar - interview conducted by a person unfamiliar to the
    patient.
Familiar - interview conducted by a person familiar to the patient.
HS - high sociable patients.
LS - low sociable patients.

Table 3. Video: Familiar

	HS v.	LS	P
Volume	10	14	NS
Tone	14	23	NS
Clarity	4	10	NS
Pitch	4	4	NS
Length	12	16	NS
Others	10	19	<.002
Self	12	14	NS
General	30	47	<.002

Table 4. Familiar: HS

	Audio	v. Video	P
Volume	3	10	<.01
Tone	,4	14	<.005
Clarity	2	4	NS
Pitch	1	4	<.05
Length	0	12	<.005
Others	9	10	NS
Self	7	12	<.01
General	16	30	<.005

Key to conditions in Tables 4 and 5

Audio - audiotaped interview.
Video - videotaped interview.
Unfamiliar - interview conducted by a person unfamiliar to the
    patient.
Familiar - interview conducted by a person familiar to the patient.
HS - high sociable patients.
LS - low sociable patients.

Table 5. Audio: LS

	Familiar	v. Unfamiliar	P
Volume	16	22	<.01
Tone	13	21	<.01
Clarity	10	26	<.01
Pitch	3	6	NS
Length	15	27	<.01
Others	13	27	<.01
Self	8	29	<.01
General	42	69	<.01

maximum amount of deviancy for that item. Therefore a rating at
either extreme of each scale would have a deviancy score of 3. This
is not true for the item of general social skill which was scored
from 1 to 7 with 7 showing a very poor level of general social skill.
The tables show total deviancy scores in each item of social skill
for each group under each condition.

Table 2 shows that when unobtrusive audiotapes are made of patients talking to an unfamiliar interviewer there are large differences between groups in the social skills ratings (all items
significant $(p < .002)$ except pitch: Mann Whitney U Test). In this
situation the LS patients show a great deal of social inadequacy.

Table 3 shows the ratings of videotapes taken when patients are
talking to a familiar interviewer. Here many of the differences are
reduced and are not significant (Mann Whitney U Test). Only general
social skill remained significant $(p < .002)$, although the absolute
difference in ratings between groups is reduced by 30 points.
Interest in others is also significant $(p < .002)$. Analysis of Table
2 and 3 shows that the reduction in group differences is due to the
LS group showing less social inadequacy and the HS group showing more
social inadequacy.

By altering only the recording variable it becomes clear that
the HS group are worse in the video: familiar condition because they
are reacting to the video equipment. Table 4 shows that when interviewed by the same person and recorded on audiotape their social
performance improves (6 out of 8 differences are reasonably significant: Wilcoxon Matched Pairs Test). Here their scores are very
similar to the audio: unfamiliar condition in Table 2.

Table 5 provides an explanation of the large reductions in
social inadequacy shown by the LS group in the video: familiar condition. In the audio: familiar condition the LS group still shows
a much improved level of performance and when this is compared to
the ratings in the audio: unfamiliar condition the differences are
consistently significant $(p < .01$, Wilcoxon Matched Pairs Test),
except for item 4. The indication here is that patients who are
considered to have poor social ability show more social skills when
talking to a familiar interviewer.

Table 6 compares the HS and LS groups under the audio: familiar
condition. The differences between groups are much reduced in comparison to Table 2. Three items remain significant at the $p < .002$
level, two are reduced to the $p < .02$ level and two become non-significant (Mann Whitney U Test). This time, most of the reduced difference between the groups is due to the LS group becoming more
socially skilled under the familiar condition as has been explained
by Table 5.

Table 6. Audio: Familiar

	HS v.	LS	P
Volume	3	16	< .002
Tone	4	13	< .02
Clarity	2	10	< .02
Pitch	1	3	NS
Length	0	15	< .002
Others	9	13	NS
Self	7	8	NS
General	16	42	< .002

Key to conditions in Table 6

Audio - audiotaped interview.
Video - videotaped interview.
Unfamiliar - interview conducted by a person unfamiliar to the
    patient.
Familiar - interview conducted by a person familiar to the patient.
HS - high sociable patients.
LS - low sociable patients.

DISCUSSION

In the results of this experiment we have seen that LS patients
have a low frequency of social interaction and show a great deal of
social inadequacy when talking to unfamiliar people. However, when
interacting with a familiar interviewer they show considerably improved social performance. Therefore, by assessing across situations
we can conclude that these patients have more social ability or
social potential than they would usually show. Indeed under certain
conditions (video: familiar) there is very little difference between
LS and HS patients, partly due to the HS patients deteriorating in
their social performance when being videotaped.

These results support a situational specific model of social
inadequacy consistent with Eisler et al (1975) and Trower (1980) and
as such have considerable repercussions for training social behaviour. Therapeutic strategy will be effected if we can establish
that in certain situations the patient has a greater repertoire of
coping social behaviour. The treatment goals become those of elicit-

ing the coping behaviour with the stimuli in the new target situation rather than training patients from a very low level of social skill. We may be able to assume that a patient already has a fair level of skill which he is not using in the target situation. Therefore, the problem becomes one of helping him to feel comfortable using his skills in the new situation rather than training social behaviour from the beginning.

The results also underline the often repeated assertion (Hersen and Bellack, 1976; Baer et al, 1968) that we cannot assume social behaviour evidenced in one situation would generalise to another. Indeed this study indicates that patients may possess social skills which they use in certain situations and not others.

The final point to be made in relation to the present report is that it offers a perspective on what may be happening during social skills training. Here it should be remembered that these subjects are withdrawn, long-stay psychotic patients. Even with these very unsociable patients, the data suggests that we need not assume that the patient has no social skill. We are not training social skill from nothing.

Here it is useful to note Trower's (1980) distinction between the components of social skill and the process of social skill. He feels that rather than engineer generalisation to new situation, therapists might attempt to increase patients' awareness of social cues and rules, thus helping them to deal with the processes of social behaviour, varying their responses as the situation demands.

Therefore our main tasks as therapists may be to help the patients to use their skills in a variety of new situations and perhaps also to train a few new social skills.

ACKNOWLEDGEMENT

For the period during which this research was conducted the author was in receipt of a Medical Research Council Grant.

REFERENCES

Argyle, M., Trower, P., and Bryant, B., 1974, Explorations of the treatment of personality disorders and neurosis by social skills training, Brit. J. Med. Psychol., 37:63.
Baer, D., Wolf, M., and Risley, T., 1968, Some current dimensions of applied behaviour analysis, J. App. Beh. Anal., 1:91.
Bellack, A.S., 1979, Behavioural assessment of social skills, in: "Research and Practice in Social Skills Training," A. Bellack & M. Hersen, eds., Plenum Press, New York & London.

Bryant, B., Trower, P., Yardley, K., Urbieta, H., and Letemendia, F., 1976, A survey of social inadequacy among psychiatric out-patients, Psychol. Med., 6:101-112.

Curran, J.P., Miller, I.W., Zwick, W.R., Monti, P.N., and Stout, R.L., 1980, The socially inadequate patient: incidence rate, demographic and clinical features, and hospital and post-hospital functioning, J. Cons. & Clin. Psychol., 43:375-382.

Eisler, R., Hersen, M., Miller, P., and Blanchard, E., 1975, Situational determinants of assertive behaviour, J. Cons. & Clin. Psychol., 43:330-340.

Foy, D.W., Miller, P.M., Eisler, R.M., and O'Toole, D.H., 1976, Social skills training to teach alcoholics to refuse drinks effectively, J. Stud. Alcohol, 37:1340-1345.

Frosh, S., and Callias, M., 1980, Social skills training in an infant school setting, Beh. Psychother., 8:69-79.

Goldsmith, J.B., and McFall, R.M., 1975, Development and evaluation of an interpersonal skills training program for psychiatric in-patients, J. Abn. Psychol., 84:51-58.

Hartshorne, H., and May, M., 1928, "Studies in the Nature of Character (Volume 1): Studies in Deceit," MacMillan, New York.

Hersen, M., 1979, Social skills deficits in psychiatric patients, in: "Research and Practice in Social Skills Training," A. Bellack & M. Hersen, eds., Plenum Press, New York & London.

Hersen, M., and Bellack, A., 1976, Social skills training for chronic psychiatric patients: rational, research findings, and future directions, Comp. Psychiat., 17:559-580.

Hersen, M., Eisler, R.M., and Miller, P.M., 1974, An experimental analysis of generalisation in assertive training, Beh. Res. & Ther., 12:295-310.

Lindsay, W.R., 1977, "The Analysis and Training of Social Skills with Particular Reference to Long-Stay Psychiatric Patients," Unpublished Ph.D. thesis, University of Aberdeen.

Lindsay, W.R., 1980, The training and generalisation of conversation behaviours in psychiatric in-patients: a controlled study implying multiple measures across settings, Brit. J. Soc. & Clin. Psychol., 19:85-98.

Lindsay, W.R., (in press), A comparison between schizophrenic patients and non-patient matched controls on several aspects of social skill under three conditions of labelling, in press, Amer. J. Psychiat.

Lindsay, W.R., Symons, R.S., and Sweet, T., 1979, A programme for teaching social skills to socially inept adolescents: description and evaluation, J. Adolesc., 2:215-228.

Lindsay, W.R., Taylor, V., and McDonald, S., 1976, A programme to increase the frequency of conversation in long-term psychiatric patients, Presented at Annual Conference of the Brit. Psychol. Soc. Abstract in Bull. Brit. Psychol. Soc., 29:206.

Longin, H.E., and Rooney, W.M., 1975, Teaching denial assertion to chronic hospitalised patients, J. Beh. Ther. & Exp. Psychiat., 6:219-222.

Lorr, M., and Vestre, N., 1969, The psychotic in-patient profile, J. Clin. Psychol., 25:137-139.

Mahoney, M.J., 1977, Cognitive therapy and research: a question of questions, Cog. Ther. & Res., 1:5-16.

Marzillier, J., 1978 Outcome studies of skills training: a review, in: "Social Skills and Mental Health," P. Trower, B. Bryant & M. Argyle, eds., Methuen, London.

Marzillier, J., Lambert, C., and Kelett, J.A., 1976, A controlled evaluation of systematic desensitisation and social skills training for socially inadequate psychiatric patients, Beh. Res. & Ther., 14:225-238.

Marzillier, J., and Winter, K., 1978, Success and failure in social skills training: individual differences, Beh. Res. & Ther., 16:67-84.

Matson, J., Zeiss, A., Zeiss, R., and Bowman, N., 1980, A comparison of social skills training and contingent attention to improve behavioural deficits of chronic psychiatric patients, Brit. J. Soc. & Clin. Psychol., 9:57-64.

Mischell, W., 1968, "Personality and Assessment," Wylie, New York.

McFall, R., and Lilliesand, D., 1971, Behaviour rehearsal with modelling and coaching in assertion training, J. Abn. Psychol., 77:313-320.

Serber, M., and Nelson, P., 1971, The ineffectiveness of systematic desensitisation and assertive training in hospitalised schizophrenics, J. Beh. Ther. & Exp. Psychiat., 2:107-109.

Shepherd, G., 1977, Social skills training: the generalisation problem, Beh. Ther., 8:1008-1009.

Shepherd, G., 1978, Social skills training: the generalisation problem - some further data, Beh. Res.& Ther., 16:287-288.

Thorpe, G., 1975, Desensitisation, behaviour rehearsal, self-instruction training and placebo effects in assertive-refusal behaviour, Eur. J. Beh. Anal. & Mod., 1:30-44.

Trower, P., 1979, Fundamentals of inter-personal behaviour: a social-psychological perspective, in: "Research and Practice in Social Skills Training," A. Bellack & M. Hersen, eds., Plenum Press, New York & London.

Trower, P., 1980, Situational analysis of the components and processes of behaviour of socially skilled and unskilled patients, J. Cons. & Clin. Psychol., 48:327-339.

LIST OF CONTRIBUTORS

David W. Black, Charge Nurse,
    Royal Dundee Liff Hospital, Liff, Dundee, Scotland.

Laurence E. Burns, Ph.D., Top Grade Clinical Psychologist,
    Area Department of Clinical Psychology, Birch Hill Hospital,
    Rochdale, England, OL12 9QN.

Linda Cockram, Clinical Psychologist,
    Royal Dundee Liff Hospital, Liff, Dundee, Scotland.

David J. Cooke, Senior Clinical Psychologist,
    Gartnavel Royal Hospital, Great Western Road, Glasgow, Scotland.

Chris Cullen, Ph.D., Director of the Residents' Development Project,
    Hester Adrian Research Centre, University of Manchester,
    Anson Road, Victoria Park, Manchester, England, M14 5BY.

Michael G.T. Dow, Senior Clinical Psychologist,
    Gartnavel Royal Hospital, Great Western Road, Glasgow, Scotland.

Douglas Fraser, Senior Clinical Psychologist,
    Royal Dundee Liff Hospital, Liff, Dundee, Scotland.

David Gerver, Senior Lecturer,
    University of Stirling and Honorary Clinical Psychologist,
    Forth Valley Health Board; Department of Psychology, University
    of Stirling, Stirling, Scotland, FK9 4LA.

Ana Maria Gomez, Postgraduate trainee in clinical psychology,
    Department of Psychology, University of Manchester, England.

John G. Greene, Ph.D., Principal Clinical Psychologist,
    Gartnavel Royal Hospital, Great Western Road, Glasgow, Scotland.

Joanna Grimes, Clinical Psychologist,
    Royal Dundee Liff Hospital, Liff, Dundee, Scotland.

359

Jack G. Ingham, Assistant Director,
    Medical Research Council Unit for Epidemiological Studies in
    Psychiatry, The Tower, Royal Edinburgh Hospital, Morningside
    Park, Edinburgh, Scotland.

David W.A. Jerrom, Senior Clinical Psychologist,
    Forth Valley Health Board and Clinical Research Fellow,
    Department of Psychology, University of Stirling, Stirling,
    Scotland, FK9 4LA.

William R. Lindsay, Ph.D., Senior Clinical Psychologist,
    Monklands District General Hospital, Monkscourt Avenue, Airdrie.
    Scotland, JL6 OJS.

Chris J. Main, Senior Clinical Psychologist,
    Gartnavel Royal Hospital, Great Western Road, Glasgow, Scotland.

Patrick McC. Miller, Ph.D., Senior Research Psychologist,
    Medical Research Council for Epidemiological Studies in
    Psychiatry, The Tower, Royal Edinburgh Hospital, Morningside
    Park, Edinburgh, Scotland.

Douglas J. Montgomery, Charge Nurse,
    Craig Dunain Hospital, Inverness, Scotland.

Kee-on Ng, Clinical Psychologist,
    Sub-Department of Clinical Psychology, New Medical School,
    University of Liverpool, Merseyside, England.

D.A. Pemberton, Consultant Psychiatrist,
    Forth Valley Health Board, Stirling, Scotland.

Clive Reading, Principal Clinical Psychologist,
    University Hospital of South Manchester, Withington Hospital,
    West Didsbury, Manchester, England, M20 8LR.

Brian F. Sheffield, Area Clinical Psychologist,
    Hope Hospital, Eccles Old Road, Salford, England, M6 8MD.

R.J. Simpson, General Practitioner and Hospital Practitioner in
    Psychiatry, The Health Centre, Fountain Road, Bridge of Allan,
    Scotland, FK9 4EU.

Nicola A. Stuckey, Senior Clinical Psychologist,
    Astley Ainslie Hospital, Canaan Lane, Morningside, Edinburgh 10,
    Scotland.

Valerie A. Taylor, Ph.D., Senior Clinical Psychologist,
    Leverndale Hospital, 510 Crookston Road, Glasgow, Scotland,
    G53 7TU.

Anthony A. Turvey, Clinical Psychologist,
     Royal Dundee Liff Hospital, Liff, Dundee, Scotland.

Gordon Waddell, M.D., Consultant Orthopaedic Surgeon,
     University Department of Orthopaedic Surgery, Western Infirmary,
     Dumbarton Road, Glasgow, Scotland, G11 6NT.

George Wright, Research Fellow,
     Department of Behavioural Sciences, The Polytechnic, Queensgate,
     Huddersfield, England, HD1 3DH.